尾田栄一郎

When I visited my family recently, my parents expressed
an opinion about *ONE PIECE* for the very first time.
"That story about the deer was really good."
...*Deer?*

-Eiichiro Oda, 2002

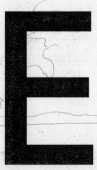iichiro Oda began his manga career at the age of
17, when his one-shot cowboy manga **Wanted!**
won second place in the coveted Tezuka manga
awards. Oda went on to work as an assistant to
some of the biggest manga artists in the industry,
including Nobuhiro Watsuki, before winning the
Hop Step Award for new artists. His pirate
adventure **One Piece**, which debuted in
Weekly Shonen Jump in 1997, quickly became
one of the most popular manga in Japan.

ONE PIECE VOL. 24
BAROQUE WORKS PART 13 &
SKYPIEA PART 1

SHONEN JUMP Manga Edition

STORY AND ART BY EIICHIRO ODA

English Adaptation/Lance Caselman
Translation/JN Productions
Touch-up Art & Lettering/Primary Graphix & HudsonYards
Design/Sean Lee
Editor/Yuki Murashige

VP, Production/Alvin Lu
VP, Sales & Product Marketing/Gonzalo Ferreyra
VP, Creative/Linda Espinosa
Publisher/Hyoe Narita

Printed in the U.S.A.

Published by VIZ Media, LLC
P.O. Box 77010
San Francisco, CA 94107

10 9 8 7 6 5 4 3 2 1
First printing, January 2010

SHONEN JUMP MANGA

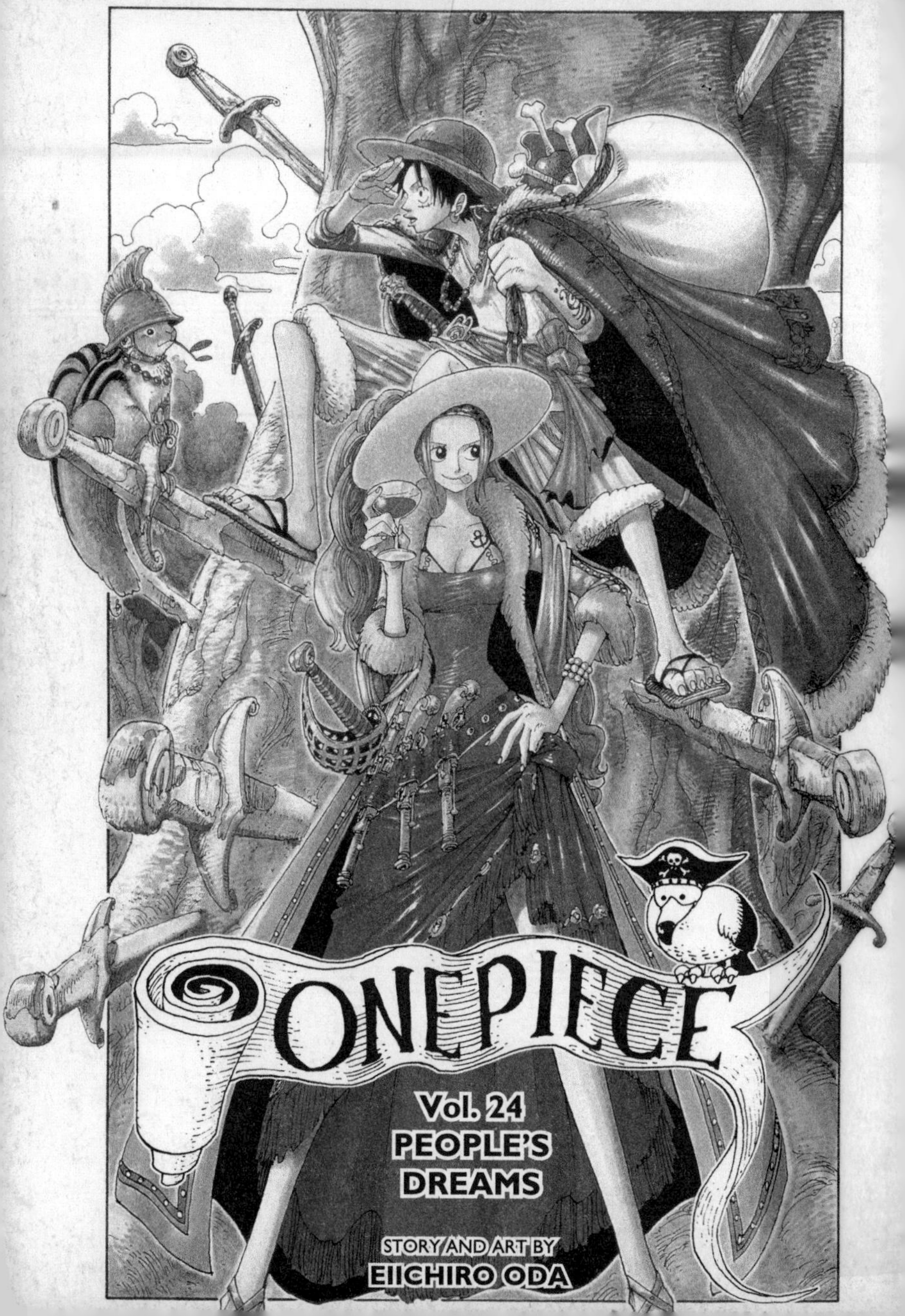

ONE PIECE

Vol. 24
PEOPLE'S DREAMS

STORY AND ART BY
EIICHIRO ODA

Boundlessly optimistic and able to stretch like rubber, he is determined to become King of the Pirates.

Monkey D. Luffy

A former bounty hunter and master of the "three-sword" style. He aspires to be the world's greatest swordsman.

Roronoa Zolo

A thief who specializes in robbing pirates. Nami hates pirates, but Luffy convinced her to be his navigator.

Nami

A village boy with a talent for telling tall tales. His father, Yasopp, is a member of Shanks's crew.

Usopp

The big-hearted cook (and ladies' man) whose dream is to find the legendary sea, the "All Blue."

Sanji

A blue-nosed man-reindeer and the ship's doctor.

Tony Tony Chopper

A pirate that Luffy idolizes. Shanks gave Luffy his trademark straw hat.

"Red-Haired" Shanks

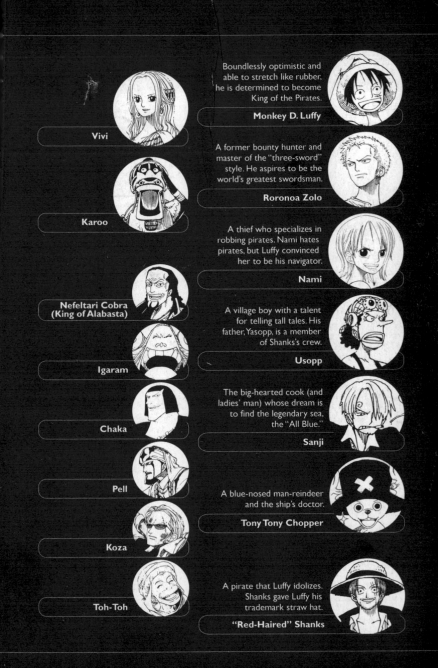

Vivi

Karoo

Nefeltari Cobra (King of Alabasta)

Igaram

Chaka

Pell

Koza

Toh-Toh

THE STORY OF ONE PIECE

Volume 24

Monkey D. Luffy started out as just a kid with a dream—to become the greatest pirate in history! Stirred by the tales of pirate "Red-Haired" Shanks, Luffy vowed to become a pirate himself. That was before the enchanted Devil Fruit gave Luffy the power to stretch like rubber, at the cost of being unable to swim—a serious handicap for an aspiring sea dog. Undeterred, Luffy set out to sea and recruited some crewmates: master swordsman Zolo, treasure-hunting thief Nami, lying sharpshooter Usopp, the high-kicking chef Sanji, and the latest addition, Chopper—the walkin' talkin' reindeer doctor.

Luffy and crew fight to help Princess Vivi save her war-torn and drought-ravaged kingdom from the evil Sir Crocodile and his secret criminal organization, the Baroque Works. But Crocodile's true objective was to get his hands on the most destructive weapon of the ancient world, the Pluton! With such a weapon, world domination would be his! After numerous hair-raising battles, Crocodile and Baroque Works are defeated and the kingdom is saved. The people rejoice and Luffy and the others recover from their wounds. But there is little time to rest as the Navy is hot on their trail! So Luffy and crew bid farewell to Vivi and set sail once more. Their hearts are heavy, but they all find solace in the friendship that remains forever in their hearts.

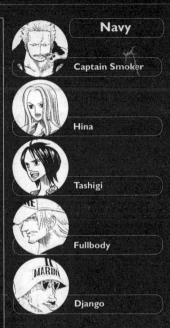

Navy

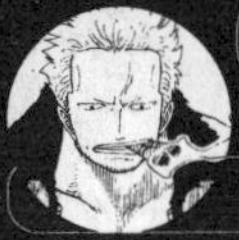

Captain Smoker

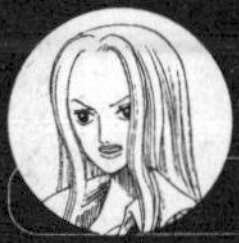

Hina

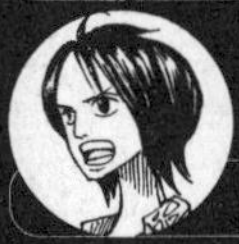

Tashigi

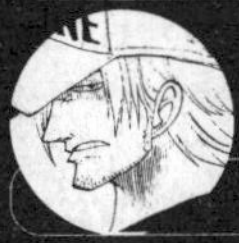

Fullbody

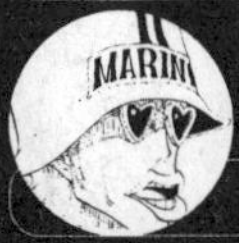
MARIN

Django

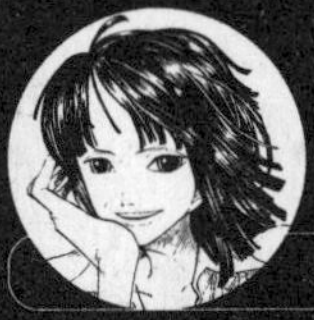

Nico Robin

SKYPIEA ONE PIECE

Vol. 24
People's Dreams

CONTENTS

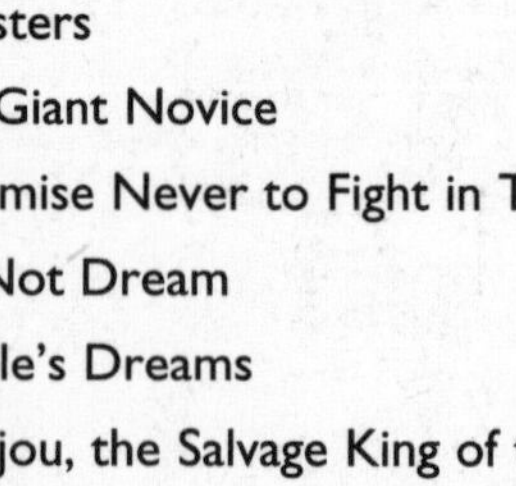

Chapter 217: STOWAWAY

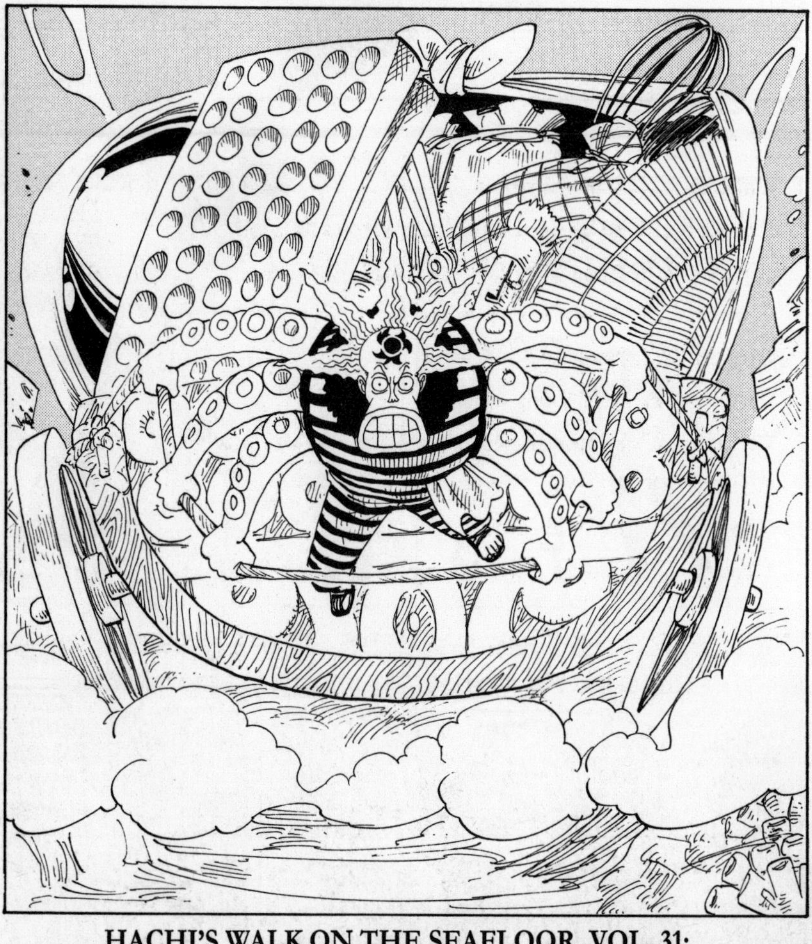

HACHI'S WALK ON THE SEAFLOOR, VOL. 31:
"SAVE THE CATFISH VILLAGE!! EXCHANGE THE TREASURE FOR COOKING EQUIPMENT"

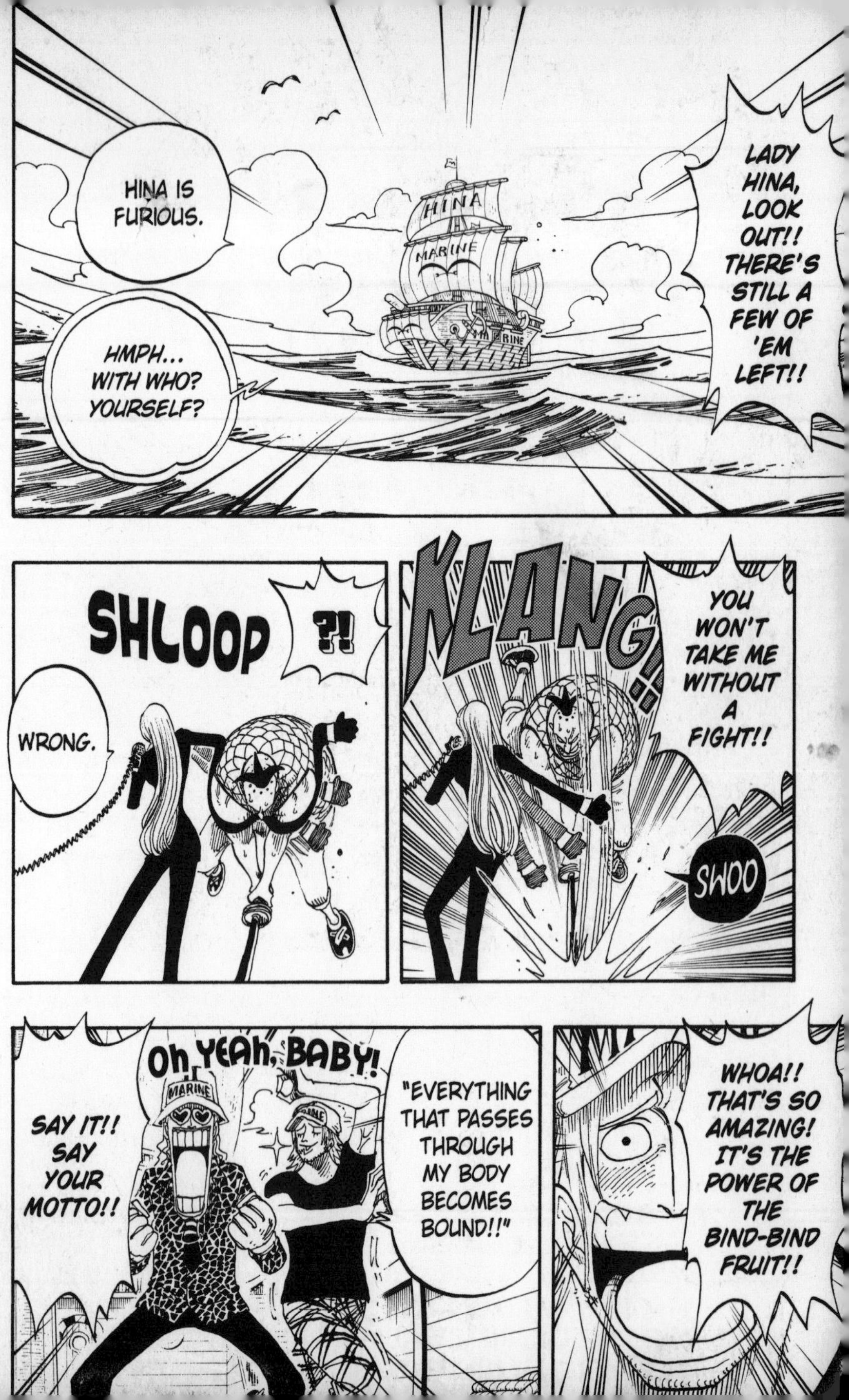
LADY HINA, LOOK OUT!! THERE'S STILL A FEW OF 'EM LEFT!!
HINA IS FURIOUS.
HMPH... WITH WHO? YOURSELF?
KLANG!!
YOU WON'T TAKE ME WITHOUT A FIGHT!!
SWOO
SHLOOP
?!
WRONG.
WHOA!! THAT'S SO AMAZING! IT'S THE POWER OF THE BIND-BIND FRUIT!!
"EVERYTHING THAT PASSES THROUGH MY BODY BECOMES BOUND!!"
Oh YEAH, BABY!
SAY IT!! SAY YOUR MOTTO!!

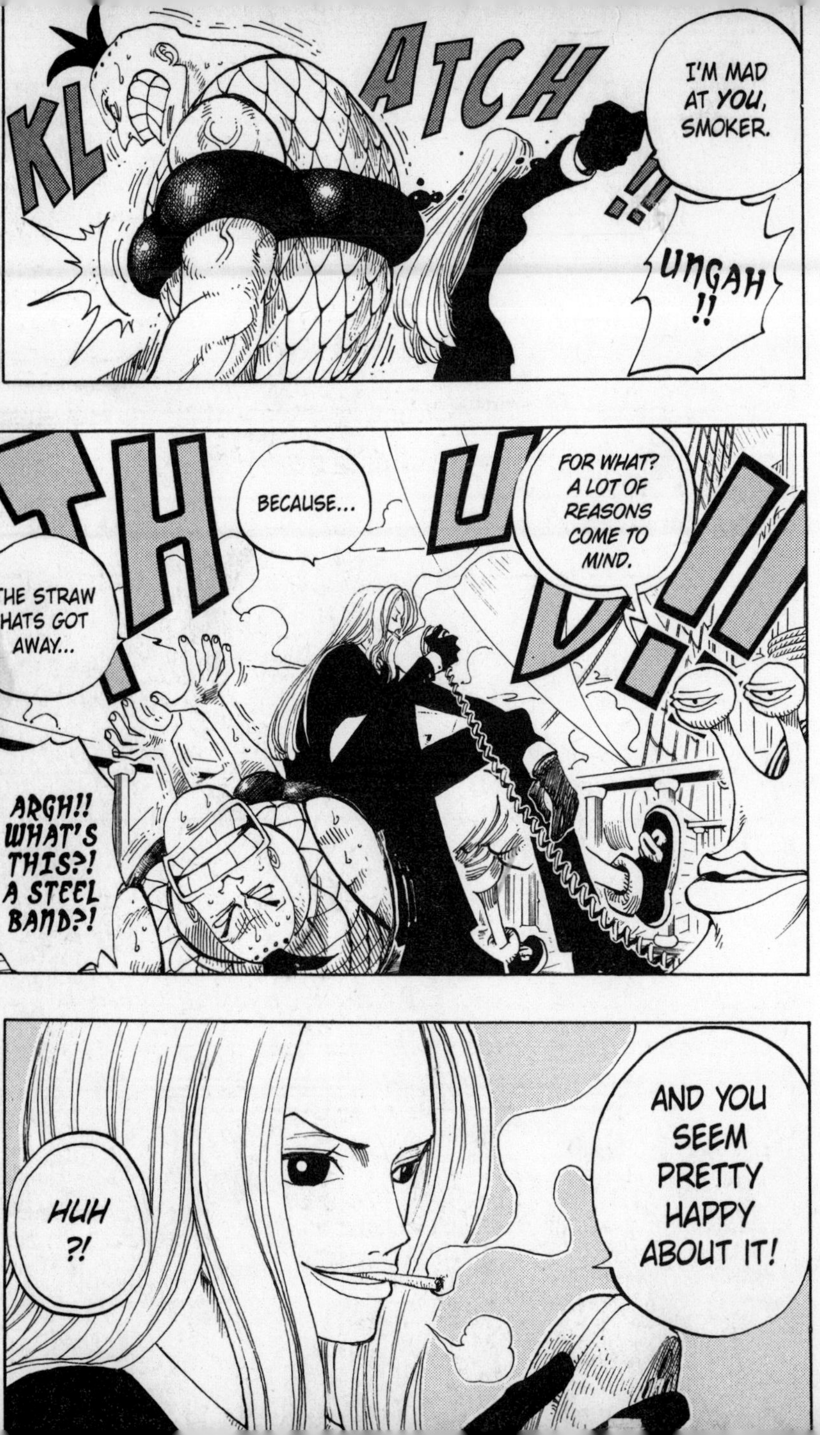

I'M MAD AT YOU, SMOKER.
KLATCH!!
UNGAH !!
FOR WHAT? A LOT OF REASONS COME TO MIND.
THUD!!
BECAUSE...
THE STRAW HATS GOT AWAY...
ARGH!! WHAT'S THIS?! A STEEL BAND?!
AND YOU SEEM PRETTY HAPPY ABOUT IT!
HUH ?!

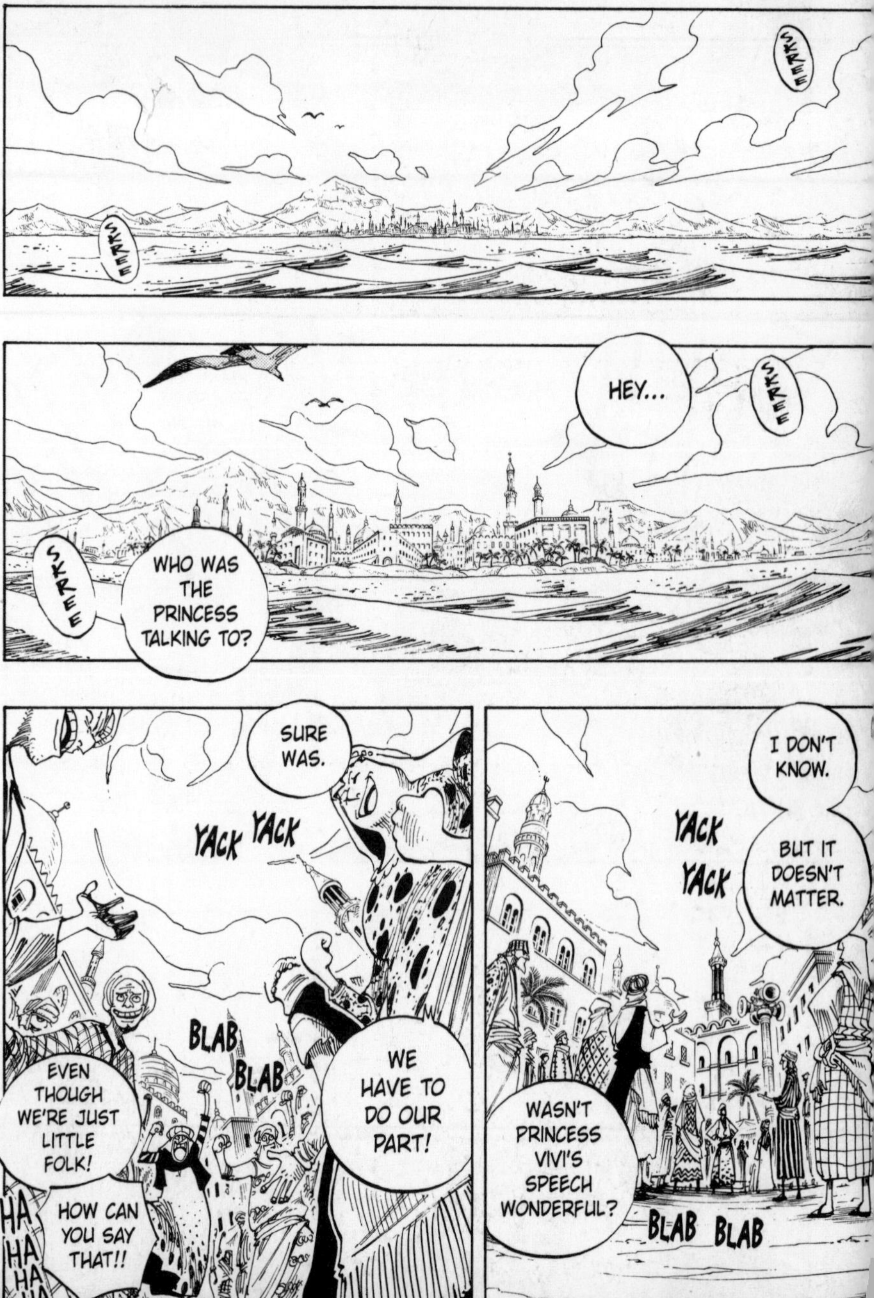
SKREE
SKREE
HEY...
SKREE
WHO WAS THE PRINCESS TALKING TO?
SKREE
I DON'T KNOW.
BUT IT DOESN'T MATTER.
YACK YACK
WASN'T PRINCESS VIVI'S SPEECH WONDERFUL?
BLAB BLAB
SURE WAS.
YACK YACK
WE HAVE TO DO OUR PART!
BLAB BLAB
EVEN THOUGH WE'RE JUST LITTLE FOLK!
HOW CAN YOU SAY THAT!!
HA HA HA HA HA

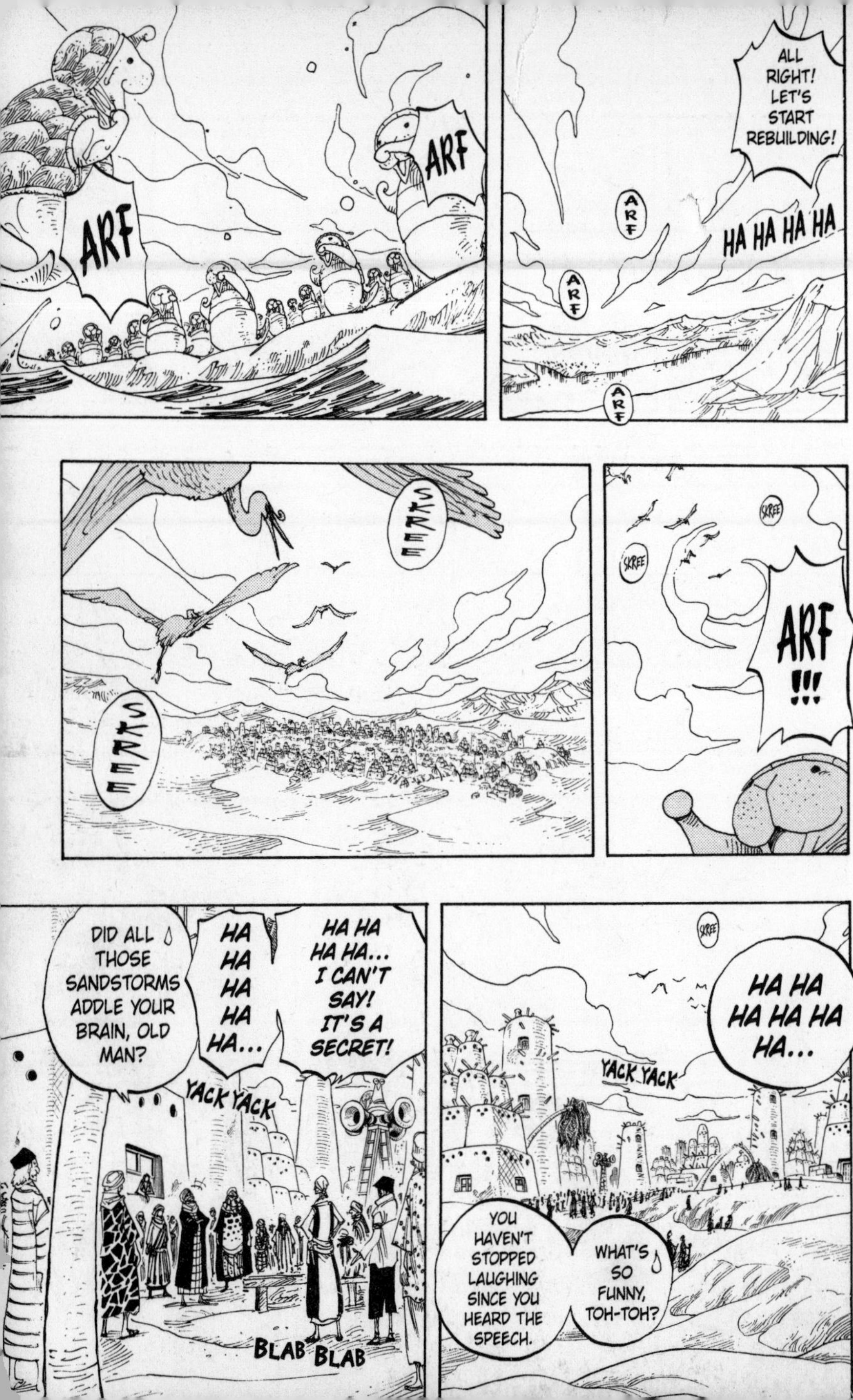
ALL RIGHT! LET'S START REBUILDING!
HA HA HA HA
ARF
ARF
ARF
ARF
ARF
SKREE
SKREE
ARF!!!
SKREE
SKREE
SKREE
HA HA HA HA HA HA...
YACK YACK
WHAT'S SO FUNNY, TOH-TOH?
YOU HAVEN'T STOPPED LAUGHING SINCE YOU HEARD THE SPEECH.
HA HA HA HA... I CAN'T SAY! IT'S A SECRET!
HA HA HA HA HA...
DID ALL THOSE SANDSTORMS ADDLE YOUR BRAIN, OLD MAN?
YACK YACK
BLAB BLAB

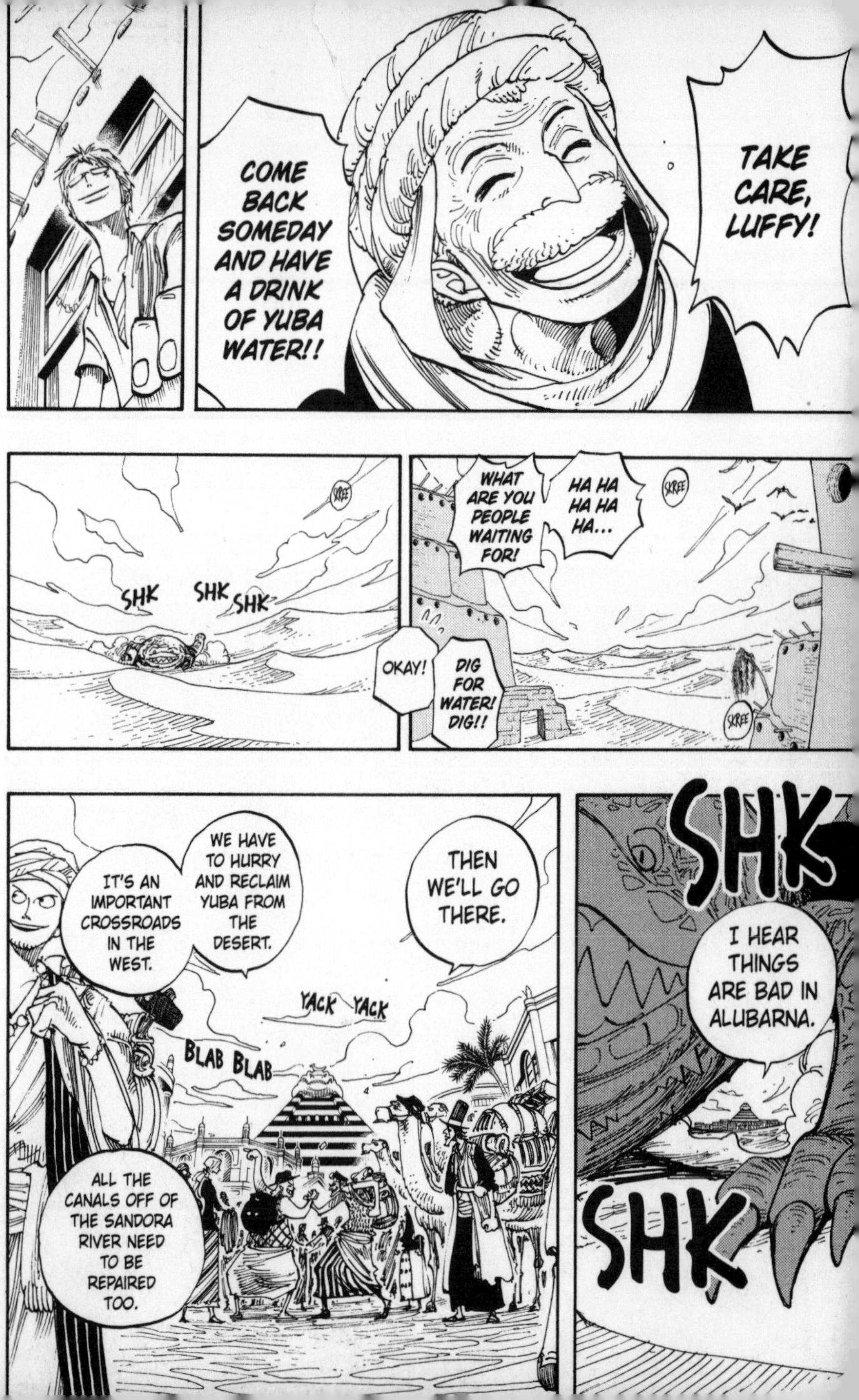
TAKE CARE, LUFFY!
COME BACK SOMEDAY AND HAVE A DRINK OF YUBA WATER!!
SKREE
HA HA HA HA HA...
WHAT ARE YOU PEOPLE WAITING FOR!
SKREE
DIG FOR WATER! DIG!!
OKAY!
SKREE
SHK SHK SHK
SHK
I HEAR THINGS ARE BAD IN ALUBARNA.
SHK
THEN WE'LL GO THERE.
WE HAVE TO HURRY AND RECLAIM YUBA FROM THE DESERT.
IT'S AN IMPORTANT CROSSROADS IN THE WEST.
YACK YACK
BLAB BLAB
ALL THE CANALS OFF OF THE SANDORA RIVER NEED TO BE REPAIRED TOO.

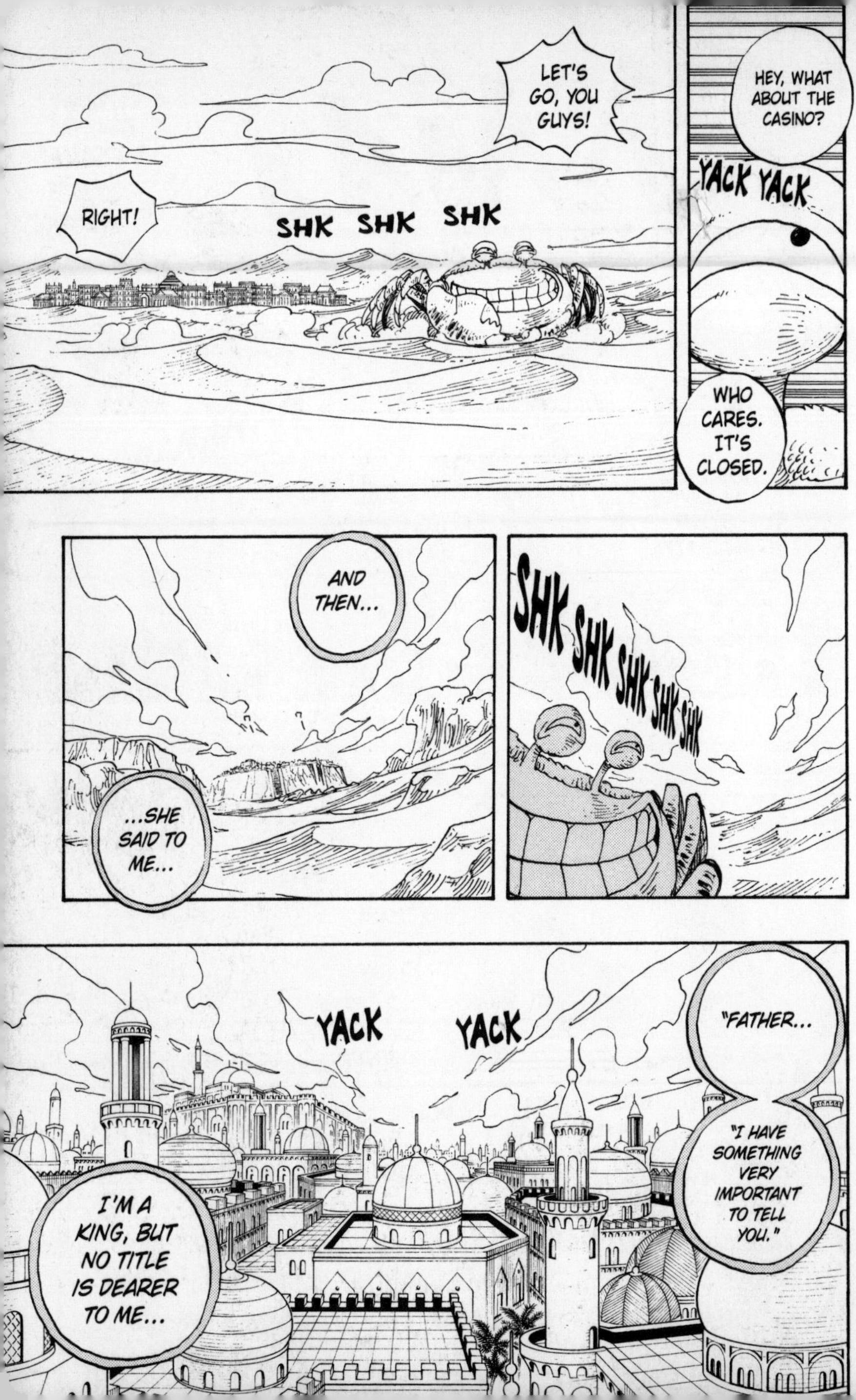
HEY, WHAT ABOUT THE CASINO?
YACK YACK
WHO CARES. IT'S CLOSED.
LET'S GO, YOU GUYS!
RIGHT!
SHK SHK SHK
SHK SHK SHK SHK SHK
AND THEN...
...SHE SAID TO ME...
"FATHER...
"I HAVE SOMETHING VERY IMPORTANT TO TELL YOU."
YACK YACK
I'M A KING, BUT NO TITLE IS DEARER TO ME...

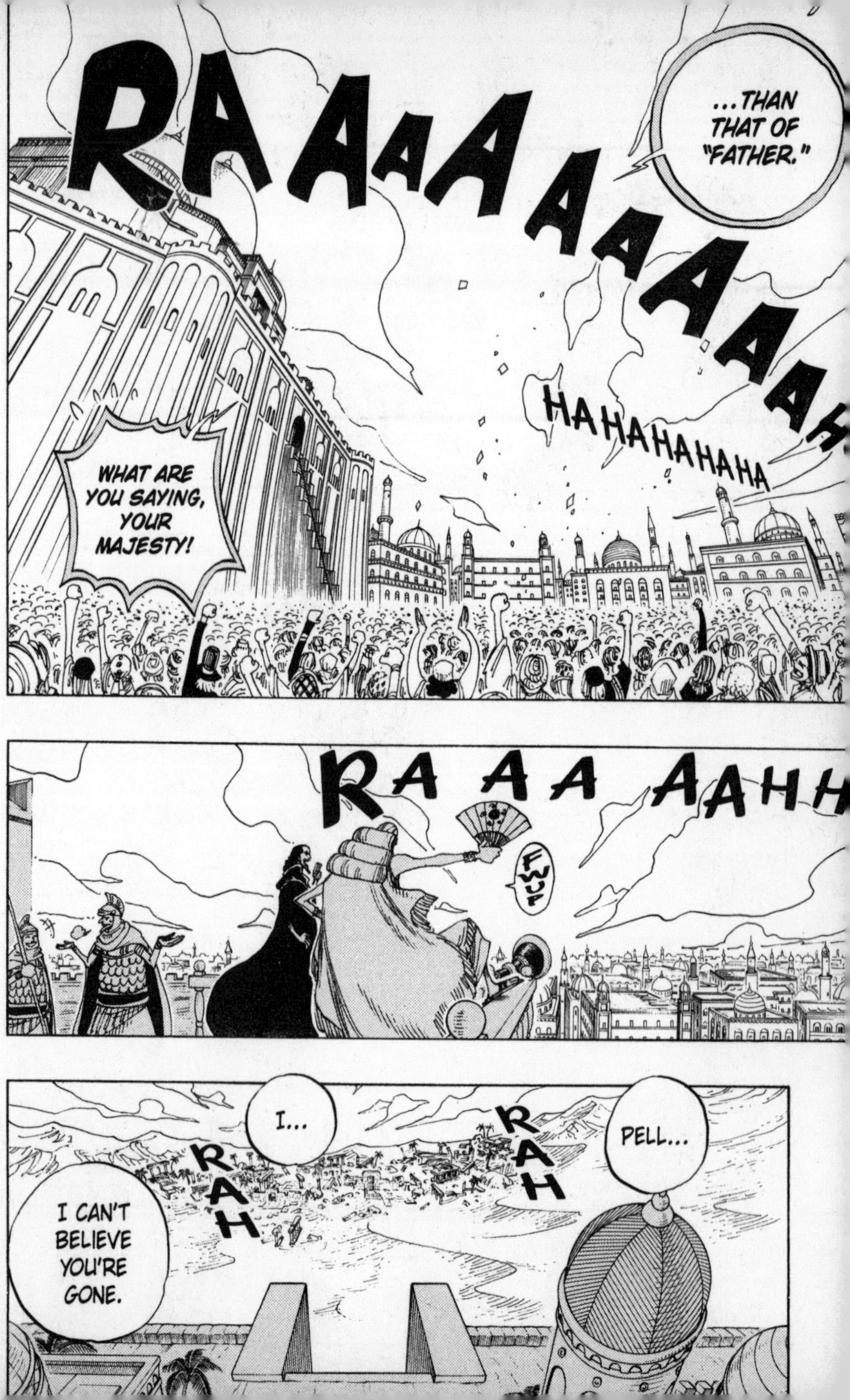
...THAN THAT OF "FATHER."
RAAAAAAAAAAH
HAHAHAHAHAHA
WHAT ARE YOU SAYING, YOUR MAJESTY!
RA A A AAHH
FWUF
PELL...
RAH
I...
RAH
I CAN'T BELIEVE YOU'RE GONE.

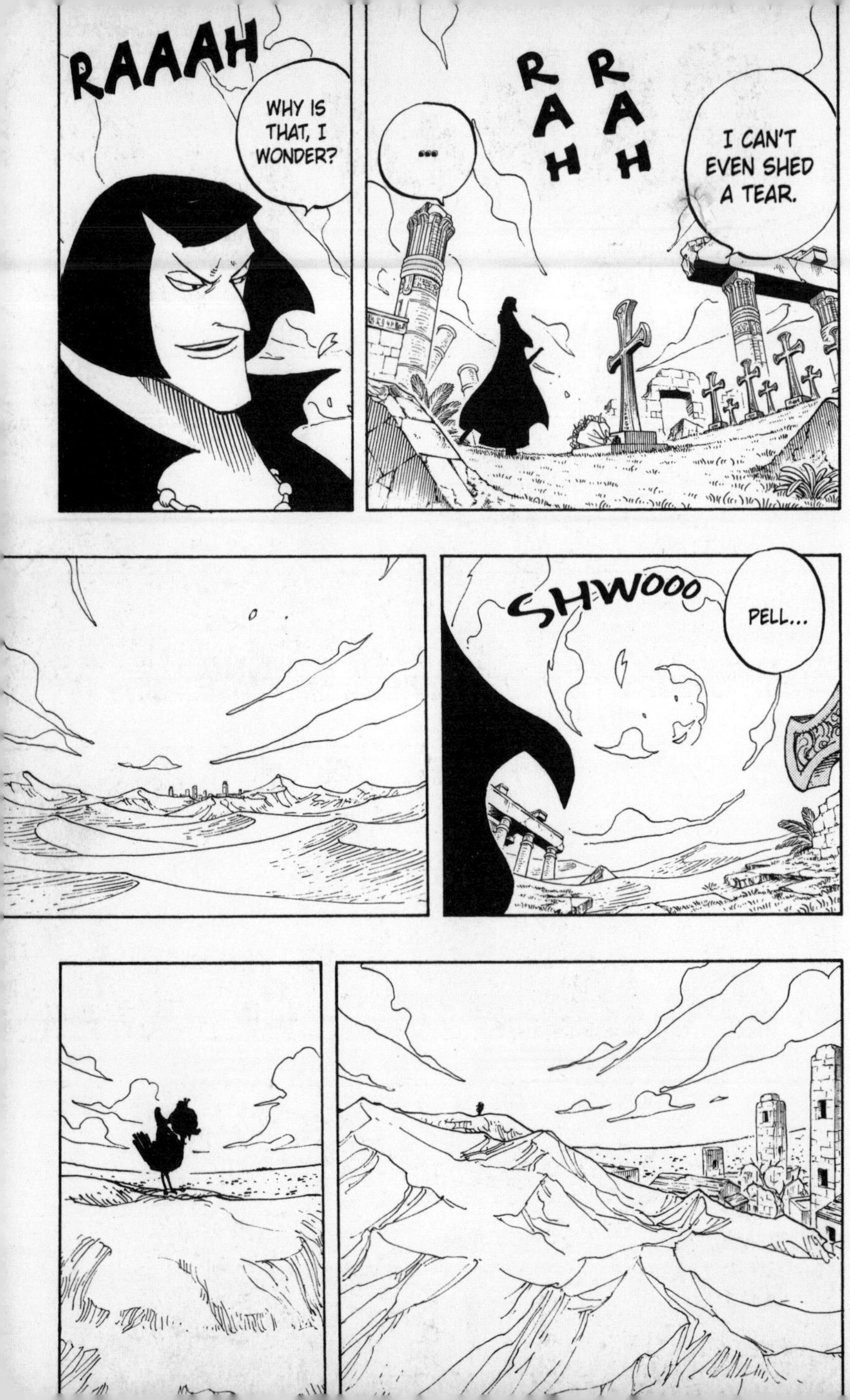
RAH RAH
I CAN'T EVEN SHED A TEAR.
...
RAAAH
WHY IS THAT, I WONDER?
SHWOOO
PELL...

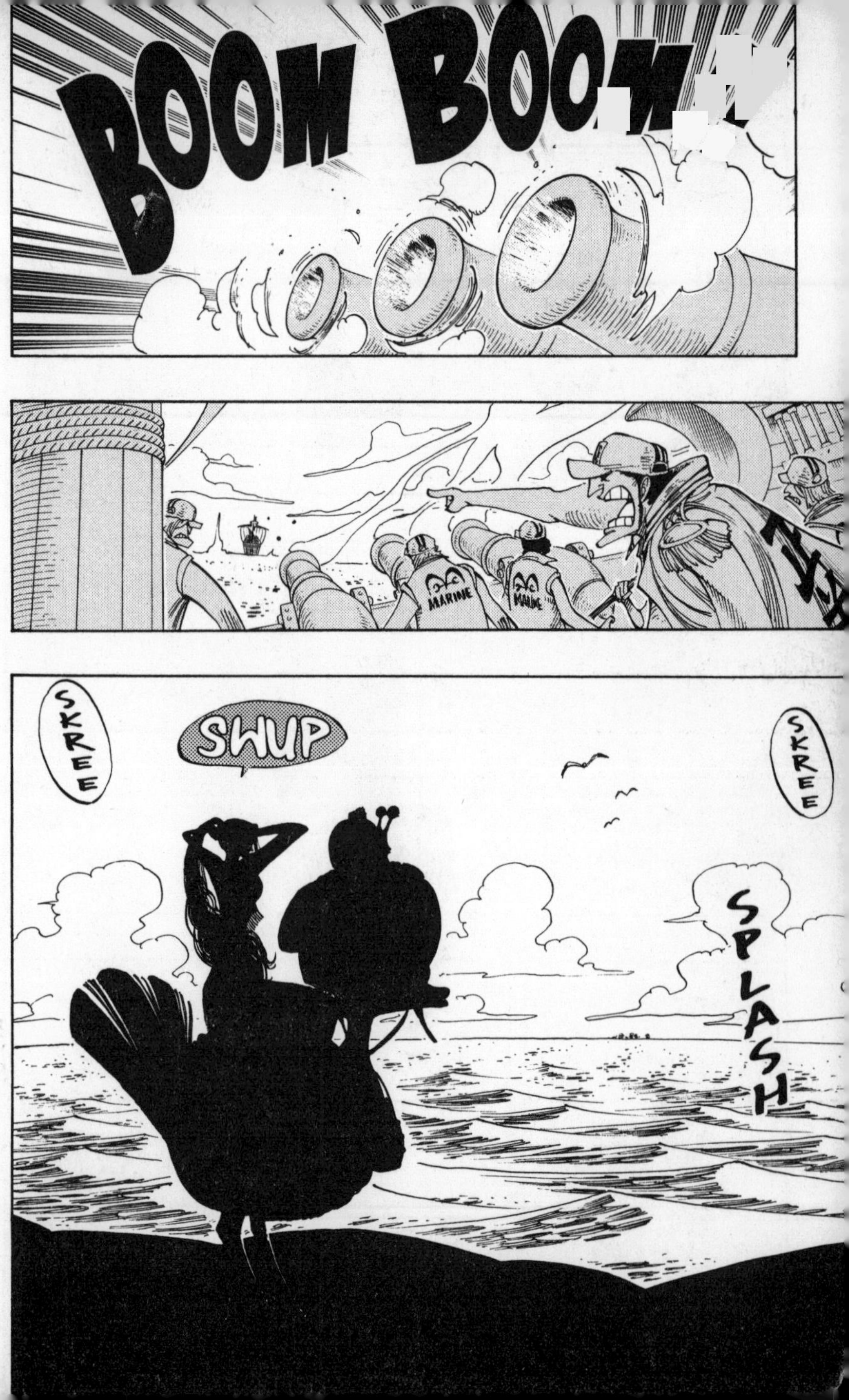
BOOM BOOM
MARINE
MARINE
SKREE
SPLASH
SWUP
SKREE

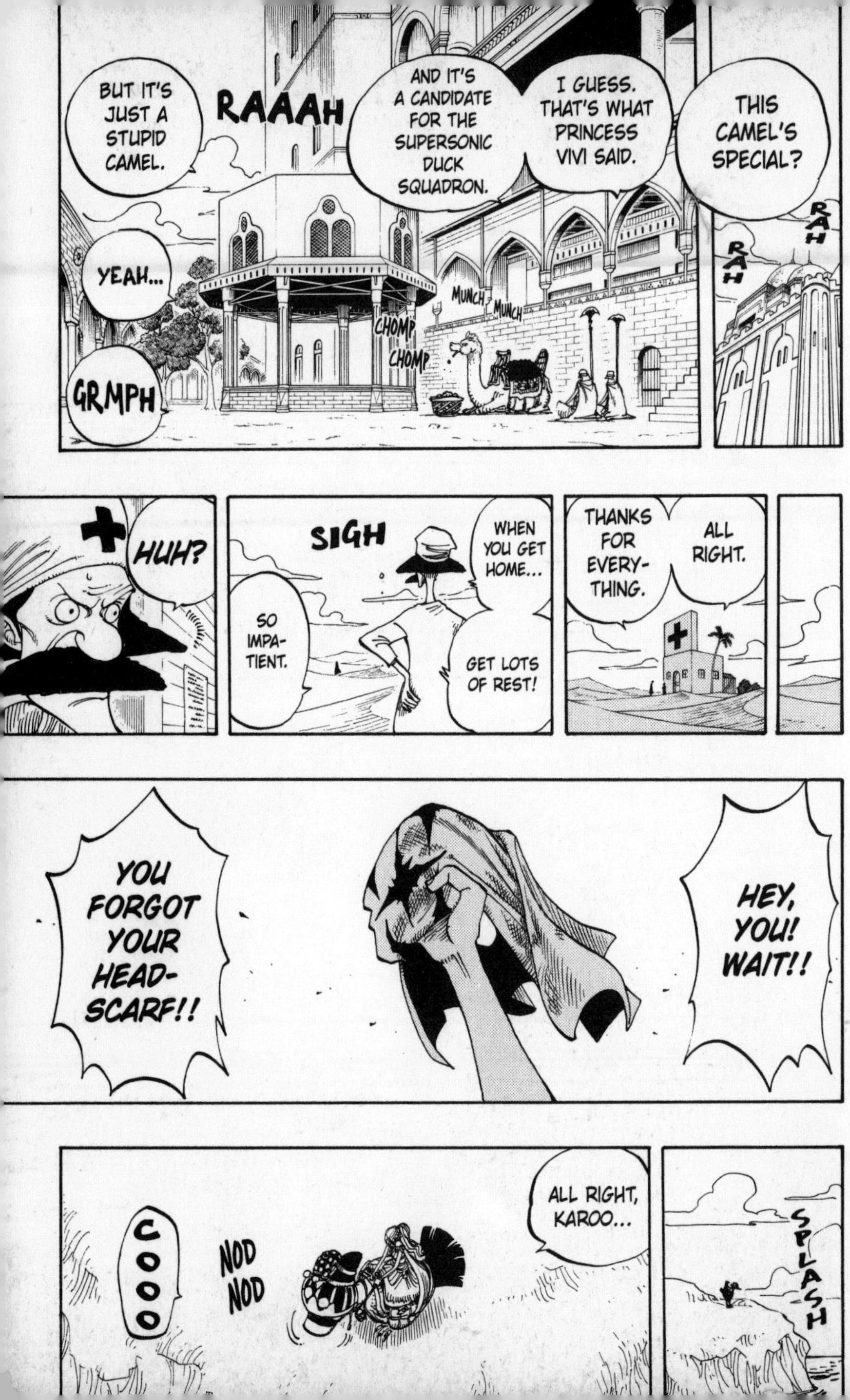
THIS CAMEL'S SPECIAL?
RAH RAH
I GUESS. THAT'S WHAT PRINCESS VIVI SAID.
AND IT'S A CANDIDATE FOR THE SUPERSONIC DUCK SQUADRON.
RAAAH
BUT IT'S JUST A STUPID CAMEL.
MUNCH MUNCH
CHOMP CHOMP
YEAH...
GRMPH
ALL RIGHT.
THANKS FOR EVERYTHING.
WHEN YOU GET HOME...
GET LOTS OF REST!
SIGH
SO IMPATIENT.
HUH?
HEY, YOU! WAIT!!
YOU FORGOT YOUR HEAD-SCARF!!
SPLASH
ALL RIGHT, KAROO...
NOD NOD
COOO

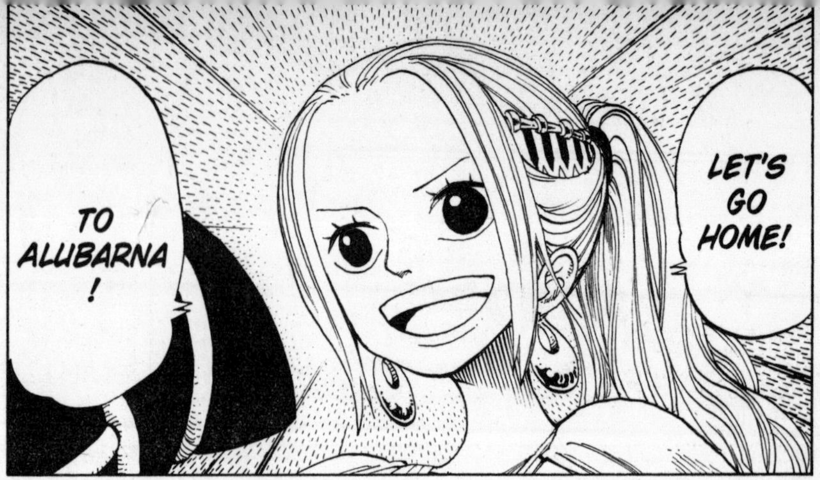
LET'S GO HOME!
TO ALUBARNA!
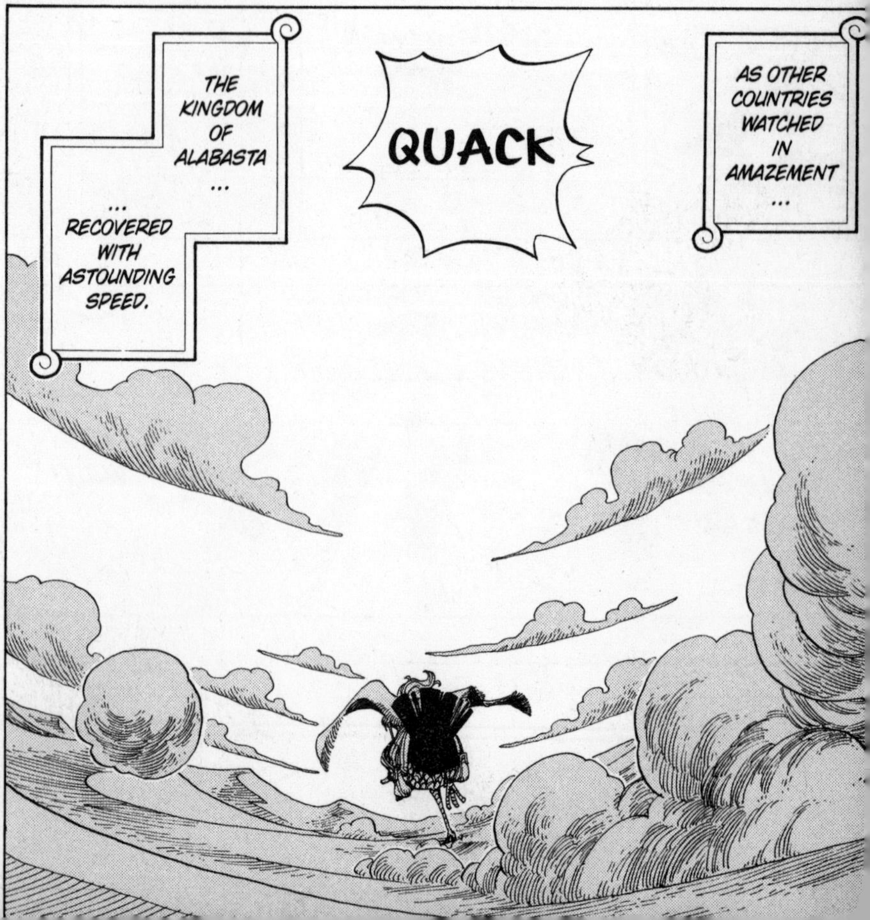
AS OTHER COUNTRIES WATCHED IN AMAZEMENT...
QUACK
THE KINGDOM OF ALABASTA...
...RECOVERED WITH ASTOUNDING SPEED.

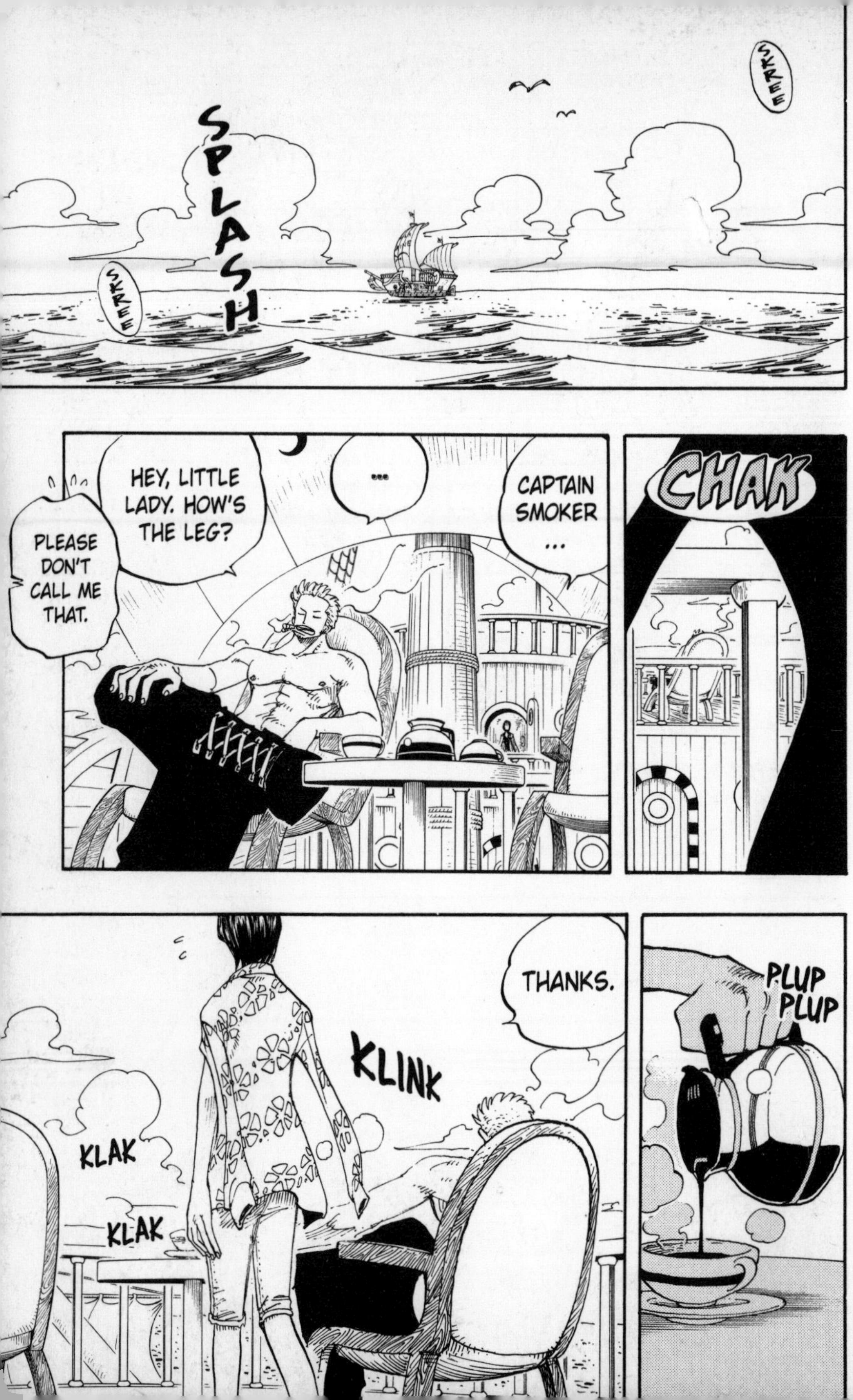
SKREE
SPLASH
SKREE
CHAK
CAPTAIN SMOKER ...
...
HEY, LITTLE LADY. HOW'S THE LEG?
PLEASE DON'T CALL ME THAT.
PLUP PLUP
THANKS.
KLINK
KLAK
KLAK

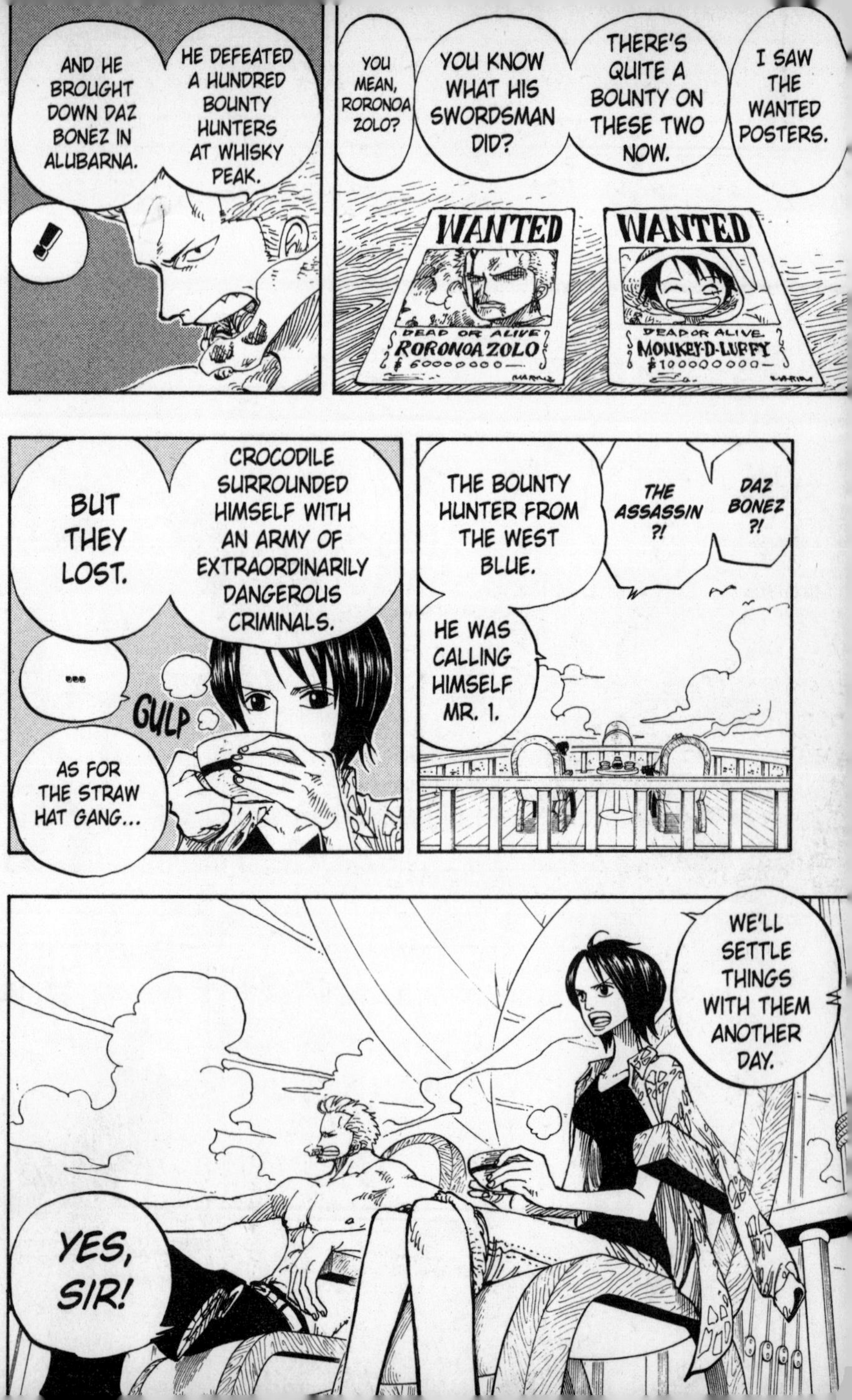
I SAW THE WANTED POSTERS.
THERE'S QUITE A BOUNTY ON THESE TWO NOW.
WANTED
DEAD OR ALIVE
MONKEY-D-LUFFY
฿100000000—
WANTED
DEAD OR ALIVE
RORONOA ZOLO
฿60000000—
YOU KNOW WHAT HIS SWORDSMAN DID?
YOU MEAN, RORONOA ZOLO?
HE DEFEATED A HUNDRED BOUNTY HUNTERS AT WHISKY PEAK.
AND HE BROUGHT DOWN DAZ BONEZ IN ALUBARNA.
!
DAZ BONEZ ?!
THE ASSASSIN ?!
THE BOUNTY HUNTER FROM THE WEST BLUE.
HE WAS CALLING HIMSELF MR. 1.
CROCODILE SURROUNDED HIMSELF WITH AN ARMY OF EXTRAORDINARILY DANGEROUS CRIMINALS.
BUT THEY LOST.
...
GULP
AS FOR THE STRAW HAT GANG...
WE'LL SETTLE THINGS WITH THEM ANOTHER DAY.
YES, SIR!

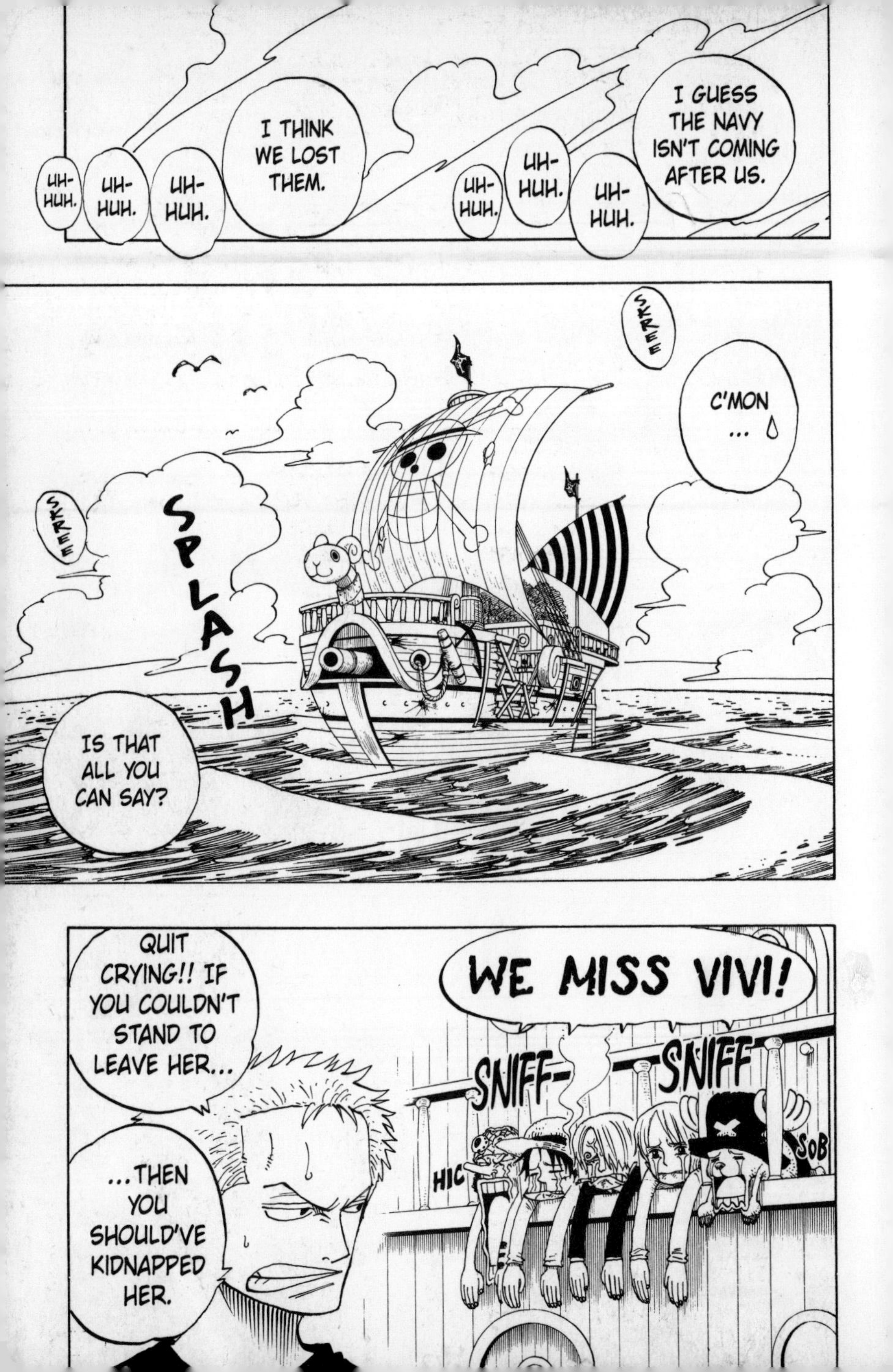

I GUESS THE NAVY ISN'T COMING AFTER US.
UH-HUH.
UH-HUH.
UH-HUH.
I THINK WE LOST THEM.
UH-HUH.
UH-HUH.
UH-HUH.
SKREE
C'MON ...
SPLASH
SKREE
IS THAT ALL YOU CAN SAY?
WE MISS VIVI!
SNIFF
SNIFF
SOB
HIC
QUIT CRYING!! IF YOU COULDN'T STAND TO LEAVE HER...
...THEN YOU SHOULD'VE KIDNAPPED HER.

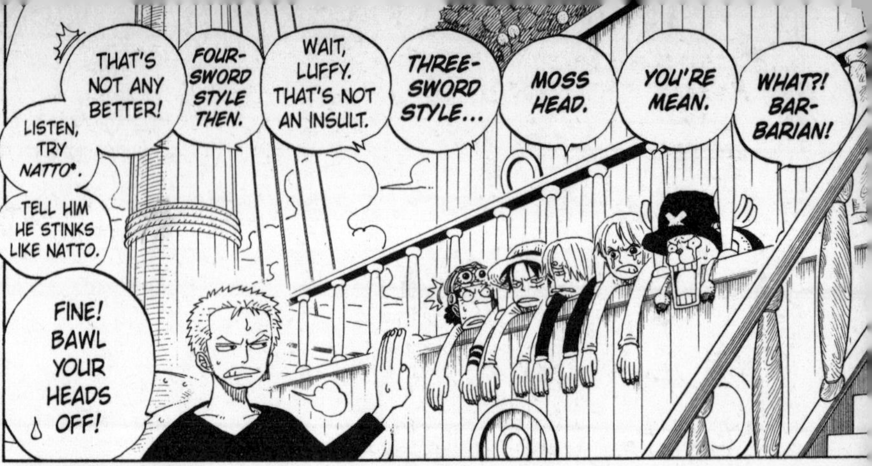
WHAT?! BAR-BARIAN!
YOU'RE MEAN.
MOSS HEAD.
THREE-SWORD STYLE...
WAIT, LUFFY. THAT'S NOT AN INSULT.
FOUR-SWORD STYLE THEN.
THAT'S NOT ANY BETTER!
LISTEN, TRY NATTO*.
TELL HIM HE STINKS LIKE NATTO.
FINE! BAWL YOUR HEADS OFF!

*FERMENTED SOYBEANS

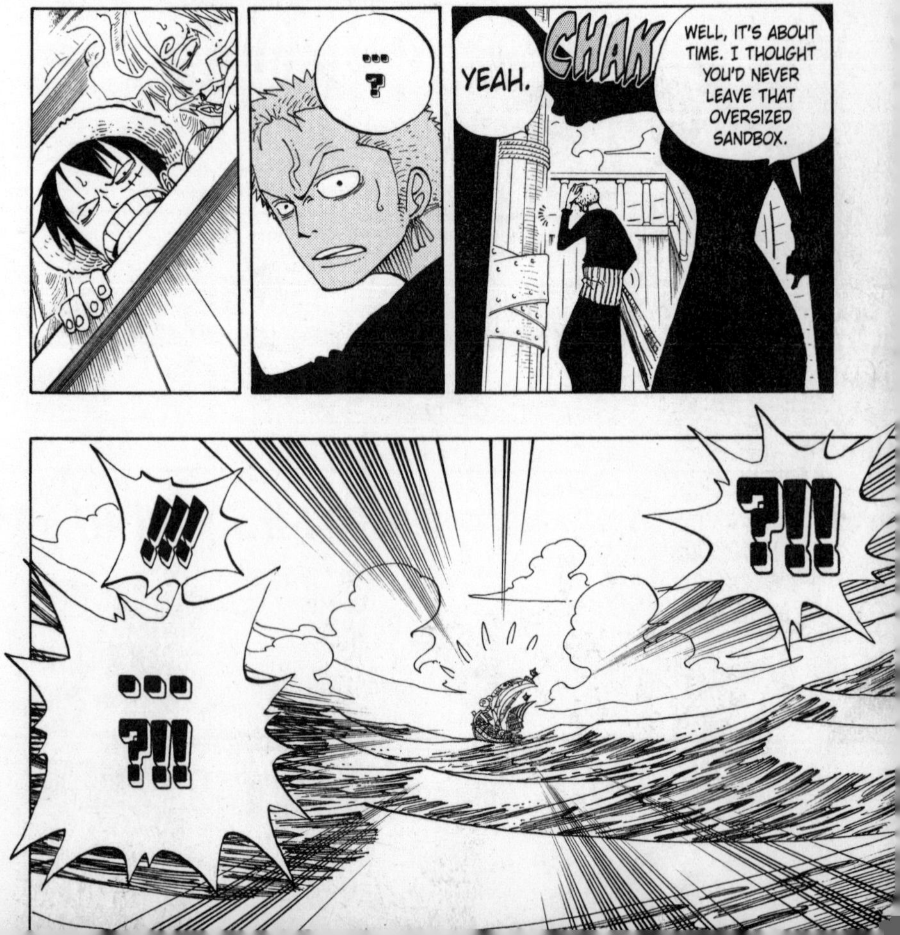
WELL, IT'S ABOUT TIME. I THOUGHT YOU'D NEVER LEAVE THAT OVERSIZED SANDBOX.
CHAK
YEAH.
...?
?!!
!!!
...?!!

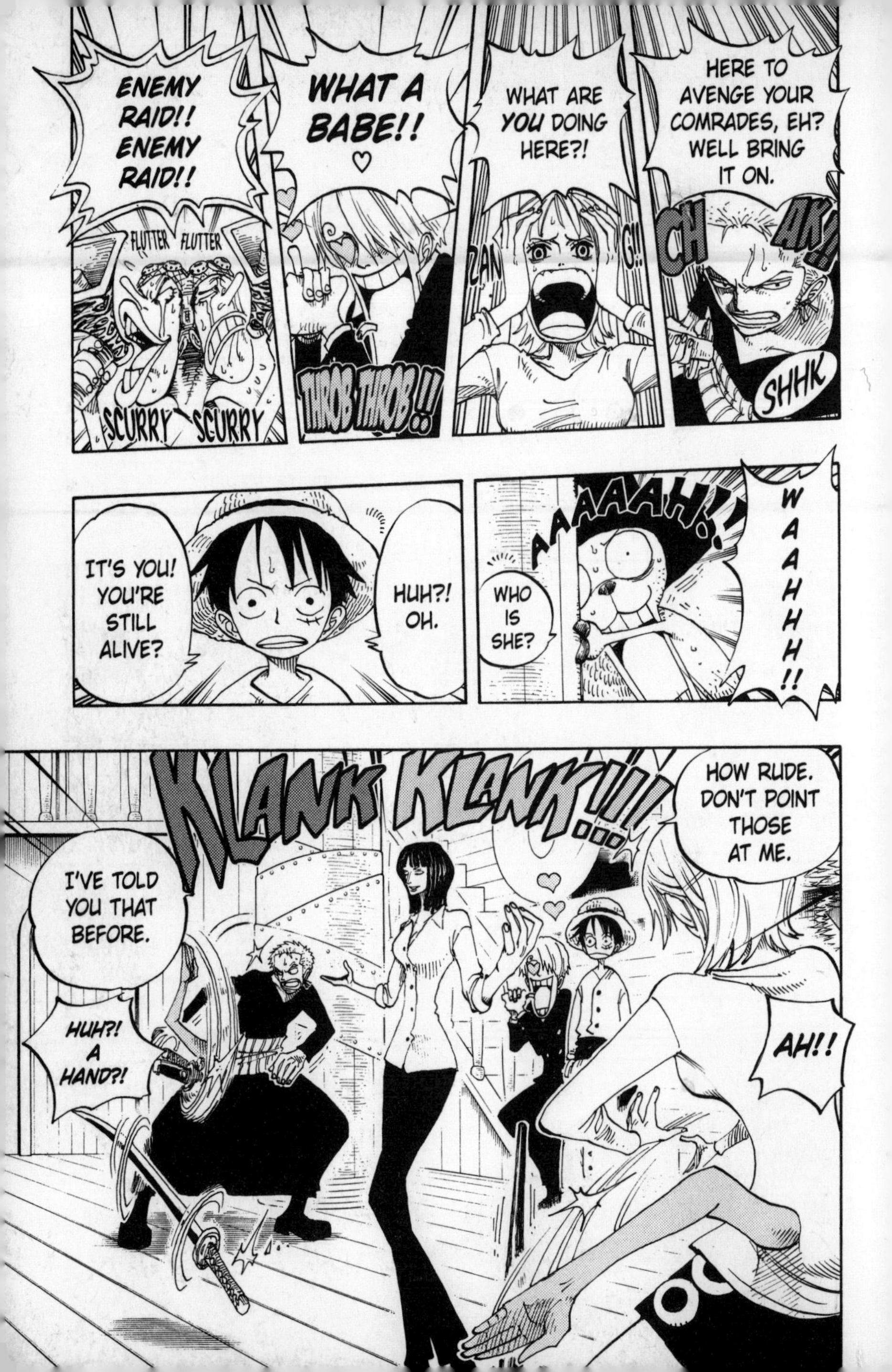
HERE TO AVENGE YOUR COMRADES, EH? WELL BRING IT ON.
CHAK!!
SHHK
WHAT ARE YOU DOING HERE?!
ZANG!!
WHAT A BABE!! ♥
THROB THROB!!
ENEMY RAID!! ENEMY RAID!!
FLUTTER FLUTTER
SCURRY SCURRY
WAAHHH!!
AAAAAH!!
WHO IS SHE?
HUH?! OH.
IT'S YOU! YOU'RE STILL ALIVE?
HOW RUDE. DON'T POINT THOSE AT ME.
KLANK KLANK!!!
I'VE TOLD YOU THAT BEFORE.
AH!!
HUH?! A HAND?!

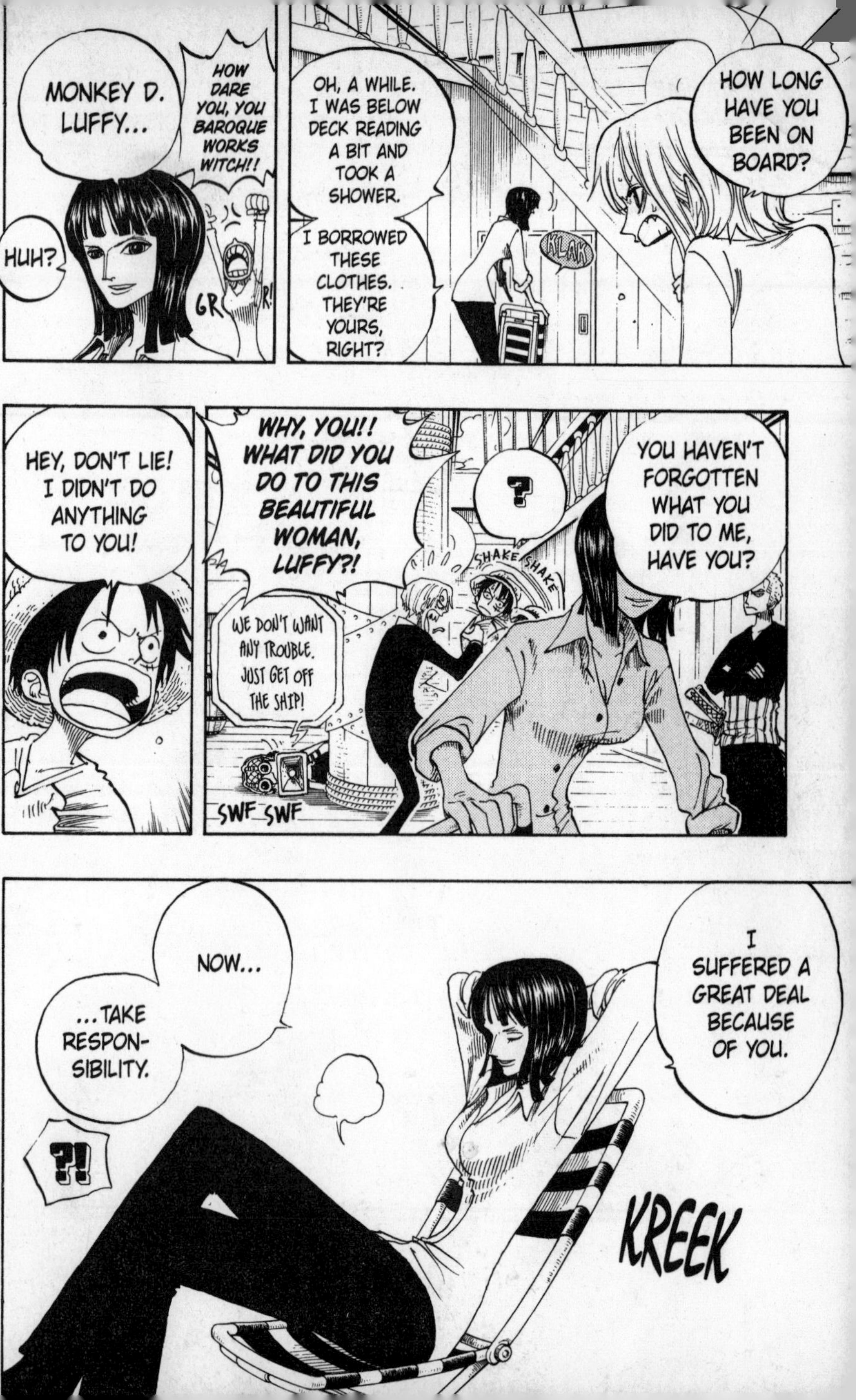
HOW LONG HAVE YOU BEEN ON BOARD?
KLAK
OH, A WHILE. I WAS BELOW DECK READING A BIT AND TOOK A SHOWER.
I BORROWED THESE CLOTHES. THEY'RE YOURS, RIGHT?
HOW DARE YOU, YOU BAROQUE WORKS WITCH!!
MONKEY D. LUFFY...
HUH?
YOU HAVEN'T FORGOTTEN WHAT YOU DID TO ME, HAVE YOU?
?
SHAKE SHAKE
WHY, YOU!! WHAT DID YOU DO TO THIS BEAUTIFUL WOMAN, LUFFY?!
WE DON'T WANT ANY TROUBLE. JUST GET OFF THE SHIP!
SWF SWF
HEY, DON'T LIE! I DIDN'T DO ANYTHING TO YOU!
I SUFFERED A GREAT DEAL BECAUSE OF YOU.
KREEK
NOW...
...TAKE RESPONSIBILITY.
?!

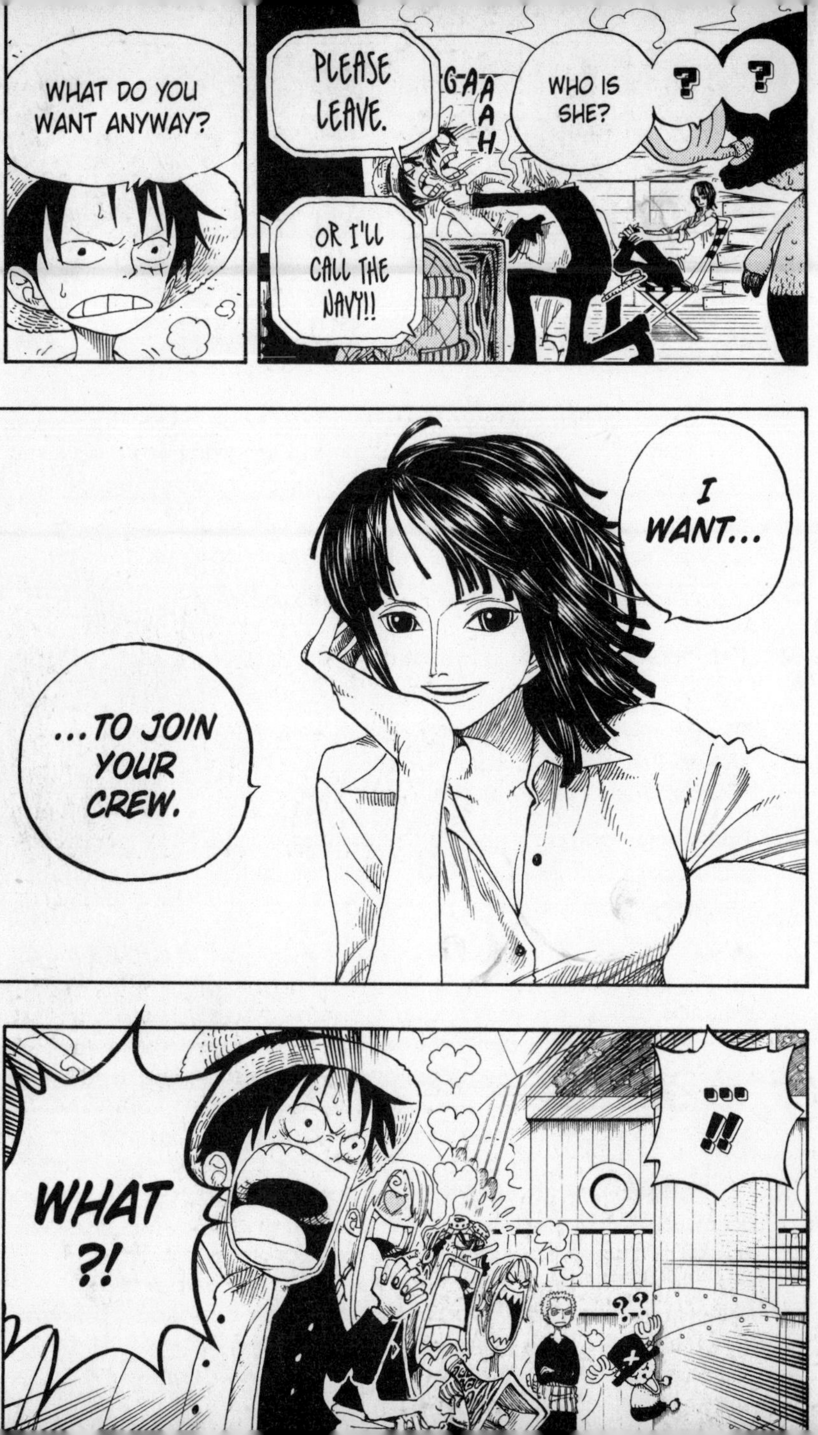
? ?
WHO IS SHE?
GAAAH
PLEASE LEAVE.
OR I'LL CALL THE NAVY!!
WHAT DO YOU WANT ANYWAY?
I WANT...
...TO JOIN YOUR CREW.
...!!
WHAT ?!

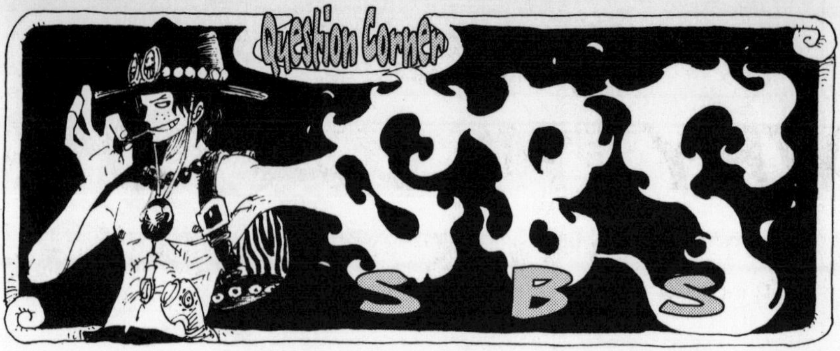
Question Corner
SBS
S B S

Reader: Huh? What, Eiichiro? Hold on! I'm in a hurry! Huh? Say it? Say what?! No, I won't say it! I'm leaving now! I'm outta here! (running off into the distance)

The Question Corner will now begin! (Being nice)

Oda: You said it after all?! ...Have a nice day.

Q: Oda Sensei, just how many liters are you?

--Nori (liquid glue)

A: That's right. It must have been in elementary school...
When I was in the fourth grade...
That's when I saw a kappa (water sprite).

Q: I have a question for you, Oda Sensei. Some of the Navy guys wear uniforms and others don't. Is that based on rank or what? Or do they just get to choose whatever they want?

A: Hmm... I guess you could say that. When you join the Navy, you're issued the standard Navy uniform and cap. (see drawing) This is a very proud moment for the new

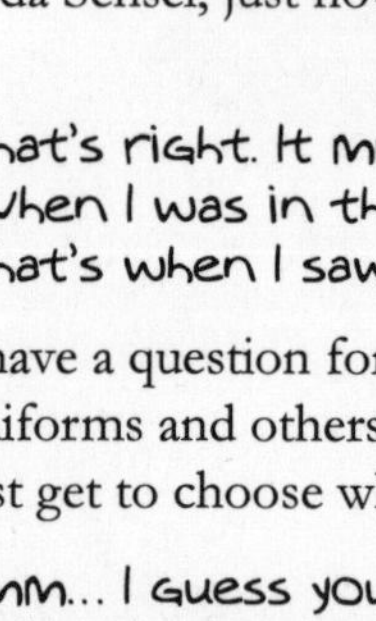
MARINE

recruits, and many of them call home via Transponder Snail to share the news. All the lower ranks have to wear the uniform. (Django and Fullbody are violating regulations.) Once they reach the rank of petty officer, they're allowed to choose different types of uniforms, and civilian clothes are okay too. But all clothing must conform to Navy standards. Those above the rank of lieutenant are also allowed to wear the word "Justice" on their backs. It seems the preferred attire for those above the rank of captain is a Justice coat over a suit. (See volume 8 for more details on the Navy ranks.)

Chapter 218:
WHY THE LOG POSE IS DOME-SHAPED

SIGN SAYS "TAKOYAKI (OCTOPUS FRITTERS)" --ED.

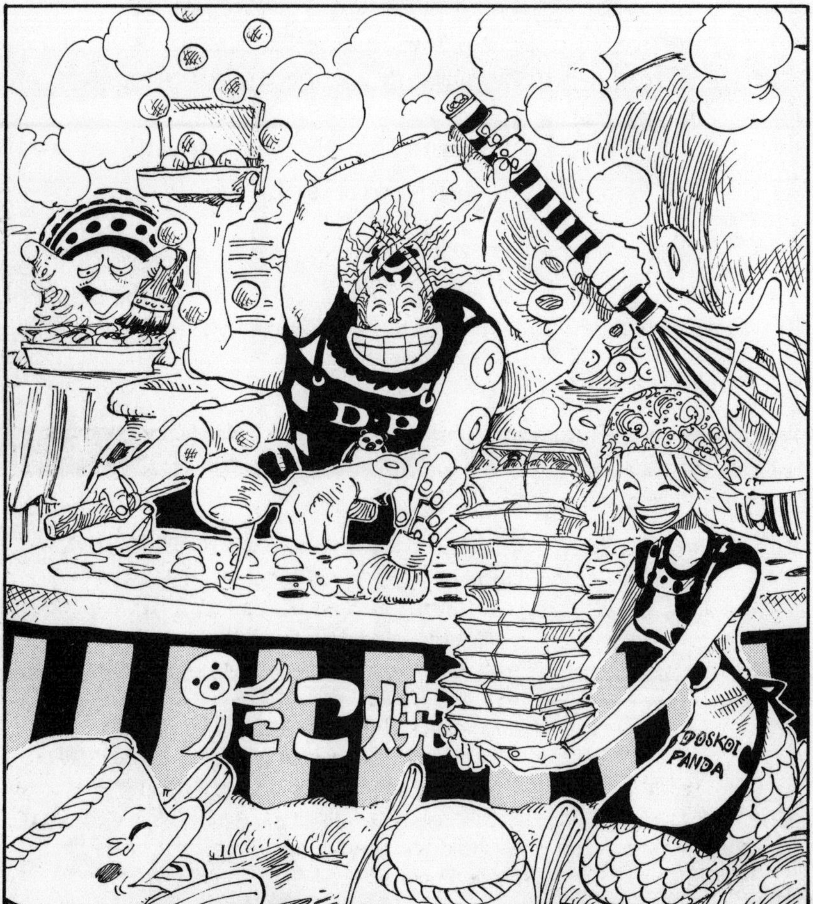
D.P
DOSKOI PANDA

HACHI'S WALK ON THE SEAFLOOR, VOL. 32:
"THE SUDDEN GRAND OPENING OF THE LEGENDARY OCTOPUS FRITTER SHOP"

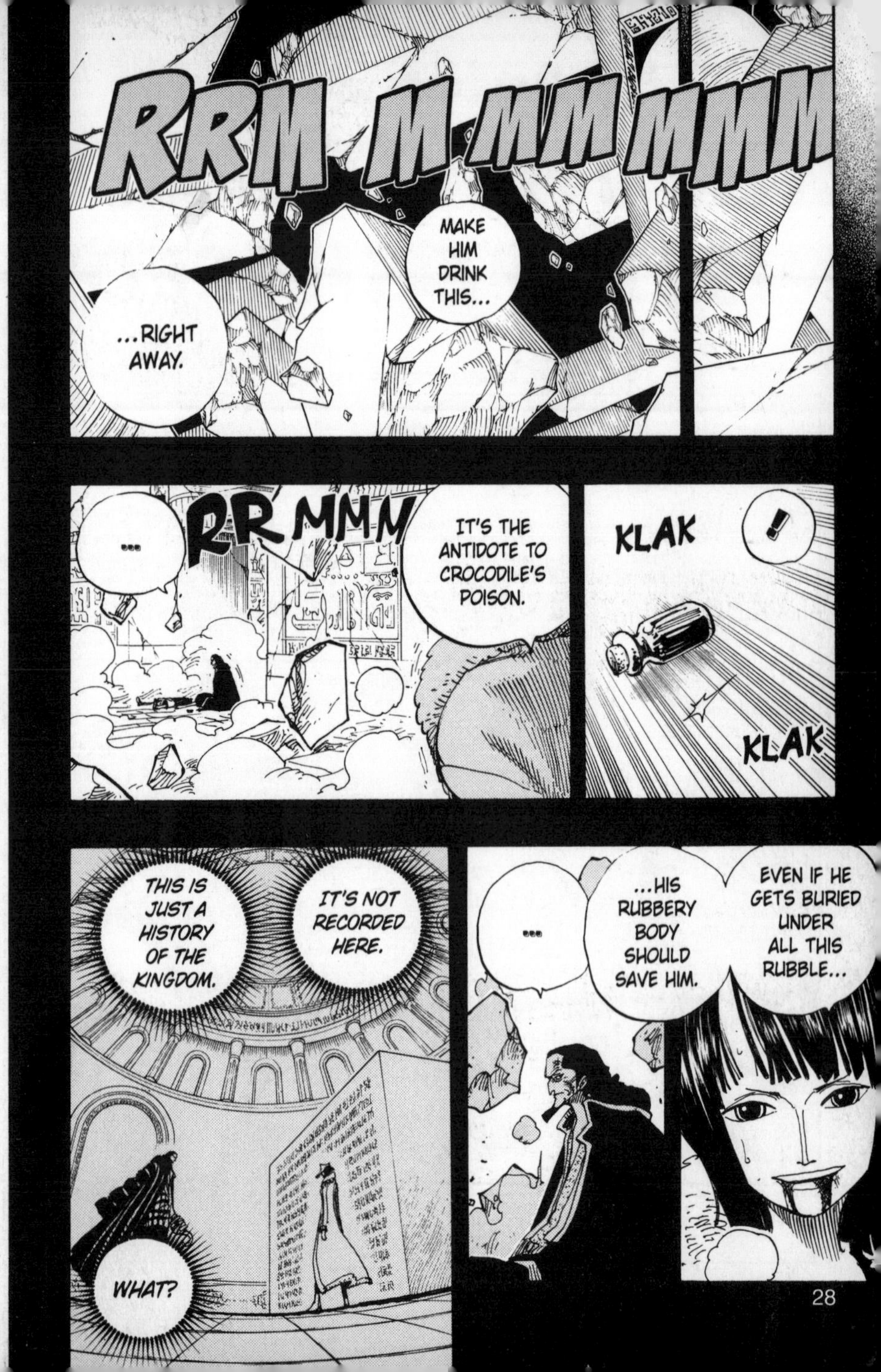
RRM M MM MMMM
MAKE HIM DRINK THIS...
...RIGHT AWAY.
!
KLAK
KLAK
IT'S THE ANTIDOTE TO CROCODILE'S POISON.
RRMMM
...
EVEN IF HE GETS BURIED UNDER ALL THIS RUBBLE...
...HIS RUBBERY BODY SHOULD SAVE HIM.
...
IT'S NOT RECORDED HERE.
THIS IS JUST A HISTORY OF THE KINGDOM.
WHAT?

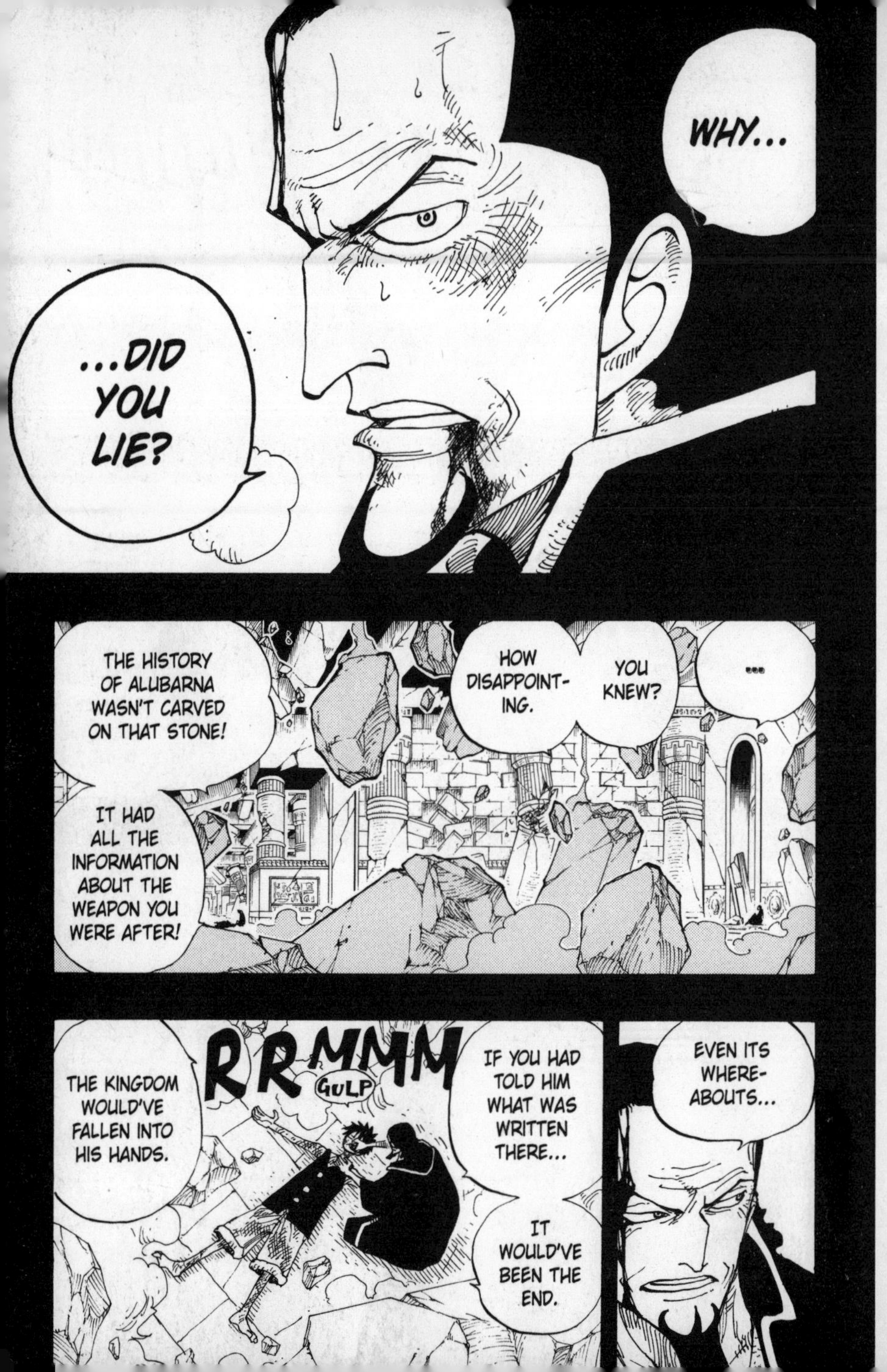
WHY...
...DID YOU LIE?
...
YOU KNEW?
HOW DISAPPOINTING.
THE HISTORY OF ALUBARNA WASN'T CARVED ON THAT STONE!
IT HAD ALL THE INFORMATION ABOUT THE WEAPON YOU WERE AFTER!
EVEN ITS WHERE-ABOUTS...
IF YOU HAD TOLD HIM WHAT WAS WRITTEN THERE...
IT WOULD'VE BEEN THE END.
RRMMM
GULP
THE KINGDOM WOULD'VE FALLEN INTO HIS HANDS.

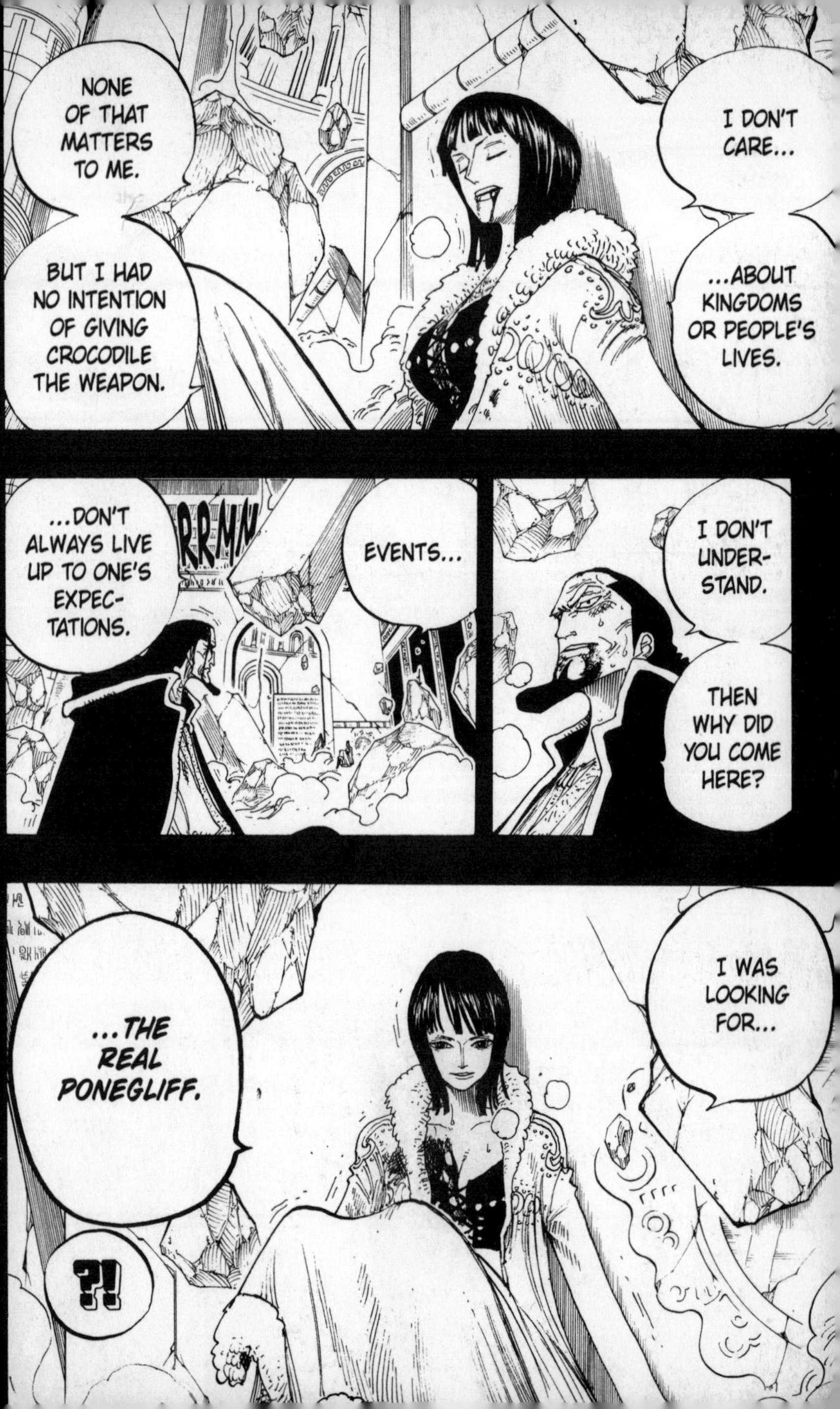
I DON'T CARE...
...ABOUT KINGDOMS OR PEOPLE'S LIVES.
NONE OF THAT MATTERS TO ME.
BUT I HAD NO INTENTION OF GIVING CROCODILE THE WEAPON.
I DON'T UNDER-STAND.
THEN WHY DID YOU COME HERE?
EVENTS...
RRMN
...DON'T ALWAYS LIVE UP TO ONE'S EXPEC-TATIONS.
I WAS LOOKING FOR...
...THE REAL PONEGLIFF.
?!

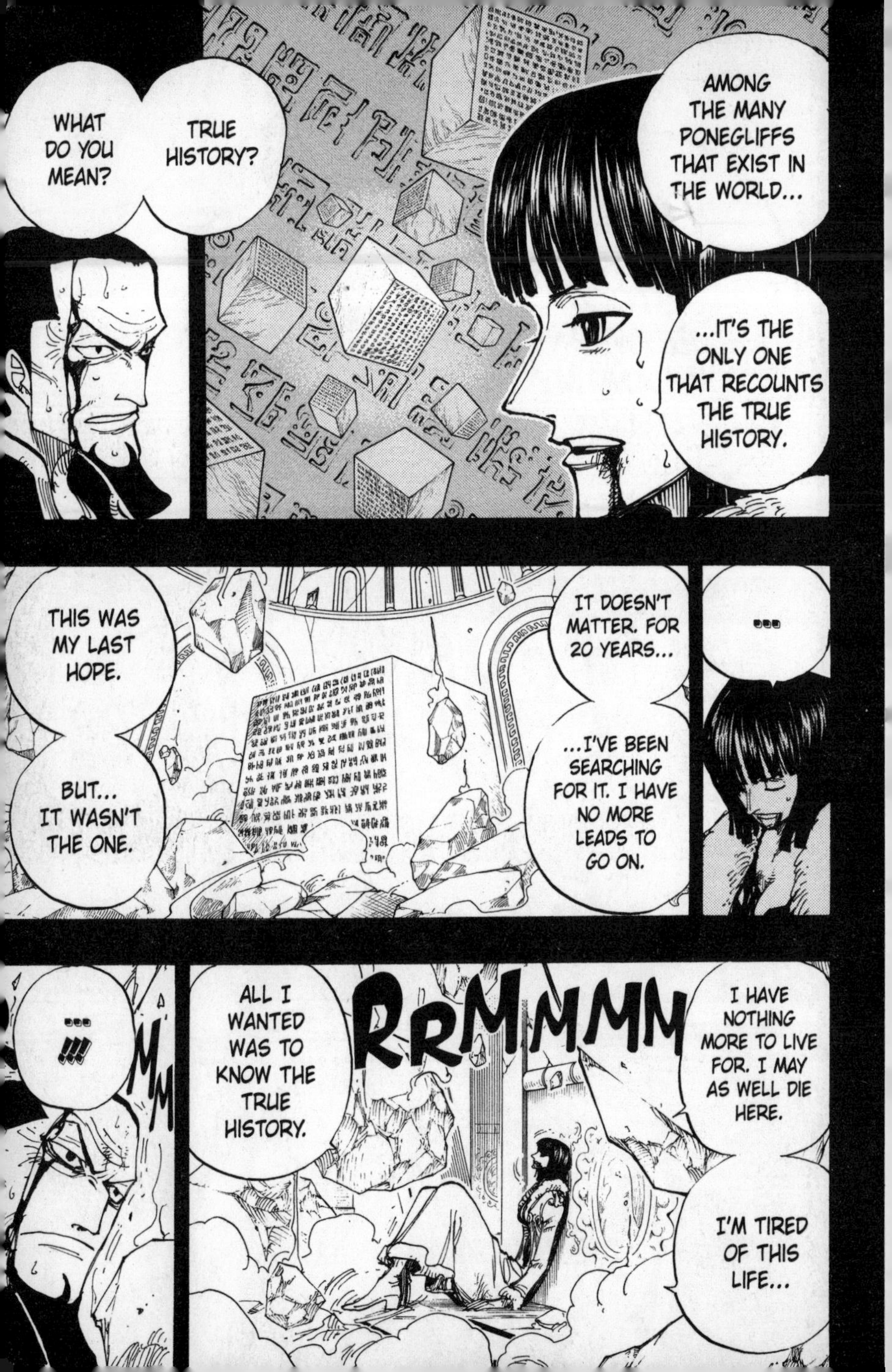
AMONG THE MANY PONEGLIFFS THAT EXIST IN THE WORLD...
...IT'S THE ONLY ONE THAT RECOUNTS THE TRUE HISTORY.
TRUE HISTORY?
WHAT DO YOU MEAN?
...
IT DOESN'T MATTER. FOR 20 YEARS...
...I'VE BEEN SEARCHING FOR IT. I HAVE NO MORE LEADS TO GO ON.
THIS WAS MY LAST HOPE.
BUT... IT WASN'T THE ONE.
I HAVE NOTHING MORE TO LIVE FOR. I MAY AS WELL DIE HERE.
I'M TIRED OF THIS LIFE...
RRMMMM
ALL I WANTED WAS TO KNOW THE TRUE HISTORY.
MM
...
!!!

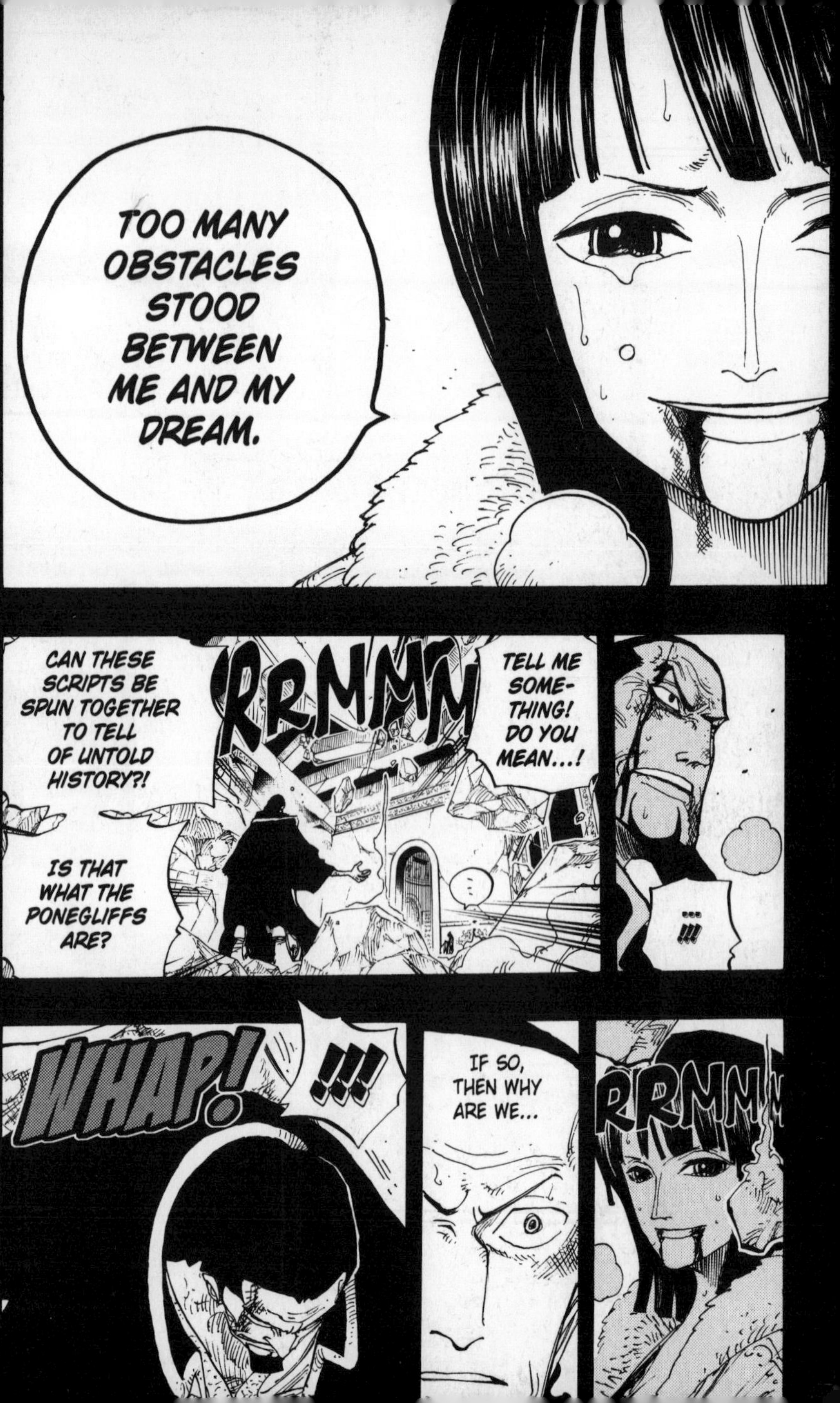
TOO MANY OBSTACLES STOOD BETWEEN ME AND MY DREAM.
...!!!
TELL ME SOME-THING! DO YOU MEAN...!
RRMMM
CAN THESE SCRIPTS BE SPUN TOGETHER TO TELL OF UNTOLD HISTORY?!
IS THAT WHAT THE PONEGLIFFS ARE?
...
RRMMM
IF SO, THEN WHY ARE WE...
WHAP!
!!!

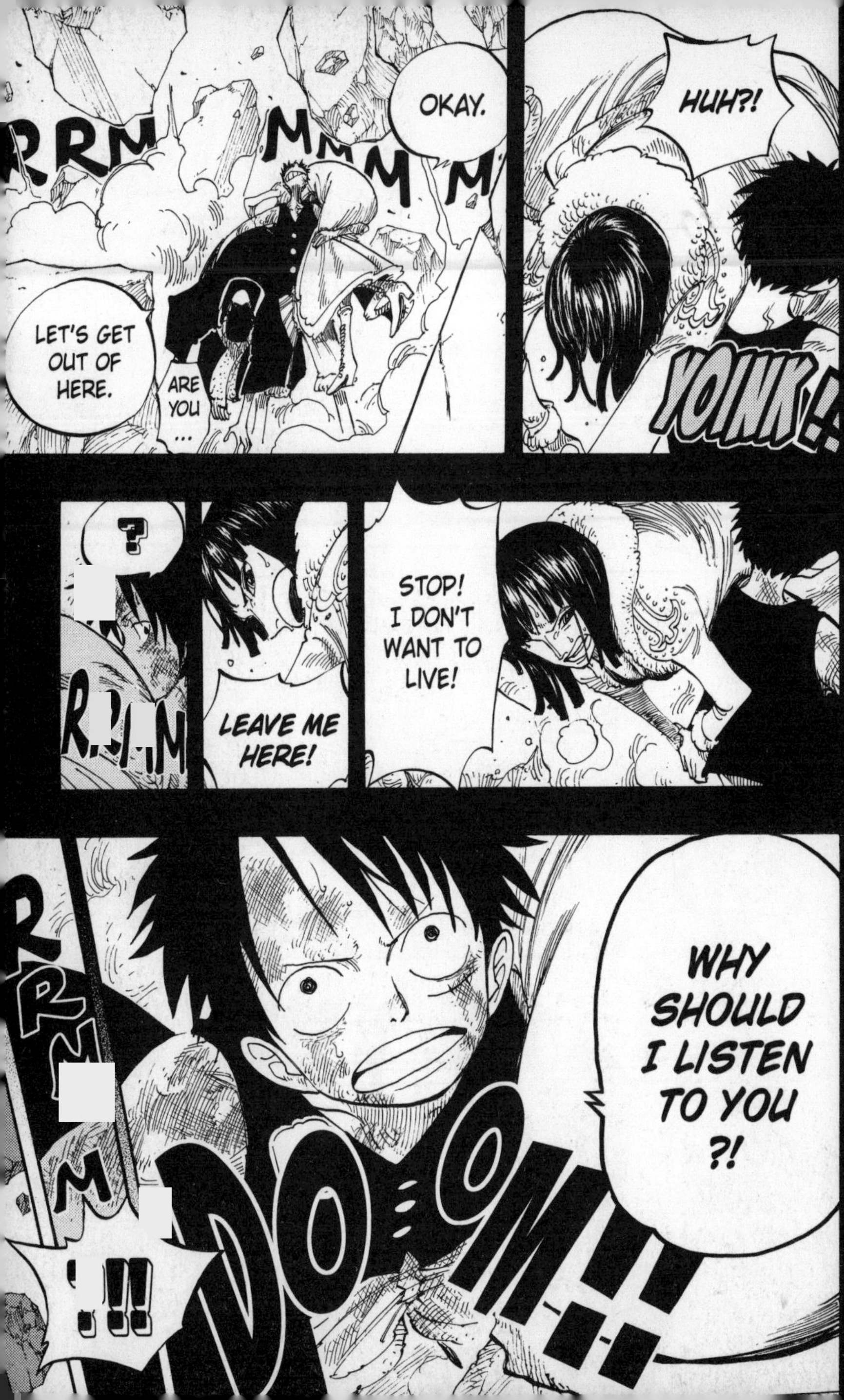
HUH?!
YOINK!!
OKAY.
RRMMMMM
LET'S GET OUT OF HERE.
ARE YOU ...
STOP! I DON'T WANT TO LIVE!
LEAVE ME HERE!
?
WHY SHOULD I LISTEN TO YOU ?!
DOOOM!!

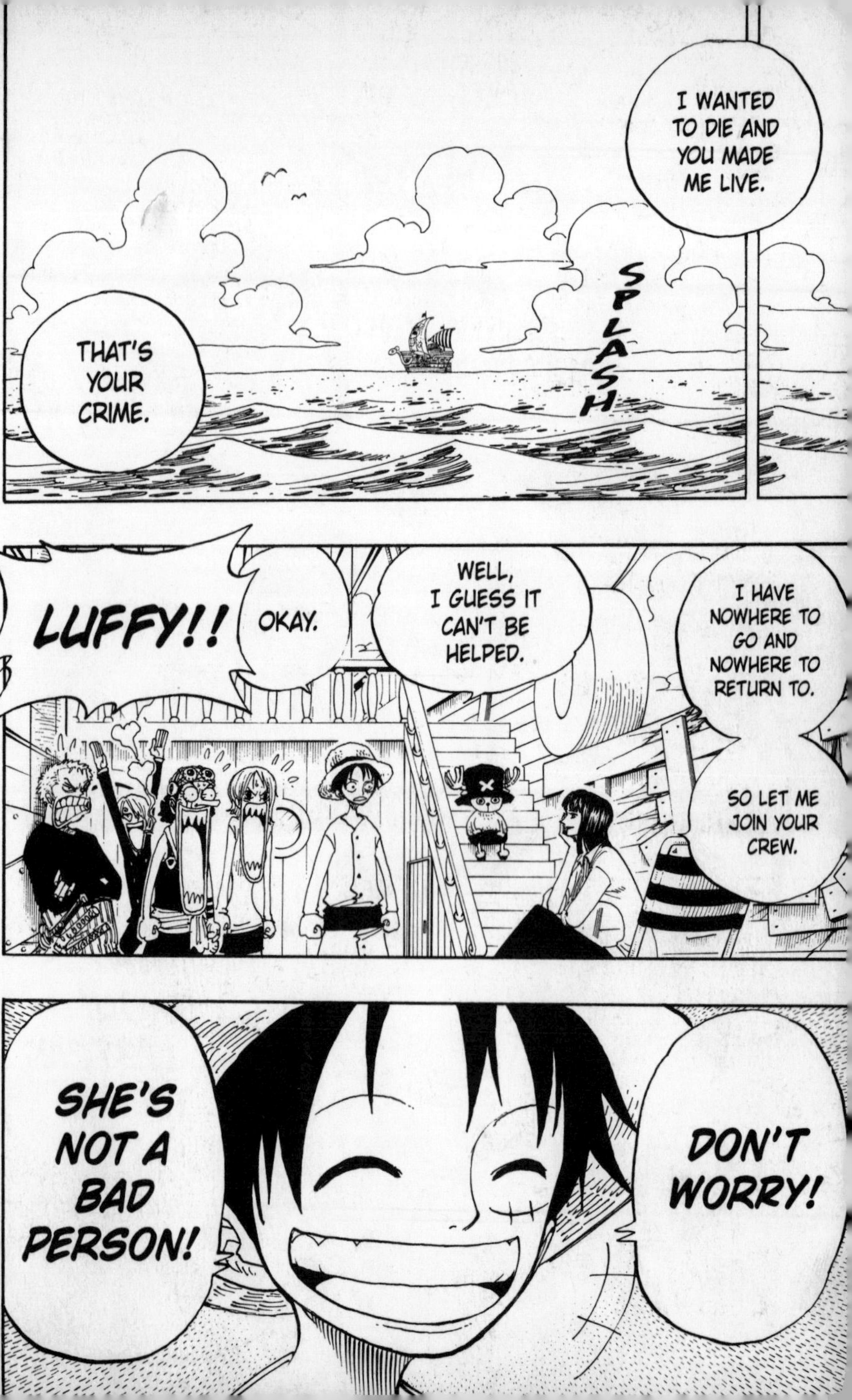
I WANTED TO DIE AND YOU MADE ME LIVE.
SPLASH
THAT'S YOUR CRIME.
I HAVE NOWHERE TO GO AND NOWHERE TO RETURN TO.
SO LET ME JOIN YOUR CREW.
WELL, I GUESS IT CAN'T BE HELPED.
OKAY.
LUFFY!!
DON'T WORRY!
SHE'S NOT A BAD PERSON!

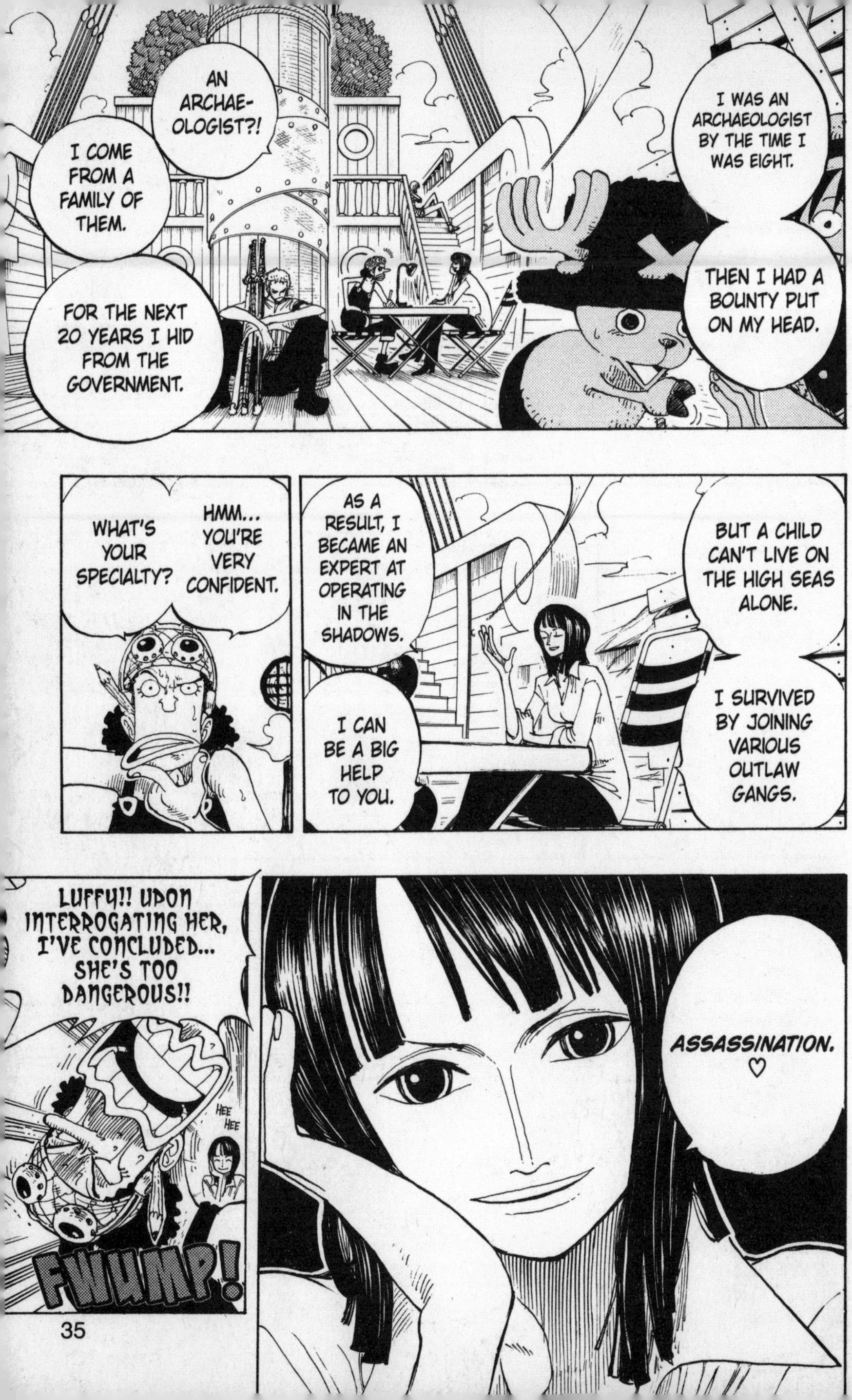
I WAS AN ARCHAEOLOGIST BY THE TIME I WAS EIGHT.
THEN I HAD A BOUNTY PUT ON MY HEAD.
AN ARCHAE-OLOGIST?!
I COME FROM A FAMILY OF THEM.
FOR THE NEXT 20 YEARS I HID FROM THE GOVERNMENT.
BUT A CHILD CAN'T LIVE ON THE HIGH SEAS ALONE.
I SURVIVED BY JOINING VARIOUS OUTLAW GANGS.
AS A RESULT, I BECAME AN EXPERT AT OPERATING IN THE SHADOWS.
I CAN BE A BIG HELP TO YOU.
HMM... YOU'RE VERY CONFIDENT.
WHAT'S YOUR SPECIALTY?
ASSASSINATION. ♡
LUFFY!! UPON INTERROGATING HER, I'VE CONCLUDED... SHE'S TOO DANGEROUS!!
HEE HEE
FWUMP!

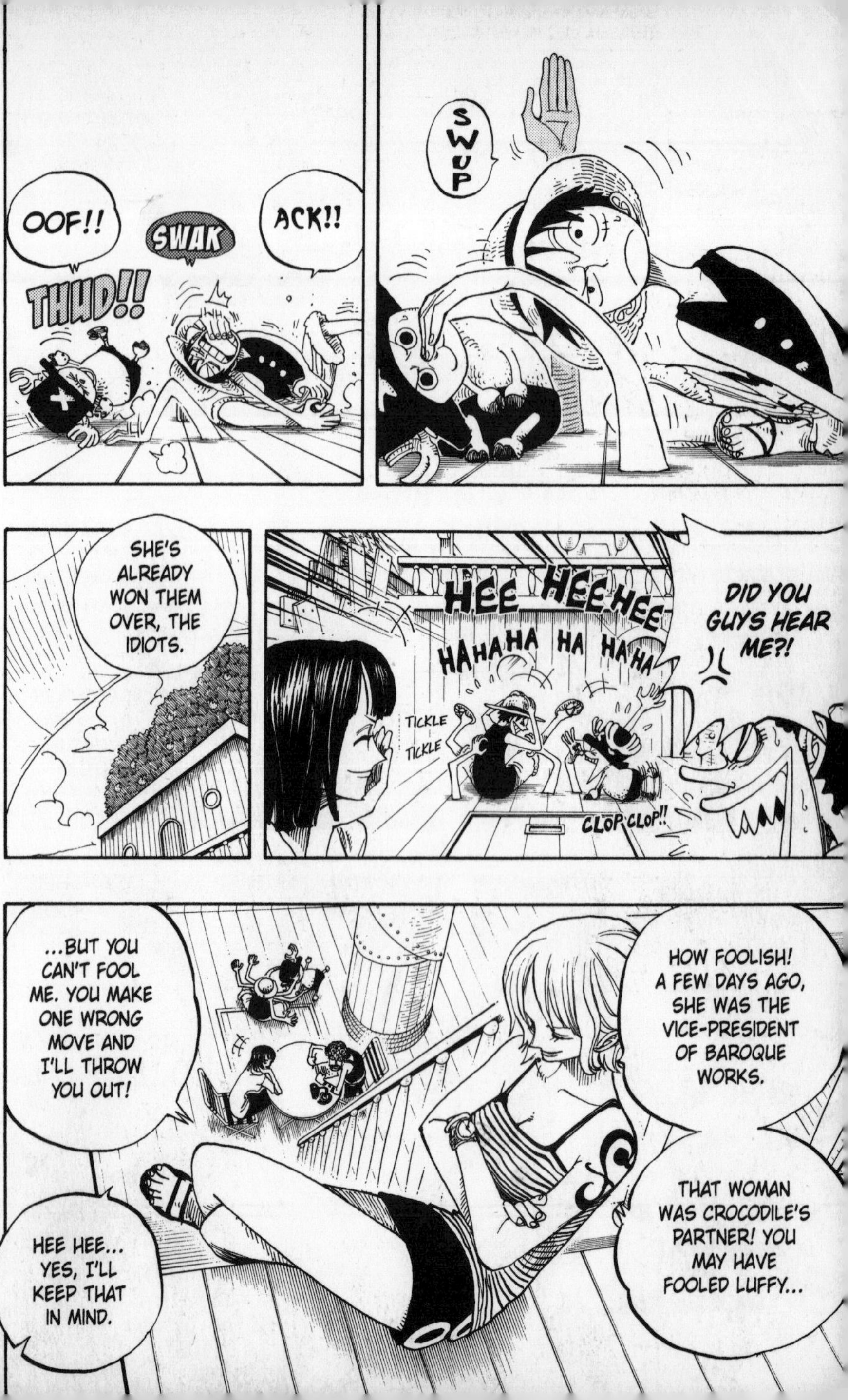
SWUP
ACK!!
SWAK
OOF!!
THUD!!
DID YOU GUYS HEAR ME?!
HEE HEE HEE HEE
HA HA HA HA HA HA
TICKLE TICKLE
CLOP CLOP!!
SHE'S ALREADY WON THEM OVER, THE IDIOTS.
HOW FOOLISH! A FEW DAYS AGO, SHE WAS THE VICE-PRESIDENT OF BAROQUE WORKS.
THAT WOMAN WAS CROCODILE'S PARTNER! YOU MAY HAVE FOOLED LUFFY...
...BUT YOU CAN'T FOOL ME. YOU MAKE ONE WRONG MOVE AND I'LL THROW YOU OUT!
HEE HEE... YES, I'LL KEEP THAT IN MIND.

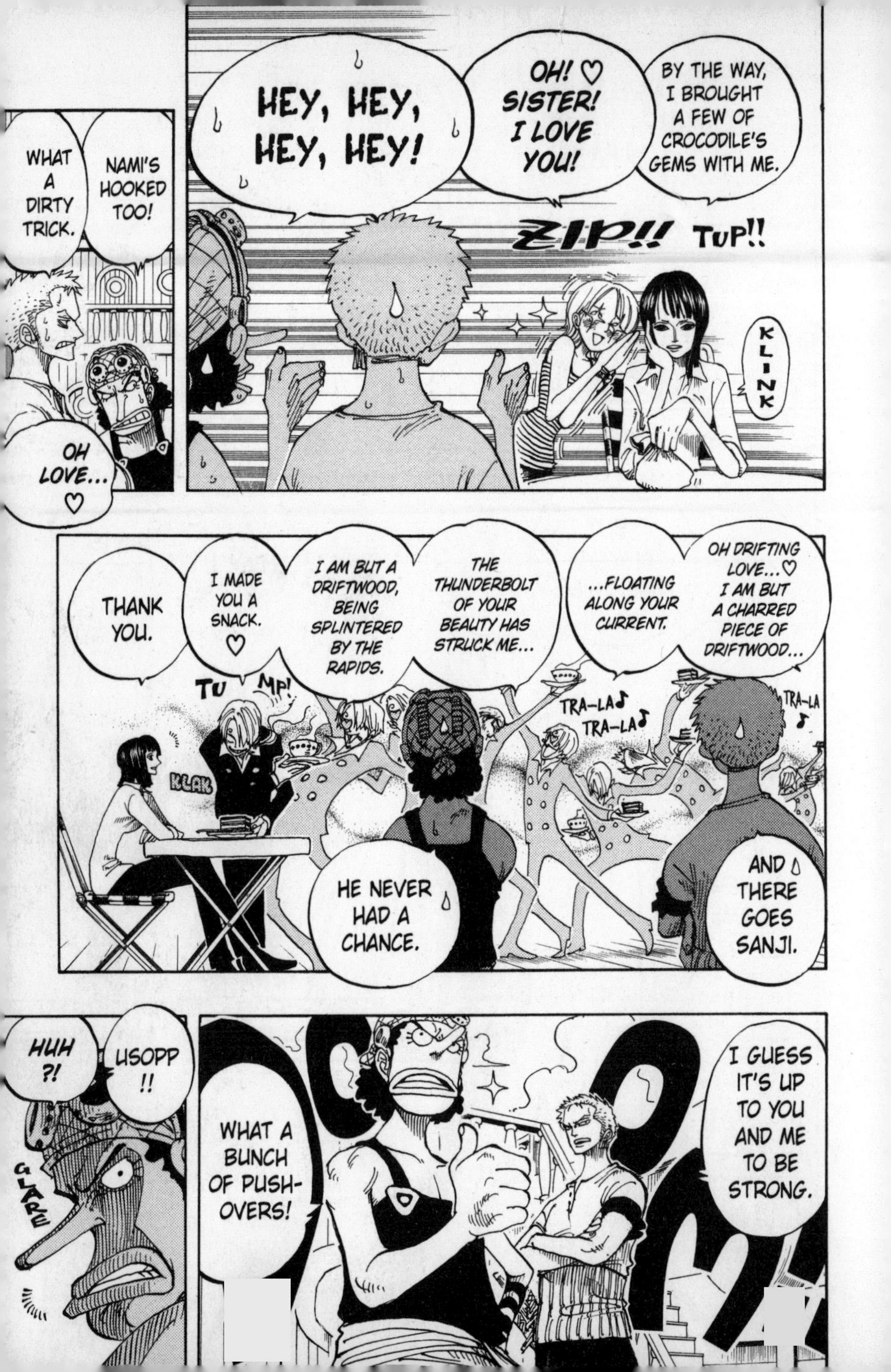
BY THE WAY, I BROUGHT A FEW OF CROCODILE'S GEMS WITH ME.
OH! ♡ SISTER! I LOVE YOU!
HEY, HEY, HEY, HEY!
ZIP!!
TUP!!
KLINK
NAMI'S HOOKED TOO!
WHAT A DIRTY TRICK.
OH LOVE... ♡
OH DRIFTING LOVE...♡ I AM BUT A CHARRED PIECE OF DRIFTWOOD...
...FLOATING ALONG YOUR CURRENT.
THE THUNDERBOLT OF YOUR BEAUTY HAS STRUCK ME...
I AM BUT A DRIFTWOOD, BEING SPLINTERED BY THE RAPIDS.
I MADE YOU A SNACK. ♡
THANK YOU.
TU MP!
KLAK
TRA-LA♪
TRA-LA TRA-LA♪
AND THERE GOES SANJI.
HE NEVER HAD A CHANCE.
I GUESS IT'S UP TO YOU AND ME TO BE STRONG.
WHAT A BUNCH OF PUSH-OVERS!
USOPP !!
HUH ?!
GLARE

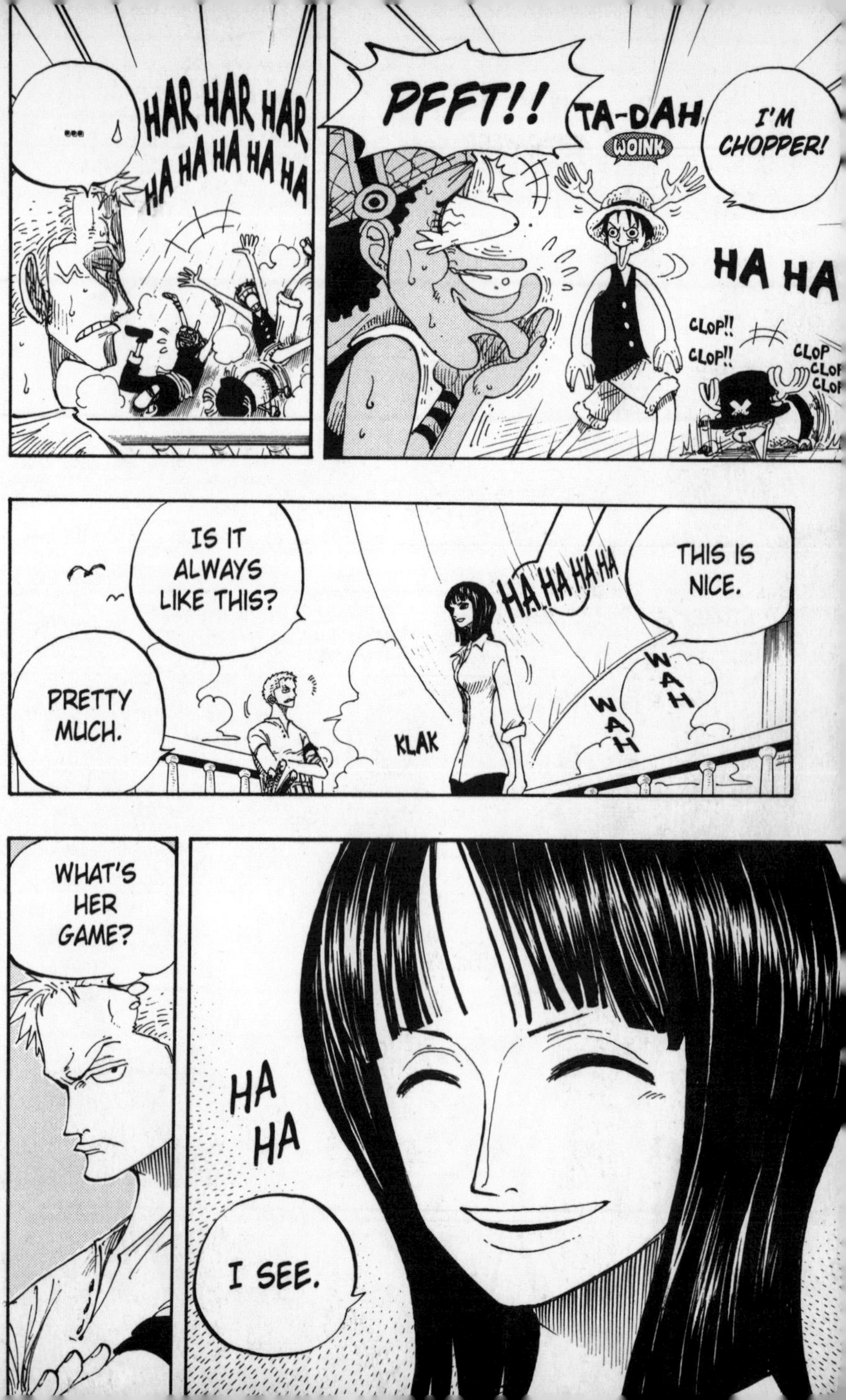
I'M CHOPPER!
TA-DAH
WOINK
PFFT!!
HA HA
CLOP!! CLOP!!
CLOP CLOP CLOP
HAR HAR HAR HA HA HA HA HA
...
THIS IS NICE.
HA HA HA HA
WAH WAH
IS IT ALWAYS LIKE THIS?
KLAK
PRETTY MUCH.
HA HA
I SEE.
WHAT'S HER GAME?

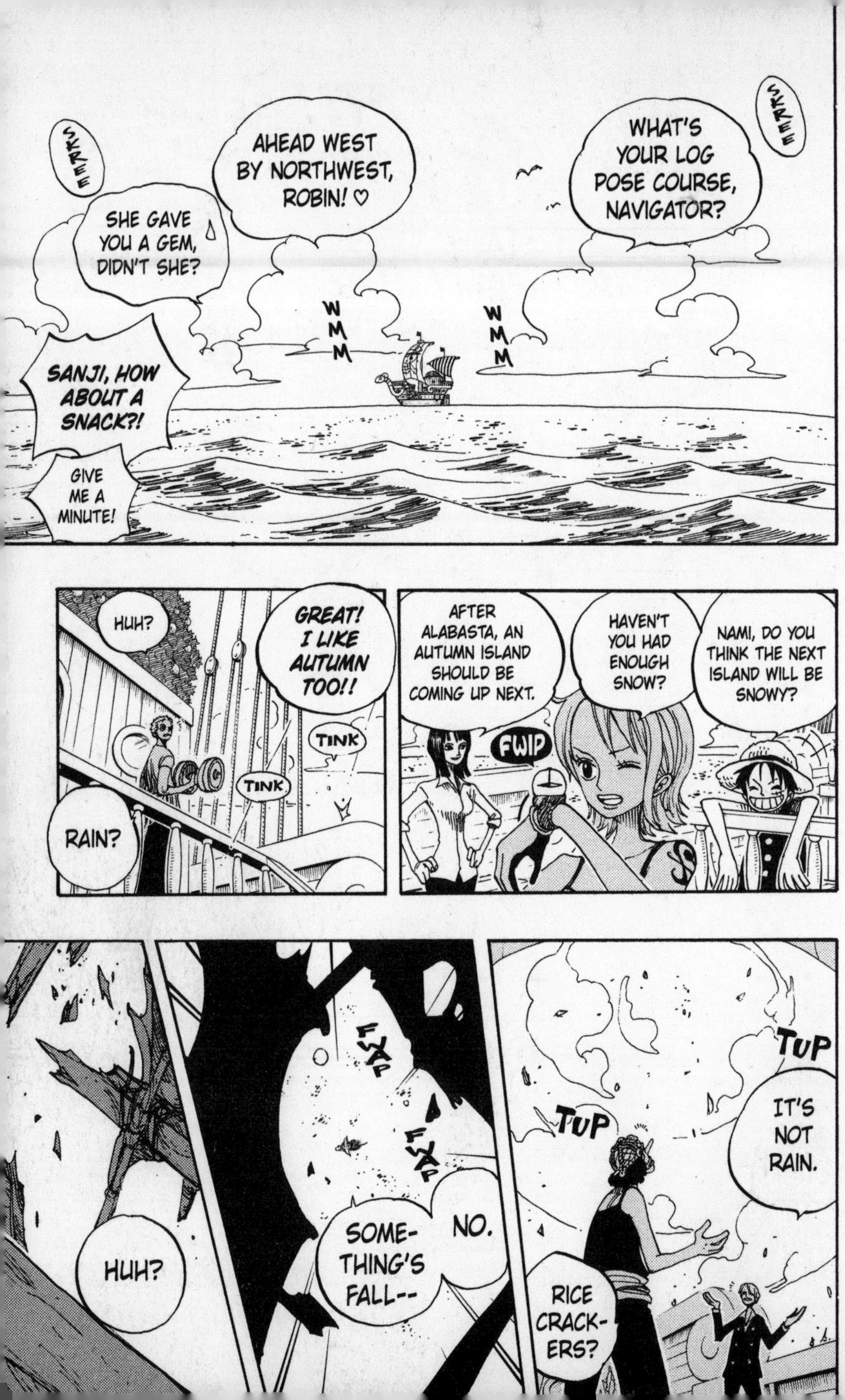
SKREE
WHAT'S YOUR LOG POSE COURSE, NAVIGATOR?
AHEAD WEST BY NORTHWEST, ROBIN! ♡
SKREE
SHE GAVE YOU A GEM, DIDN'T SHE?
WMM
WMM
SANJI, HOW ABOUT A SNACK?!
GIVE ME A MINUTE!
NAMI, DO YOU THINK THE NEXT ISLAND WILL BE SNOWY?
HAVEN'T YOU HAD ENOUGH SNOW?
AFTER ALABASTA, AN AUTUMN ISLAND SHOULD BE COMING UP NEXT.
FWIP
GREAT! I LIKE AUTUMN TOO!!
HUH?
TINK
TINK
RAIN?
TUP
IT'S NOT RAIN.
TUP
RICE CRACK-ERS?
FWAP
FWAP
NO.
SOME-THING'S FALL--
HUH?

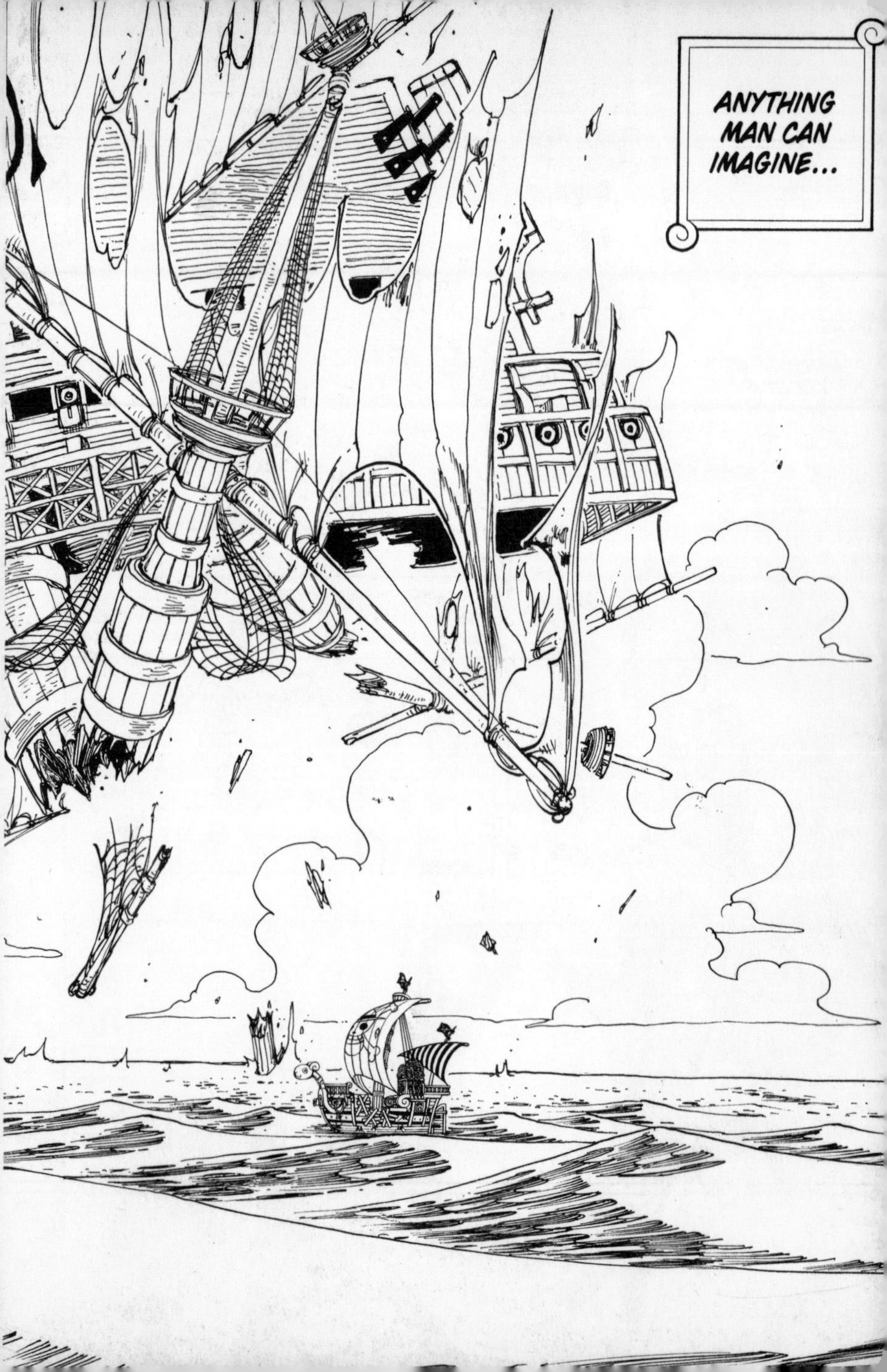
ANYTHING MAN CAN IMAGINE...

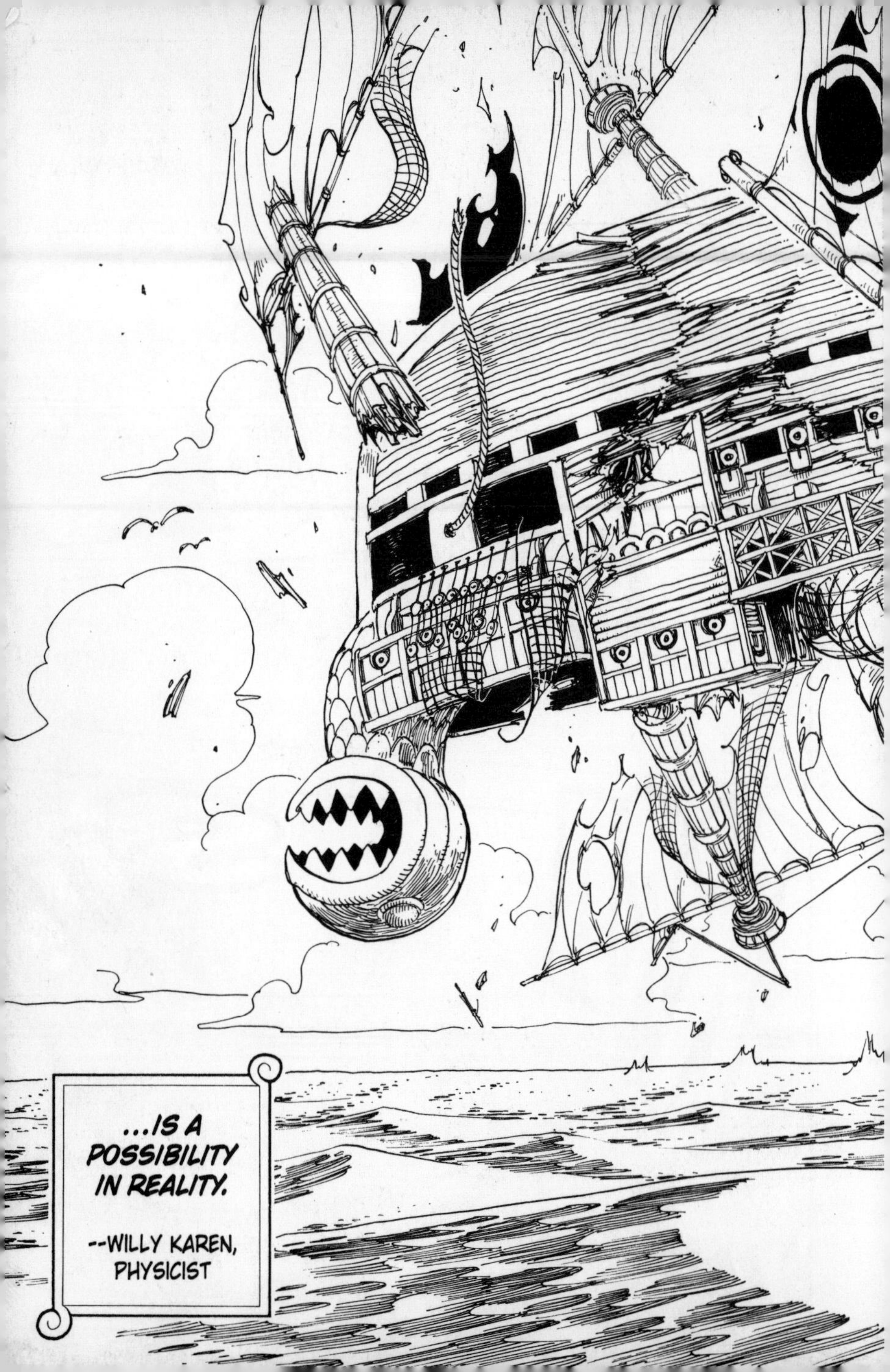
...IS A POSSIBILITY IN REALITY.
--WILLY KAREN, PHYSICIST

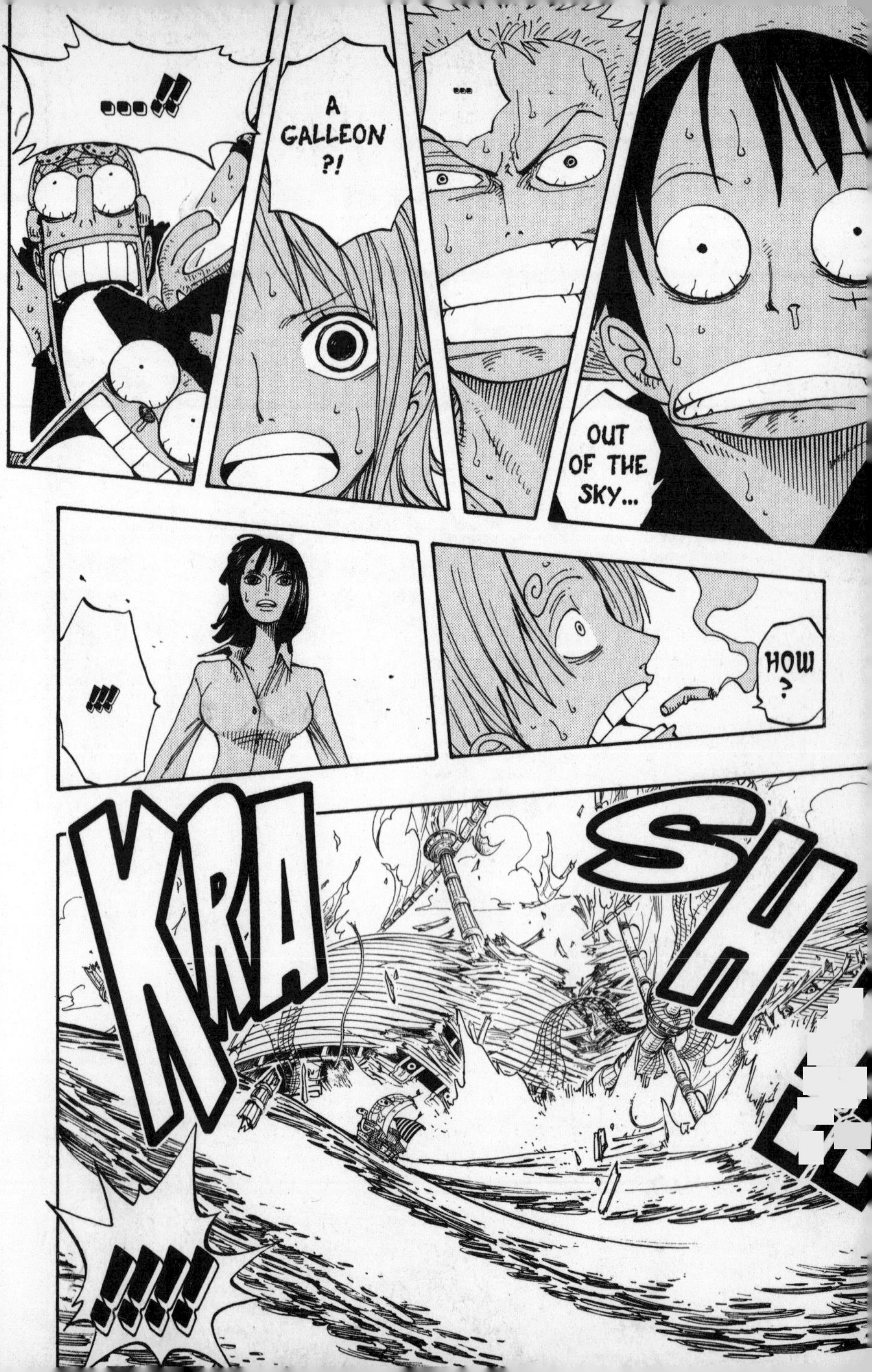
OUT OF THE SKY...
...
A GALLEON ?!
...!!
HOW ?
!!!
KRASH
!!!!

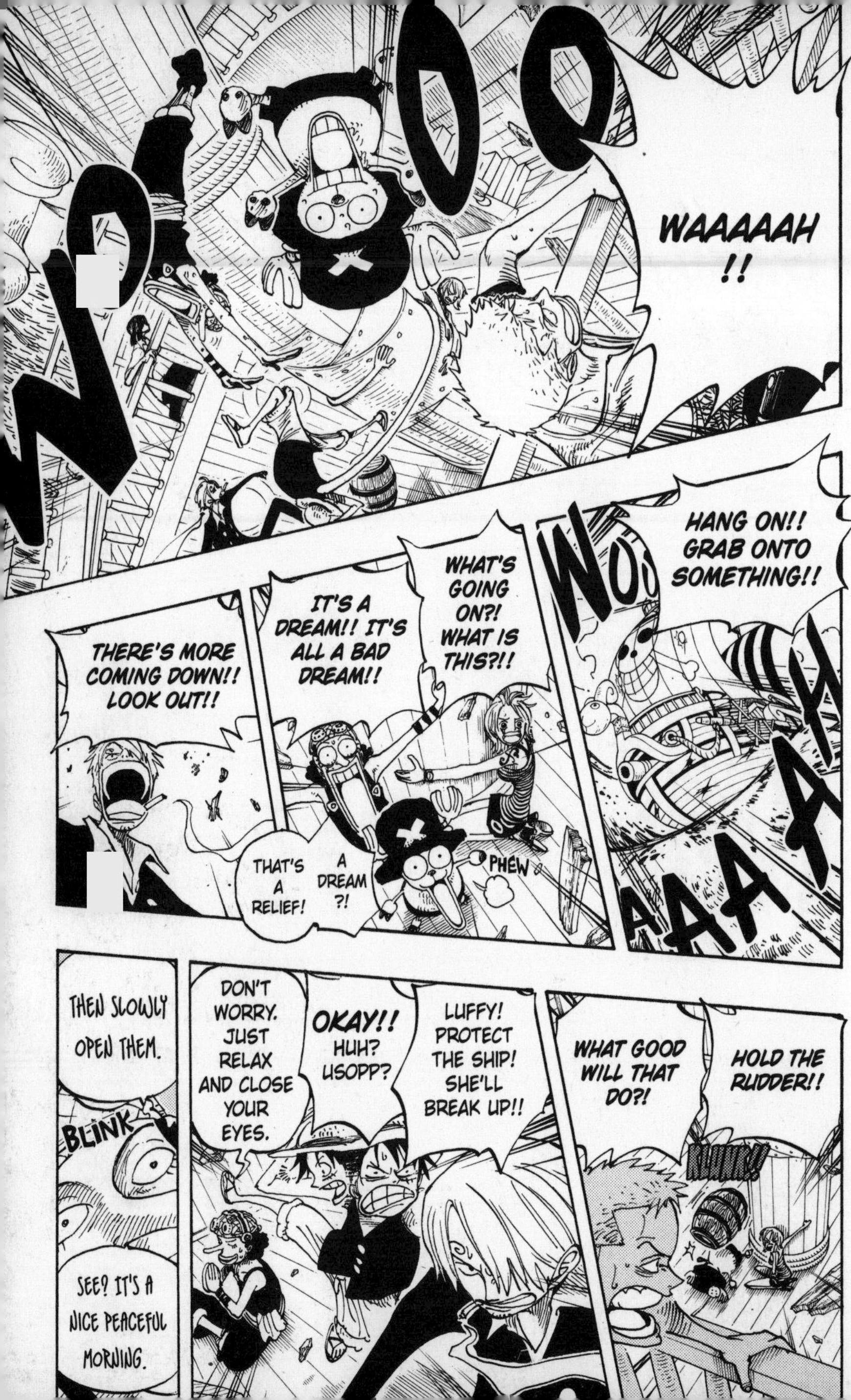
WOOO
WAAAAAH!!
HANG ON!! GRAB ONTO SOMETHING!!
WOOAAAAAH
WHAT'S GOING ON?! WHAT IS THIS?!!
IT'S A DREAM!! IT'S ALL A BAD DREAM!!
A DREAM?!
THAT'S A RELIEF!
PHEW
THERE'S MORE COMING DOWN!! LOOK OUT!!
HOLD THE RUDDER!!
WHAT GOOD WILL THAT DO?!
LUFFY! PROTECT THE SHIP! SHE'LL BREAK UP!!
OKAY!!
HUH? USOPP?
DON'T WORRY. JUST RELAX AND CLOSE YOUR EYES.
THEN SLOWLY OPEN THEM.
BLINK
SEE? IT'S A NICE PEACEFUL MORNING.

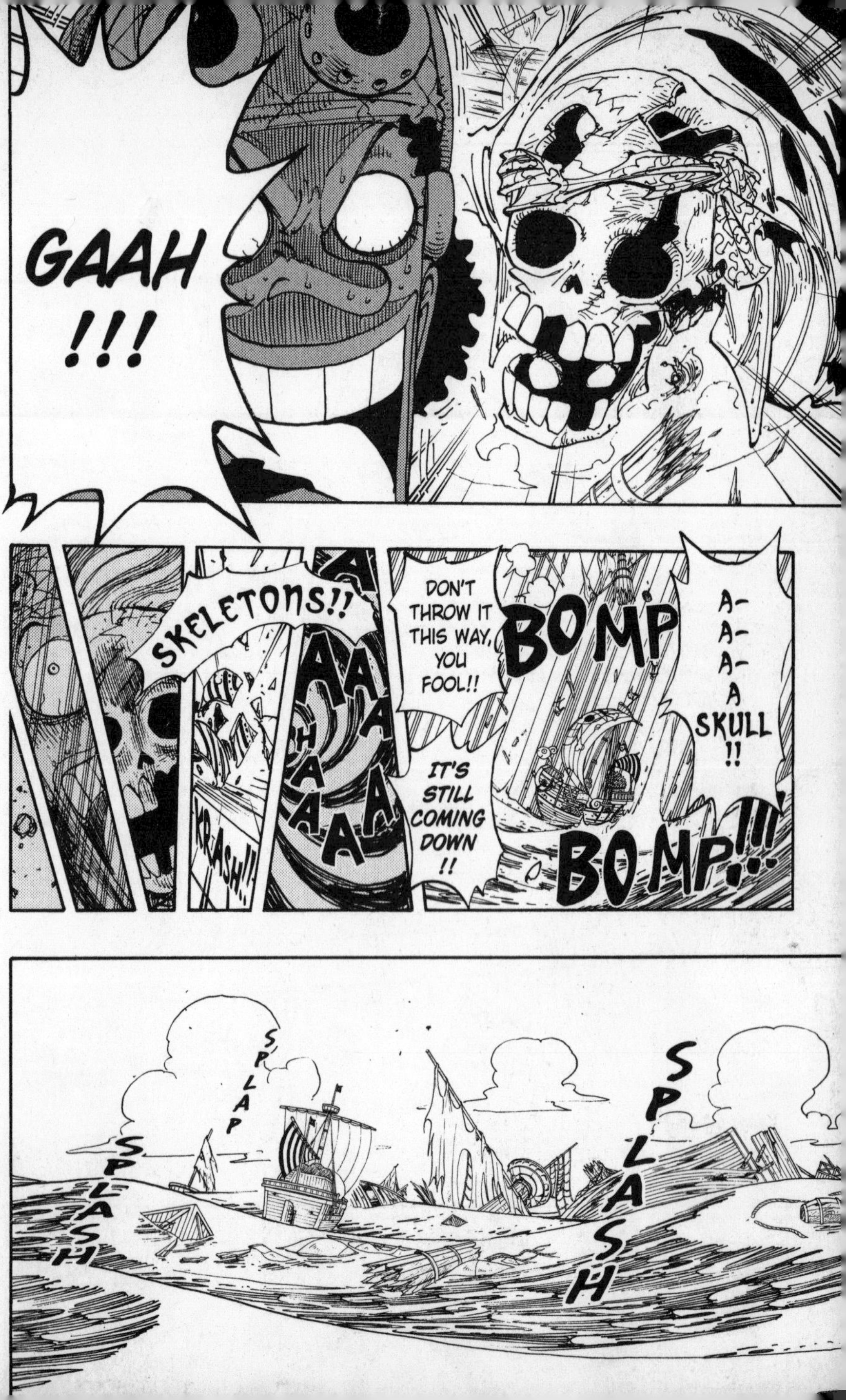
GAAH!!!
A-A-A-A SKULL!!
BOMP
BOMP!!!
DON'T THROW IT THIS WAY, YOU FOOL!!
IT'S STILL COMING DOWN!!
AAAAAHAAAAA
SKELETONS!!
KRASH!!
SPLASH
SPLAP
SPLASH

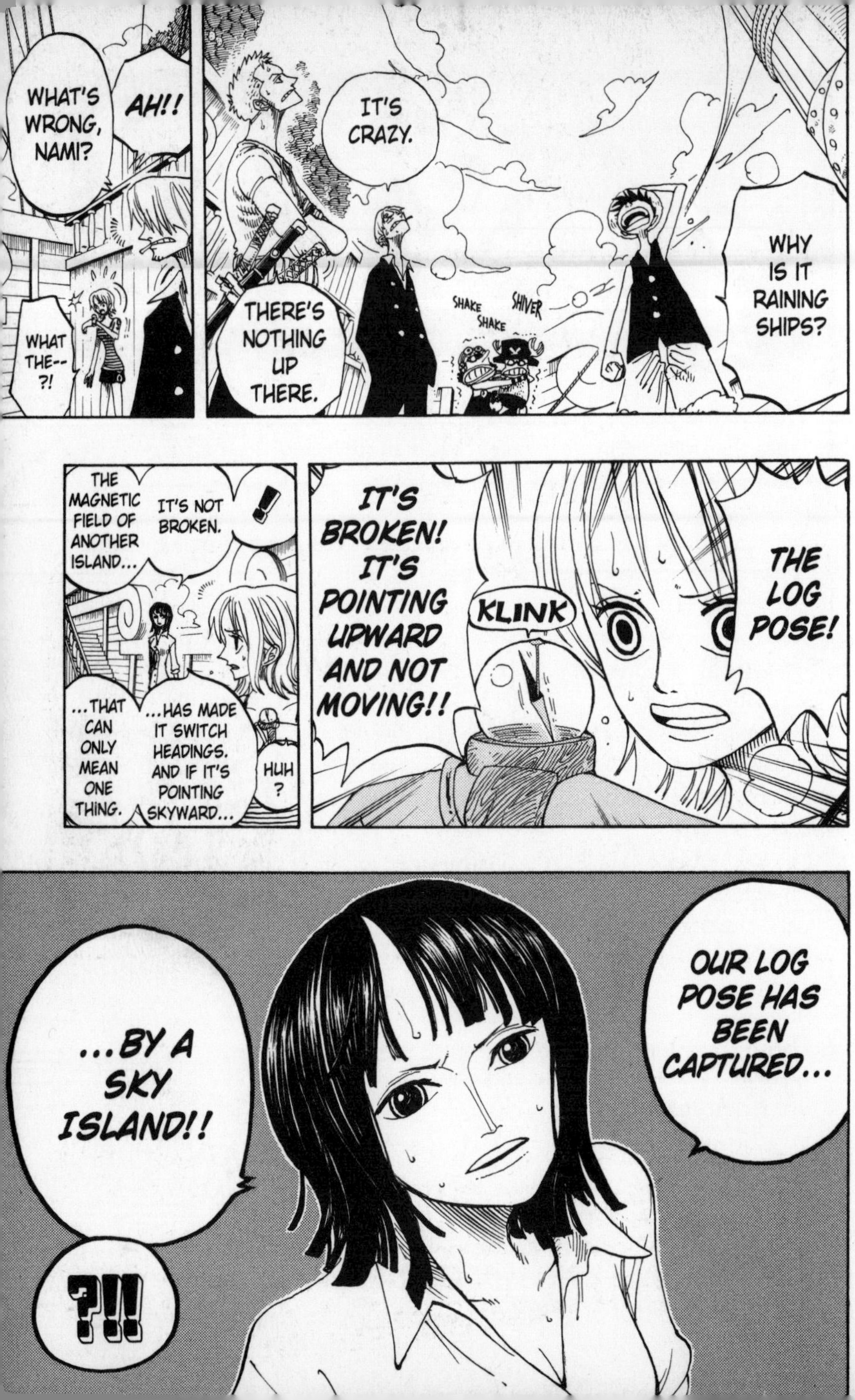
WHY IS IT RAINING SHIPS?
IT'S CRAZY.
SHIVER
SHAKE SHAKE
THERE'S NOTHING UP THERE.
AH!!
WHAT'S WRONG, NAMI?
WHAT THE-- ?!
THE LOG POSE!
IT'S BROKEN! IT'S POINTING UPWARD AND NOT MOVING!!
KLINK
!
IT'S NOT BROKEN.
THE MAGNETIC FIELD OF ANOTHER ISLAND...
HUH?
...HAS MADE IT SWITCH HEADINGS. AND IF IT'S POINTING SKYWARD...
...THAT CAN ONLY MEAN ONE THING.
OUR LOG POSE HAS BEEN CAPTURED...
...BY A SKY ISLAND!!
?!!

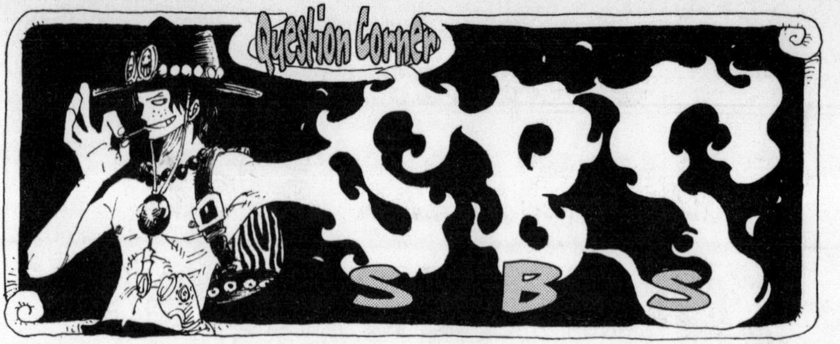
Question Corner
SBS

Q: Time passes more slowly in the manga world, doesn't it? Does that mean that we'll have to wait another two years before it's Luffy's birthday?

A: No, no, Luffy has a birthday every year. It's just that he turns 17 every year. Isn't he lucky?

Q: Say, Oda Sensei, in chapter 216 of volume 23 in the second panel of page 215, one of the passersby is Mr. 3. He's walking along like nothing happened! What's going on? Didn't he die? Please explain in exactly 75 letters! (Not including punctuation marks.)

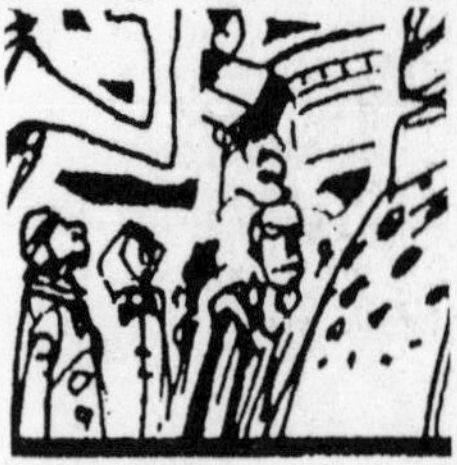

A: Oh yes, that's him. But explaining it in 75 letters won't be easy. The reason he's there? Easy. I felt like it. Oh!! Shucks, I was too long.

Q: How do you do, Oda Sensei. Here's a question for you. Who takes the pictures for those wanted posters the Navy put out?

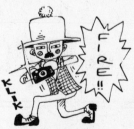

A: That's him (→). Real name: Atatchi. Also known as: Atacchan. He's very agile and can sneak into any place. When he snaps a picture, he yells out: "Fire!!" Hence, his nickname "Fire Atacchan."

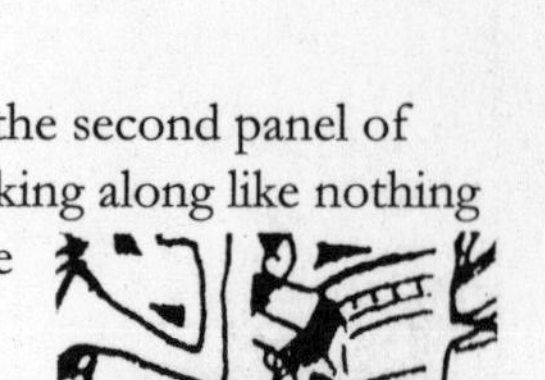
FIRE!!
KLIK

FIRE ATACCHAN
HEAD OF THE NAVY
PHOTOGRAPHY DEPARTMENT

Chapter 219:
MASIRA THE SALVAGE KING

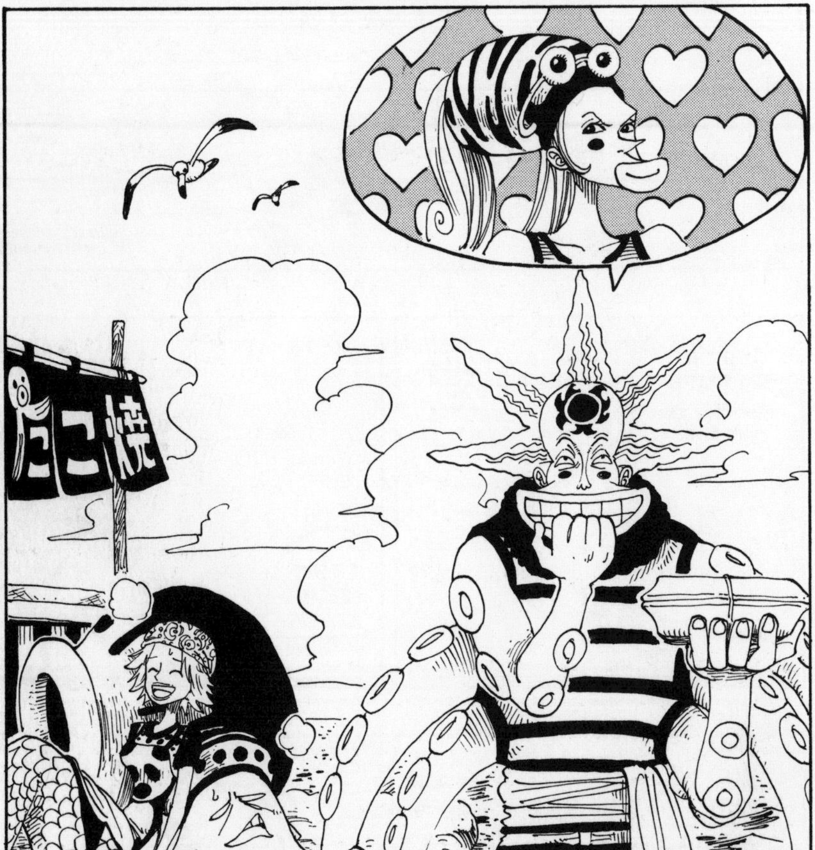

HACHI'S WALK ON THE SEAFLOOR, VOL. 33:
"THE CATFISH VILLAGE IS SAVED;
PROPOSING WITH THE LAST BOX ♡"

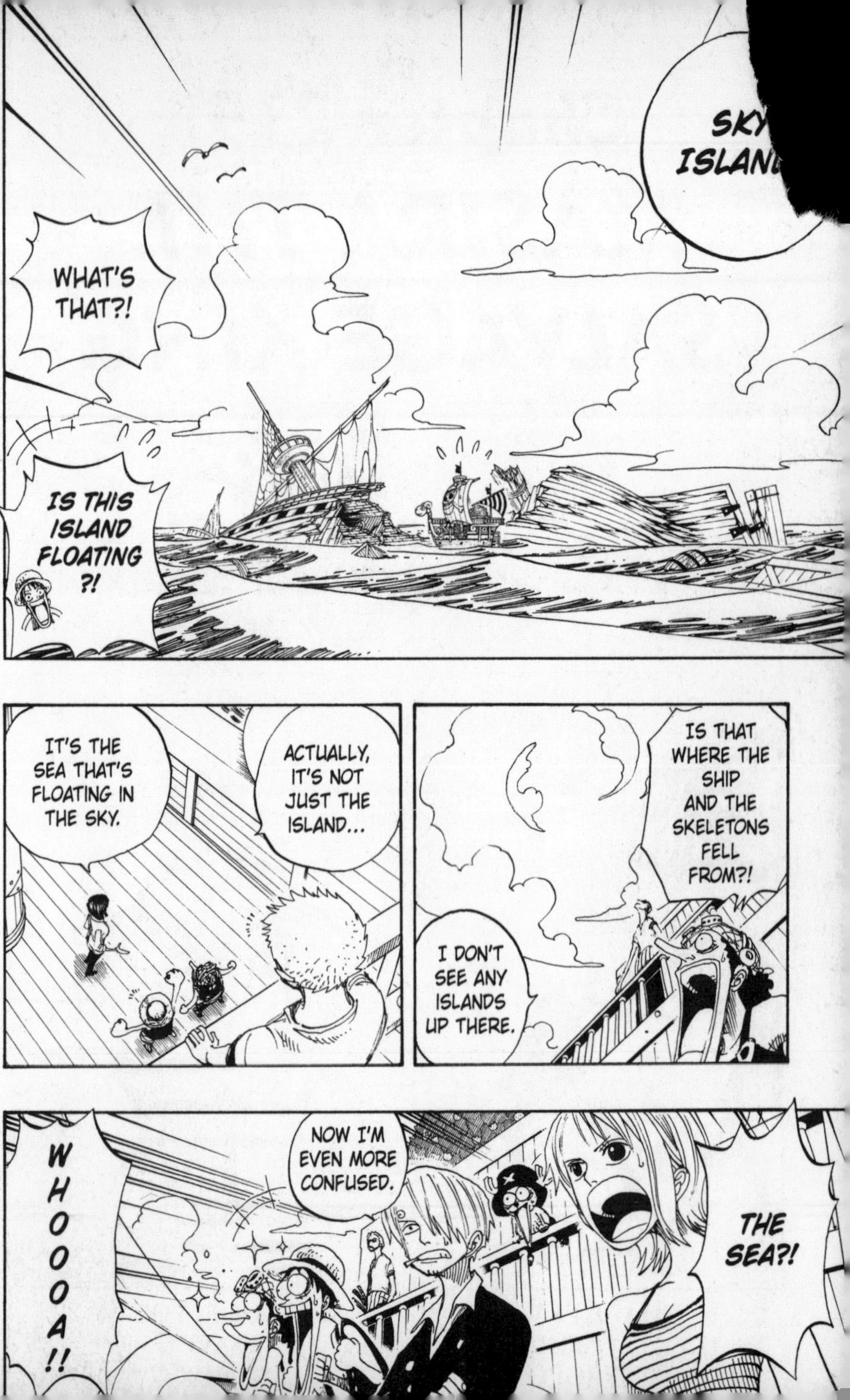
SKY ISLAN
WHAT'S THAT?!
IS THIS ISLAND FLOATING?!
IS THAT WHERE THE SHIP AND THE SKELETONS FELL FROM?!
I DON'T SEE ANY ISLANDS UP THERE.
ACTUALLY, IT'S NOT JUST THE ISLAND...
IT'S THE SEA THAT'S FLOATING IN THE SKY.
THE SEA?!
NOW I'M EVEN MORE CONFUSED.
WHOOOOA!!

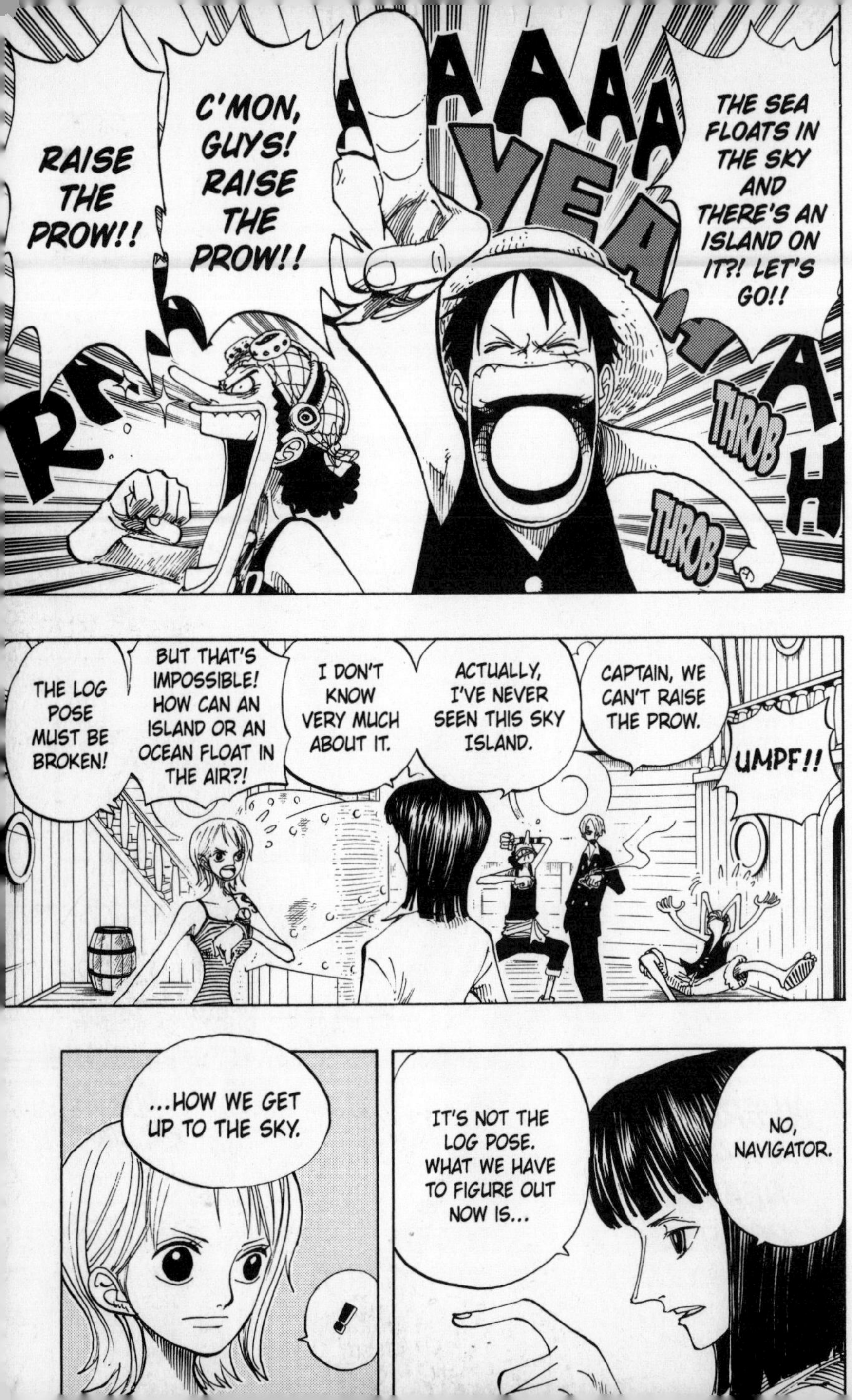
THE SEA FLOATS IN THE SKY AND THERE'S AN ISLAND ON IT?! LET'S GO!!
YEA
THROB
THROB
C'MON, GUYS! RAISE THE PROW!!
RAISE THE PROW!!
UMPF!!
CAPTAIN, WE CAN'T RAISE THE PROW.
ACTUALLY, I'VE NEVER SEEN THIS SKY ISLAND.
I DON'T KNOW VERY MUCH ABOUT IT.
BUT THAT'S IMPOSSIBLE! HOW CAN AN ISLAND OR AN OCEAN FLOAT IN THE AIR?!
THE LOG POSE MUST BE BROKEN!
NO, NAVIGATOR.
IT'S NOT THE LOG POSE. WHAT WE HAVE TO FIGURE OUT NOW IS...
...HOW WE GET UP TO THE SKY.
!

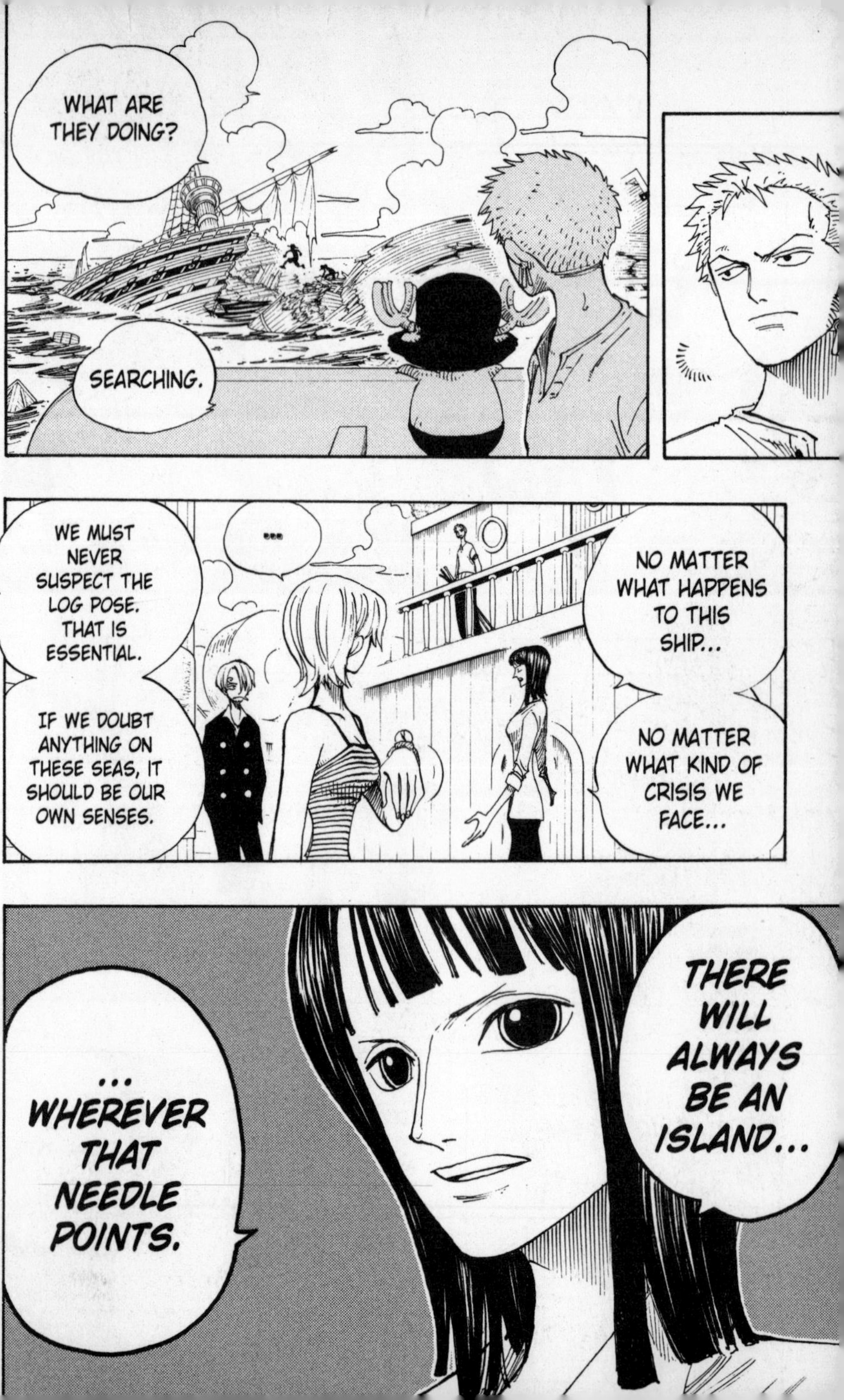
WHAT ARE THEY DOING?
SEARCHING.
NO MATTER WHAT HAPPENS TO THIS SHIP...
NO MATTER WHAT KIND OF CRISIS WE FACE...
...
WE MUST NEVER SUSPECT THE LOG POSE. THAT IS ESSENTIAL.
IF WE DOUBT ANYTHING ON THESE SEAS, IT SHOULD BE OUR OWN SENSES.
THERE WILL ALWAYS BE AN ISLAND...
...WHEREVER THAT NEEDLE POINTS.

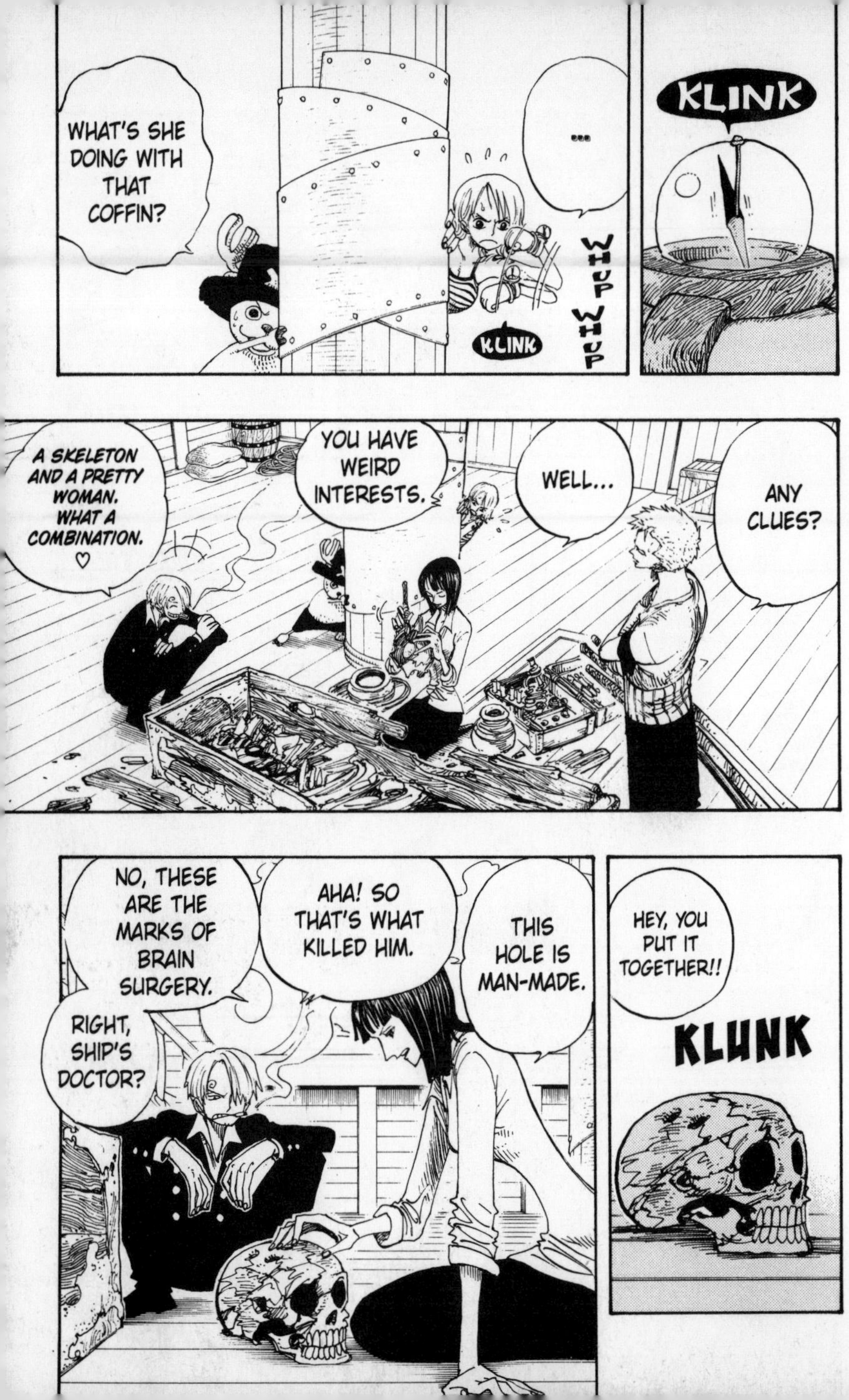
KLINK
...
WHUP WHUP
KLINK
WHAT'S SHE DOING WITH THAT COFFIN?
ANY CLUES?
WELL...
YOU HAVE WEIRD INTERESTS.
A SKELETON AND A PRETTY WOMAN. WHAT A COMBINATION. ♡
HEY, YOU PUT IT TOGETHER!!
KLUNK
THIS HOLE IS MAN-MADE.
AHA! SO THAT'S WHAT KILLED HIM.
NO, THESE ARE THE MARKS OF BRAIN SURGERY.
RIGHT, SHIP'S DOCTOR?

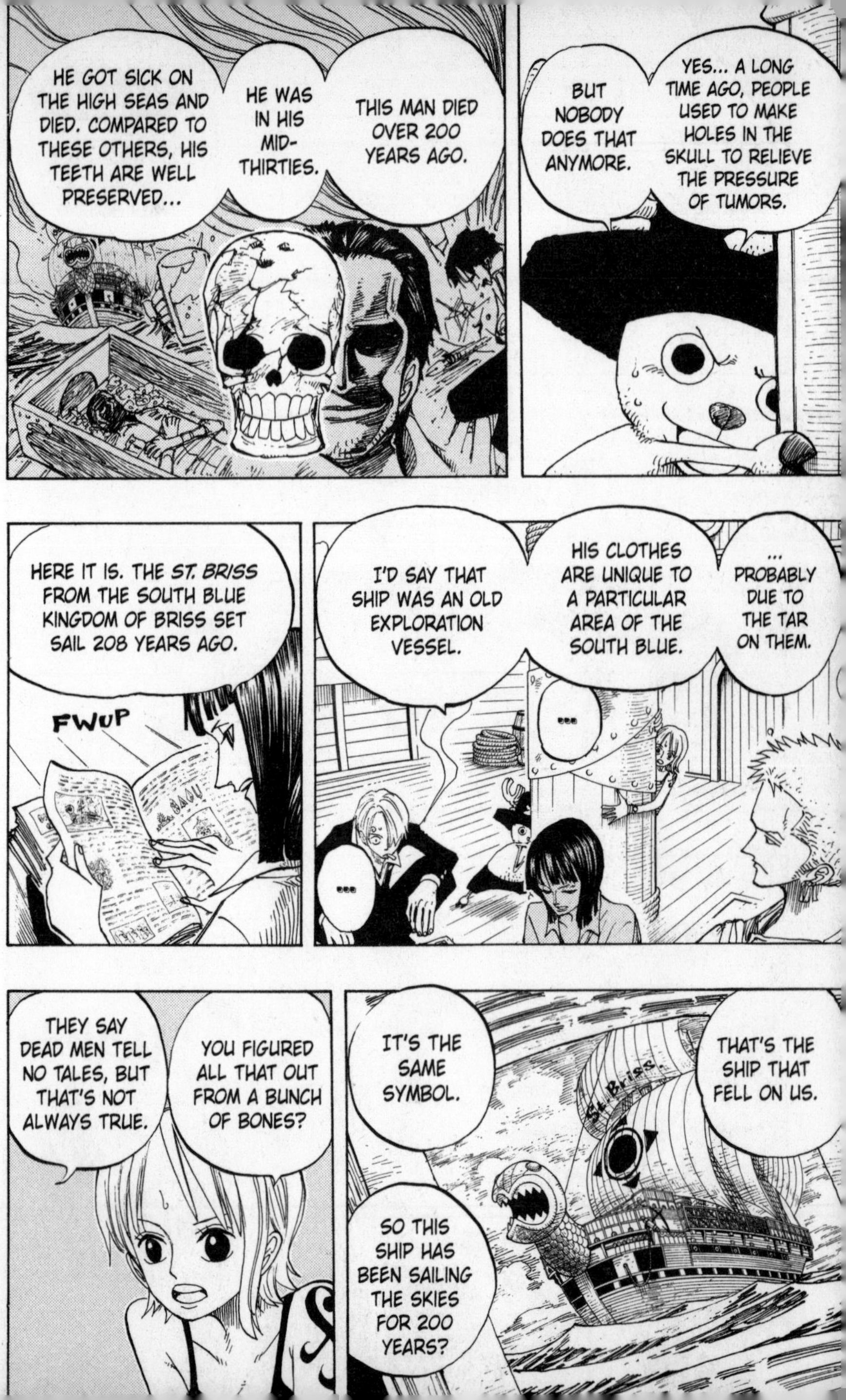
YES... A LONG TIME AGO, PEOPLE USED TO MAKE HOLES IN THE SKULL TO RELIEVE THE PRESSURE OF TUMORS.
BUT NOBODY DOES THAT ANYMORE.
THIS MAN DIED OVER 200 YEARS AGO.
HE WAS IN HIS MID-THIRTIES.
HE GOT SICK ON THE HIGH SEAS AND DIED. COMPARED TO THESE OTHERS, HIS TEETH ARE WELL PRESERVED...
... PROBABLY DUE TO THE TAR ON THEM.
HIS CLOTHES ARE UNIQUE TO A PARTICULAR AREA OF THE SOUTH BLUE.
I'D SAY THAT SHIP WAS AN OLD EXPLORATION VESSEL.
...
...
HERE IT IS. THE *ST. BRISS* FROM THE SOUTH BLUE KINGDOM OF BRISS SET SAIL 208 YEARS AGO.
FWUP
THAT'S THE SHIP THAT FELL ON US.
IT'S THE SAME SYMBOL.
St. Briss
SO THIS SHIP HAS BEEN SAILING THE SKIES FOR 200 YEARS?
YOU FIGURED ALL THAT OUT FROM A BUNCH OF BONES?
THEY SAY DEAD MEN TELL NO TALES, BUT THAT'S NOT ALWAYS TRUE.

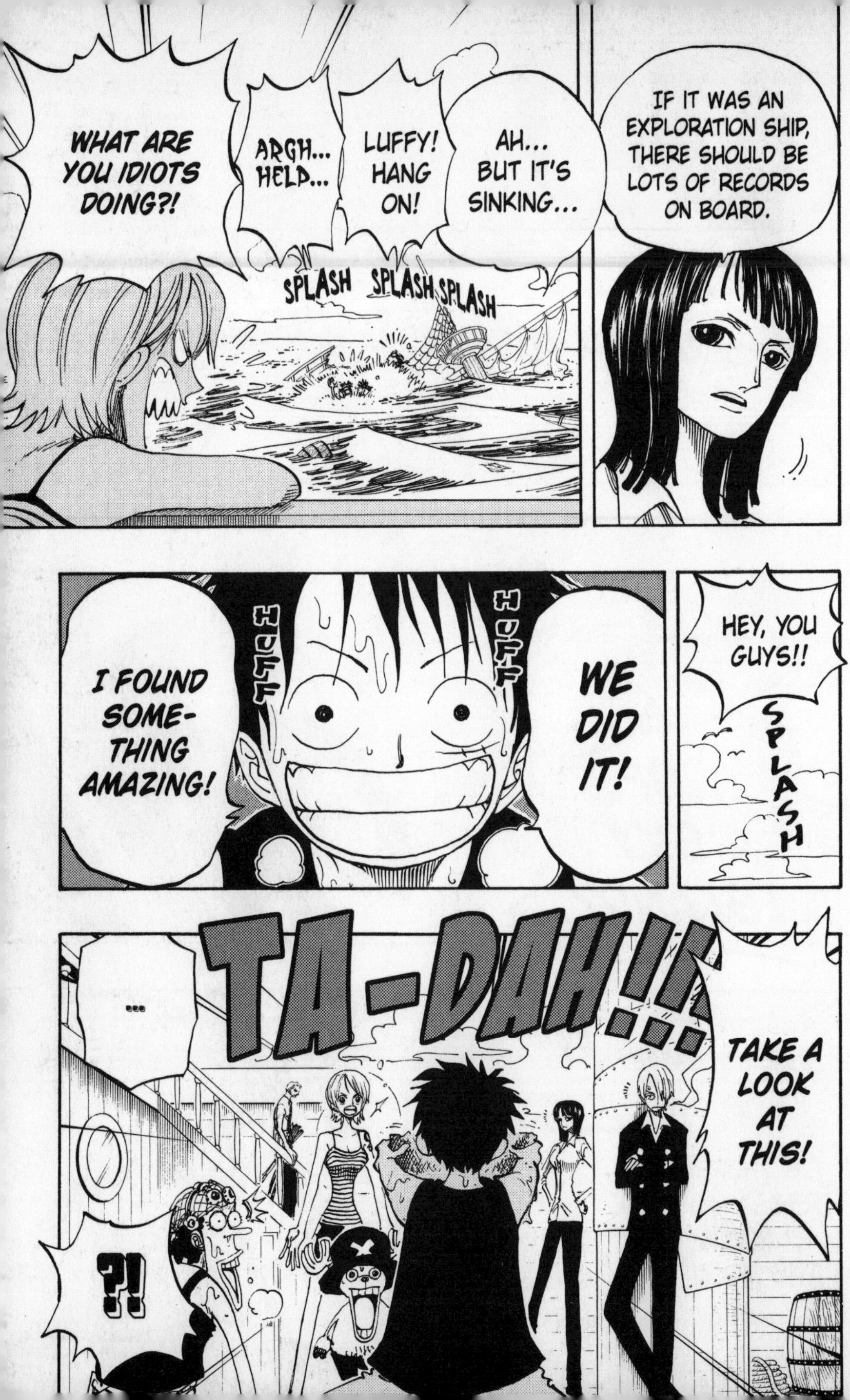
IF IT WAS AN EXPLORATION SHIP, THERE SHOULD BE LOTS OF RECORDS ON BOARD.
AH... BUT IT'S SINKING...
LUFFY! HANG ON!
ARGH... HELP...
WHAT ARE YOU IDIOTS DOING?!
SPLASH SPLASH SPLASH
HEY, YOU GUYS!!
SPLASH
HUFF
WE DID IT!
HUFF
I FOUND SOME-THING AMAZING!
TA-DAH!!
TAKE A LOOK AT THIS!
...
?!

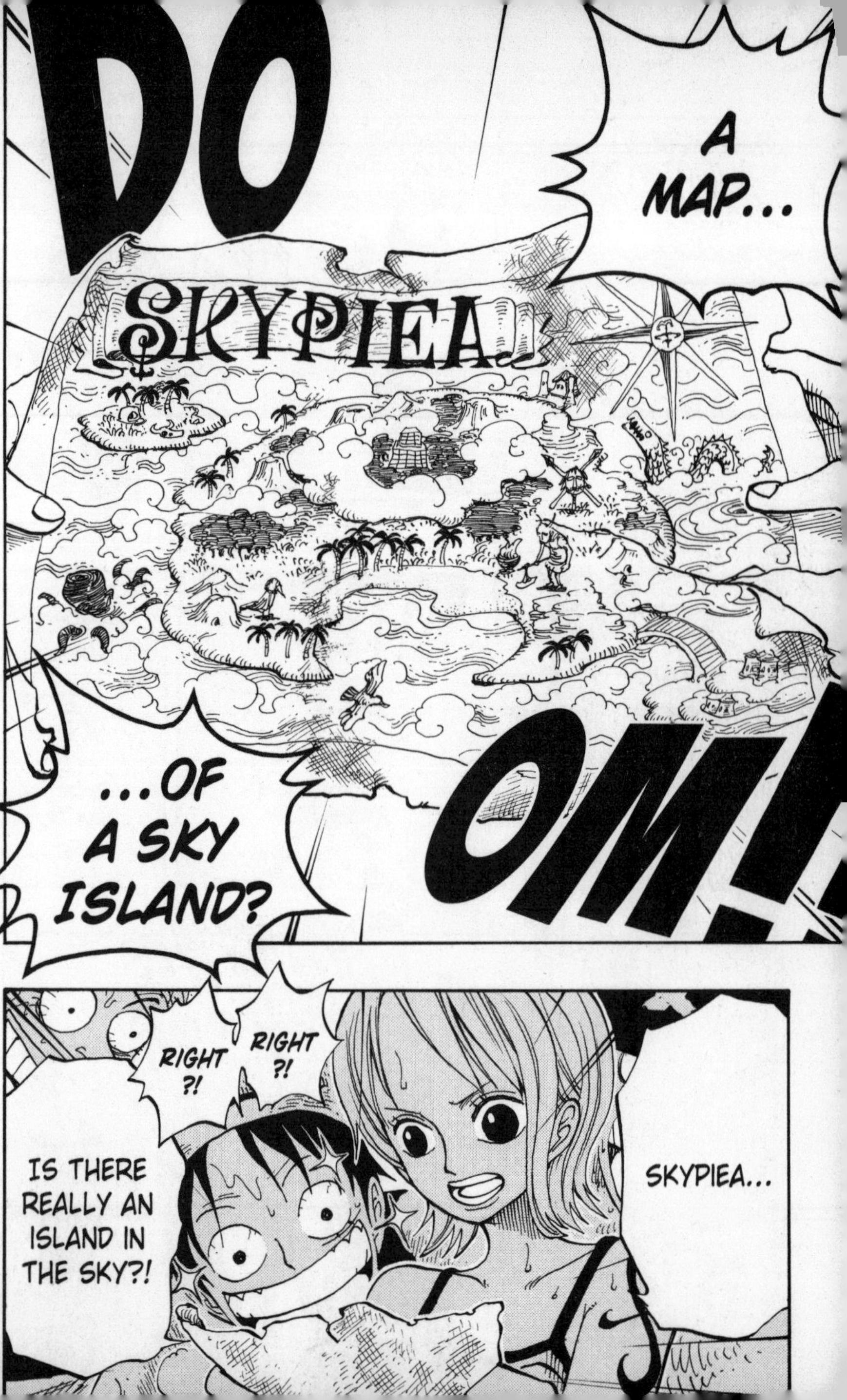
A MAP...
DO
SKYPIEA
OM!!
...OF A SKY ISLAND?
SKYPIEA...
RIGHT ?!
RIGHT ?!
IS THERE REALLY AN ISLAND IN THE SKY?!

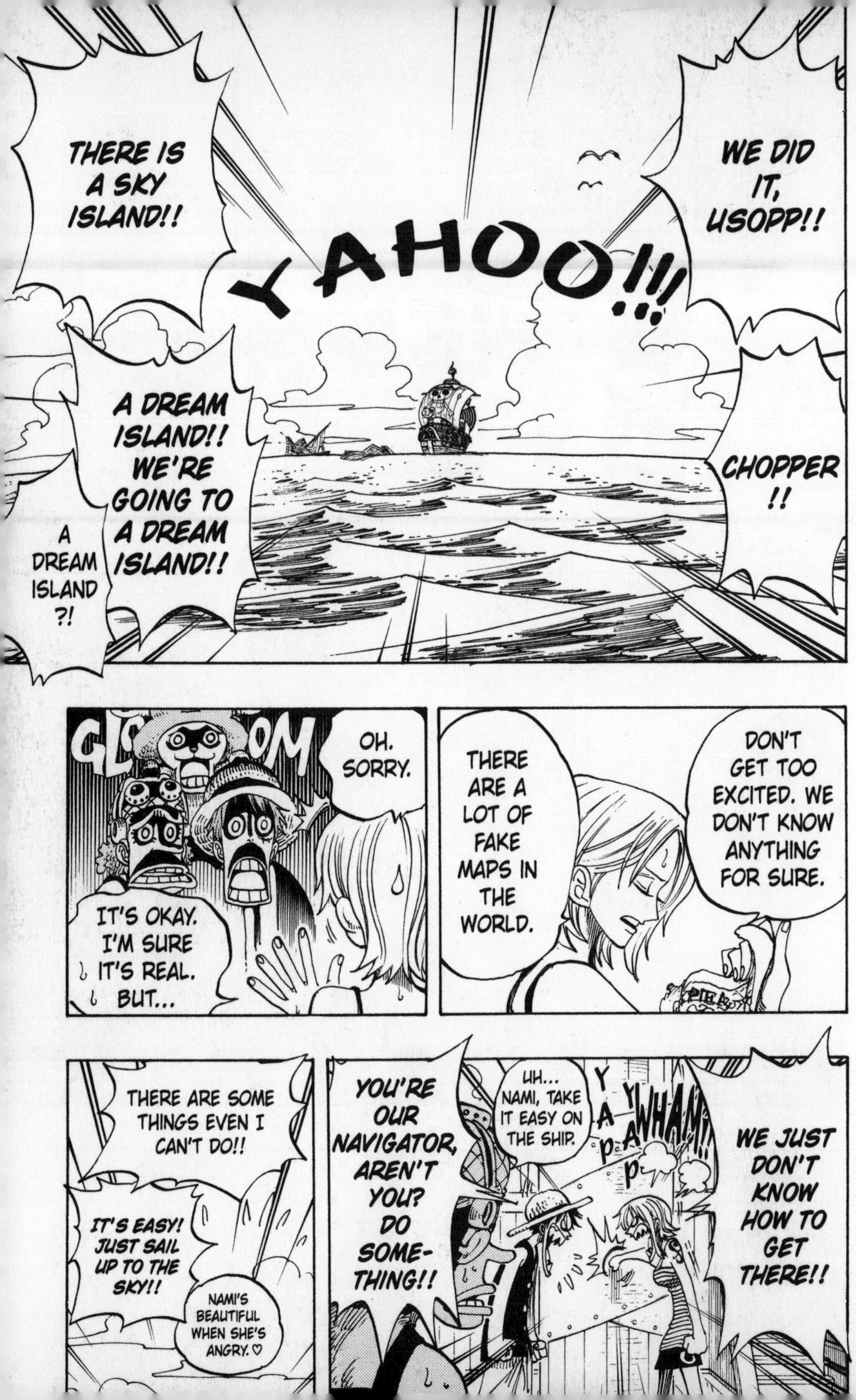
WE DID IT, USOPP!!
CHOPPER !!
YAHOO!!!
THERE IS A SKY ISLAND!!
A DREAM ISLAND!! WE'RE GOING TO A DREAM ISLAND!!
A DREAM ISLAND ?!
DON'T GET TOO EXCITED. WE DON'T KNOW ANYTHING FOR SURE.
THERE ARE A LOT OF FAKE MAPS IN THE WORLD.
OH. SORRY.
IT'S OKAY. I'M SURE IT'S REAL. BUT...
WE JUST DON'T KNOW HOW TO GET THERE!!
WHAM!!
YAP YAP
UH... NAMI, TAKE IT EASY ON THE SHIP.
YOU'RE OUR NAVIGATOR, AREN'T YOU? DO SOMETHING!!
THERE ARE SOME THINGS EVEN I CAN'T DO!!
IT'S EASY! JUST SAIL UP TO THE SKY!!
NAMI'S BEAUTIFUL WHEN SHE'S ANGRY.♡

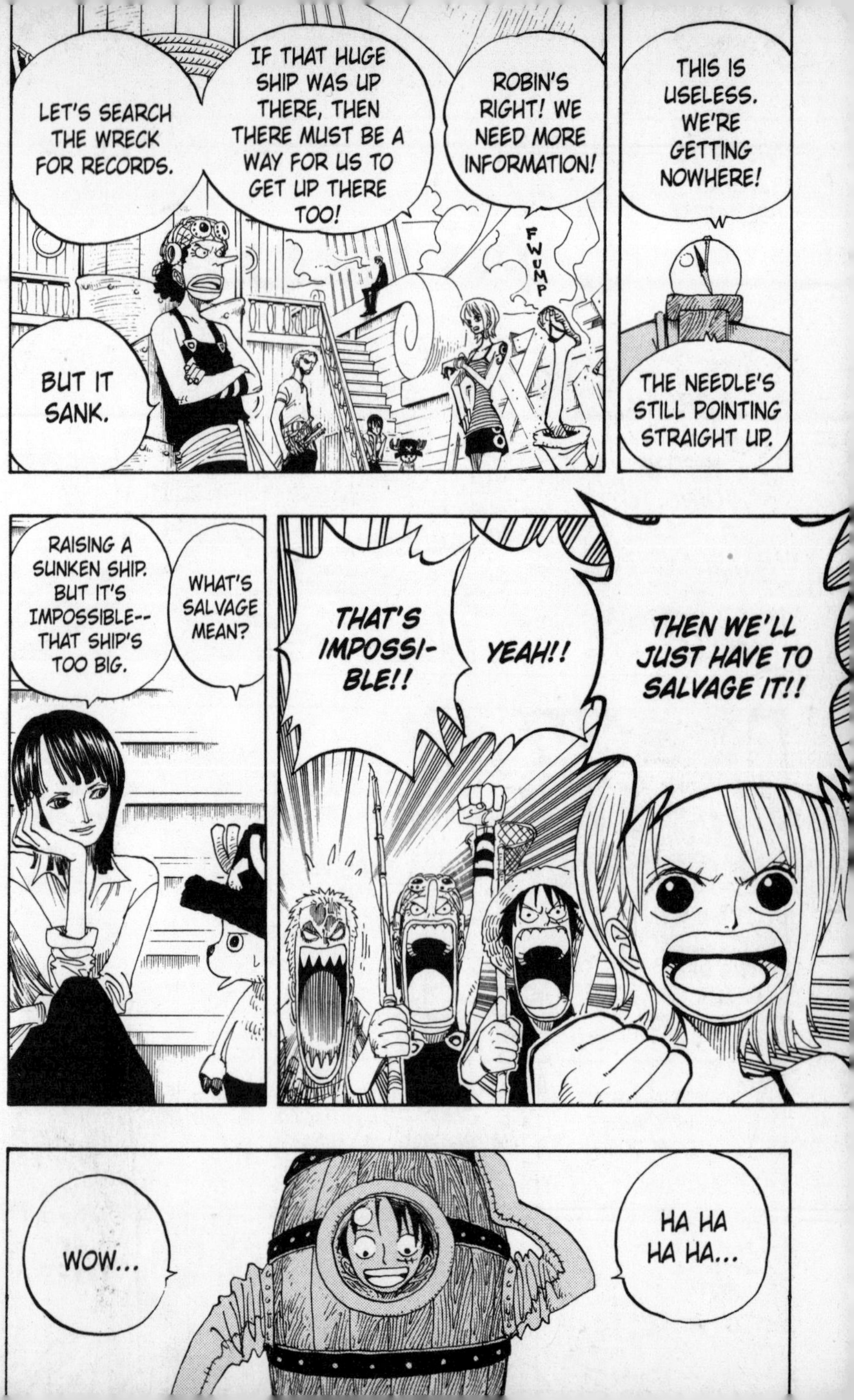
THIS IS USELESS. WE'RE GETTING NOWHERE!
THE NEEDLE'S STILL POINTING STRAIGHT UP.
ROBIN'S RIGHT! WE NEED MORE INFORMATION!
FWUMP
IF THAT HUGE SHIP WAS UP THERE, THEN THERE MUST BE A WAY FOR US TO GET UP THERE TOO!
LET'S SEARCH THE WRECK FOR RECORDS.
BUT IT SANK.
THEN WE'LL JUST HAVE TO SALVAGE IT!!
YEAH!!
THAT'S IMPOSSI-BLE!!
WHAT'S SALVAGE MEAN?
RAISING A SUNKEN SHIP. BUT IT'S IMPOSSIBLE-- THAT SHIP'S TOO BIG.
HA HA HA HA...
WOW...

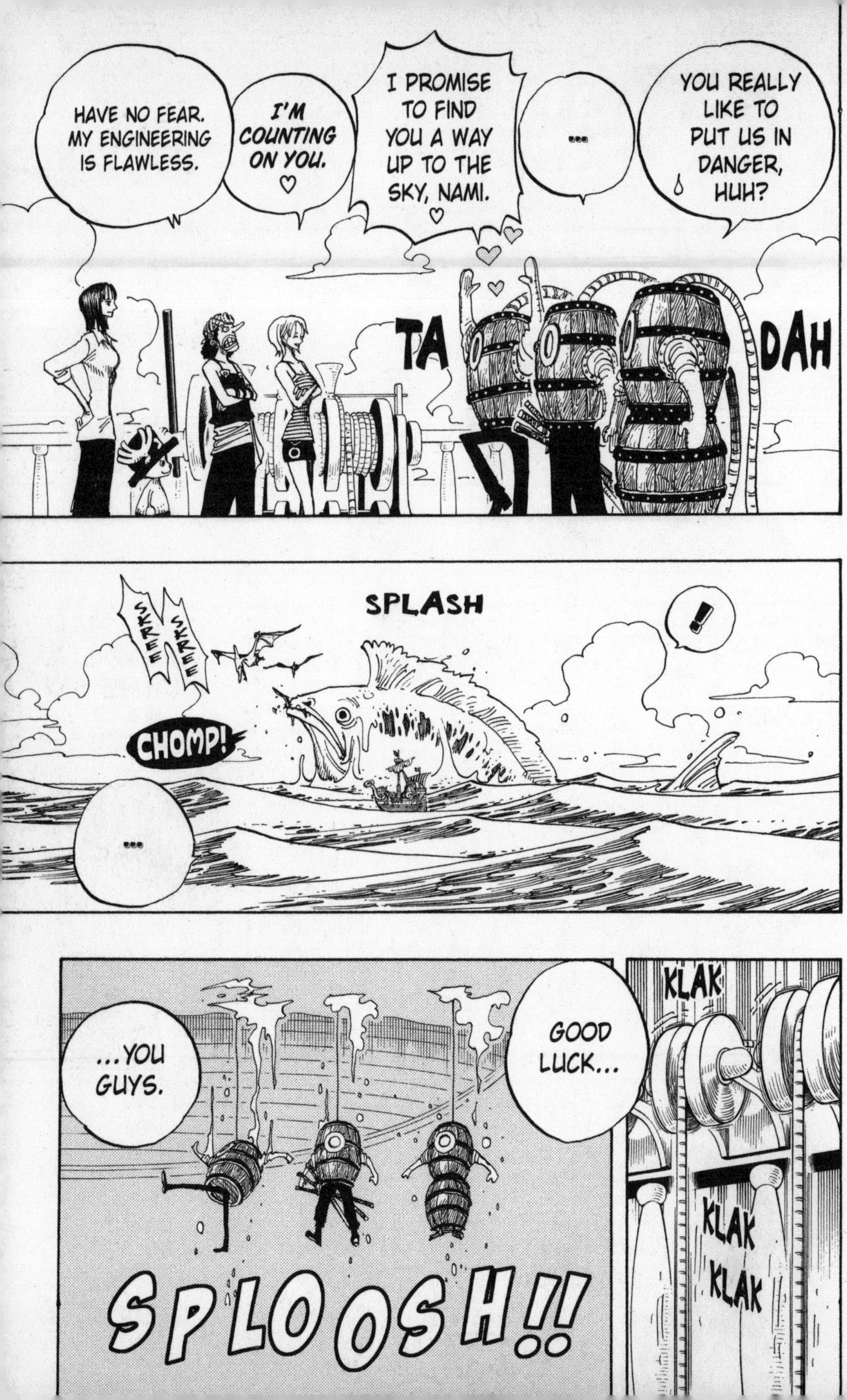
YOU REALLY LIKE TO PUT US IN DANGER, HUH?
...
I PROMISE TO FIND YOU A WAY UP TO THE SKY, NAMI.
I'M COUNTING ON YOU.
HAVE NO FEAR. MY ENGINEERING IS FLAWLESS.
TA DAH
!
SPLASH
SKREE SKREE
CHOMP!
...
KLAK
KLAK
KLAK
GOOD LUCK...
...YOU GUYS.
SPLOOSH!!

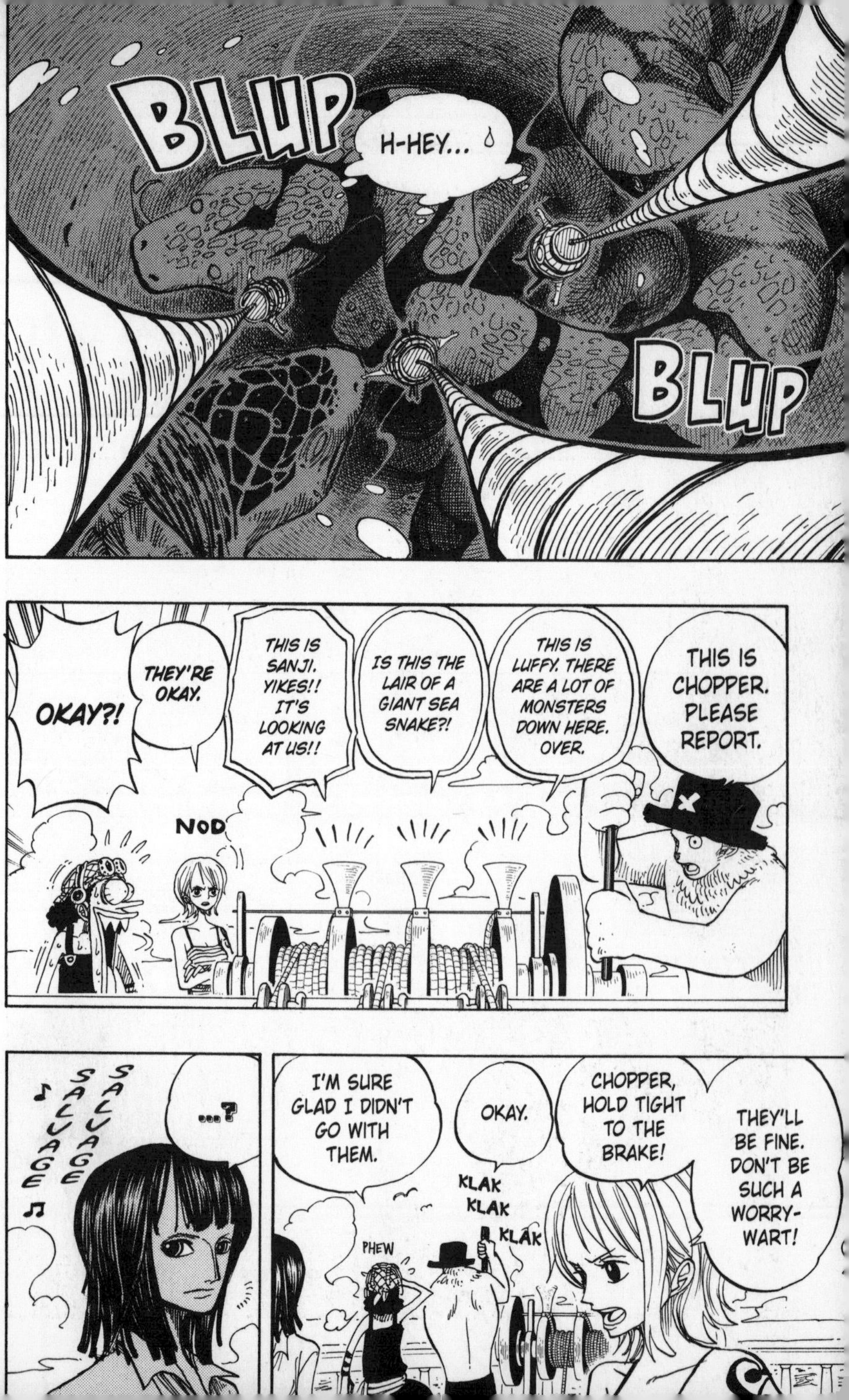

H-HEY...
BLUP
BLUP
THIS IS CHOPPER. PLEASE REPORT.
THIS IS LUFFY. THERE ARE A LOT OF MONSTERS DOWN HERE. OVER.
IS THIS THE LAIR OF A GIANT SEA SNAKE?!
THIS IS SANJI. YIKES!! IT'S LOOKING AT US!!
THEY'RE OKAY.
OKAY?!
NOD
THEY'LL BE FINE. DON'T BE SUCH A WORRY-WART!
CHOPPER, HOLD TIGHT TO THE BRAKE!
OKAY.
I'M SURE GLAD I DIDN'T GO WITH THEM.
KLAK
KLAK
KLAK
PHEW
...?
SALVAGE SALVAGE ♪ ♫

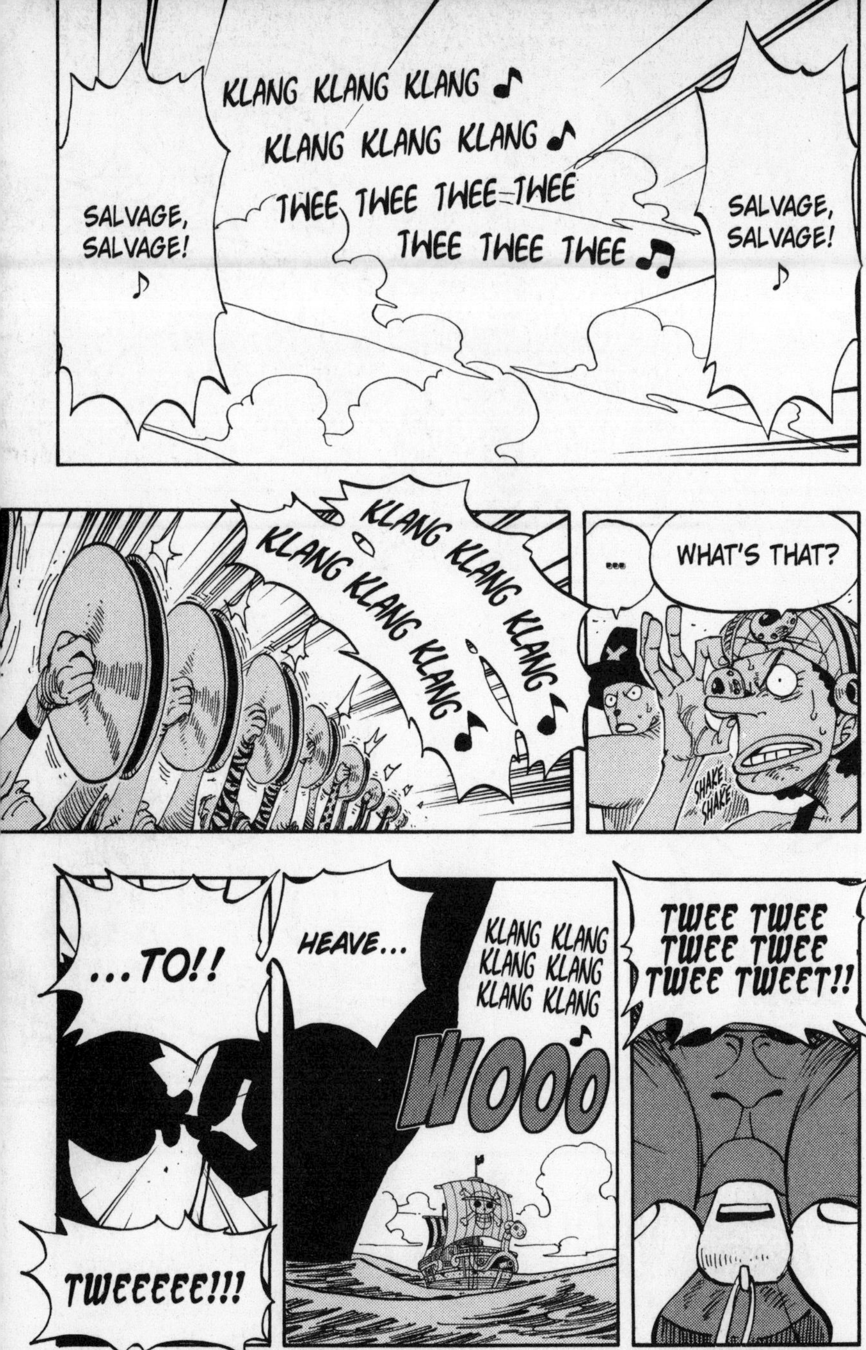
SALVAGE, SALVAGE! ♪
KLANG KLANG KLANG ♪
KLANG KLANG KLANG ♪
TWEE TWEE TWEE TWEE
TWEE TWEE TWEE ♫
SALVAGE, SALVAGE! ♪
WHAT'S THAT?
...
SHAKE SHAKE
KLANG KLANG KLANG KLANG ♪
KLANG KLANG KLANG ♪
TWEE TWEE TWEE TWEE TWEE TWEET!!
KLANG KLANG KLANG KLANG KLANG KLANG ♪
HEAVE...
WOOO
...TO!!
TWEEEEEE!!!

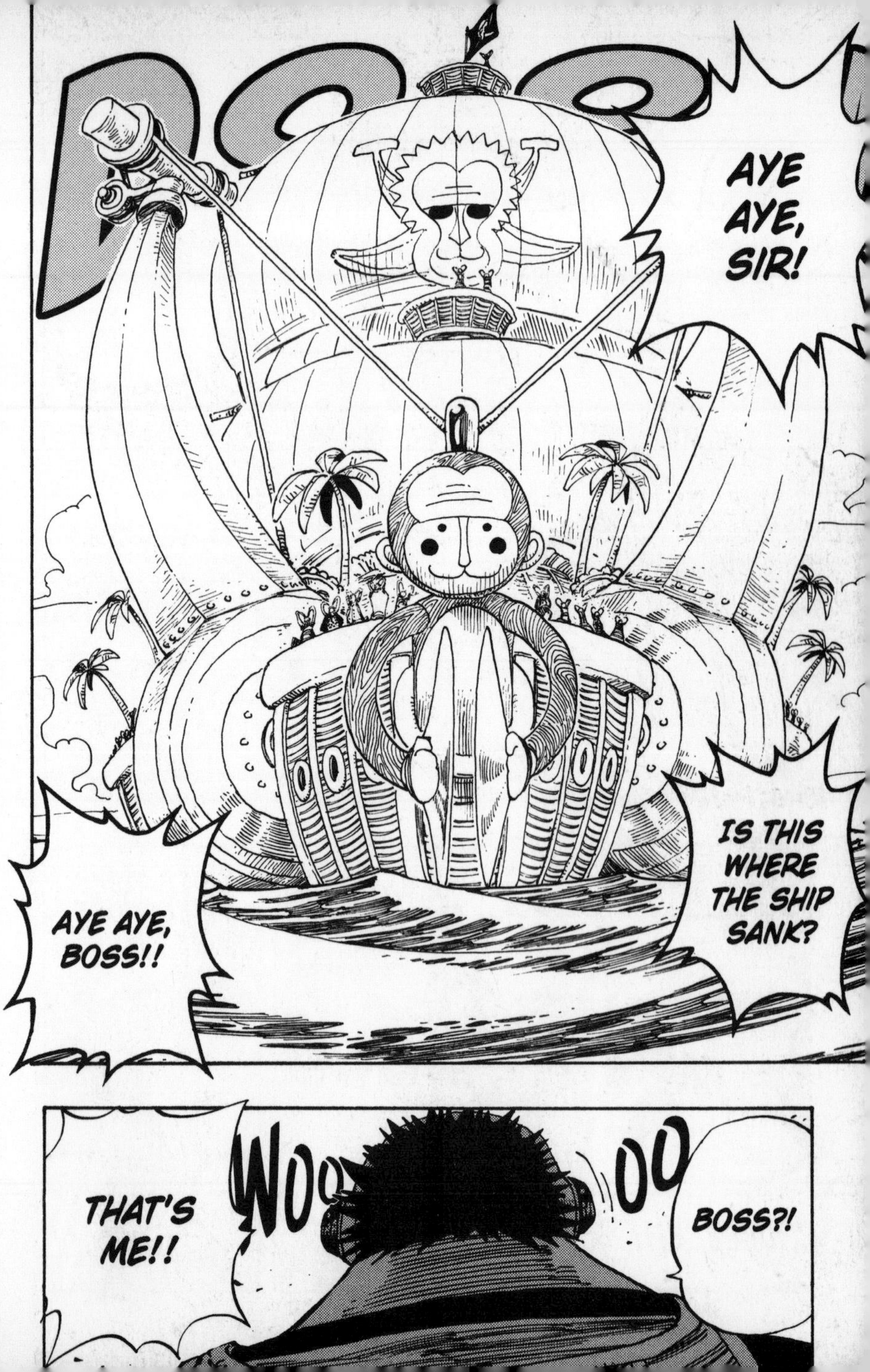
AYE AYE, SIR!
IS THIS WHERE THE SHIP SANK?
AYE AYE, BOSS!!
BOSS?!
THAT'S ME!!

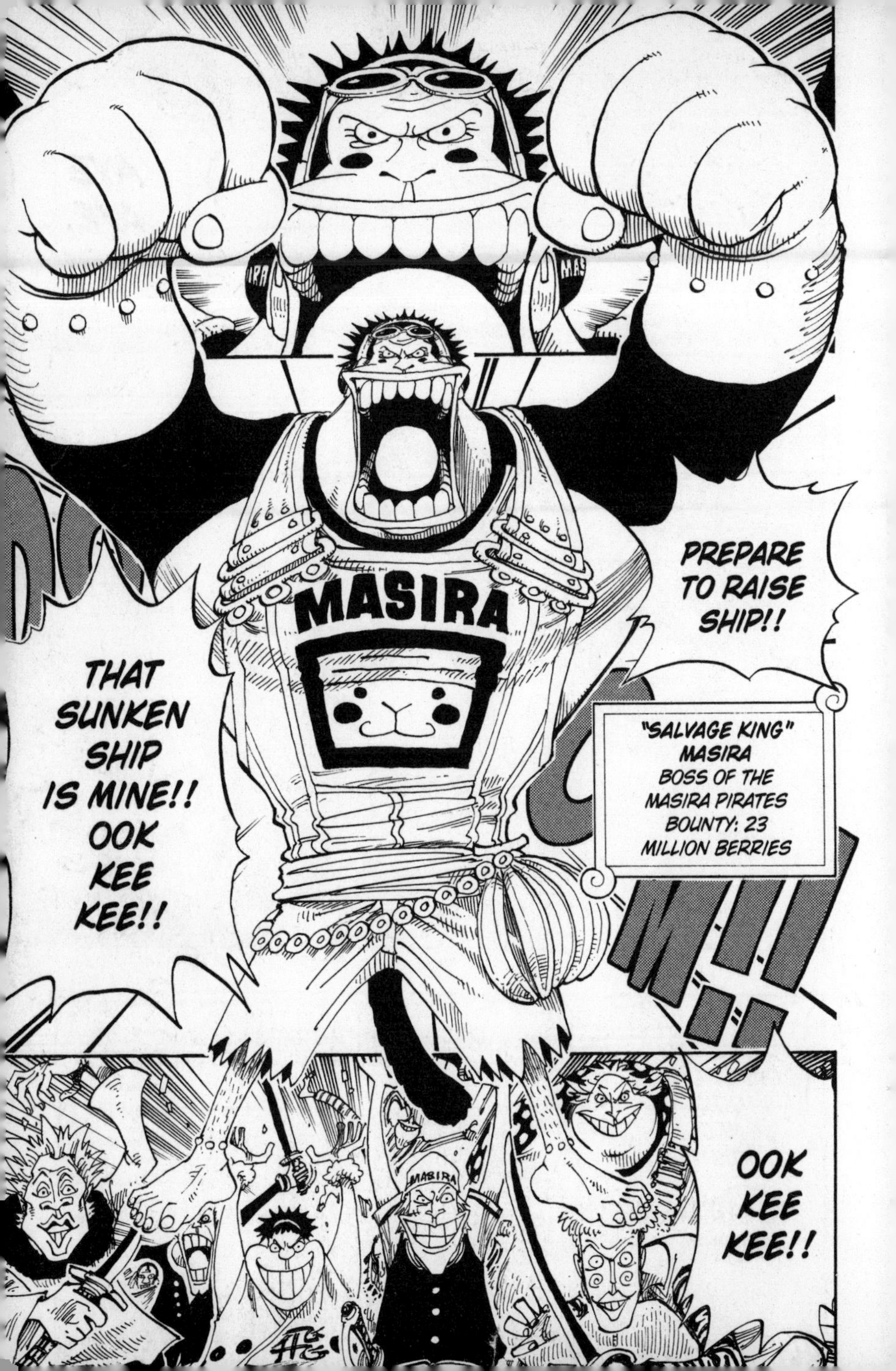
PREPARE TO RAISE SHIP!!
"SALVAGE KING" MASIRA BOSS OF THE MASIRA PIRATES BOUNTY: 23 MILLION BERRIES
THAT SUNKEN SHIP IS MINE!! OOK KEE KEE!!
MASIRA
OOK KEE KEE!!

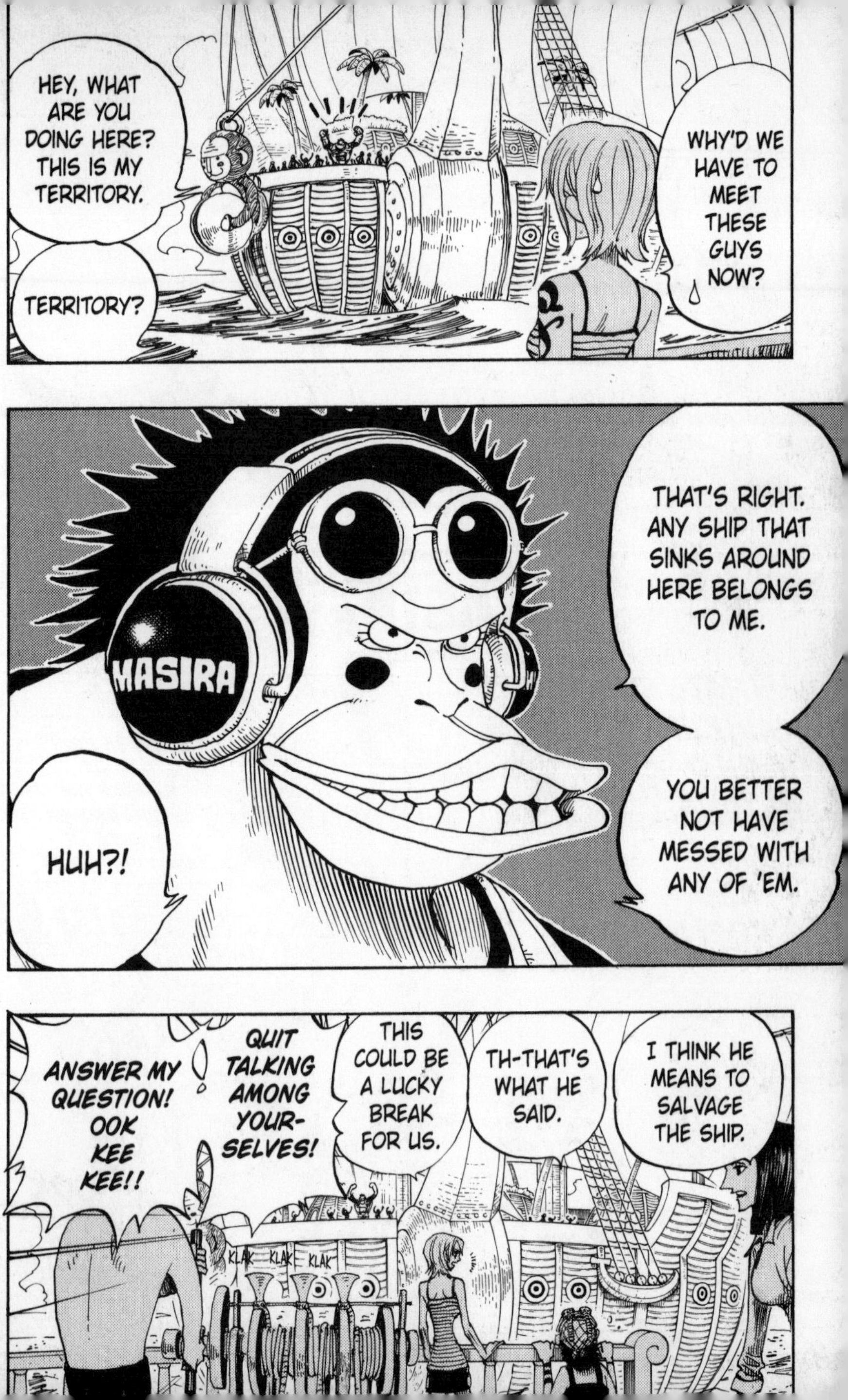
WHY'D WE HAVE TO MEET THESE GUYS NOW?
HEY, WHAT ARE YOU DOING HERE? THIS IS MY TERRITORY.
TERRITORY?
MASIRA
THAT'S RIGHT. ANY SHIP THAT SINKS AROUND HERE BELONGS TO ME.
YOU BETTER NOT HAVE MESSED WITH ANY OF 'EM.
HUH?!
I THINK HE MEANS TO SALVAGE THE SHIP.
TH-THAT'S WHAT HE SAID.
THIS COULD BE A LUCKY BREAK FOR US.
QUIT TALKING AMONG YOUR-SELVES!
ANSWER MY QUESTION! OOK KEE KEE!!
KLAK KLAK KLAK

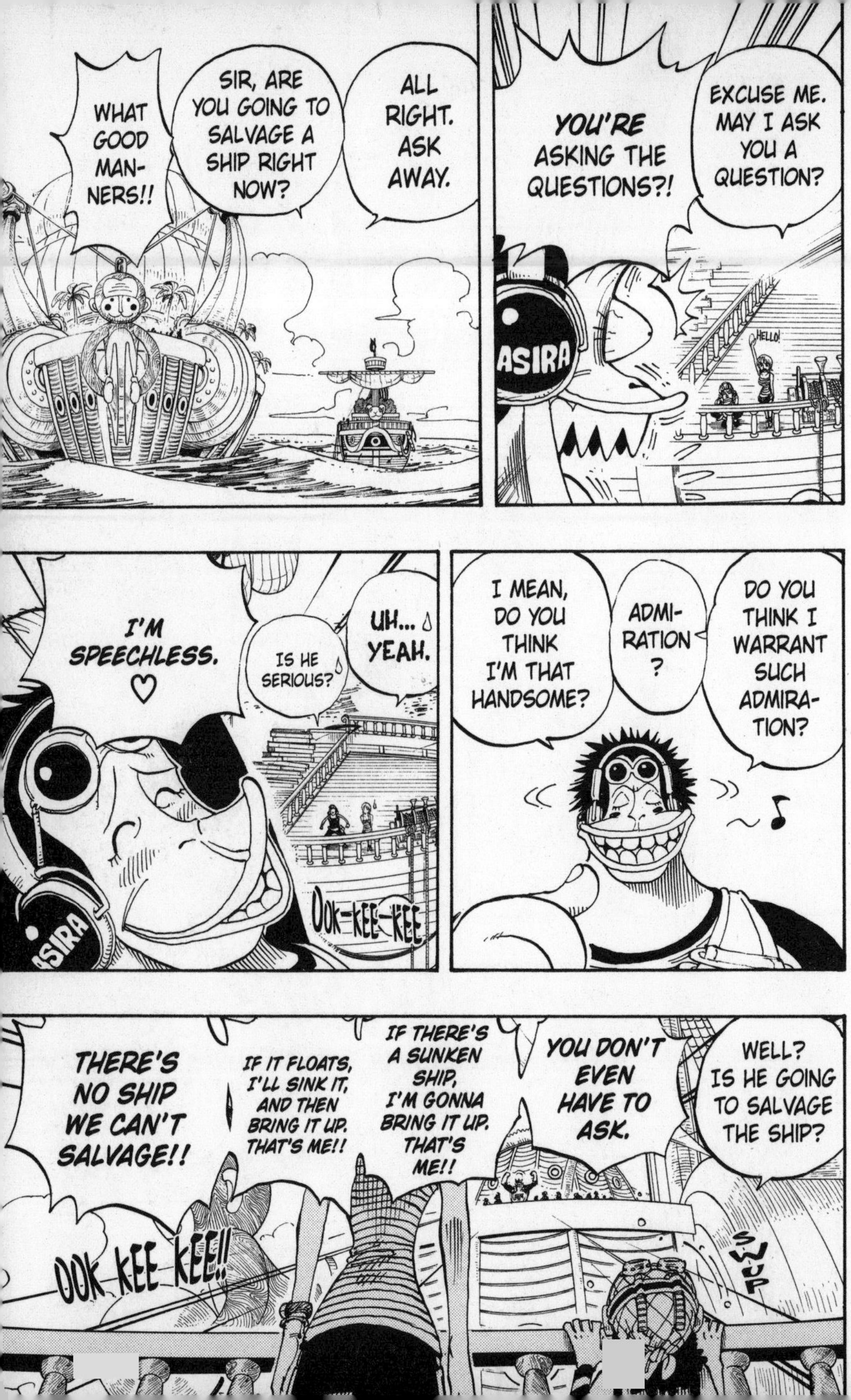
EXCUSE ME. MAY I ASK YOU A QUESTION?
YOU'RE ASKING THE QUESTIONS?!
ASIRA
HELLO!
ALL RIGHT. ASK AWAY.
SIR, ARE YOU GOING TO SALVAGE A SHIP RIGHT NOW?
WHAT GOOD MAN-NERS!!
DO YOU THINK I WARRANT SUCH ADMIRA-TION?
ADMI-RATION?
I MEAN, DO YOU THINK I'M THAT HANDSOME?
UH... YEAH.
IS HE SERIOUS?
I'M SPEECHLESS. ♡
OOK-KEE-KEE
ASIRA
WELL? IS HE GOING TO SALVAGE THE SHIP?
YOU DON'T EVEN HAVE TO ASK.
IF THERE'S A SUNKEN SHIP, I'M GONNA BRING IT UP. THAT'S ME!!
IF IT FLOATS, I'LL SINK IT, AND THEN BRING IT UP. THAT'S ME!!
THERE'S NO SHIP WE CAN'T SALVAGE!!
SWUP
OOK KEE KEE!!

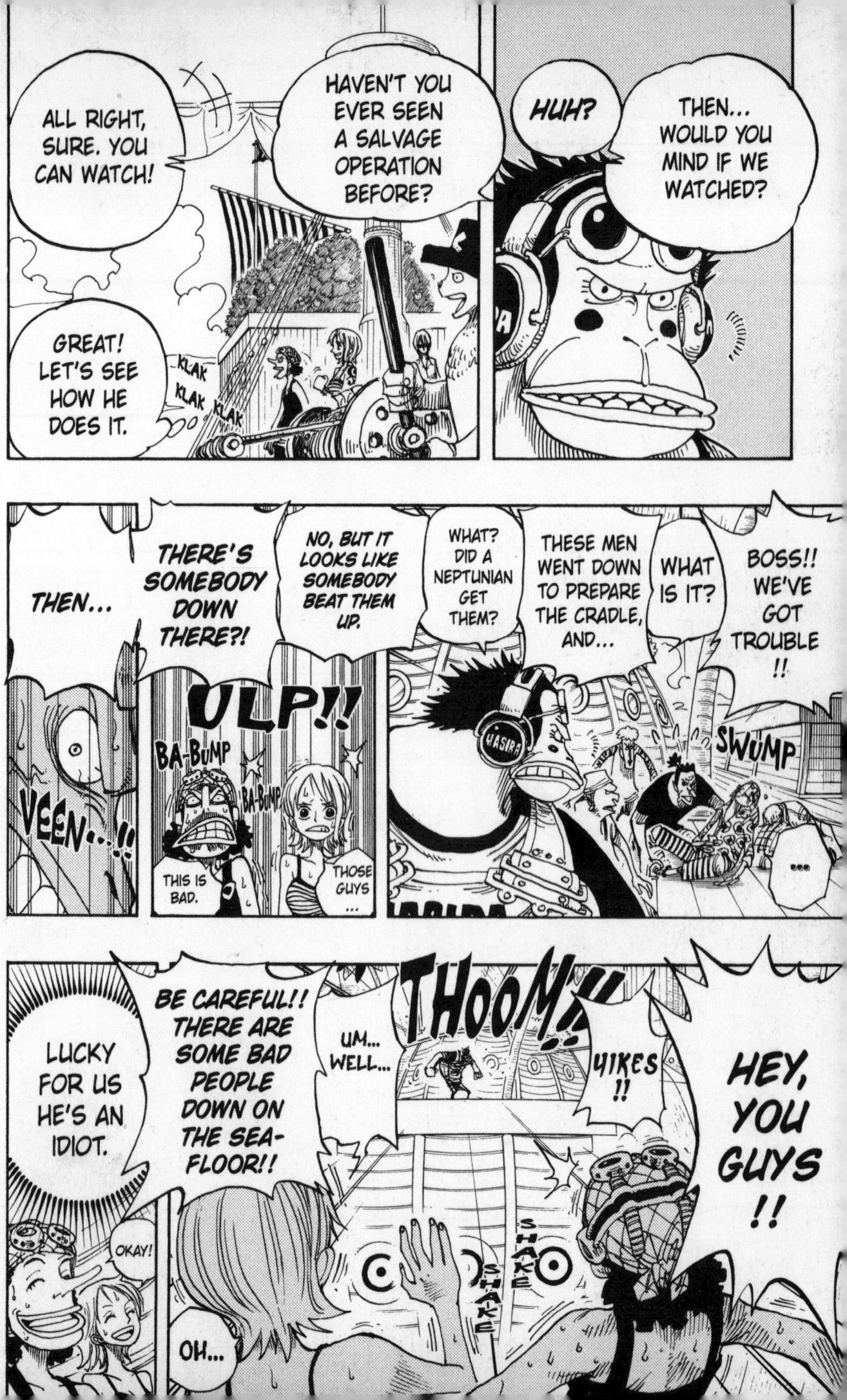
THEN... WOULD YOU MIND IF WE WATCHED?
HUH?
HAVEN'T YOU EVER SEEN A SALVAGE OPERATION BEFORE?
ALL RIGHT, SURE. YOU CAN WATCH!
GREAT! LET'S SEE HOW HE DOES IT.
KLAK KLAK KLAK
BOSS!! WE'VE GOT TROUBLE!!
WHAT IS IT?
THESE MEN WENT DOWN TO PREPARE THE CRADLE, AND...
SWUMP
...
WHAT? DID A NEPTUNIAN GET THEM?
NO, BUT IT LOOKS LIKE SOMEBODY BEAT THEM UP.
ULP!!
BA-BUMP
BA-BUMP
THOSE GUYS...
THIS IS BAD.
THERE'S SOMEBODY DOWN THERE?!
THEN...
VEEN...!!
HEY, YOU GUYS!!
YIKES!!
THOOM!!
UM... WELL...
SHAKE
SHAKE
BE CAREFUL!! THERE ARE SOME BAD PEOPLE DOWN ON THE SEA-FLOOR!!
LUCKY FOR US HE'S AN IDIOT.
OKAY!
OH...

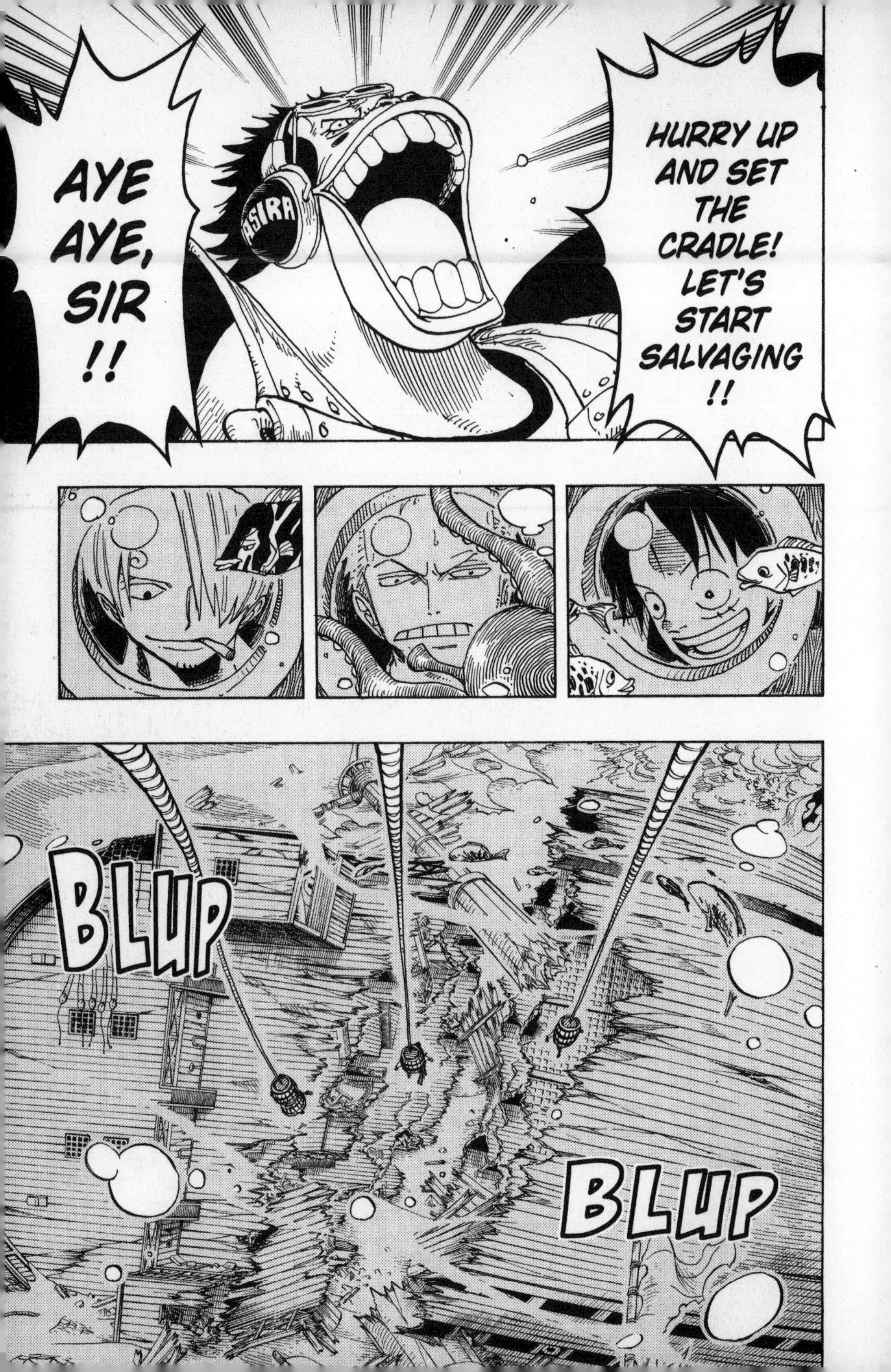
HURRY UP AND SET THE CRADLE! LET'S START SALVAGING!!
AYE AYE, SIR!!
BLUP
BLUP

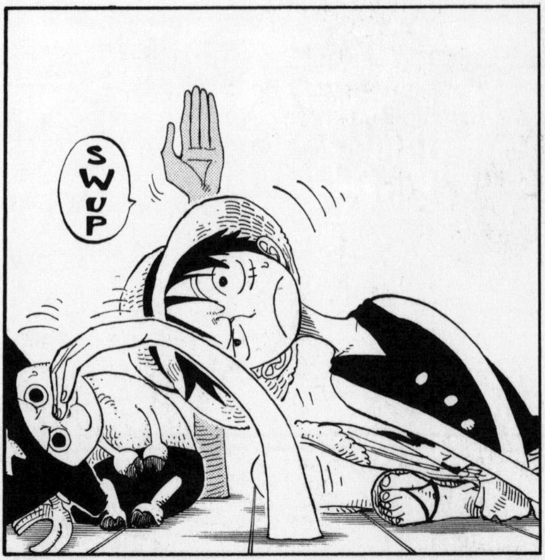
SWUP

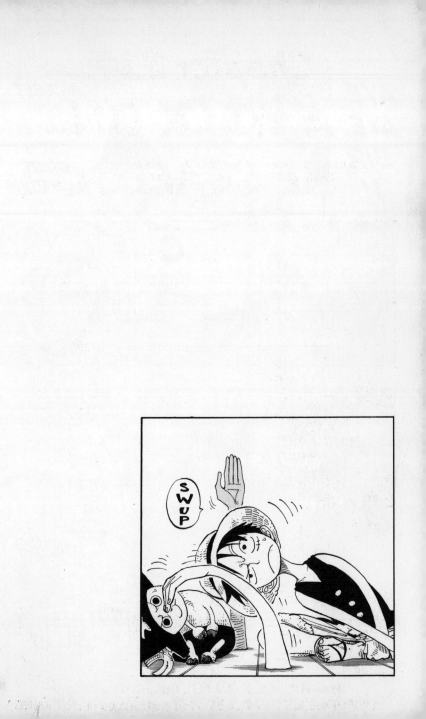

Chapter 220:

A WALK ON THE SEAFLOOR

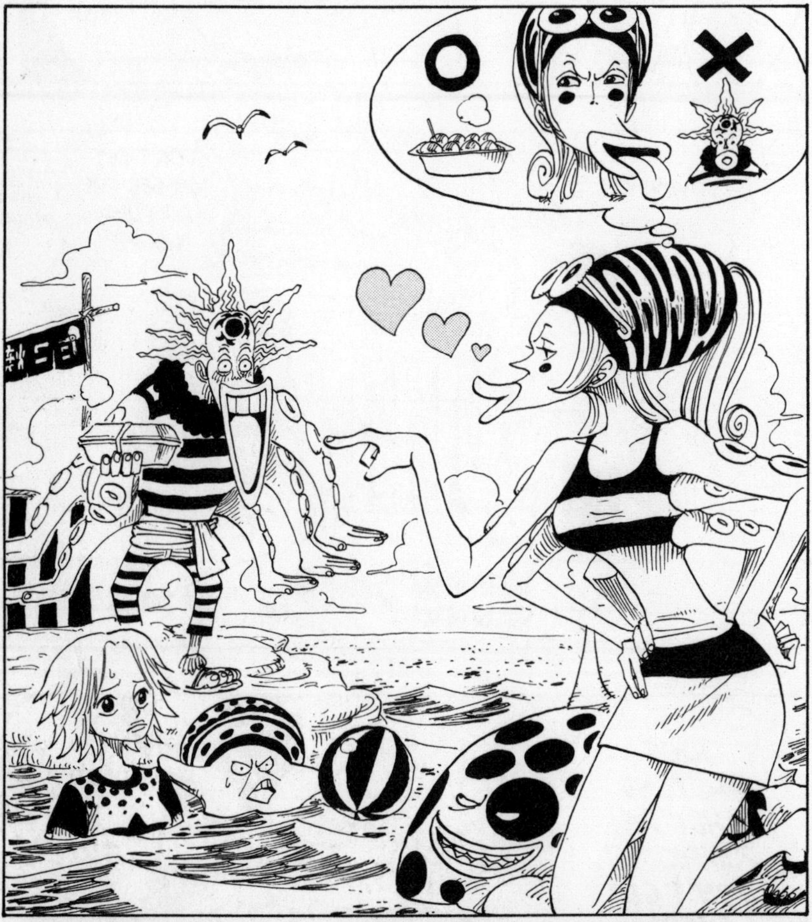

HACHI'S WALK ON THE SEAFLOOR, VOL. 34:
"OCTOPAKO IS DRAWN BY THE AROMA OF THE SAUCE"

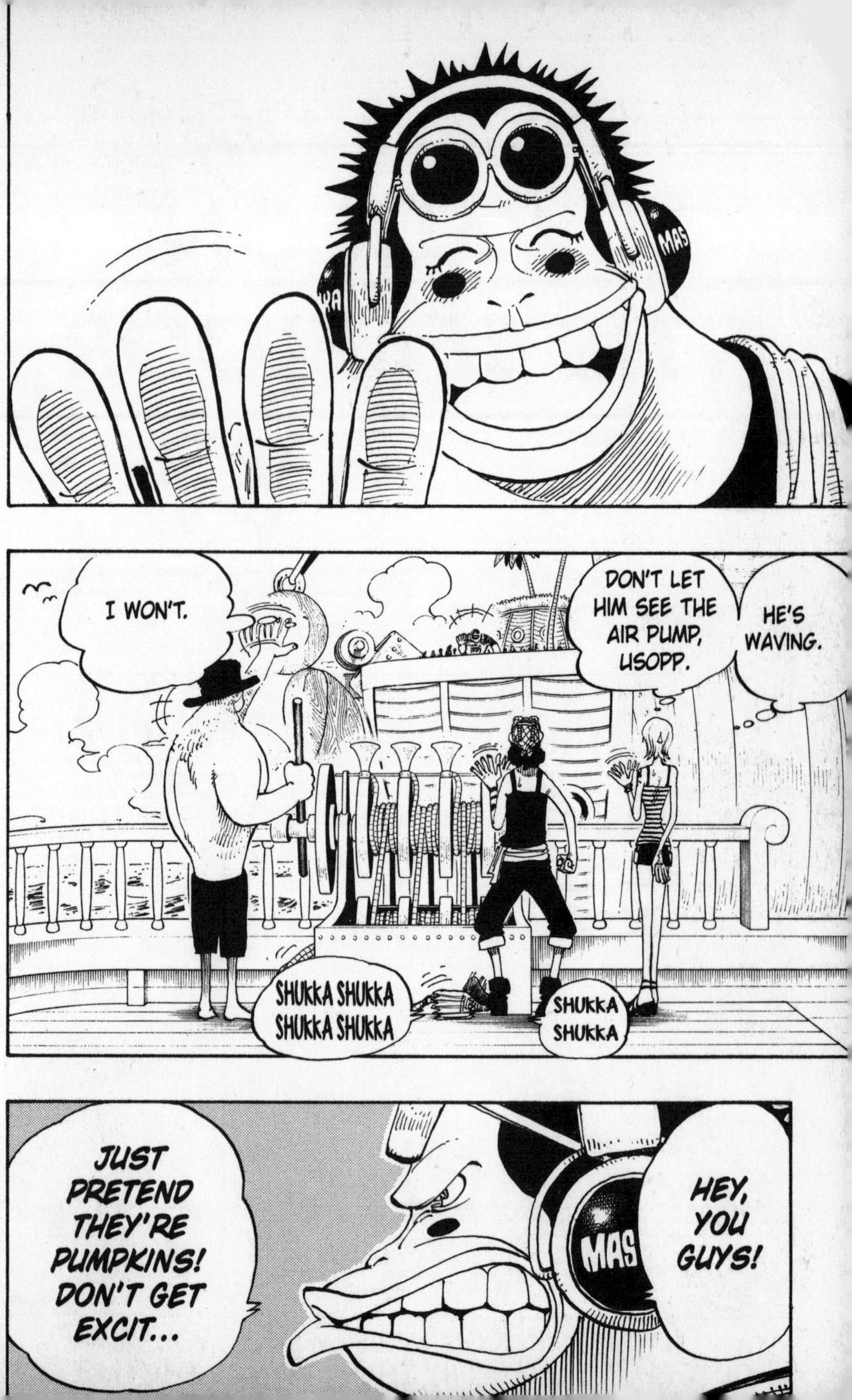
MAS
HE'S WAVING.
DON'T LET HIM SEE THE AIR PUMP, USOPP.
I WON'T.
SHUKKA SHUKKA
SHUKKA SHUKKA SHUKKA SHUKKA
HEY, YOU GUYS!
MAS
JUST PRETEND THEY'RE PUMPKINS! DON'T GET EXCIT...

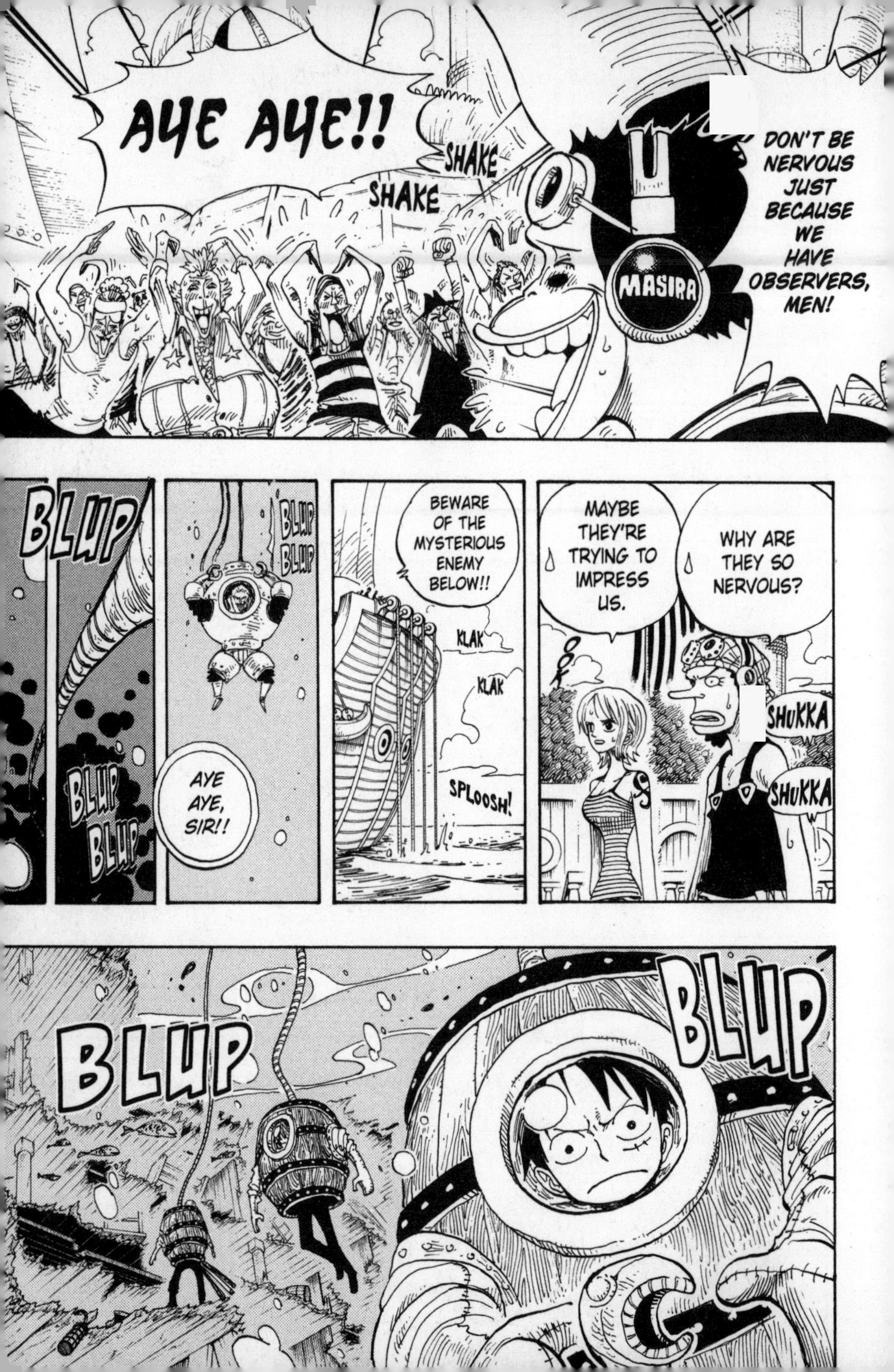
DON'T BE NERVOUS JUST BECAUSE WE HAVE OBSERVERS, MEN!
SHAKE
SHAKE
AYE AYE!!
WHY ARE THEY SO NERVOUS?
MAYBE THEY'RE TRYING TO IMPRESS US.
SHUKKA
SHUKKA
BEWARE OF THE MYSTERIOUS ENEMY BELOW!!
KLAK
KLAK
SPLOOSH!
BLUP
BLUP
AYE AYE, SIR!!
BLUP
BLUP
BLUP
BLUP
BLUP

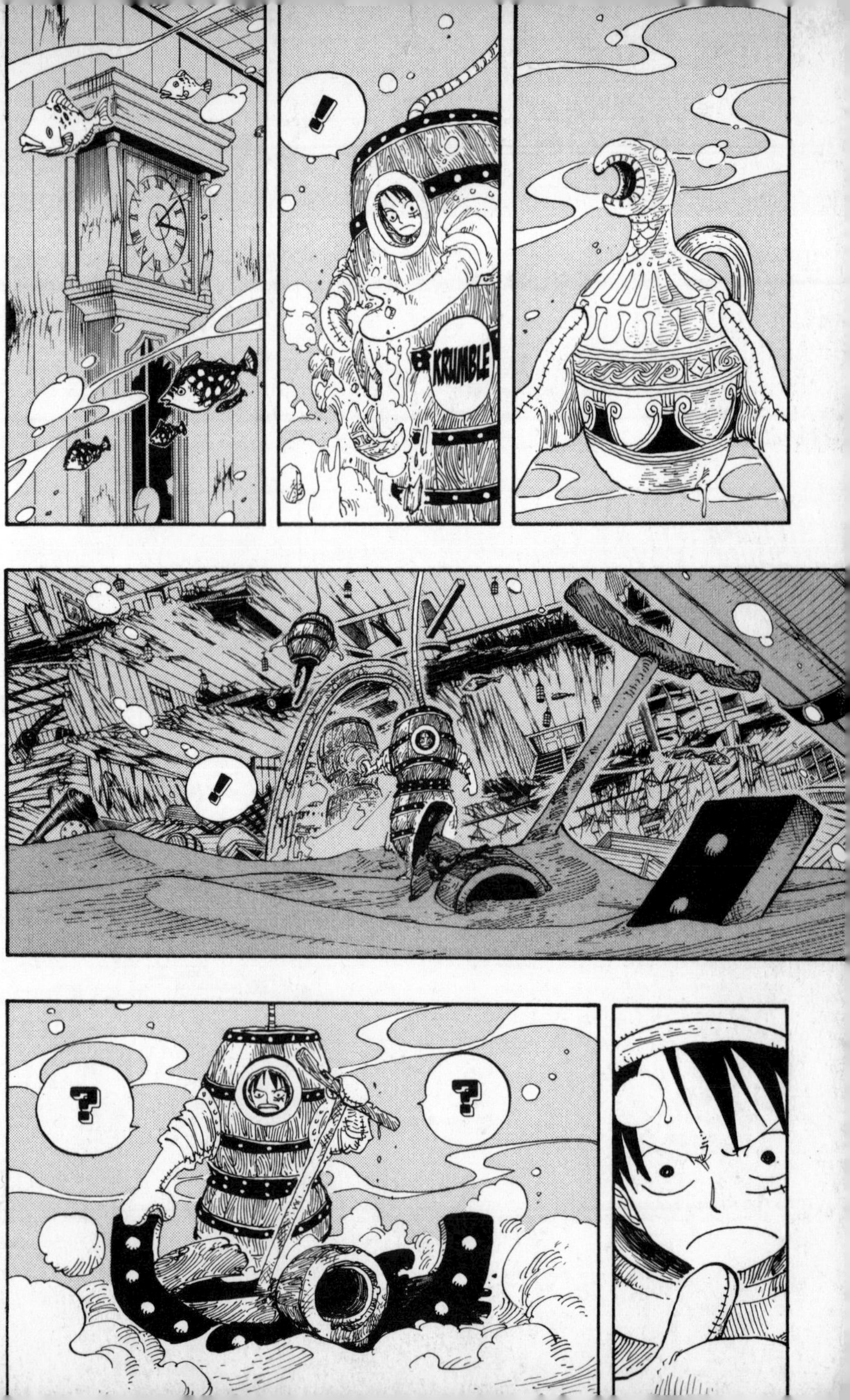
!
KRUMBLE
!
?
?

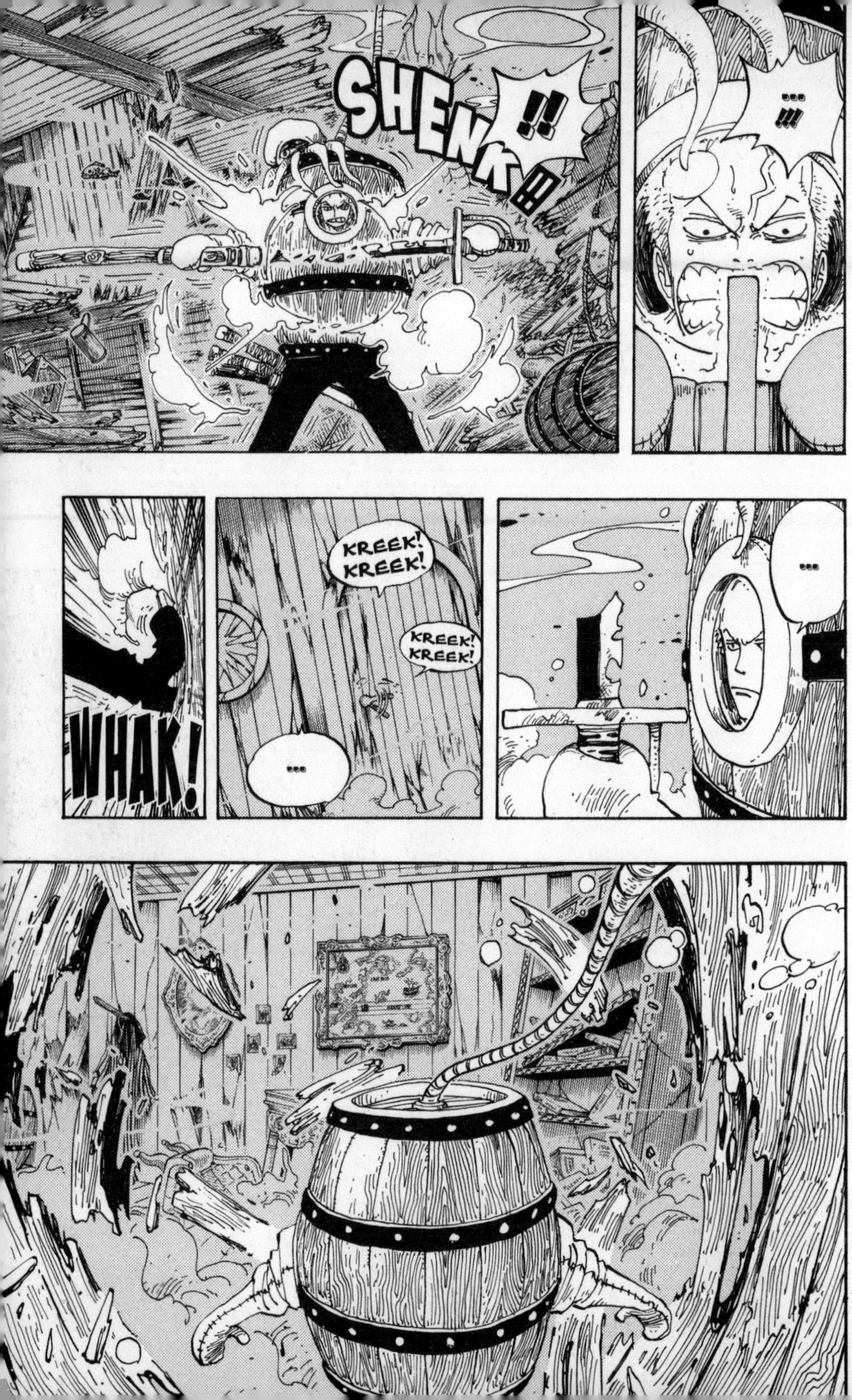

...!!!
!!
SHENK!!
...
KREEK! KREEK!
KREEK! KREEK!
...
WHAK!

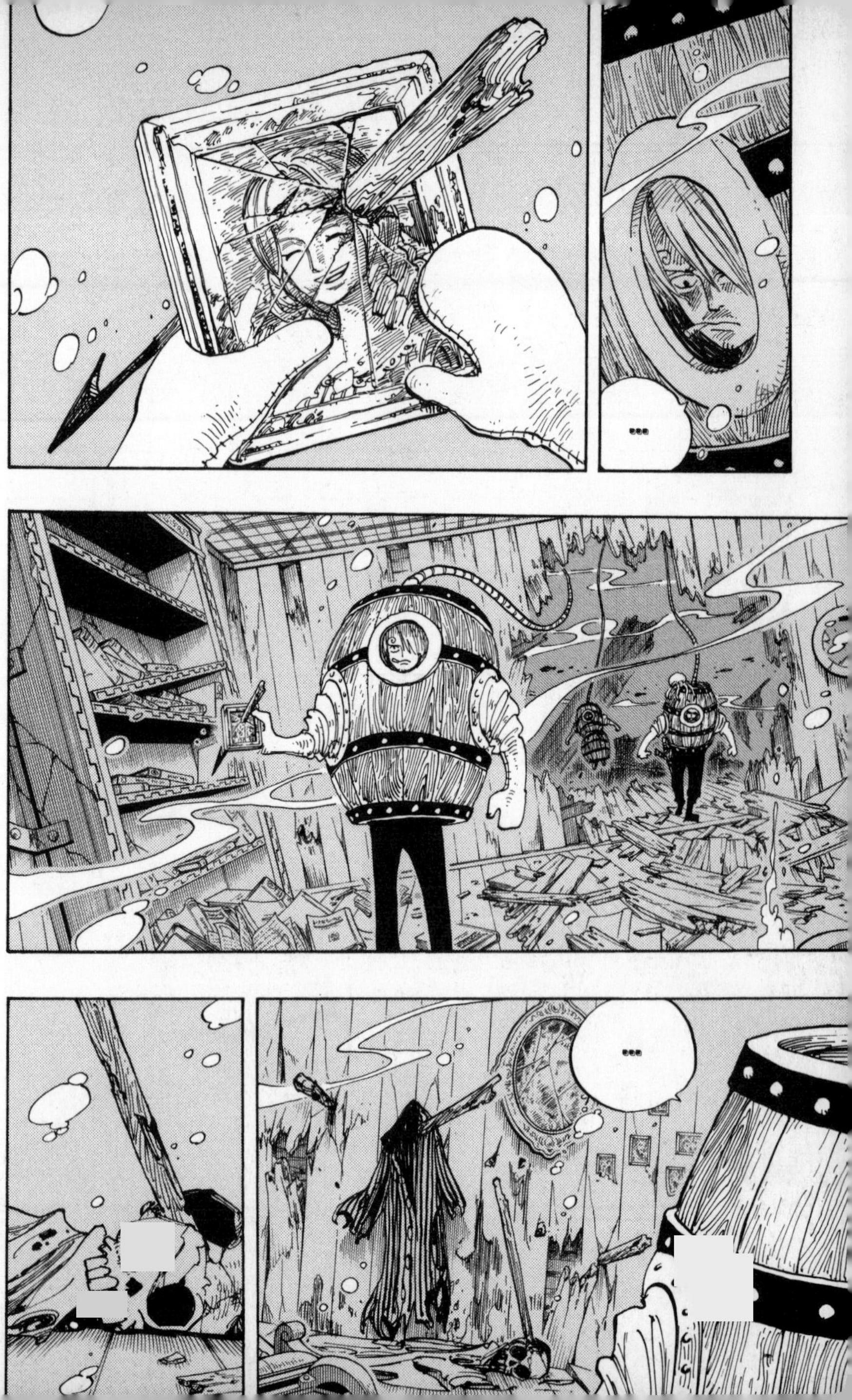
...
...

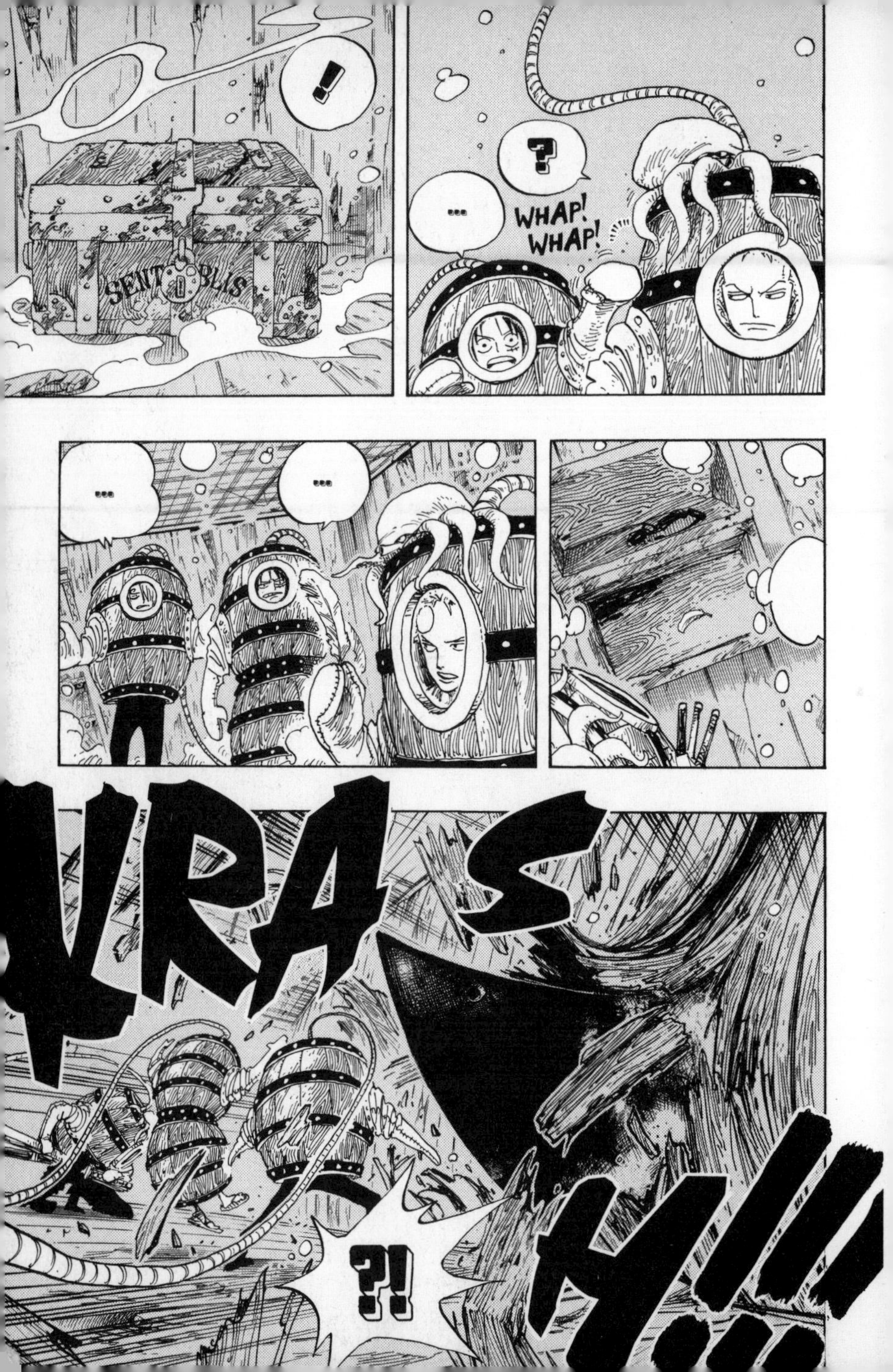

?
...
WHAP! WHAP!
!
...
...
?!

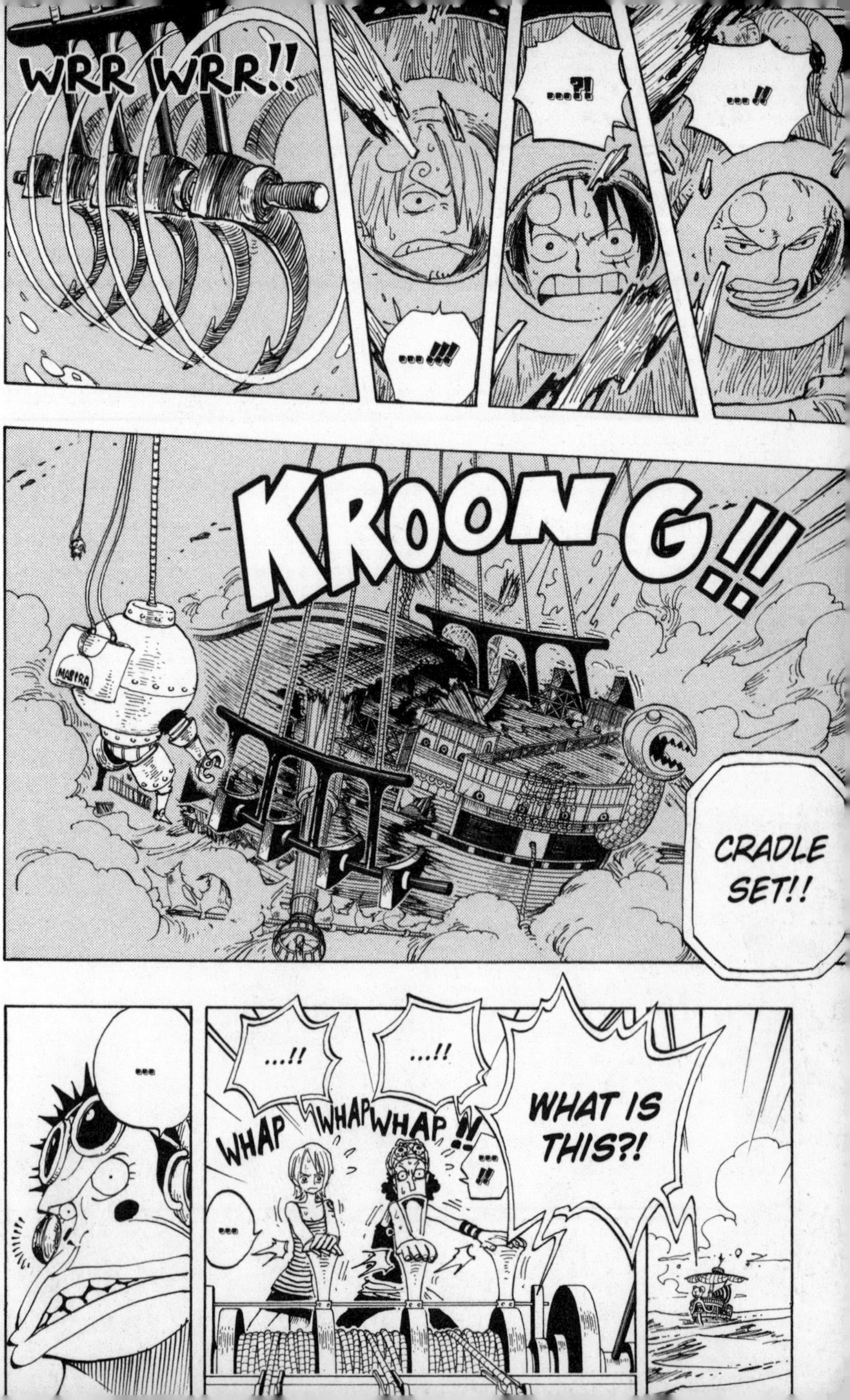

...!!
...?!
...!!!
WRR WRR!!
KROONG!!!
CRADLE SET!!
...!!
...!!
WHAT IS THIS?!
...!!
WHAPWHAP!!
WHAP
...
...

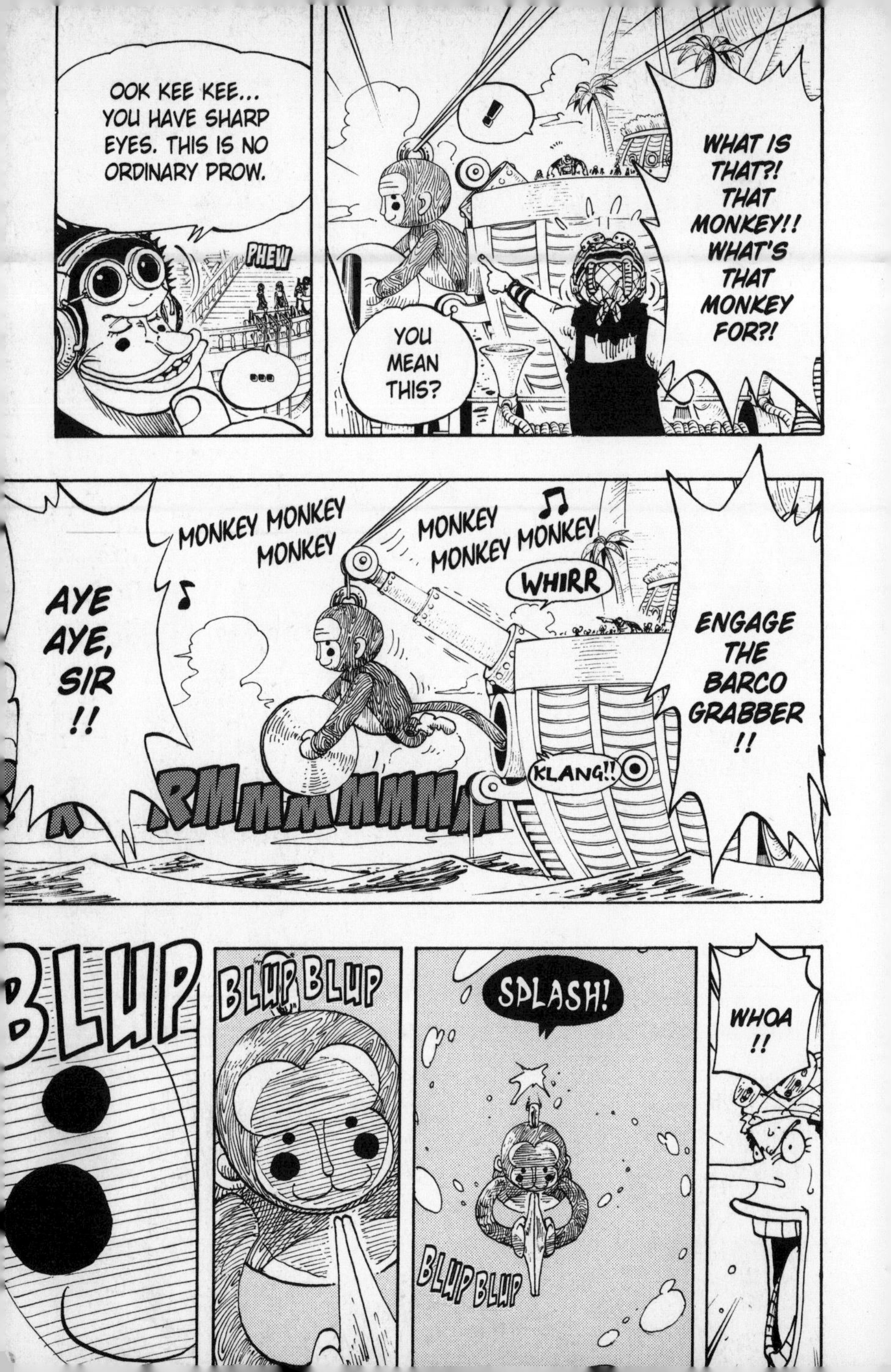
WHAT IS THAT?! THAT MONKEY!! WHAT'S THAT MONKEY FOR?!
!
YOU MEAN THIS?
OOK KEE KEE... YOU HAVE SHARP EYES. THIS IS NO ORDINARY PROW.
PHEW
...
ENGAGE THE BARCO GRABBER!!
MONKEY MONKEY MONKEY
WHIRR
KLANG!!
MONKEY MONKEY MONKEY
AYE AYE, SIR!!
RMMMMMMMM
WHOA!!
SPLASH!
BLUP BLUP
BLUP BLUP
BLUP

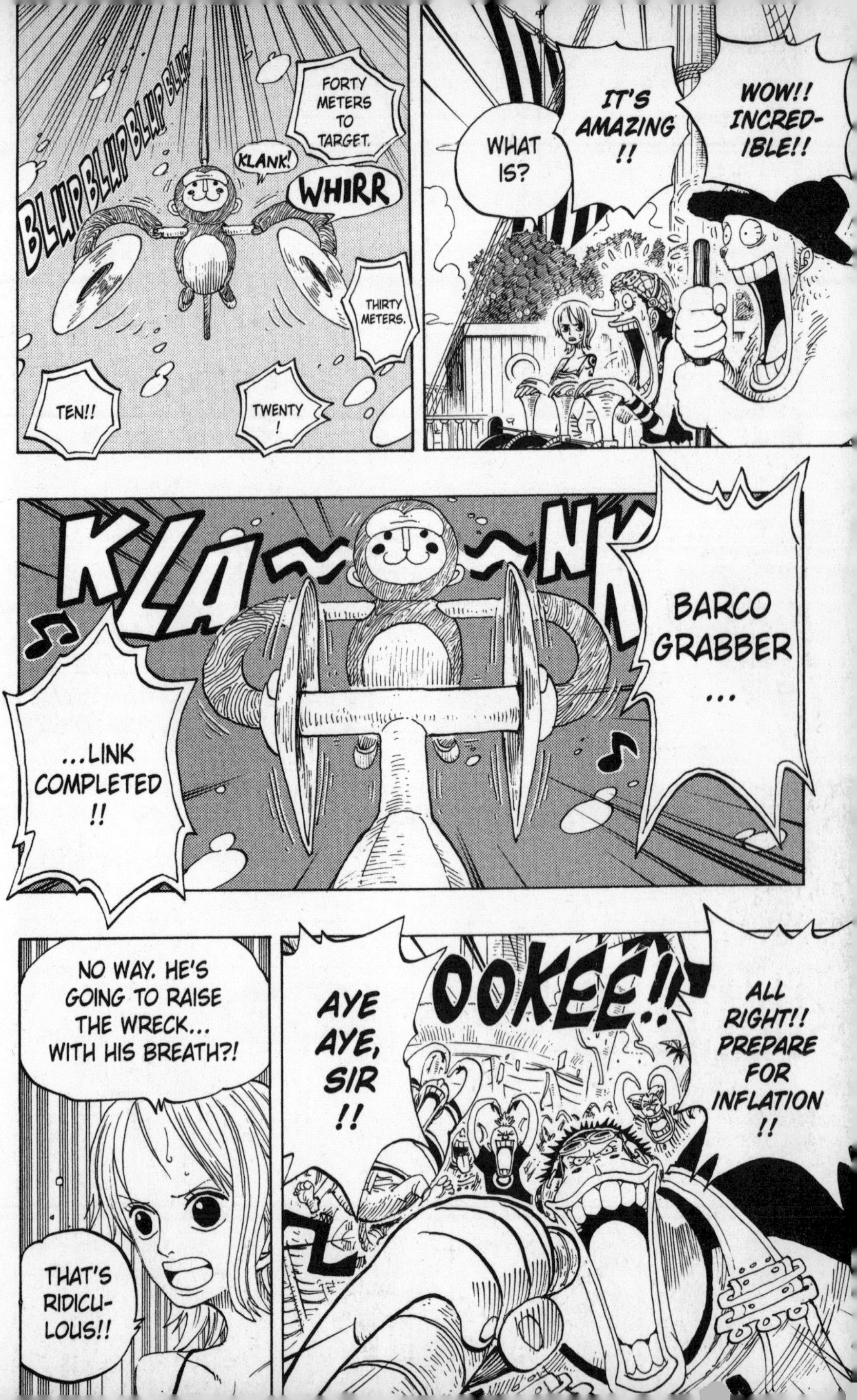
WOW!! INCRED-IBLE!!
IT'S AMAZING!!
WHAT IS?
FORTY METERS TO TARGET.
KLANK!
WHIRR
BLUP BLUP BLUP BLUP
THIRTY METERS.
TWENTY!
TEN!!
BARCO GRABBER ...
KLA~~~NK
...LINK COMPLETED!!
ALL RIGHT!! PREPARE FOR INFLATION!!
OOKEE!!
AYE AYE, SIR!!
NO WAY. HE'S GOING TO RAISE THE WRECK... WITH HIS BREATH?!
THAT'S RIDICU-LOUS!!

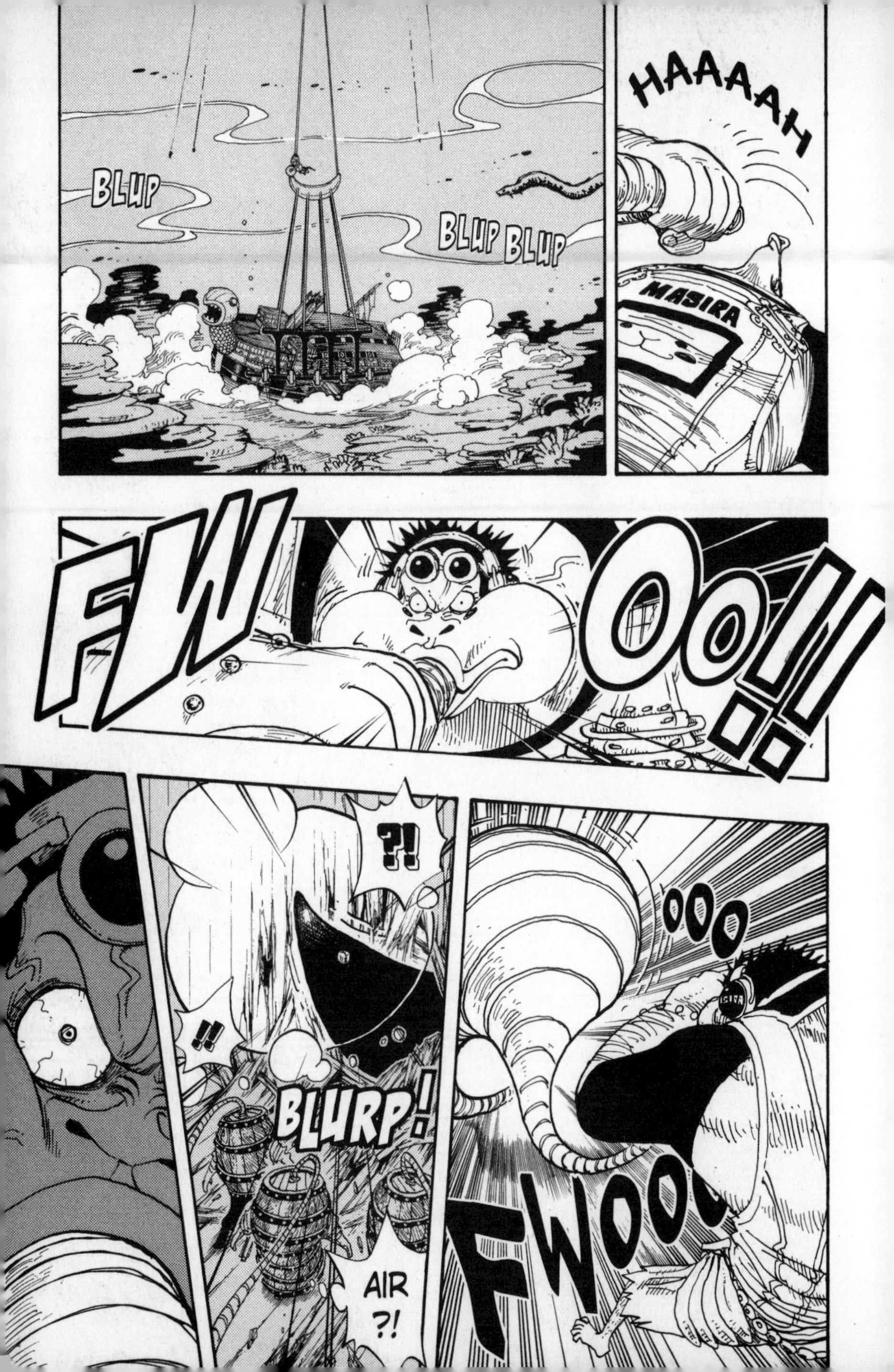

HAAAAH
MASIRA
BLUP
BLUP BLUP BLUP
FWOO!!
OOO
FWOO
?!
!!
BLURP!
AIR ?!

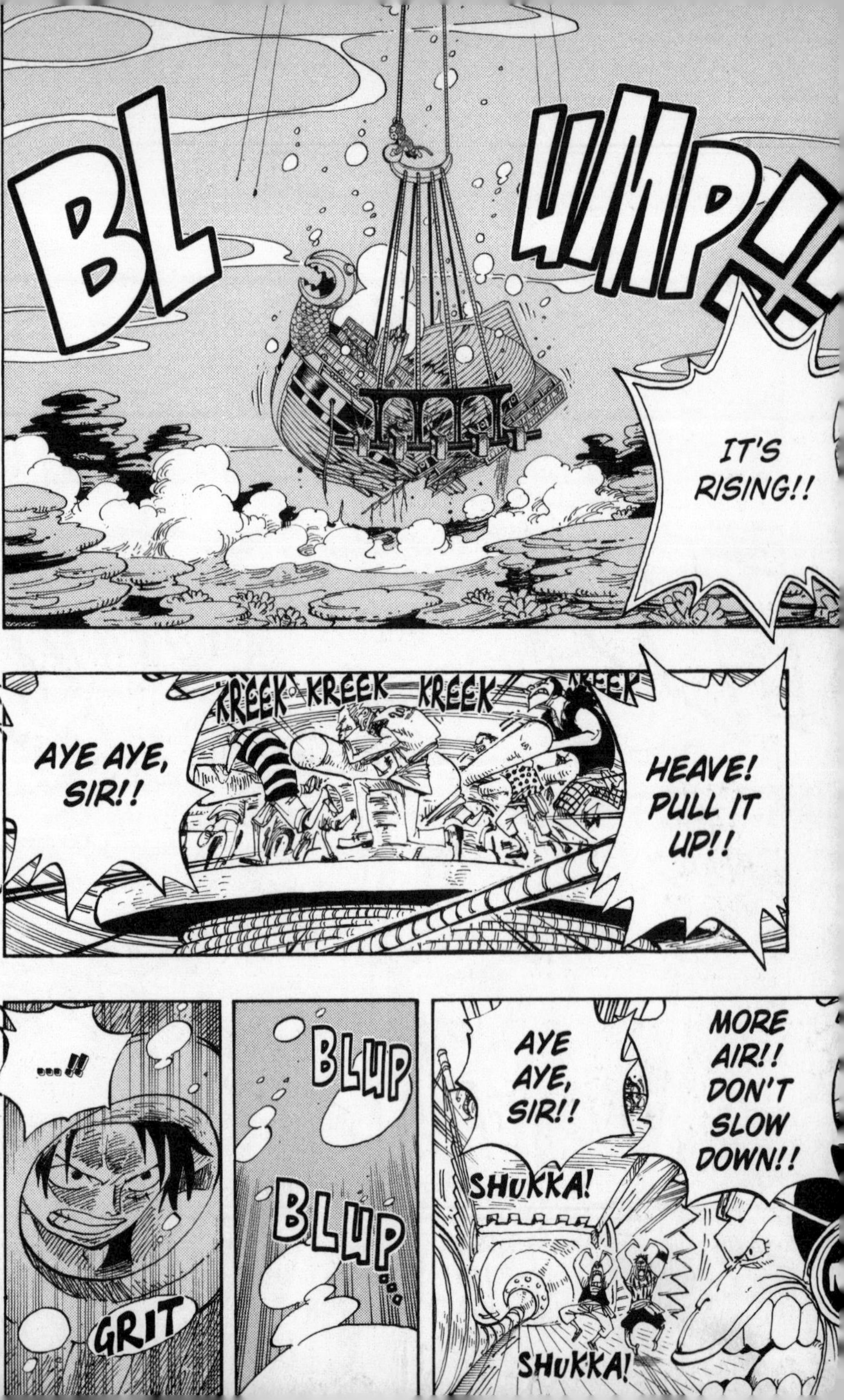
BL
UMP!!
IT'S RISING!!
HEAVE! PULL IT UP!!
KREEK KREEK KREEK
AYE AYE, SIR!!
MORE AIR!! DON'T SLOW DOWN!!
AYE AYE, SIR!!
SHUKKA!
SHUKKA!
BLUP
BLUP
...!!
GRIT

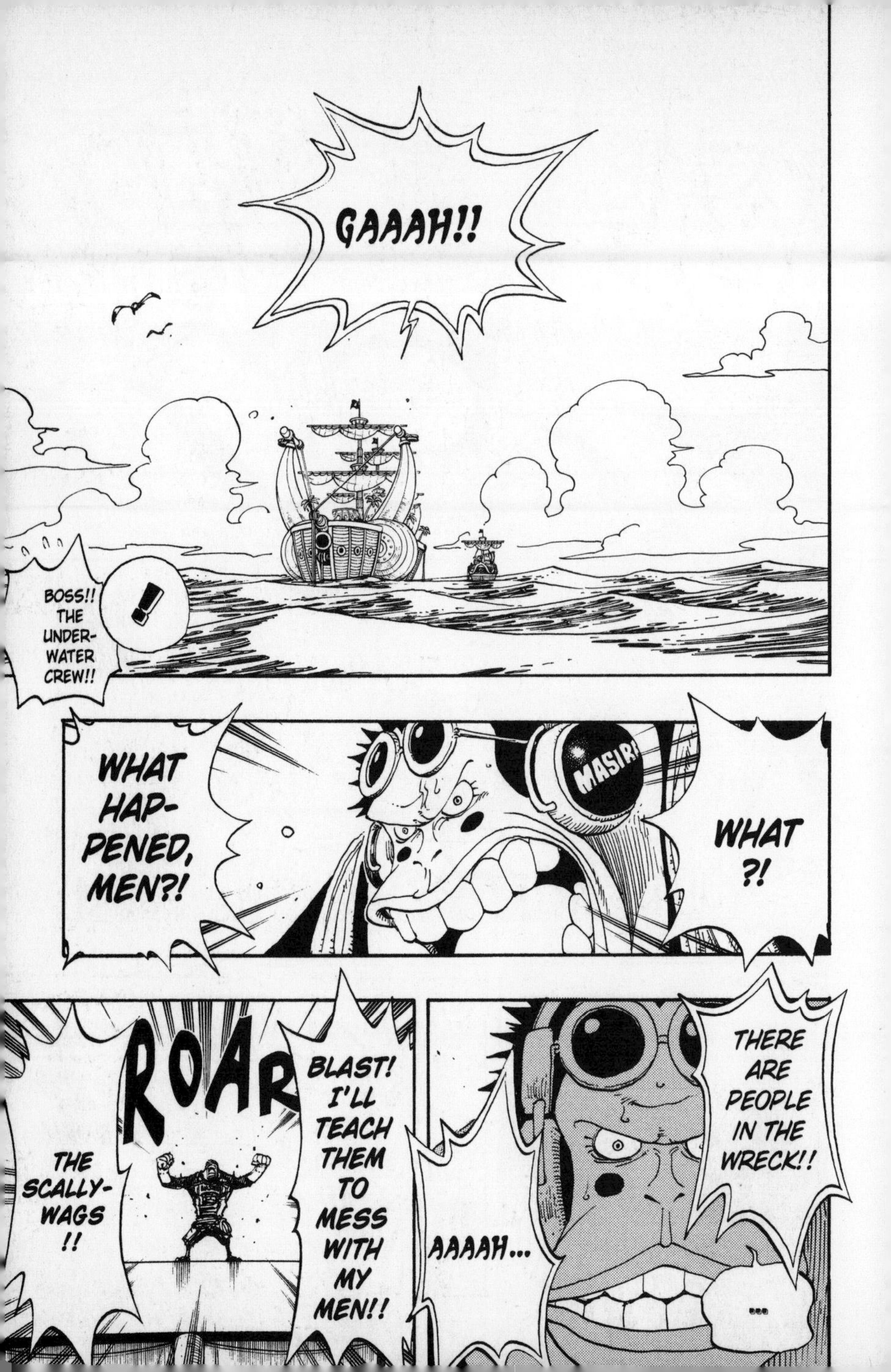
GAAAH!!
!
BOSS!! THE UNDER-WATER CREW!!
WHAT ?!
WHAT HAP-PENED, MEN?!
THERE ARE PEOPLE IN THE WRECK!!
...
AAAAH...
BLAST! I'LL TEACH THEM TO MESS WITH MY MEN!!
ROAR
THE SCALLY-WAGS !!

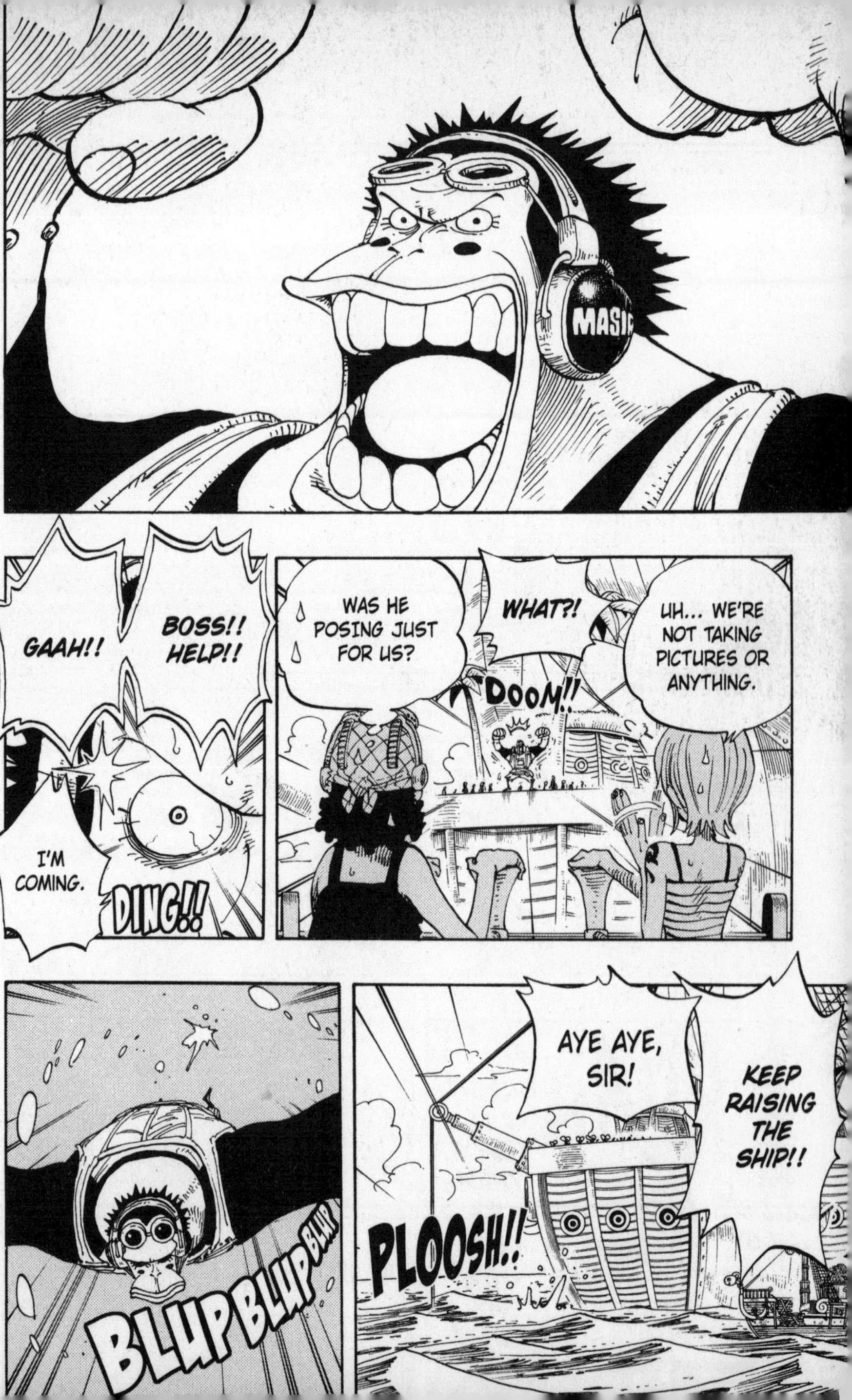
MASIC
UH... WE'RE NOT TAKING PICTURES OR ANYTHING.
WHAT?!
WAS HE POSING JUST FOR US?
DOOM!!
BOSS!! HELP!!
GAAH!!
I'M COMING.
DING!!
KEEP RAISING THE SHIP!!
AYE AYE, SIR!
PLOOSH!!
BLUP BLUP BLUP

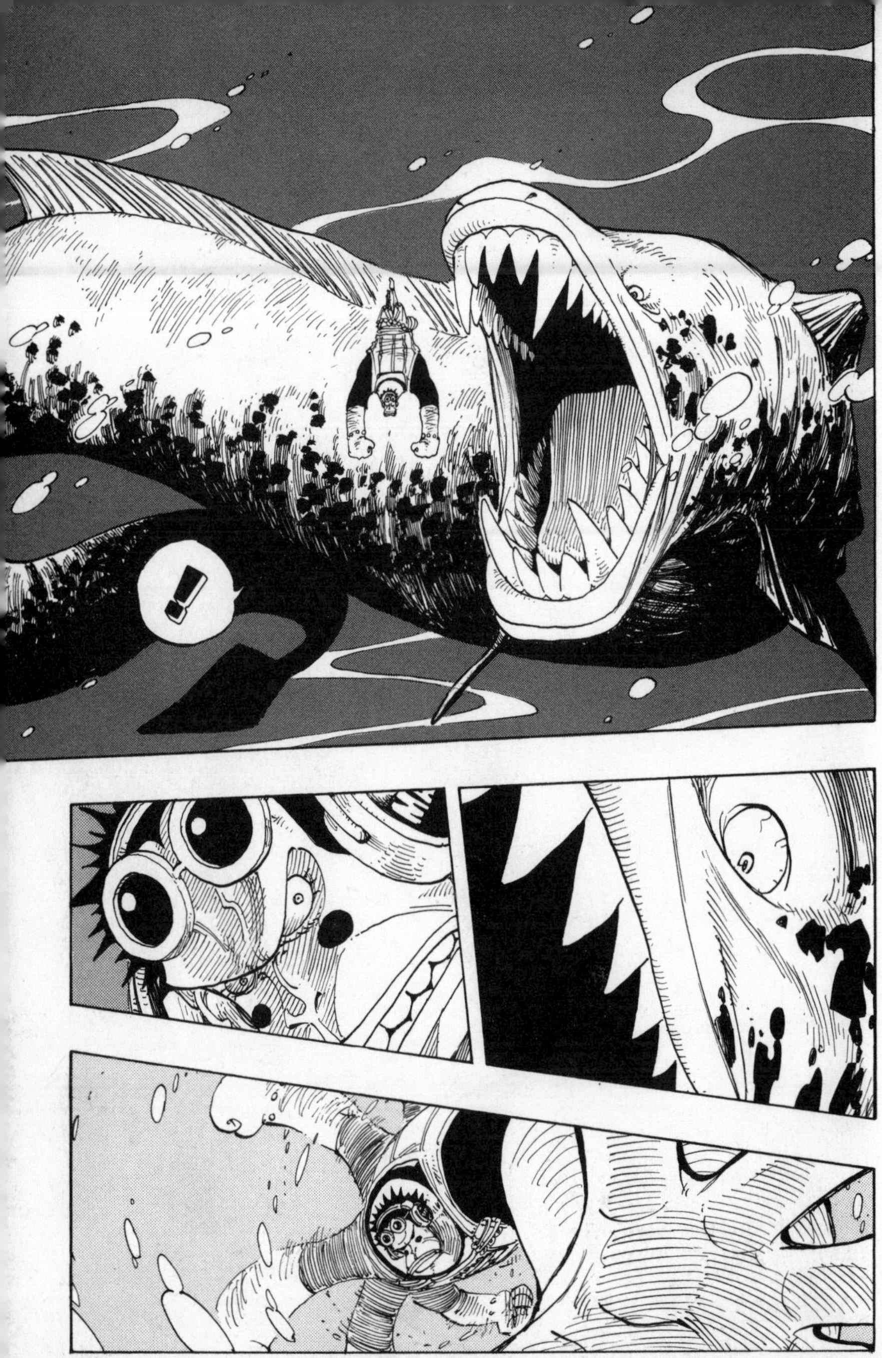
!

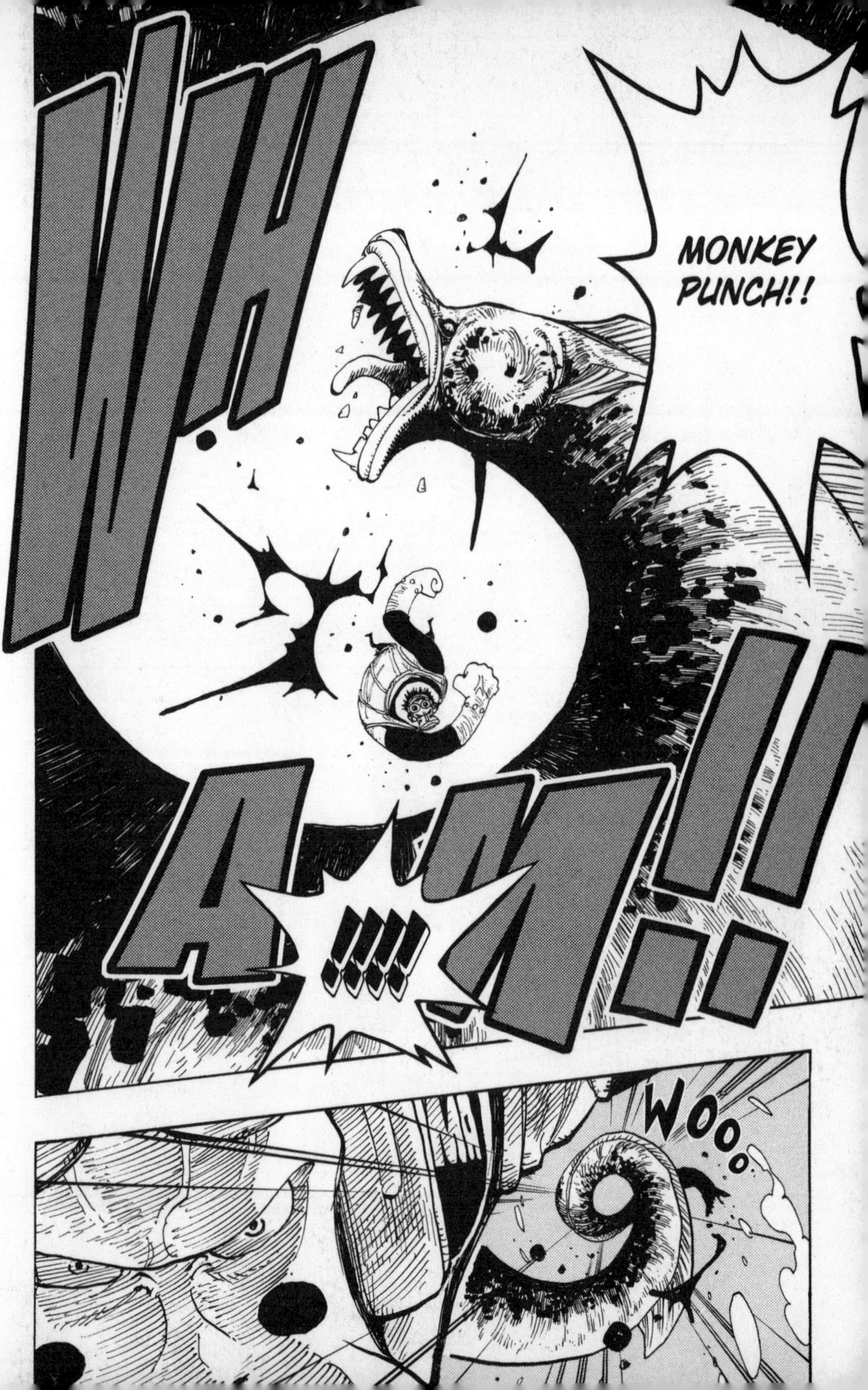
MONKEY PUNCH!!
WHAM!!
!!!!!
WOOO

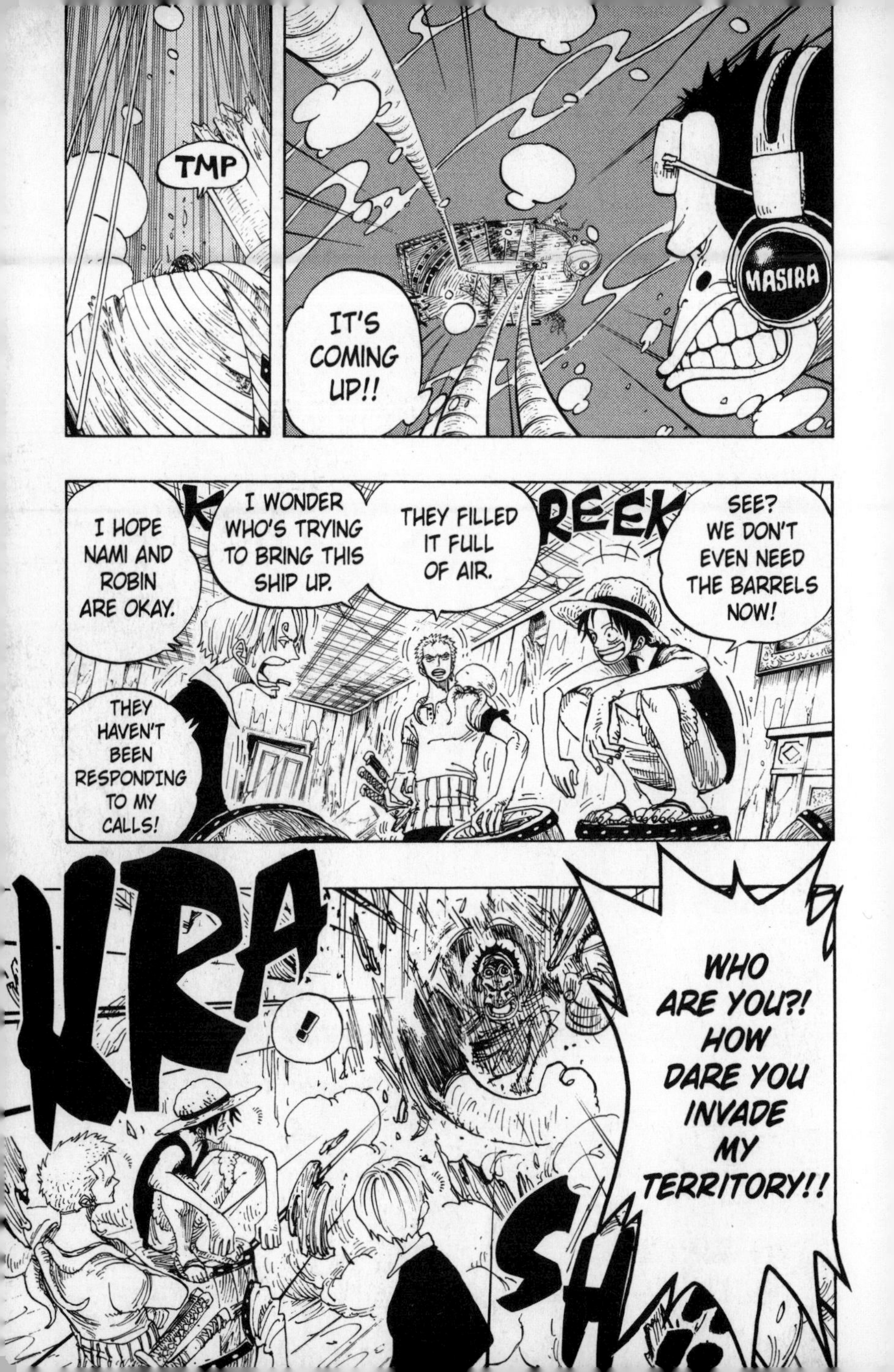
MASIRA
IT'S COMING UP!!
TMP
SEE? WE DON'T EVEN NEED THE BARRELS NOW!
KREEK
THEY FILLED IT FULL OF AIR.
I WONDER WHO'S TRYING TO BRING THIS SHIP UP.
I HOPE NAMI AND ROBIN ARE OKAY.
THEY HAVEN'T BEEN RESPONDING TO MY CALLS!
WHO ARE YOU?! HOW DARE YOU INVADE MY TERRITORY!!
KRASH
!

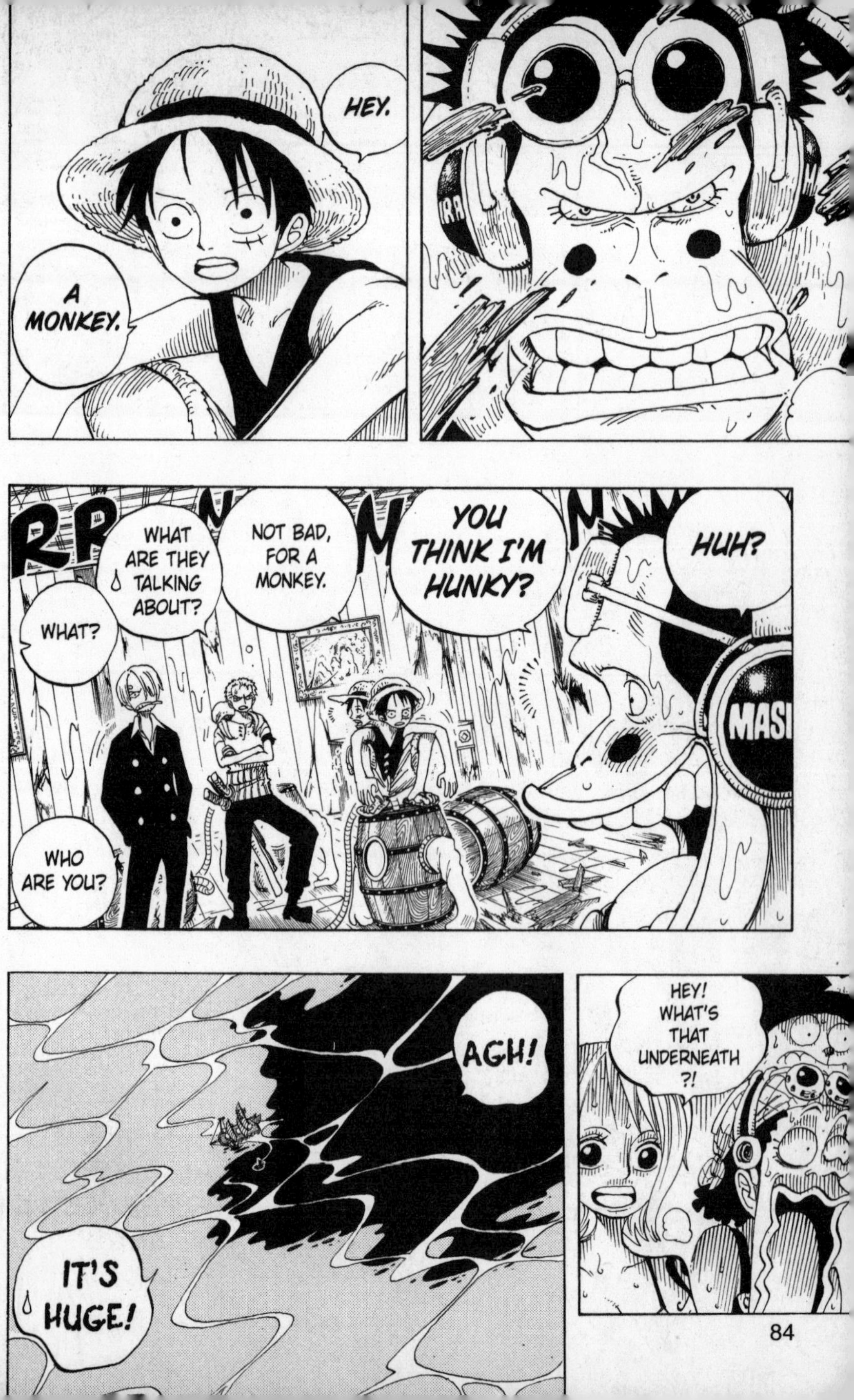
HEY.
A MONKEY.
HUH?
YOU THINK I'M HUNKY?
NOT BAD, FOR A MONKEY.
WHAT ARE THEY TALKING ABOUT?
WHAT?
WHO ARE YOU?
HEY! WHAT'S THAT UNDERNEATH ?!
AGH!
IT'S HUGE!

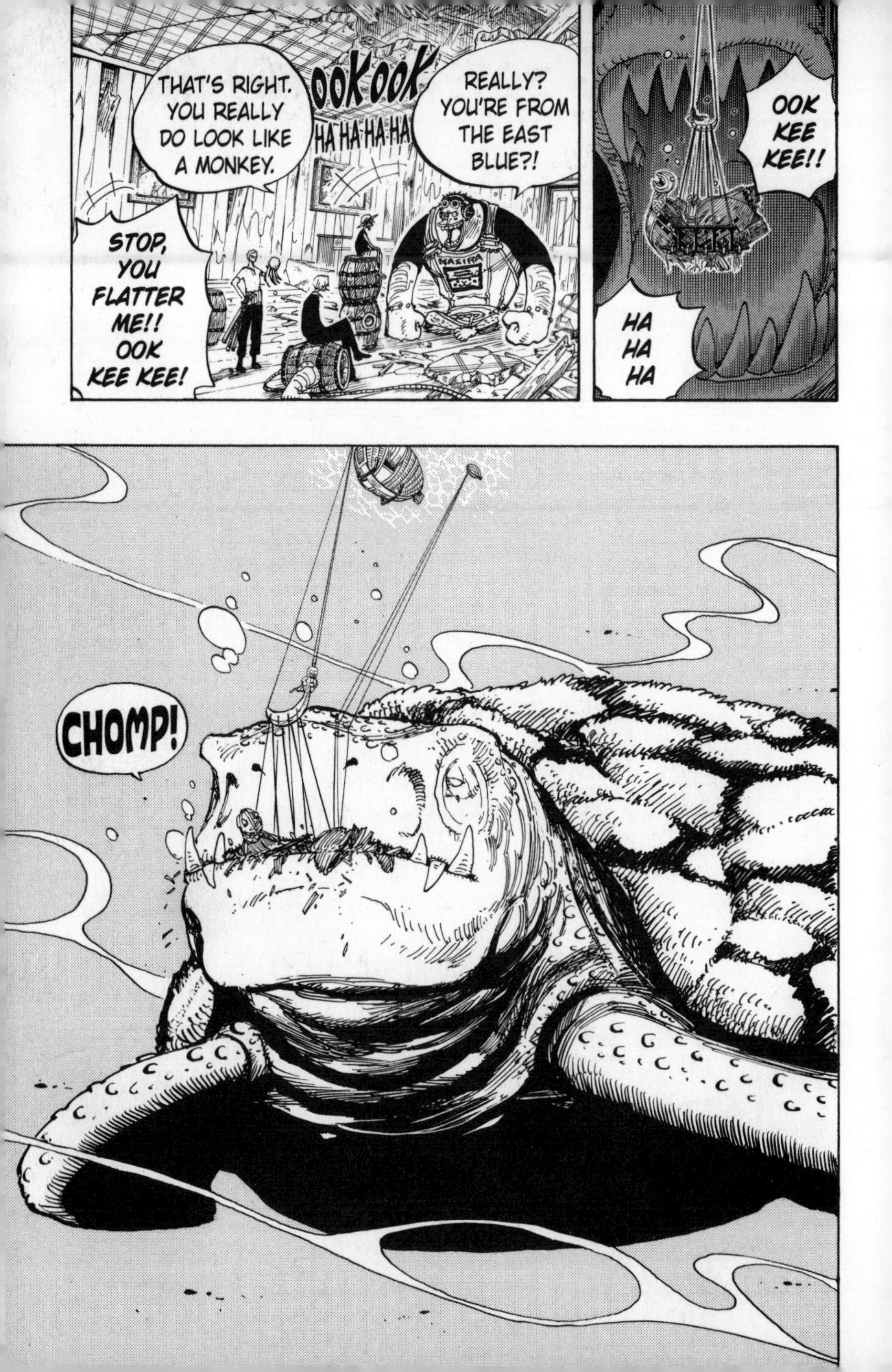
OOK KEE KEE!!
HA HA HA
REALLY? YOU'RE FROM THE EAST BLUE?!
OOKOOK
HA HA HA HA
THAT'S RIGHT. YOU REALLY DO LOOK LIKE A MONKEY.
STOP, YOU FLATTER ME!! OOK KEE KEE!
CHOMP!

Chapter 221: MONSTERS

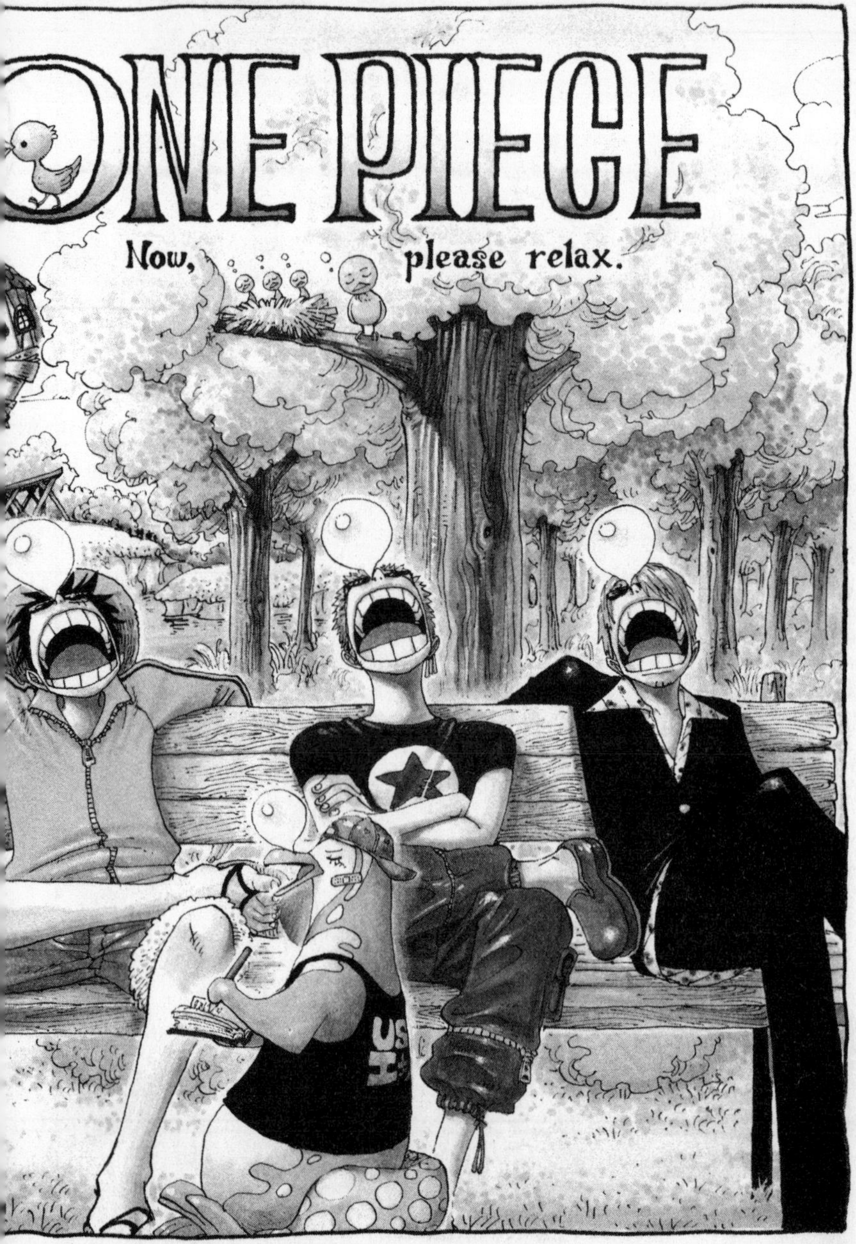
ONE PIECE
Now, please relax.

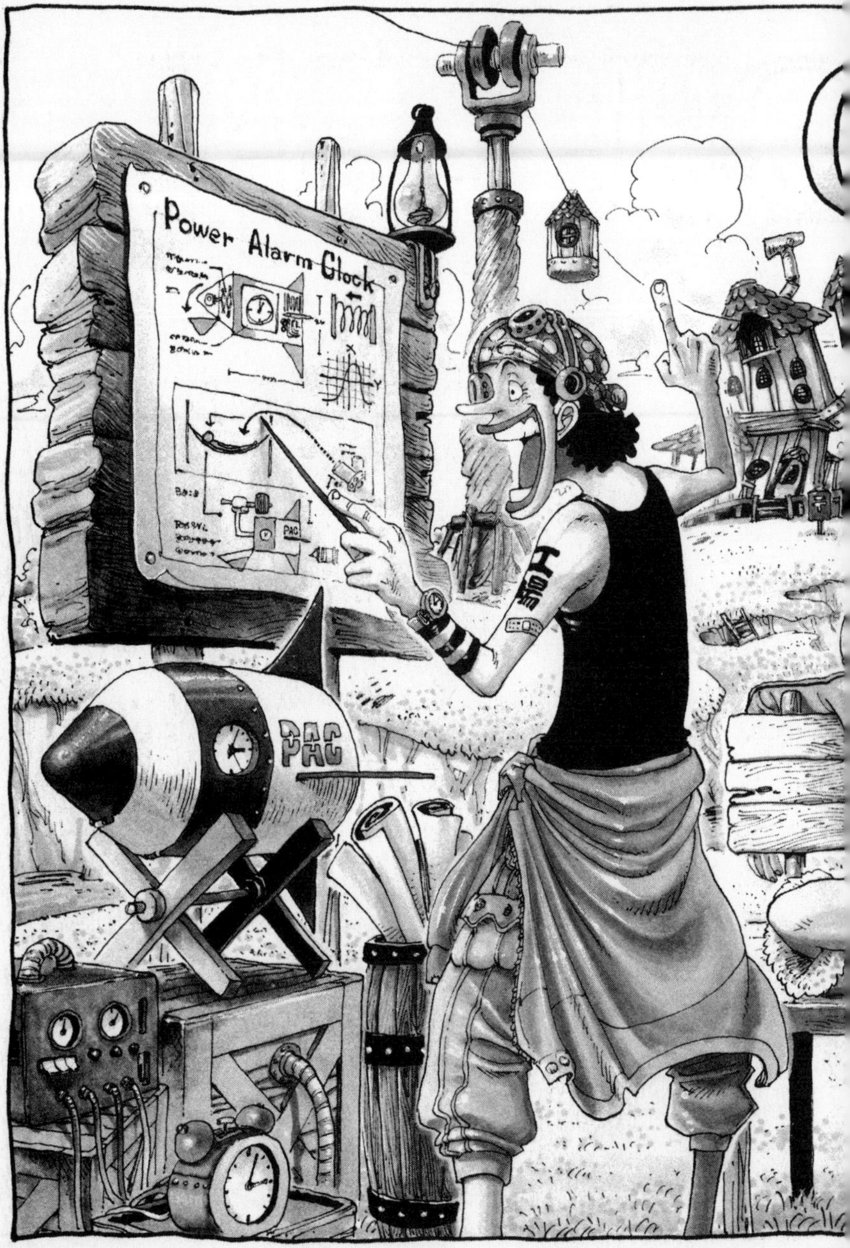
Power Alarm Clock
PAC
PAC

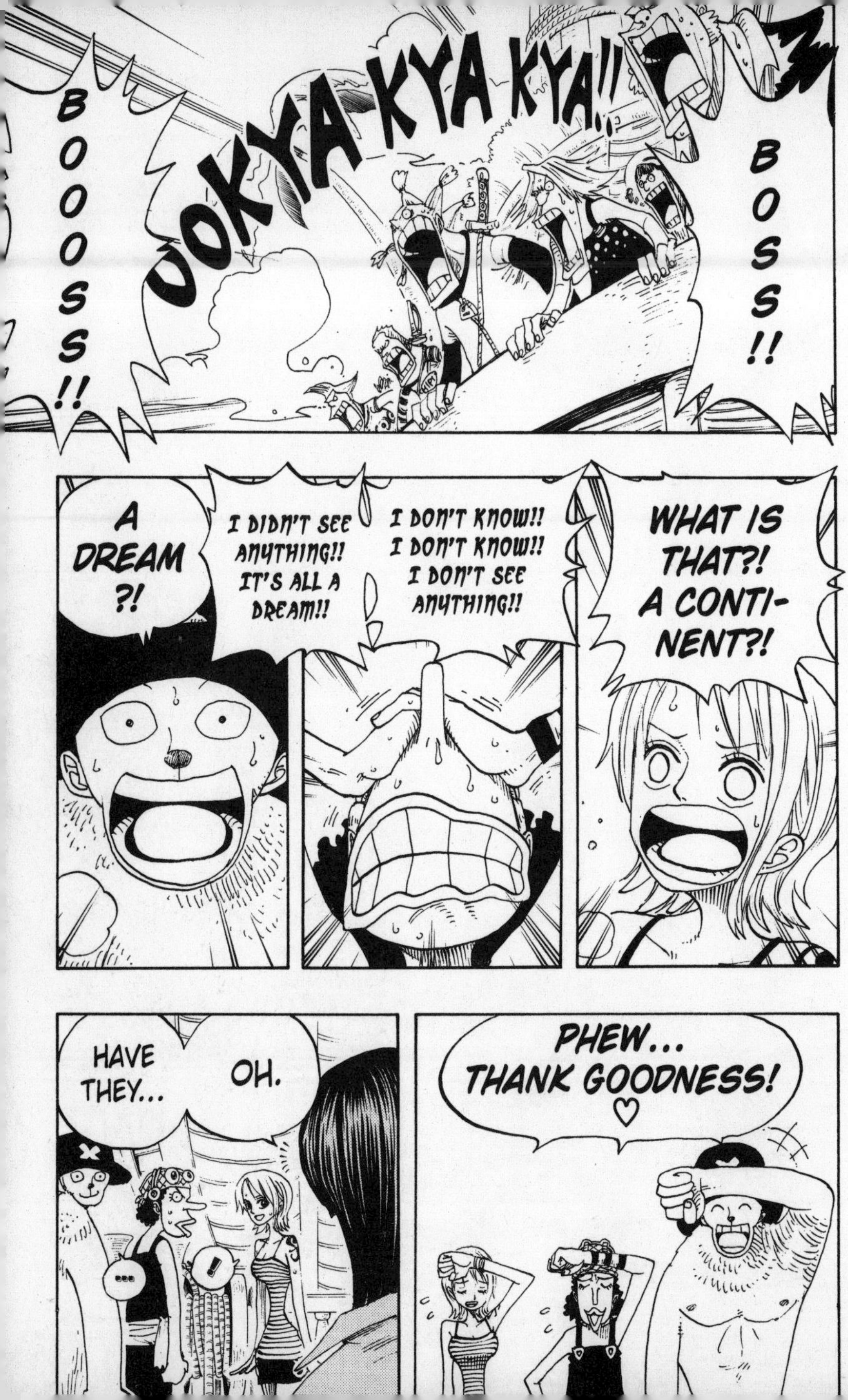
BOSS!!
UOKYA-KYA KYA!!
BOOOOSS!!
WHAT IS THAT?! A CONTI-NENT?!
I DON'T KNOW!! I DON'T KNOW!! I DON'T SEE ANYTHING!!
I DIDN'T SEE ANYTHING!! IT'S ALL A DREAM!!
A DREAM ?!
PHEW... THANK GOODNESS! ♡
HAVE THEY...
OH.
...
!

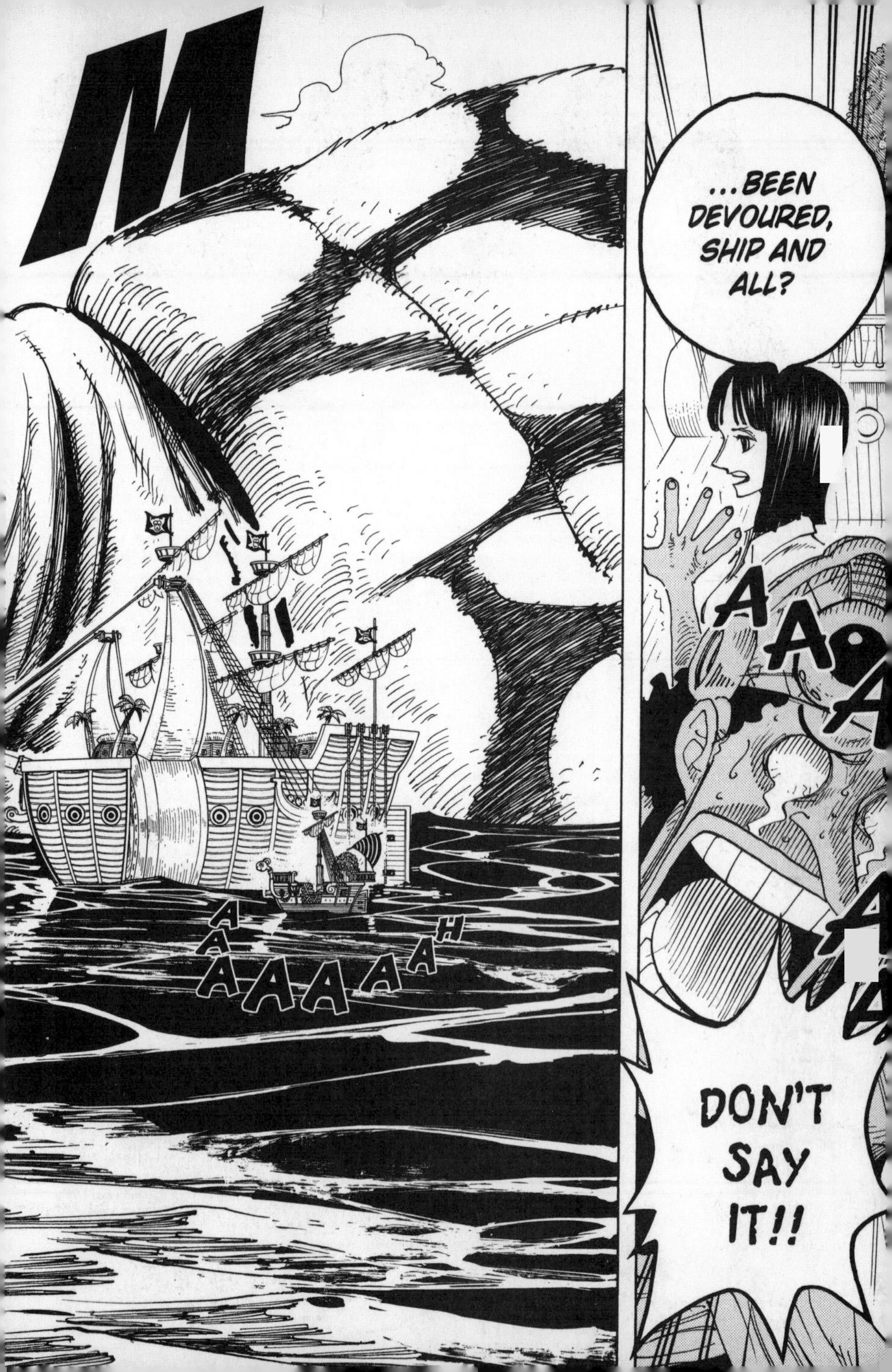
...BEEN DEVOURED, SHIP AND ALL?
AAAAAA
DON'T SAY IT!!
M
AAAAAAAAH

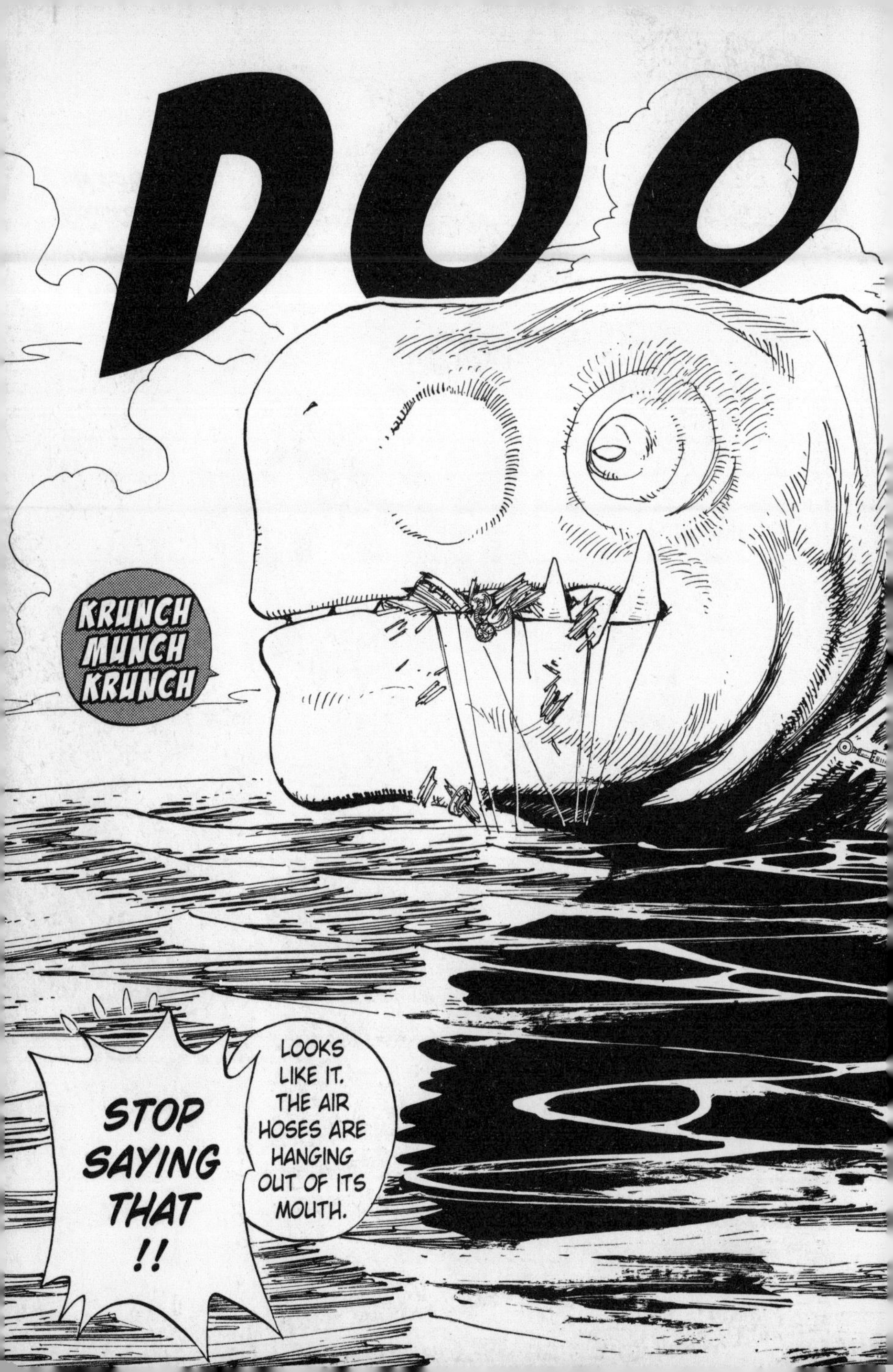
DOO
KRUNCH MUNCH KRUNCH
LOOKS LIKE IT. THE AIR HOSES ARE HANGING OUT OF ITS MOUTH.
STOP SAYING THAT !!

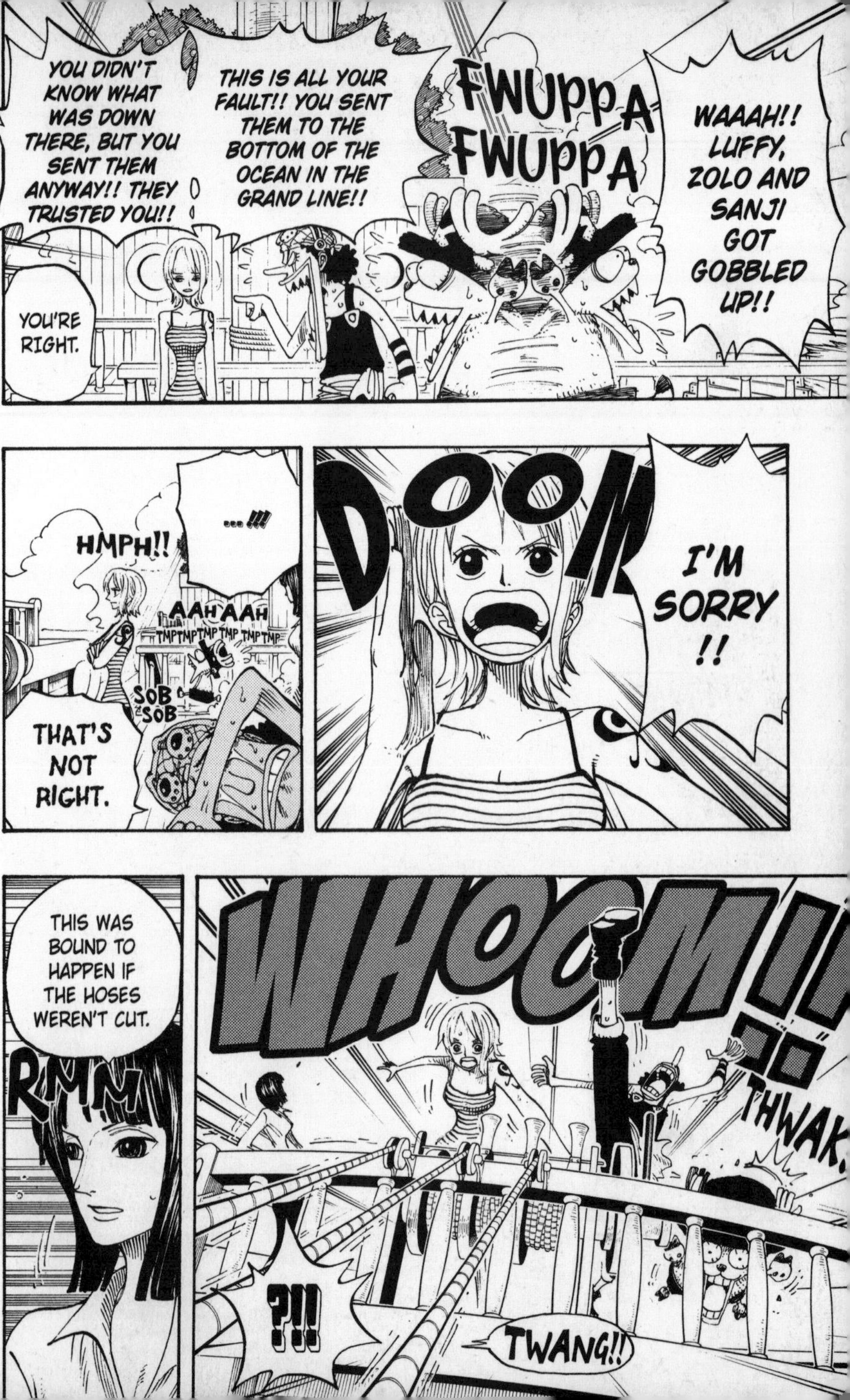

WAAAH!! LUFFY, ZOLO AND SANJI GOT GOBBLED UP!!
FWUPPA FWUPPA
THIS IS ALL YOUR FAULT!! YOU SENT THEM TO THE BOTTOM OF THE OCEAN IN THE GRAND LINE!!
YOU DIDN'T KNOW WHAT WAS DOWN THERE, BUT YOU SENT THEM ANYWAY!! THEY TRUSTED YOU!!
YOU'RE RIGHT.
I'M SORRY!!
DOOM
...!!!
HMPH!!
AAH AAH
TMPTMPTMP TMP TMPTMP
SOB SOB
THAT'S NOT RIGHT.
WHOOM!!
THWAK.
?!!
TWANG!!
THIS WAS BOUND TO HAPPEN IF THE HOSES WEREN'T CUT.
RMM

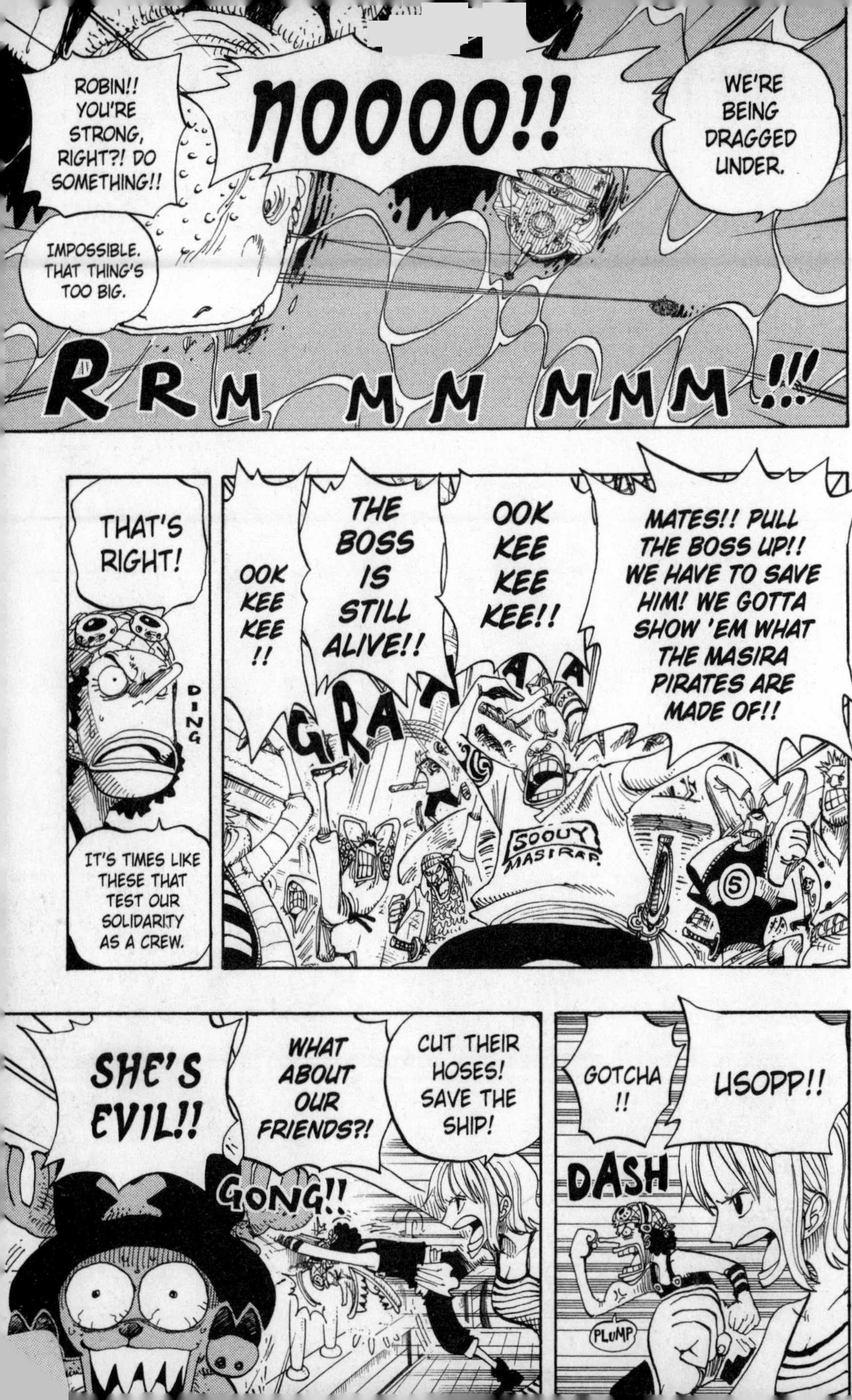
WE'RE BEING DRAGGED UNDER.
NOOOO!!
ROBIN!! YOU'RE STRONG, RIGHT?! DO SOMETHING!!
IMPOSSIBLE. THAT THING'S TOO BIG.
RRMMMMMMM!!!
MATES!! PULL THE BOSS UP!! WE HAVE TO SAVE HIM! WE GOTTA SHOW 'EM WHAT THE MASIRA PIRATES ARE MADE OF!!
OOK KEE KEE KEE!!
THE BOSS IS STILL ALIVE!!
OOK KEE KEE !!
GRA AA
SOOUY
MASIRAP
THAT'S RIGHT!
DING
IT'S TIMES LIKE THESE THAT TEST OUR SOLIDARITY AS A CREW.
USOPP!!
GOTCHA !!
DASH
PLUMP
CUT THEIR HOSES! SAVE THE SHIP!
WHAT ABOUT OUR FRIENDS?!
SHE'S EVIL!!
GONG!!

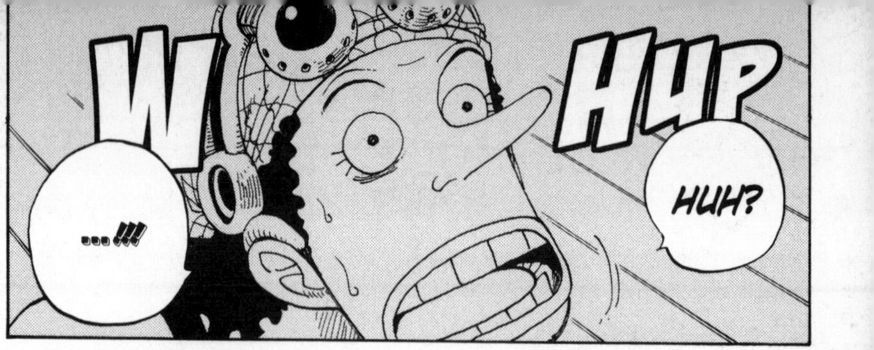
W HUP
HUH?
...!!!

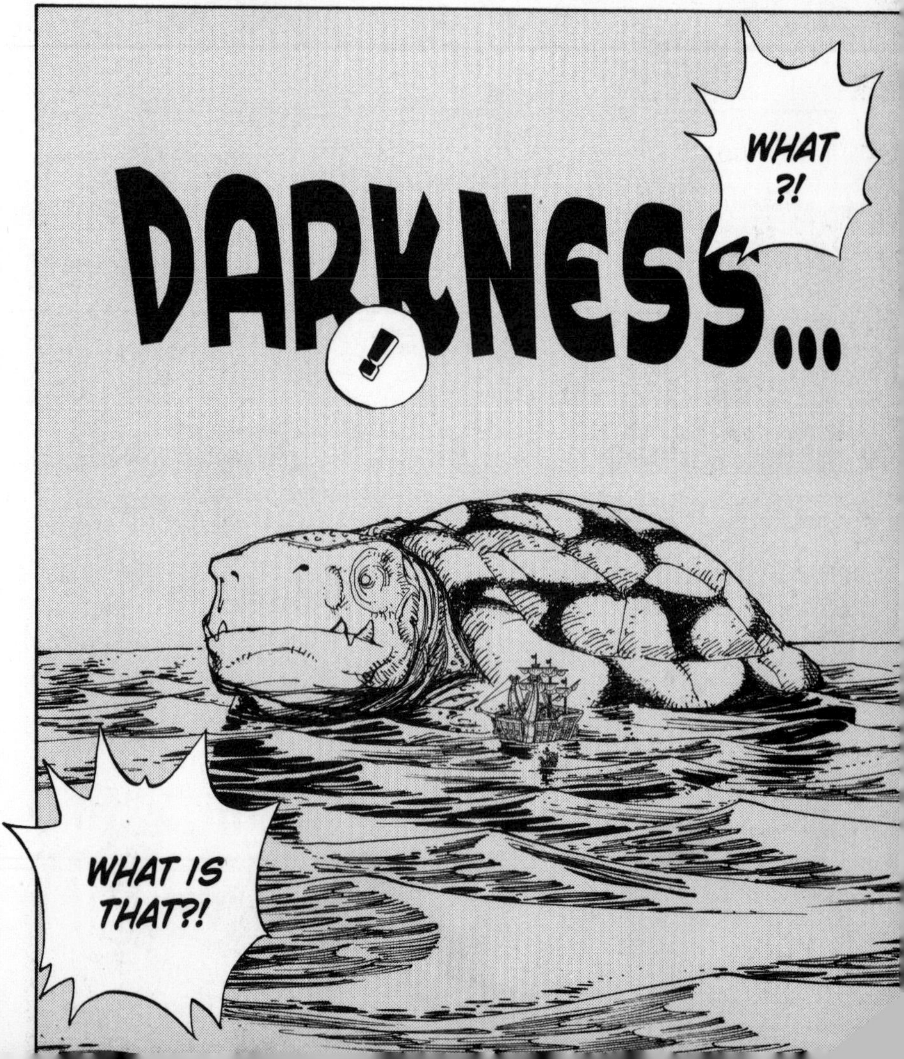
WHAT ?!
DARKNESS...
!
WHAT IS THAT?!

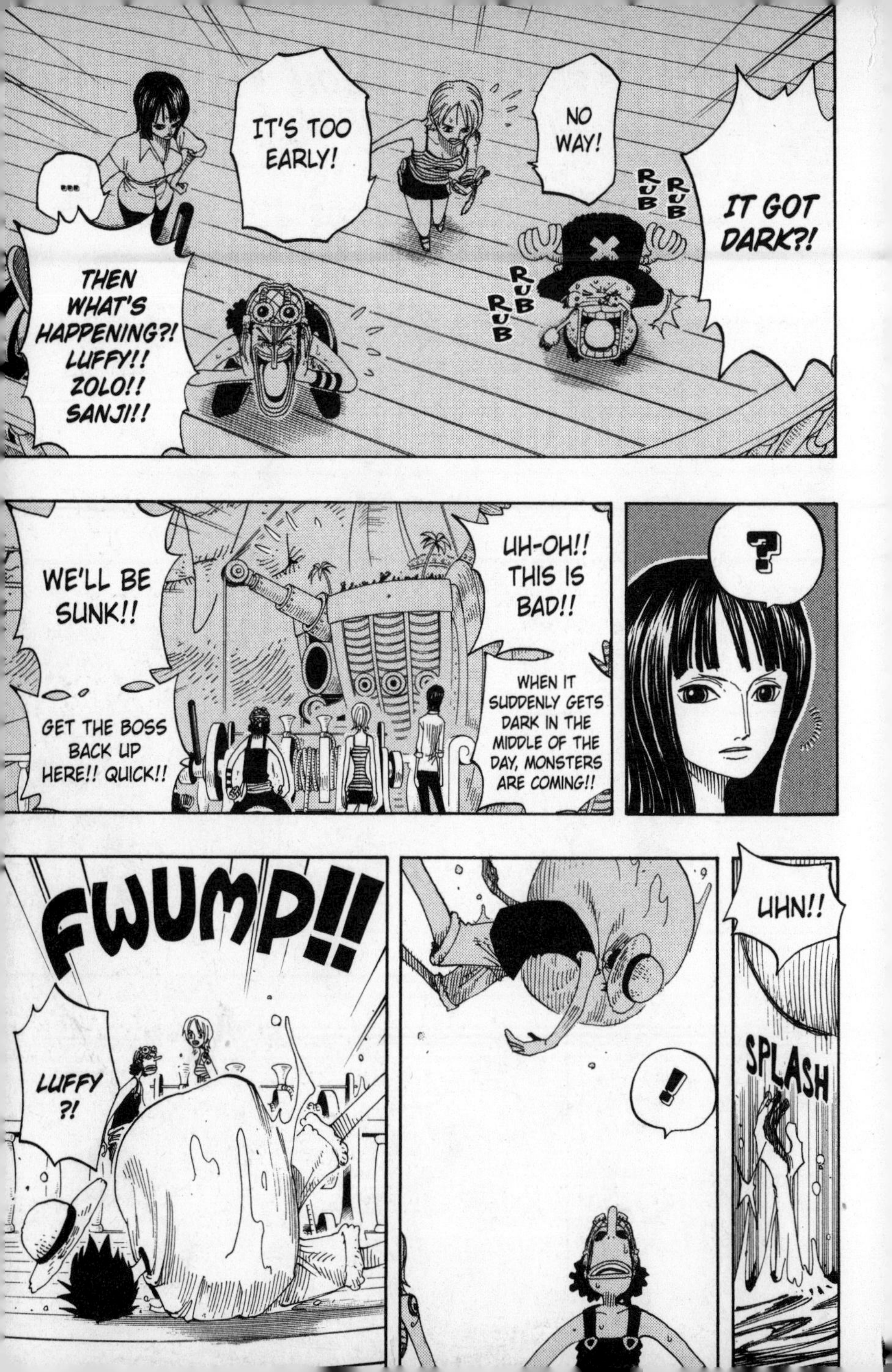
IT GOT DARK?!
NO WAY!
RUB RUB
IT'S TOO EARLY!
RUB RUB
...
THEN WHAT'S HAPPENING?! LUFFY!! ZOLO!! SANJI!!
?
UH-OH!! THIS IS BAD!!
WHEN IT SUDDENLY GETS DARK IN THE MIDDLE OF THE DAY, MONSTERS ARE COMING!!
WE'LL BE SUNK!!
GET THE BOSS BACK UP HERE!! QUICK!!
UHN!!
SPLASH
!
FWUMP!!
LUFFY ?!

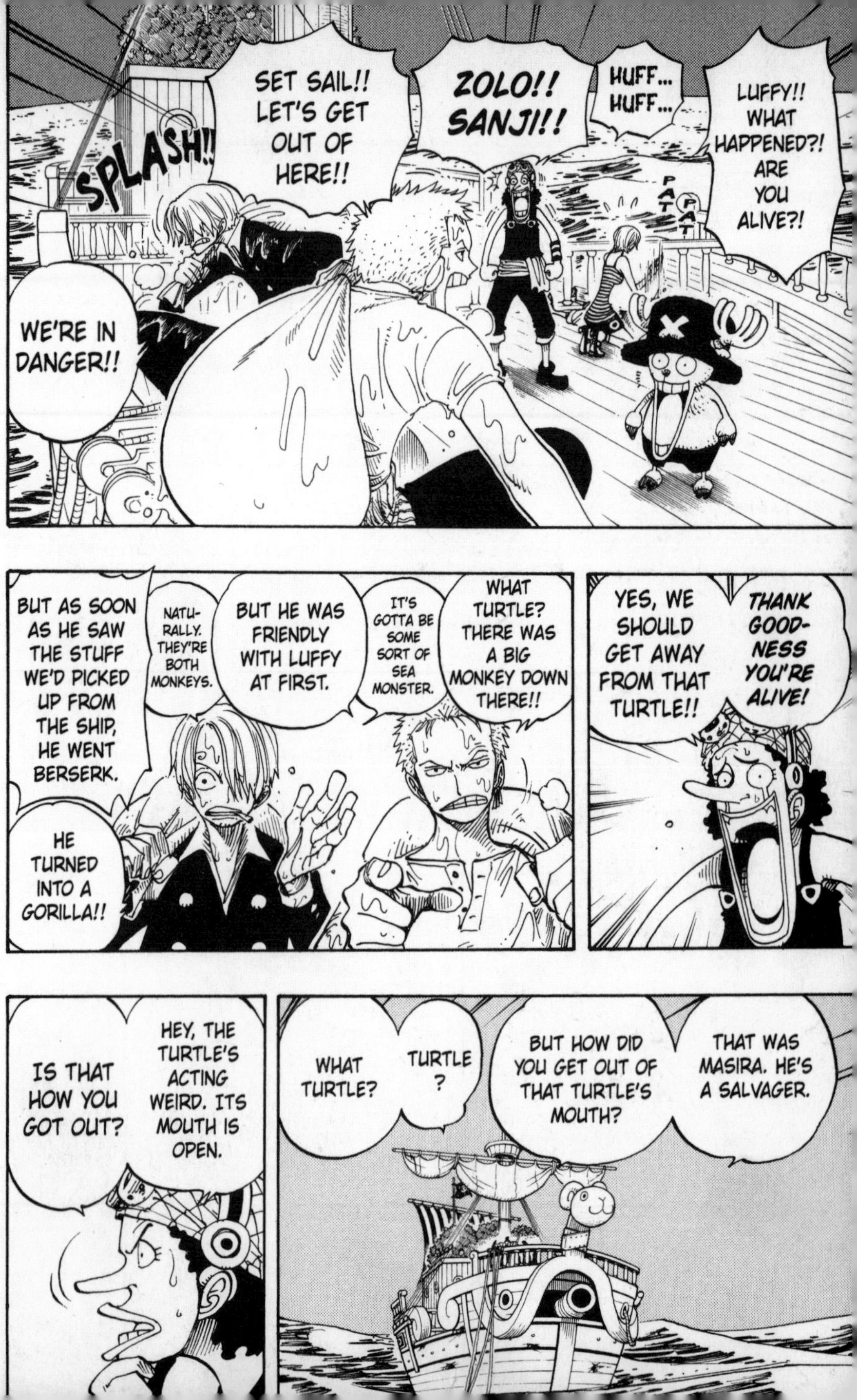
LUFFY!! WHAT HAPPENED?! ARE YOU ALIVE?!
PAT PAT
HUFF... HUFF...
ZOLO!! SANJI!!
SET SAIL!! LET'S GET OUT OF HERE!!
SPLASH!!
WE'RE IN DANGER!!
THANK GOOD-NESS YOU'RE ALIVE!
YES, WE SHOULD GET AWAY FROM THAT TURTLE!!
WHAT TURTLE? THERE WAS A BIG MONKEY DOWN THERE!!
IT'S GOTTA BE SOME SORT OF SEA MONSTER.
BUT HE WAS FRIENDLY WITH LUFFY AT FIRST.
NATU-RALLY. THEY'RE BOTH MONKEYS.
BUT AS SOON AS HE SAW THE STUFF WE'D PICKED UP FROM THE SHIP, HE WENT BERSERK.
HE TURNED INTO A GORILLA!!
THAT WAS MASIRA. HE'S A SALVAGER.
BUT HOW DID YOU GET OUT OF THAT TURTLE'S MOUTH?
TURTLE ?
WHAT TURTLE?
HEY, THE TURTLE'S ACTING WEIRD. ITS MOUTH IS OPEN.
IS THAT HOW YOU GOT OUT?

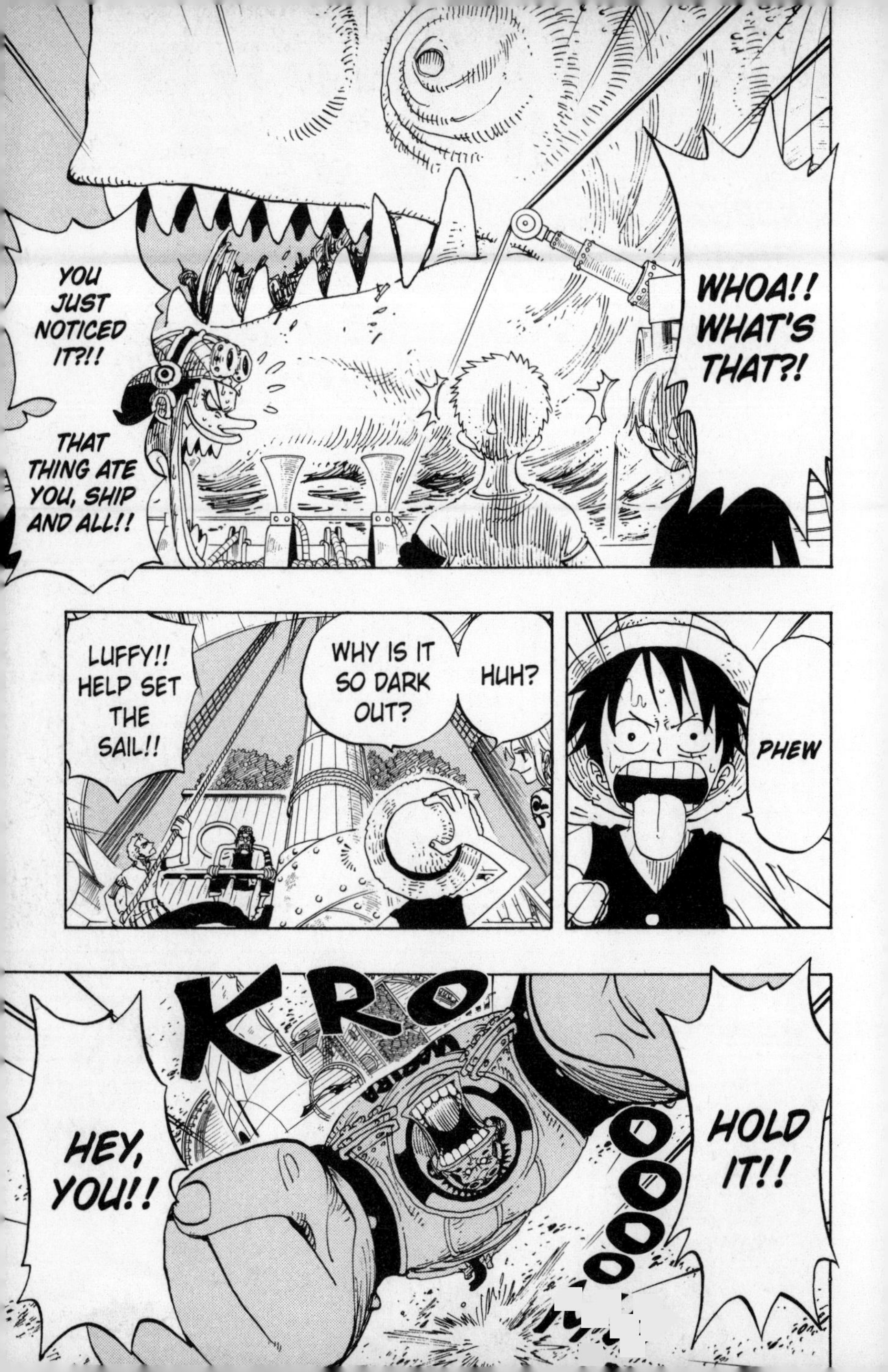
WHOA!! WHAT'S THAT?!
YOU JUST NOTICED IT?!!
THAT THING ATE YOU, SHIP AND ALL!!
PHEW
HUH?
WHY IS IT SO DARK OUT?
LUFFY!! HELP SET THE SAIL!!
HOLD IT!!
KRO... OOOOOO
HEY, YOU!!

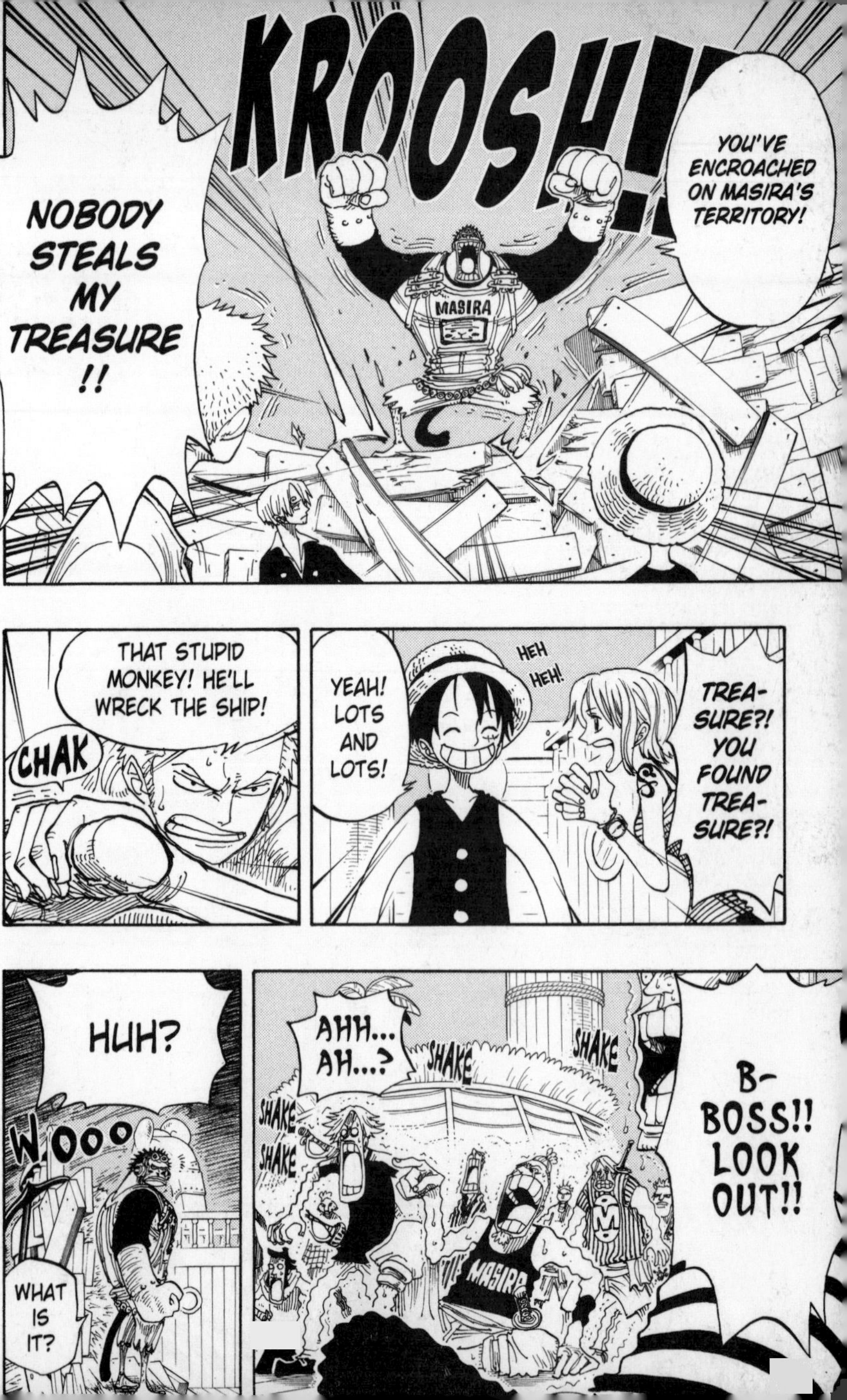

YOU'VE ENCROACHED ON MASIRA'S TERRITORY!
KROOSH!!
NOBODY STEALS MY TREASURE !!
TREA-SURE?! YOU FOUND TREA-SURE?!
HEH HEH!
YEAH! LOTS AND LOTS!
THAT STUPID MONKEY! HE'LL WRECK THE SHIP!
CHAK
B-BOSS!! LOOK OUT!!
SHAKE
SHAKE
AHH... AH...?
SHAKE SHAKE
HUH?
WOOO
WHAT IS IT?

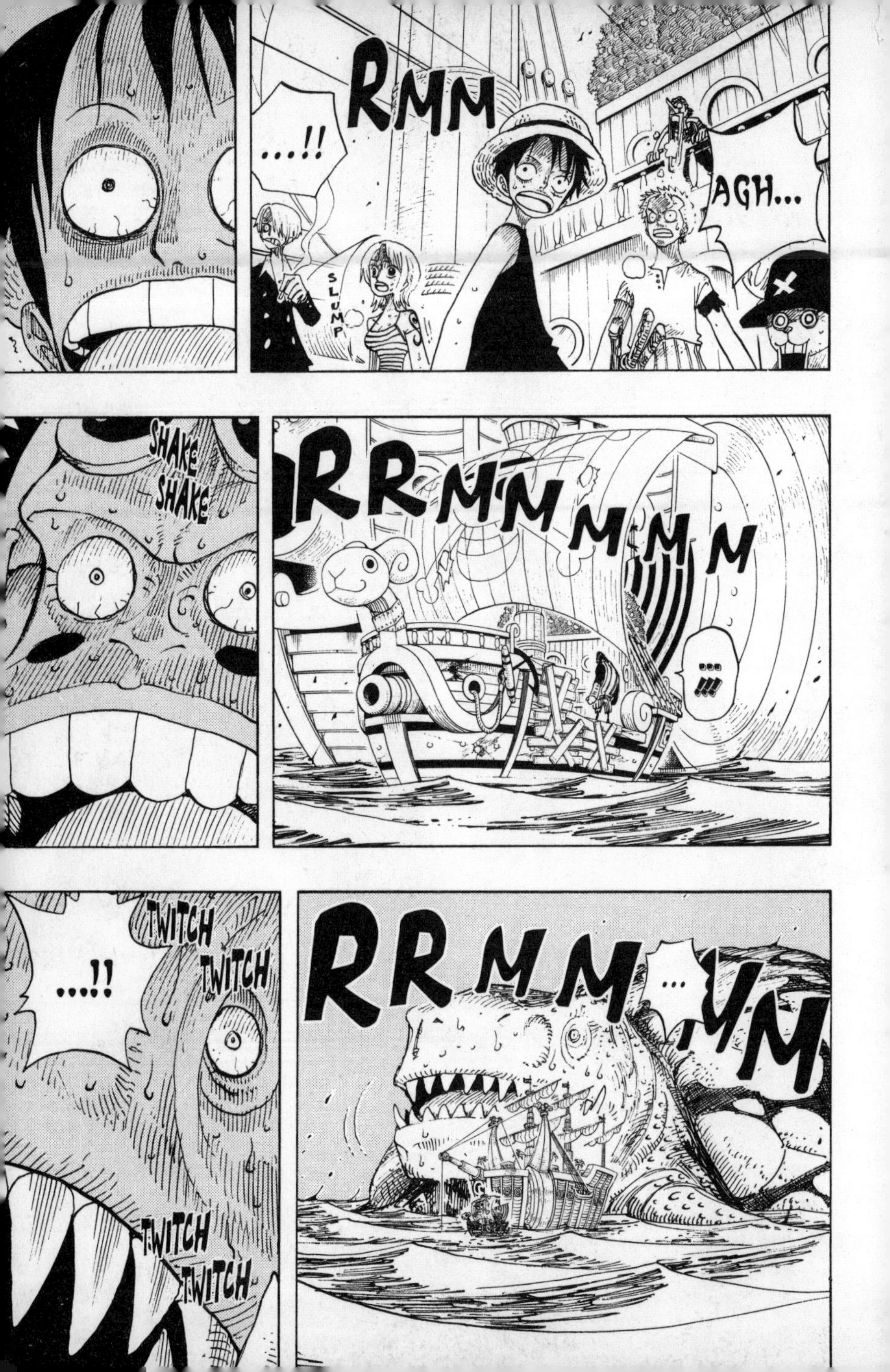
RMM
AGH...
...!!
SLUMP
RRMMMMMMM
...!!!
SHAKE SHAKE
RRMMMM
...
...!!
TWITCH TWITCH
TWITCH TWITCH

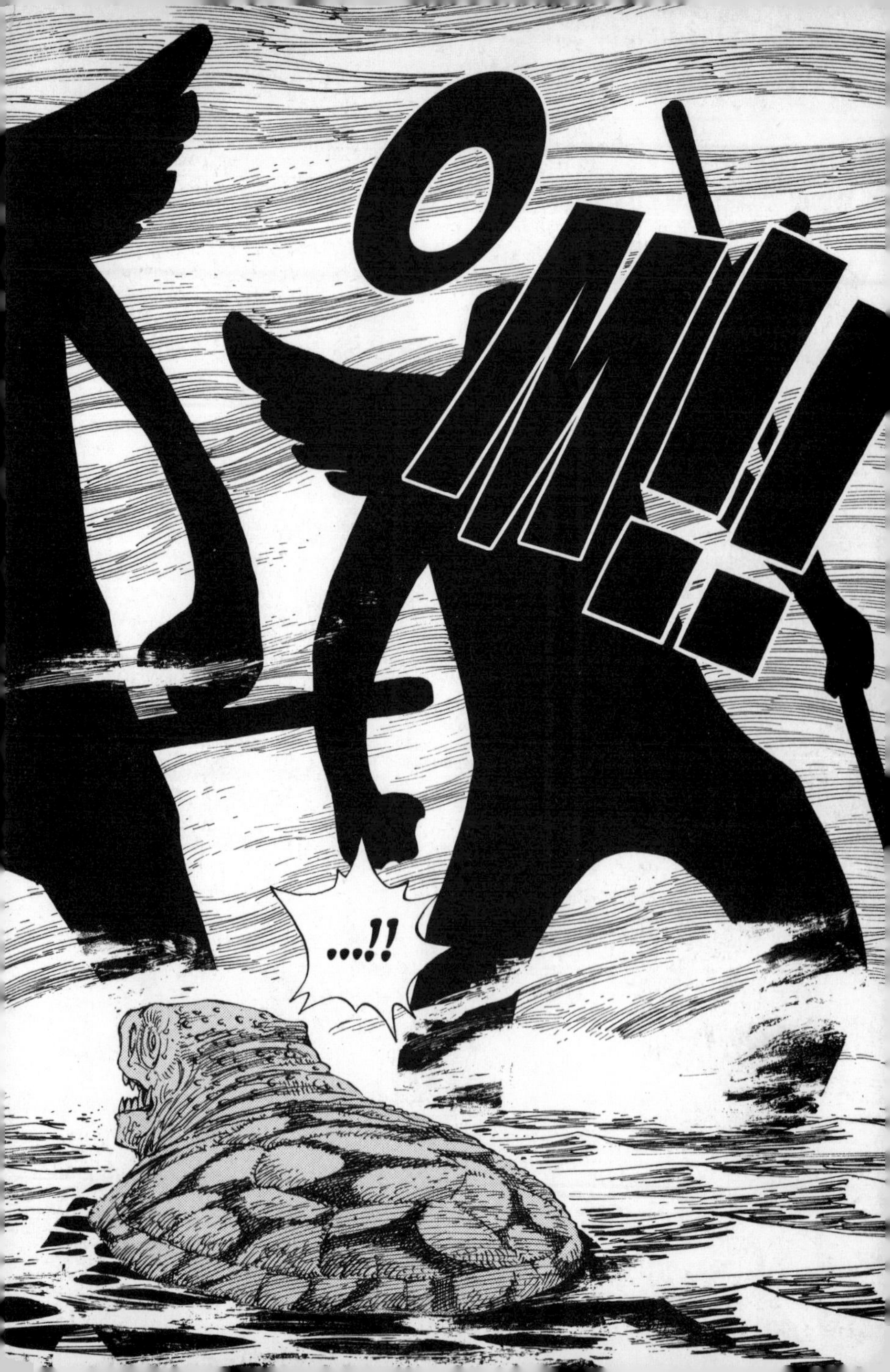
OM!!
...!!

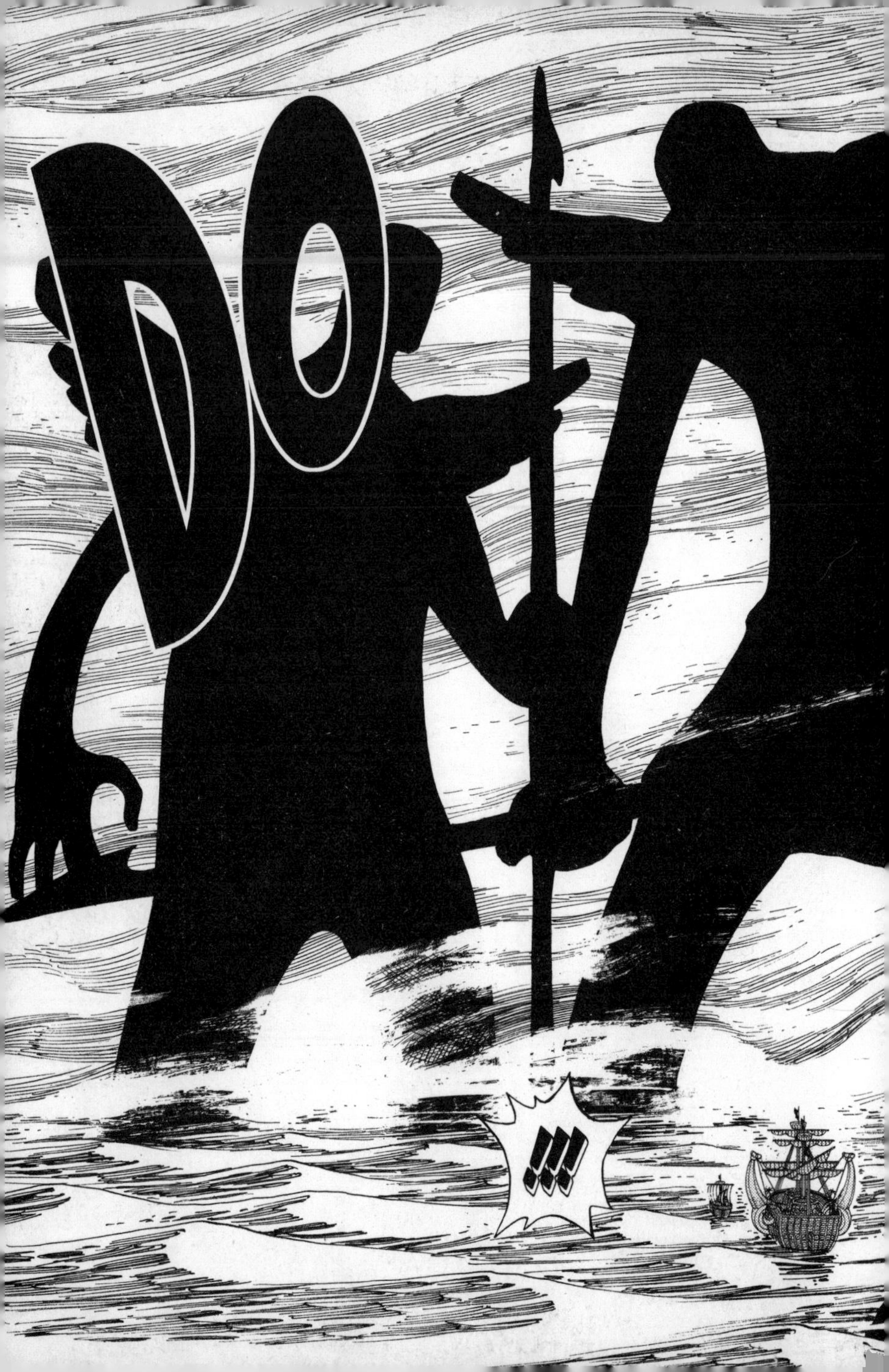
DON
!!!

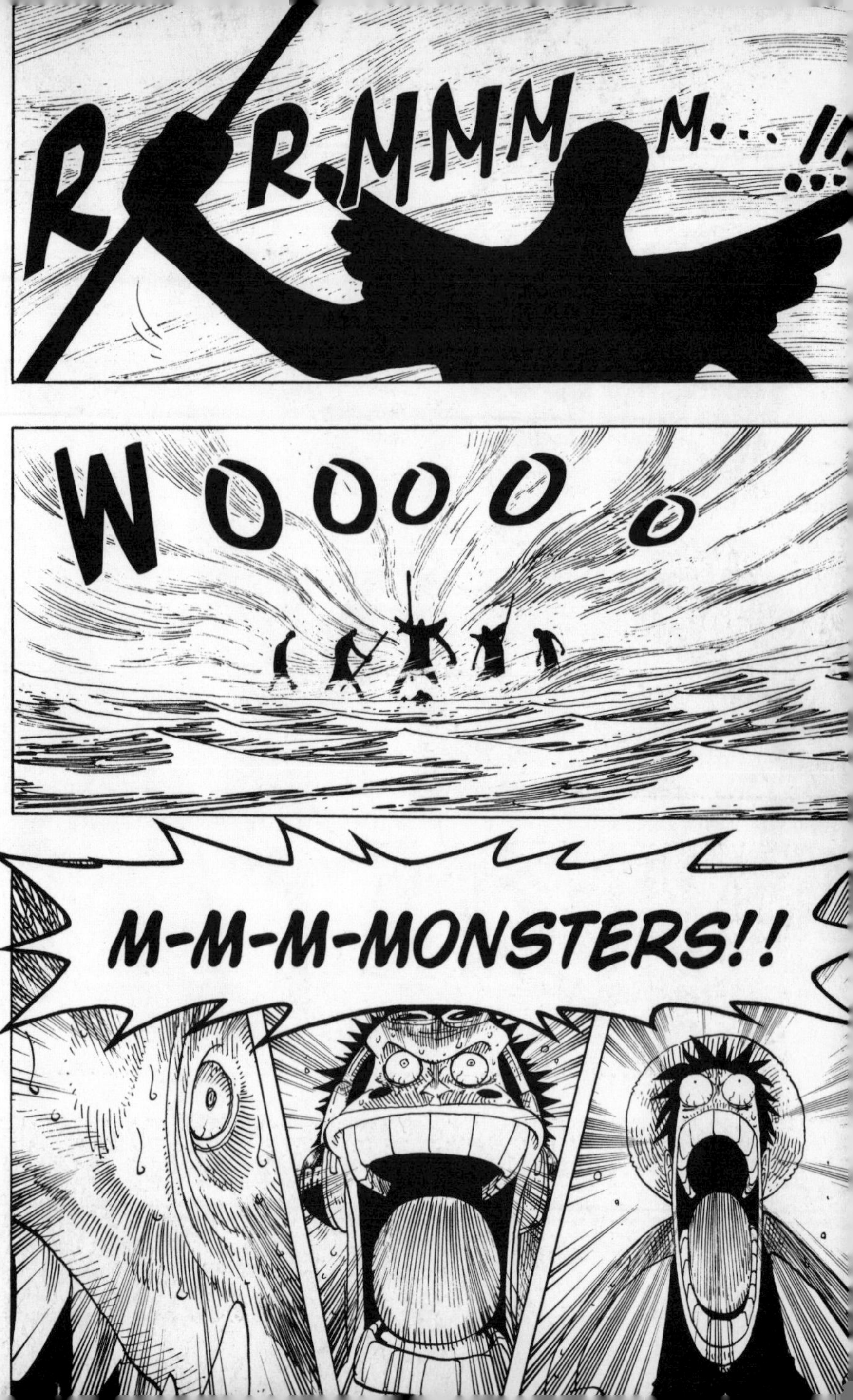
R R.MMMM M...!!
WOOOOO
M-M-M-MONSTERS!!

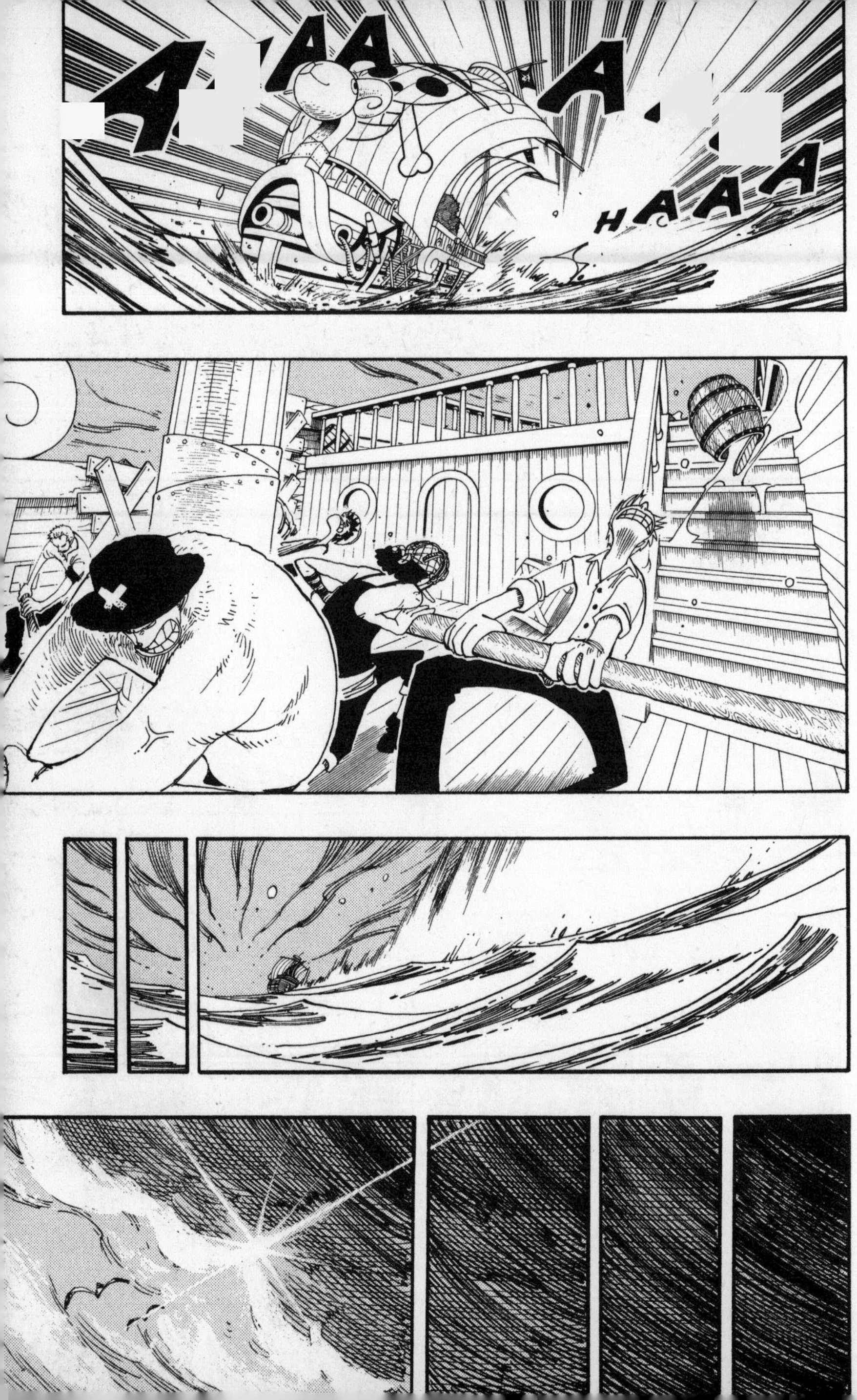
A AA A
HAAAA

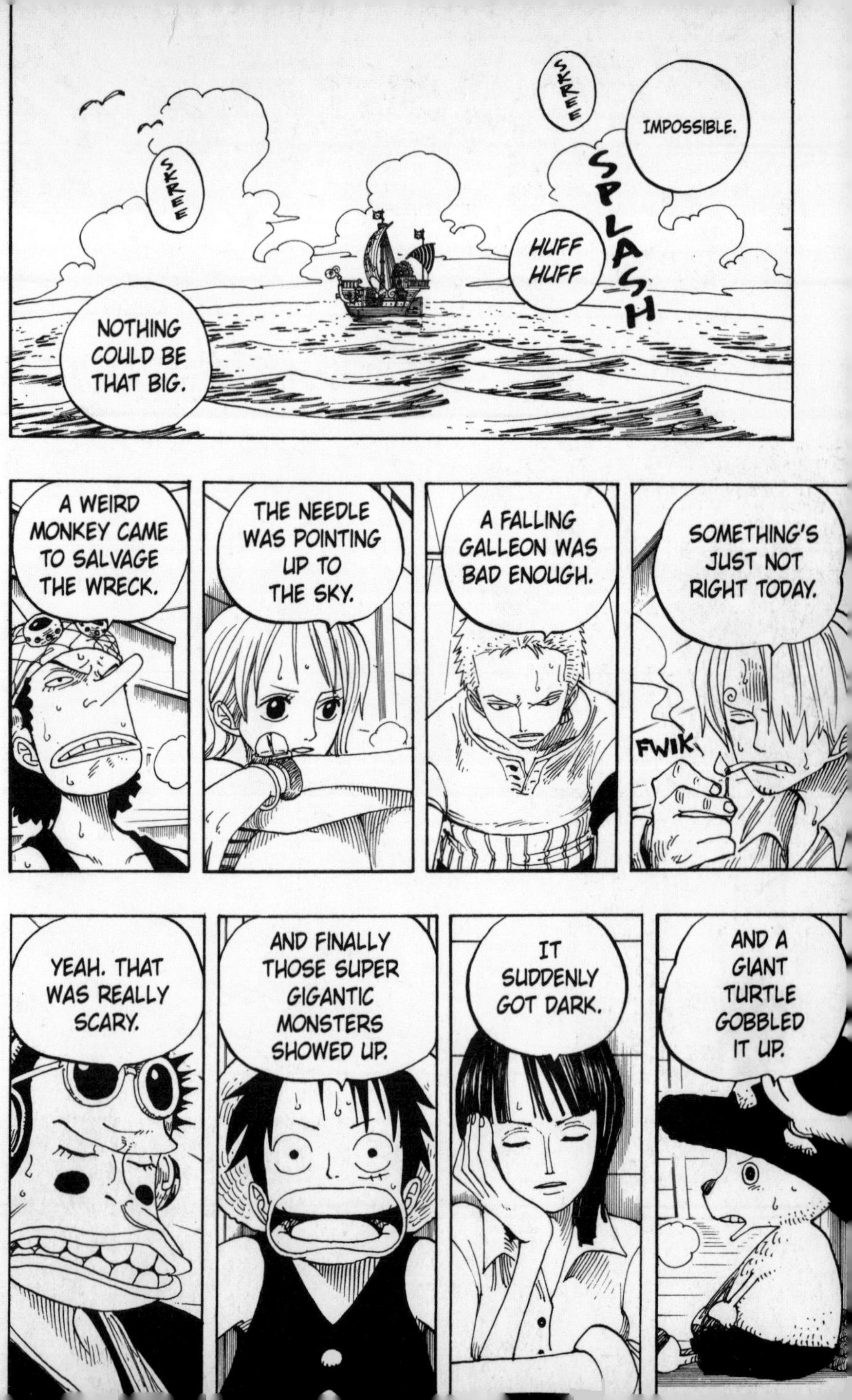
SKREE
IMPOSSIBLE.
SPLASH
HUFF HUFF
SKREE
NOTHING COULD BE THAT BIG.
SOMETHING'S JUST NOT RIGHT TODAY.
FWIK
A FALLING GALLEON WAS BAD ENOUGH.
THE NEEDLE WAS POINTING UP TO THE SKY.
A WEIRD MONKEY CAME TO SALVAGE THE WRECK.
AND A GIANT TURTLE GOBBLED IT UP.
IT SUDDENLY GOT DARK.
AND FINALLY THOSE SUPER GIGANTIC MONSTERS SHOWED UP.
YEAH. THAT WAS REALLY SCARY.

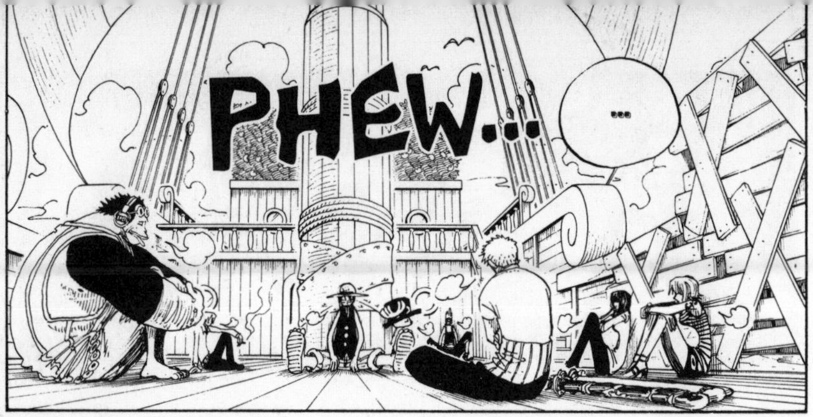
PHEW...
...

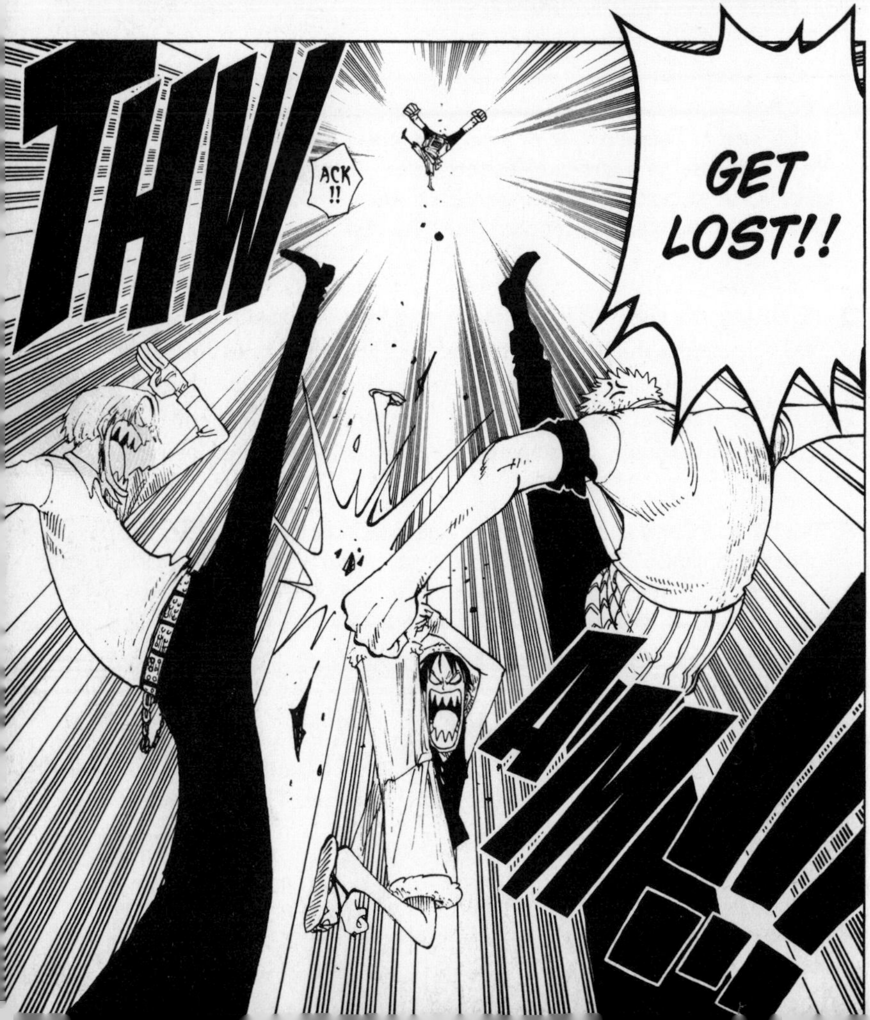
GET LOST!!
ACK !!
THW

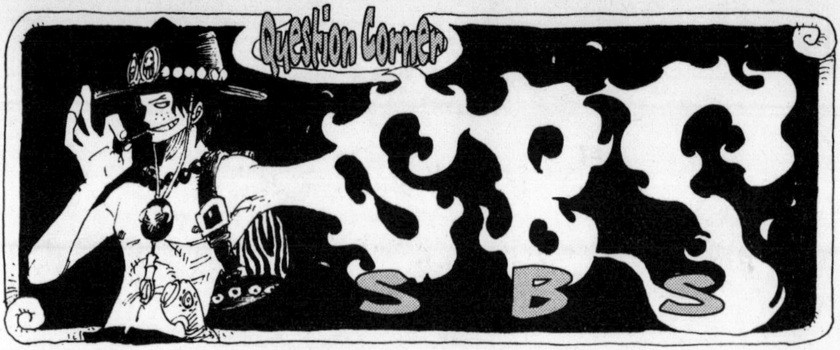
Question Corner
SBS

Q: Hello, I have a question for you, Oda Sensei. Which character in *One Piece* do you most resemble? (I'm thinking you're probably very "Usoppish.")

A: Let's see... There's the brains, the calm demeanor, the clothes... Yes, I guess I'm a lot like "Red-haired" Shanks! Yeah! I can hear everyone shouting in agreement. Ha ha ha... Huh? Ow! Don't throw things at me! That hurts!

Q: Regarding the civil war in Alabasta, originally, you said there were 300,000 men in the Royal Army and 700,000 in the rebel forces. But in volume 20, Chaka says there are two million rebels, so where did the other 1.3 million more come from? (Are they people like Toh-Toh, who didn't originally participate in the uprising but joined later?)

A: That's it. In any case, Alabasta has a population of ten million. In order to make the story easier to understand, I left out a lot of details. Alabasta has many towns and villages that weren't mentioned in the story. So two million may not seem like many compared to ten million, but two million armed people is a lot. This is a really serious uprising.

Q: Hello, Eiichiro Oda Sensei. I recently went on a homestay in England and discovered something I wanted to share with you. The toilet paper there is brown! (But kind of orange)

A: No kidding?! That's bad. Visibility is critical with toilet paper! Is that because England is tea country?! Are they evoking images of tea?!

Chapter 222:

THE GIANT NOVICE

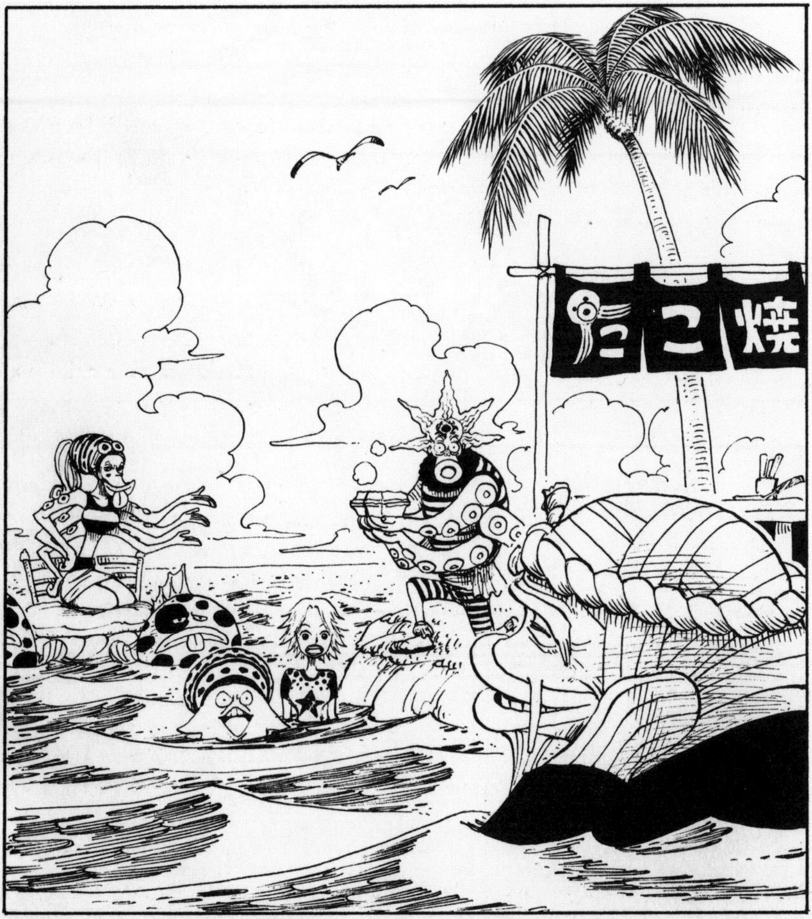

HACHI'S WALK ON THE SEAFLOOR, VOL. 35:
"THE OLD CATFISH WHO CAME LATE"

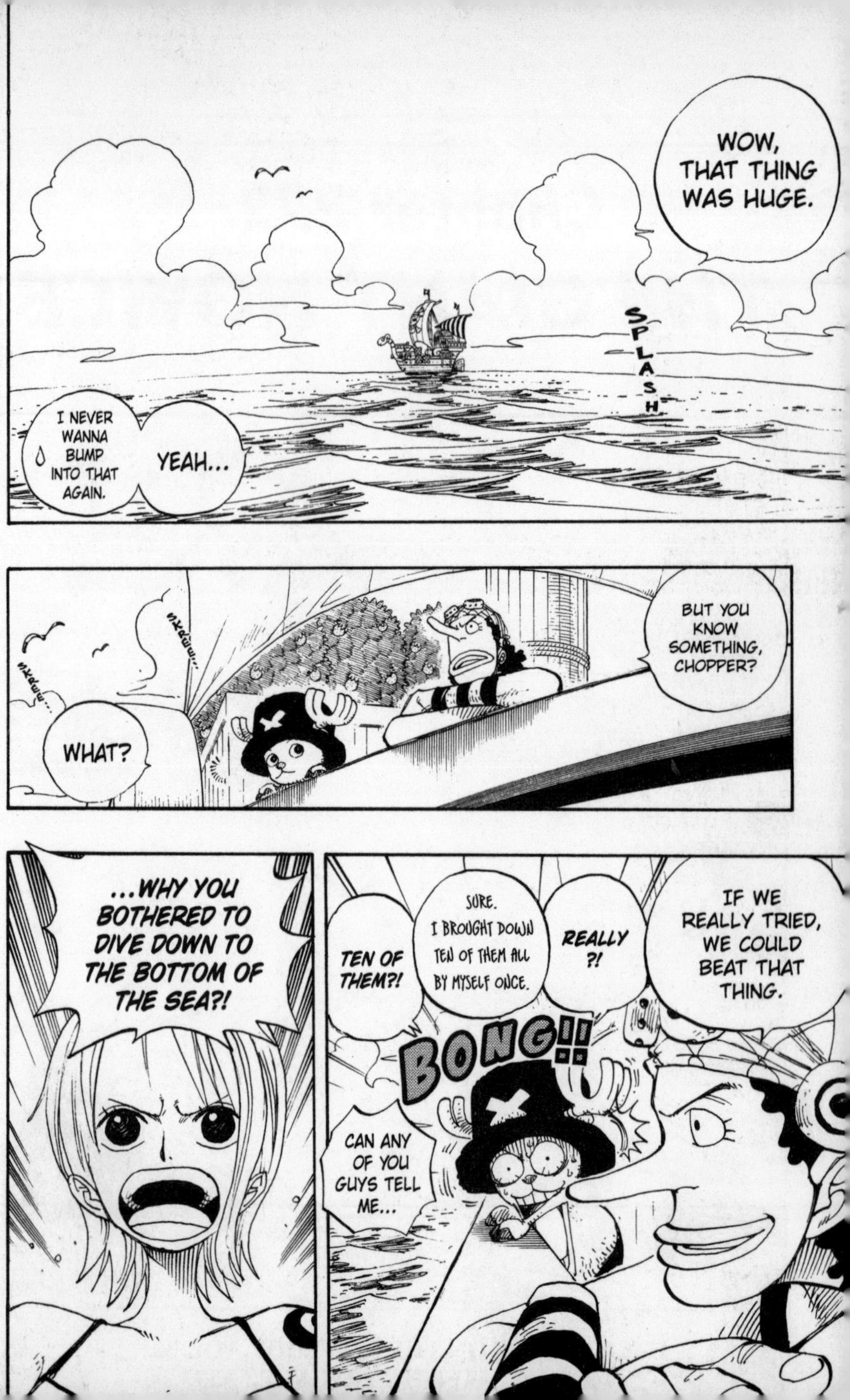
WOW, THAT THING WAS HUGE.
SPLASH
YEAH...
I NEVER WANNA BUMP INTO THAT AGAIN.
BUT YOU KNOW SOMETHING, CHOPPER?
WHAT?
IF WE REALLY TRIED, WE COULD BEAT THAT THING.
REALLY ?!
SURE. I BROUGHT DOWN TEN OF THEM ALL BY MYSELF ONCE.
TEN OF THEM?!
BONG!!
CAN ANY OF YOU GUYS TELL ME...
...WHY YOU BOTHERED TO DIVE DOWN TO THE BOTTOM OF THE SEA?!

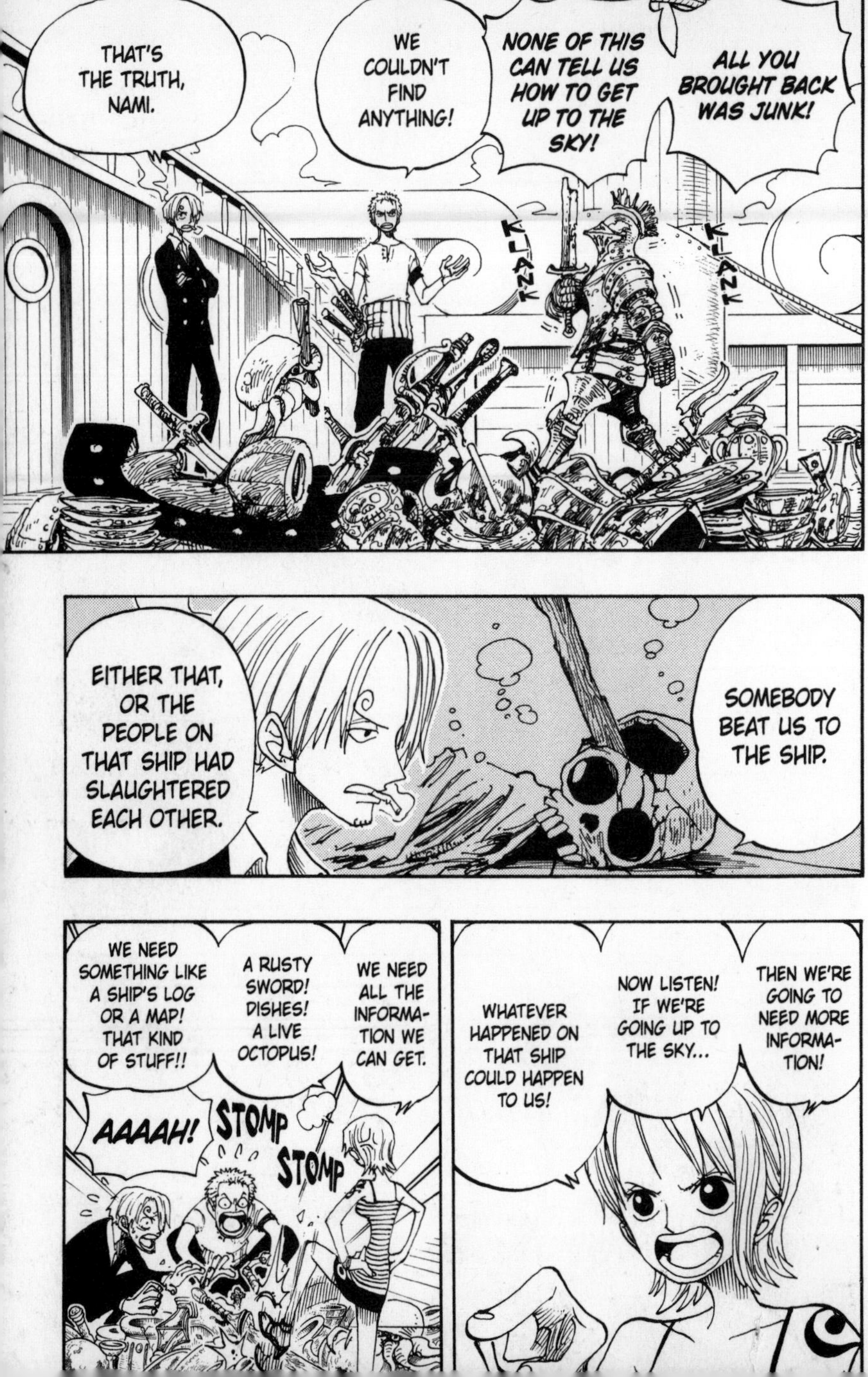
ALL YOU BROUGHT BACK WAS JUNK!
NONE OF THIS CAN TELL US HOW TO GET UP TO THE SKY!
WE COULDN'T FIND ANYTHING!
THAT'S THE TRUTH, NAMI.
KLANK
KLANK
SOMEBODY BEAT US TO THE SHIP.
EITHER THAT, OR THE PEOPLE ON THAT SHIP HAD SLAUGHTERED EACH OTHER.
THEN WE'RE GOING TO NEED MORE INFORMATION!
NOW LISTEN! IF WE'RE GOING UP TO THE SKY...
WHATEVER HAPPENED ON THAT SHIP COULD HAPPEN TO US!
WE NEED ALL THE INFORMATION WE CAN GET.
A RUSTY SWORD! DISHES! A LIVE OCTOPUS!
WE NEED SOMETHING LIKE A SHIP'S LOG OR A MAP! THAT KIND OF STUFF!!
STOMP
STOMP
AAAAH!

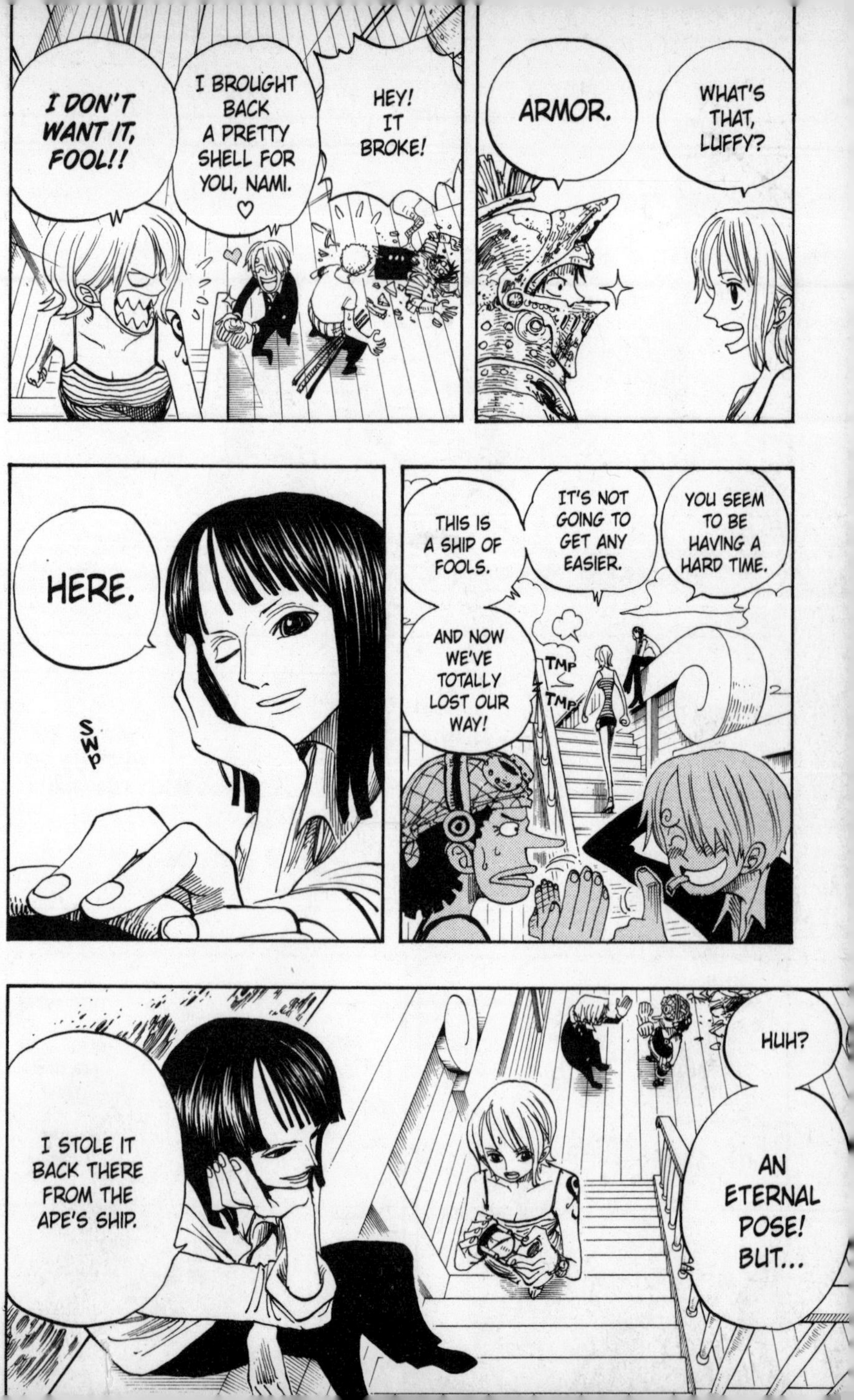
WHAT'S THAT, LUFFY?
ARMOR.
HEY! IT BROKE!
I BROUGHT BACK A PRETTY SHELL FOR YOU, NAMI. ♡
I DON'T WANT IT, FOOL!!
YOU SEEM TO BE HAVING A HARD TIME.
IT'S NOT GOING TO GET ANY EASIER.
THIS IS A SHIP OF FOOLS.
AND NOW WE'VE TOTALLY LOST OUR WAY!
TMP
TMP
HERE.
SWP
HUH?
AN ETERNAL POSE! BUT...
I STOLE IT BACK THERE FROM THE APE'S SHIP.

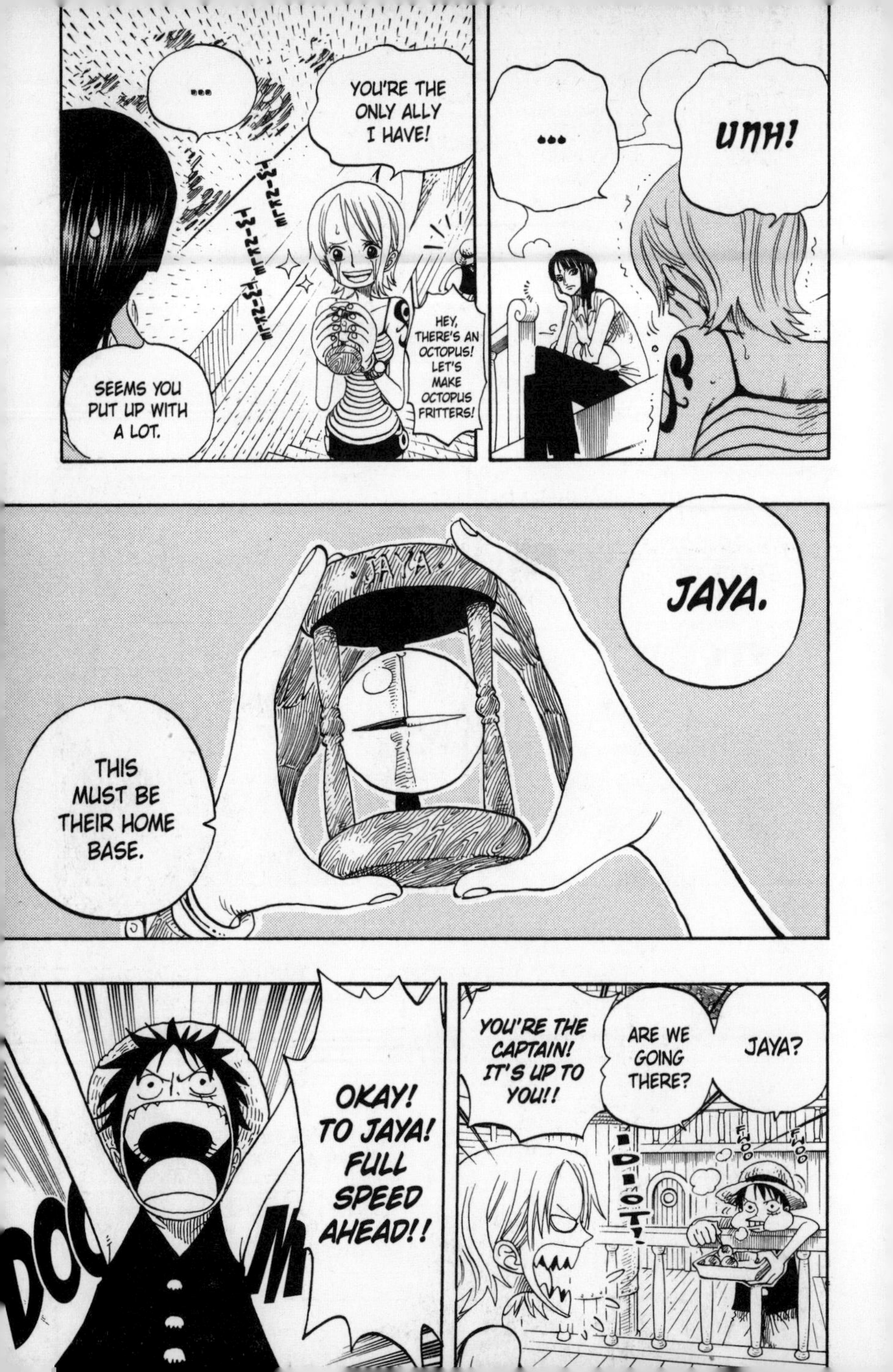
UNH!
...
YOU'RE THE ONLY ALLY I HAVE!
...
HEY, THERE'S AN OCTOPUS! LET'S MAKE OCTOPUS FRITTERS!
TWINKLE TWINKLE TWINKLE
SEEMS YOU PUT UP WITH A LOT.
JAYA.
THIS MUST BE THEIR HOME BASE.
JAYA?
ARE WE GOING THERE?
YOU'RE THE CAPTAIN! IT'S UP TO YOU!!
FWOO FWOO
IDIOT!
OKAY! TO JAYA! FULL SPEED AHEAD!!
DOOM

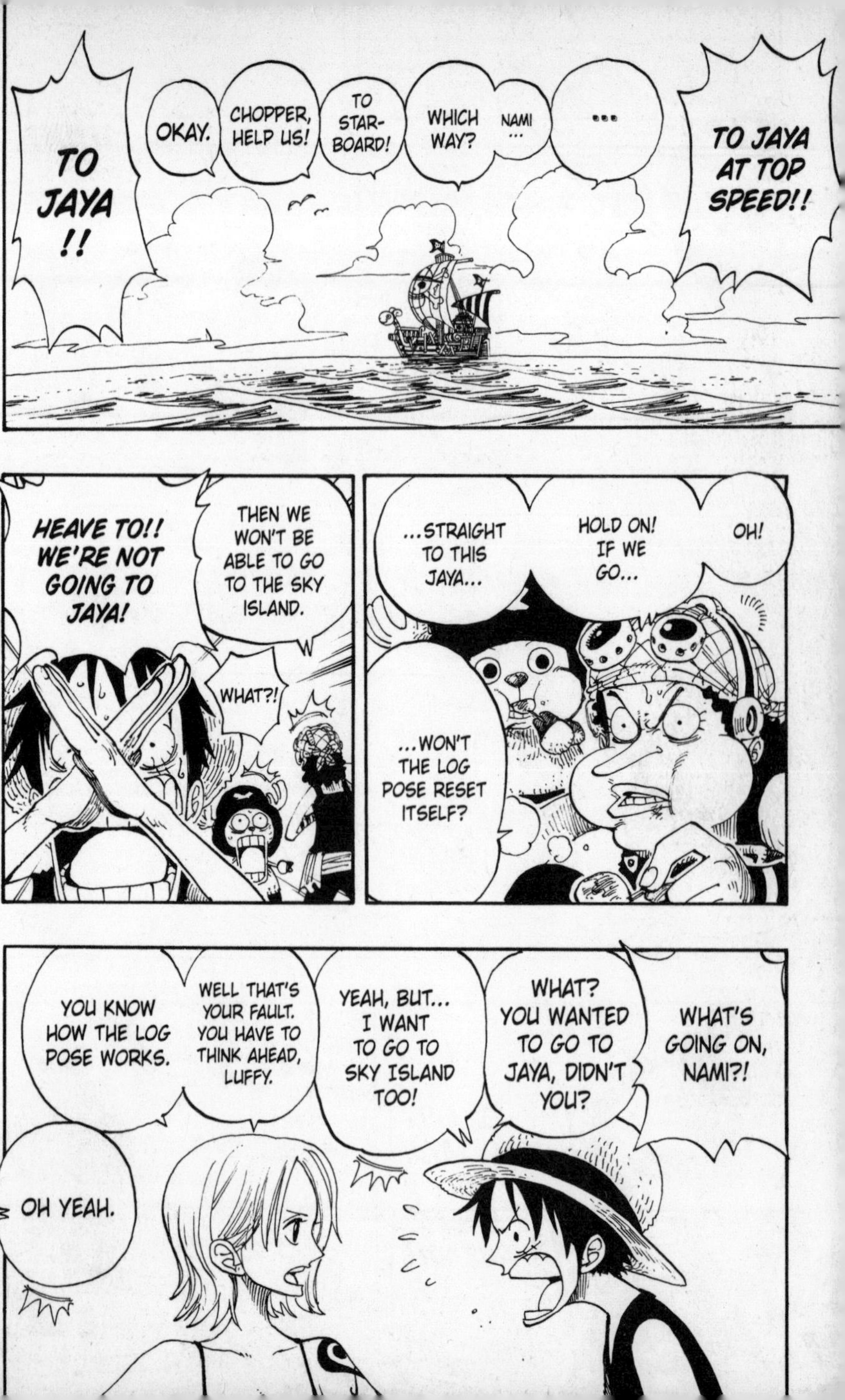
TO JAYA AT TOP SPEED!!
...
NAMI...
WHICH WAY?
TO STARBOARD!
CHOPPER, HELP US!
OKAY.
TO JAYA!!
OH!
HOLD ON! IF WE GO...
...STRAIGHT TO THIS JAYA...
...WON'T THE LOG POSE RESET ITSELF?
THEN WE WON'T BE ABLE TO GO TO THE SKY ISLAND.
HEAVE TO!! WE'RE NOT GOING TO JAYA!
WHAT?!
WHAT'S GOING ON, NAMI?!
WHAT? YOU WANTED TO GO TO JAYA, DIDN'T YOU?
YEAH, BUT... I WANT TO GO TO SKY ISLAND TOO!
WELL THAT'S YOUR FAULT. YOU HAVE TO THINK AHEAD, LUFFY.
YOU KNOW HOW THE LOG POSE WORKS.
OH YEAH.

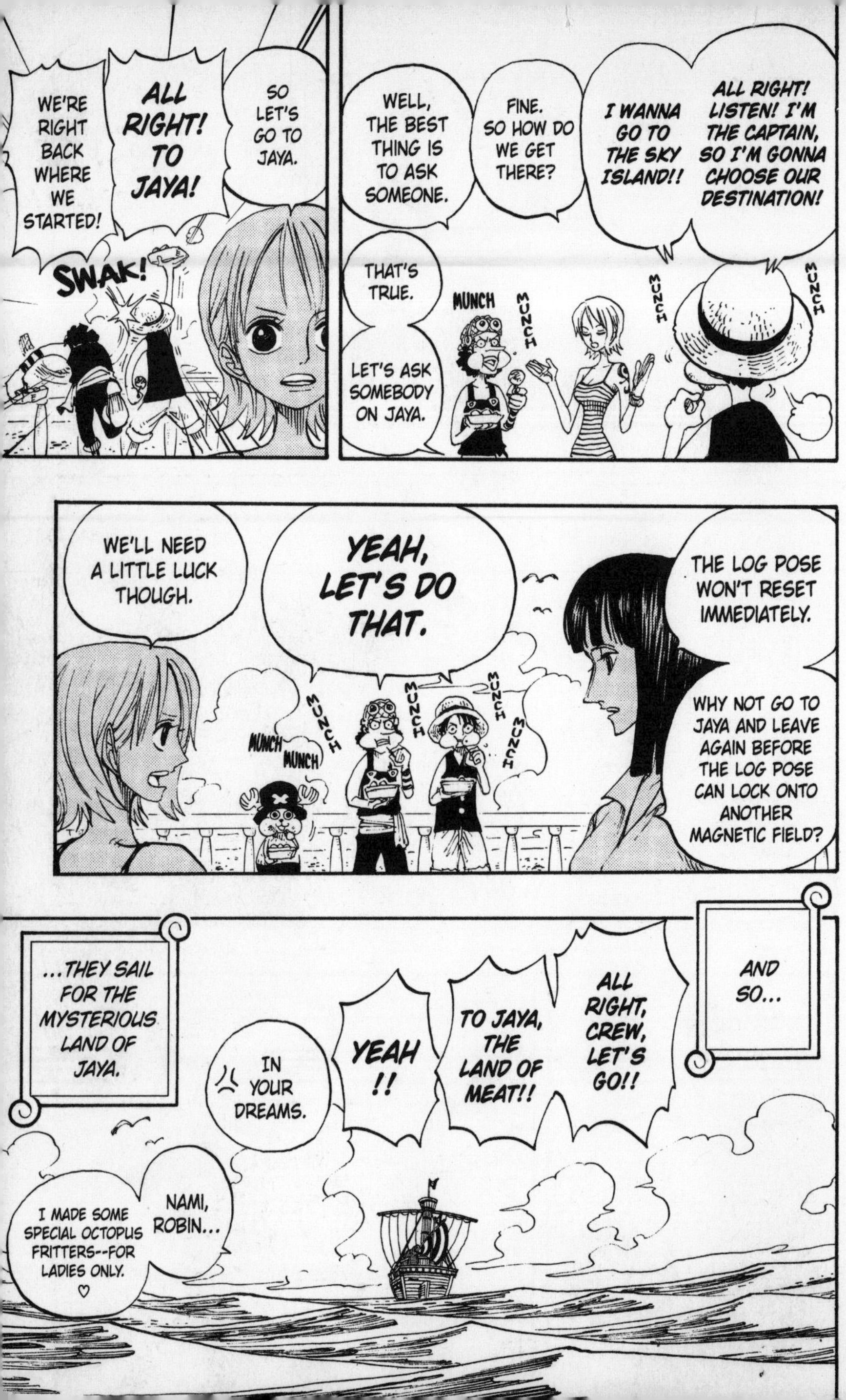
ALL RIGHT! LISTEN! I'M THE CAPTAIN, SO I'M GONNA CHOOSE OUR DESTINATION!
I WANNA GO TO THE SKY ISLAND!!
FINE. SO HOW DO WE GET THERE?
WELL, THE BEST THING IS TO ASK SOMEONE.
MUNCH
MUNCH
MUNCH
MUNCH
THAT'S TRUE.
LET'S ASK SOMEBODY ON JAYA.
SO LET'S GO TO JAYA.
ALL RIGHT! TO JAYA!
WE'RE RIGHT BACK WHERE WE STARTED!
SWAK!
THE LOG POSE WON'T RESET IMMEDIATELY.
WHY NOT GO TO JAYA AND LEAVE AGAIN BEFORE THE LOG POSE CAN LOCK ONTO ANOTHER MAGNETIC FIELD?
YEAH, LET'S DO THAT.
MUNCH
MUNCH
MUNCH
MUNCH
MUNCH
MUNCH
WE'LL NEED A LITTLE LUCK THOUGH.
AND SO...
ALL RIGHT, CREW, LET'S GO!!
TO JAYA, THE LAND OF MEAT!!
YEAH !!
IN YOUR DREAMS.
...THEY SAIL FOR THE MYSTERIOUS LAND OF JAYA.
NAMI, ROBIN...
I MADE SOME SPECIAL OCTOPUS FRITTERS--FOR LADIES ONLY. ♡

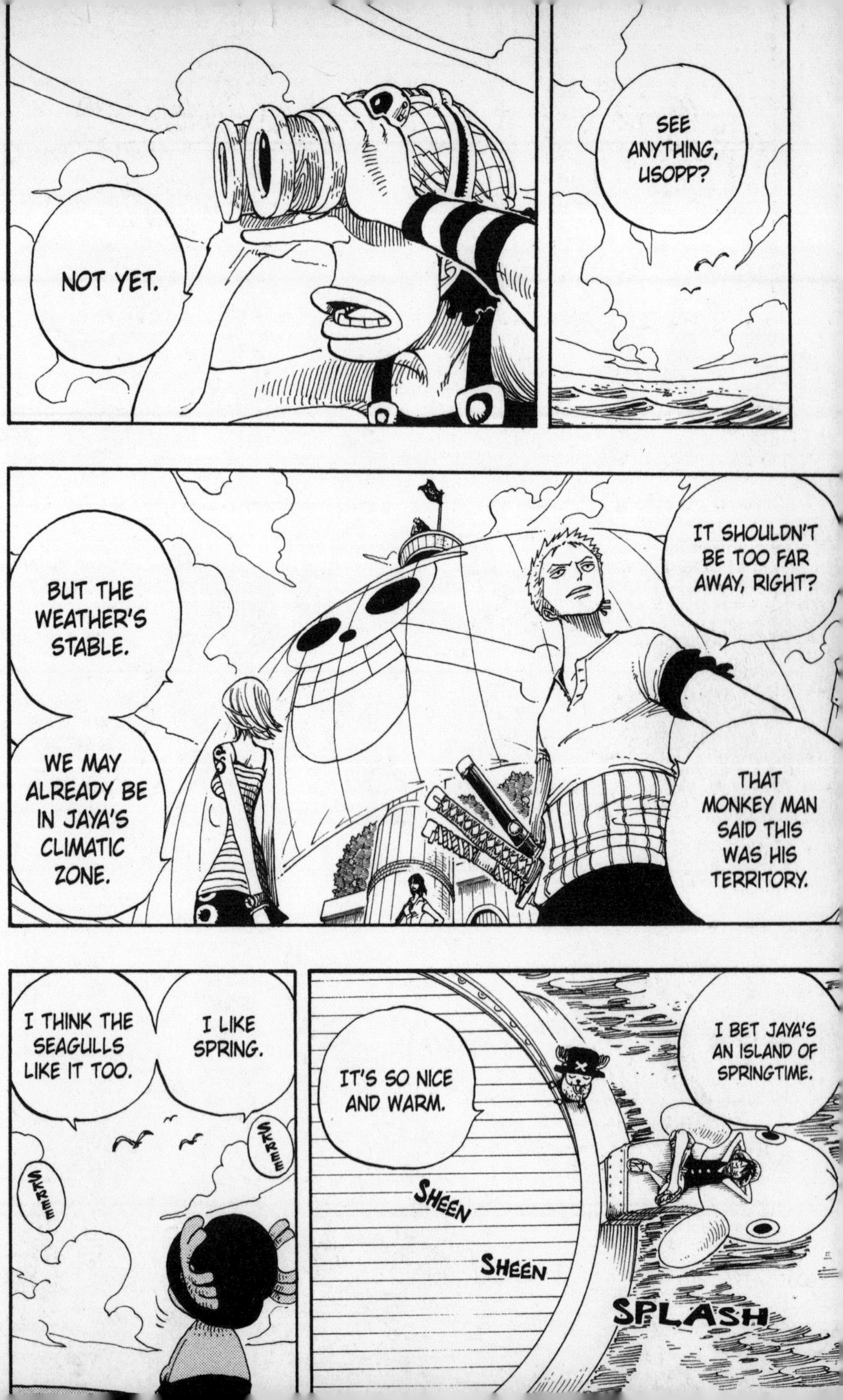
SEE ANYTHING, USOPP?
NOT YET.
IT SHOULDN'T BE TOO FAR AWAY, RIGHT?
THAT MONKEY MAN SAID THIS WAS HIS TERRITORY.
BUT THE WEATHER'S STABLE.
WE MAY ALREADY BE IN JAYA'S CLIMATIC ZONE.
I BET JAYA'S AN ISLAND OF SPRINGTIME.
IT'S SO NICE AND WARM.
SHEEN
SHEEN
SPLASH
I LIKE SPRING.
I THINK THE SEAGULLS LIKE IT TOO.
SKREE
SKREE

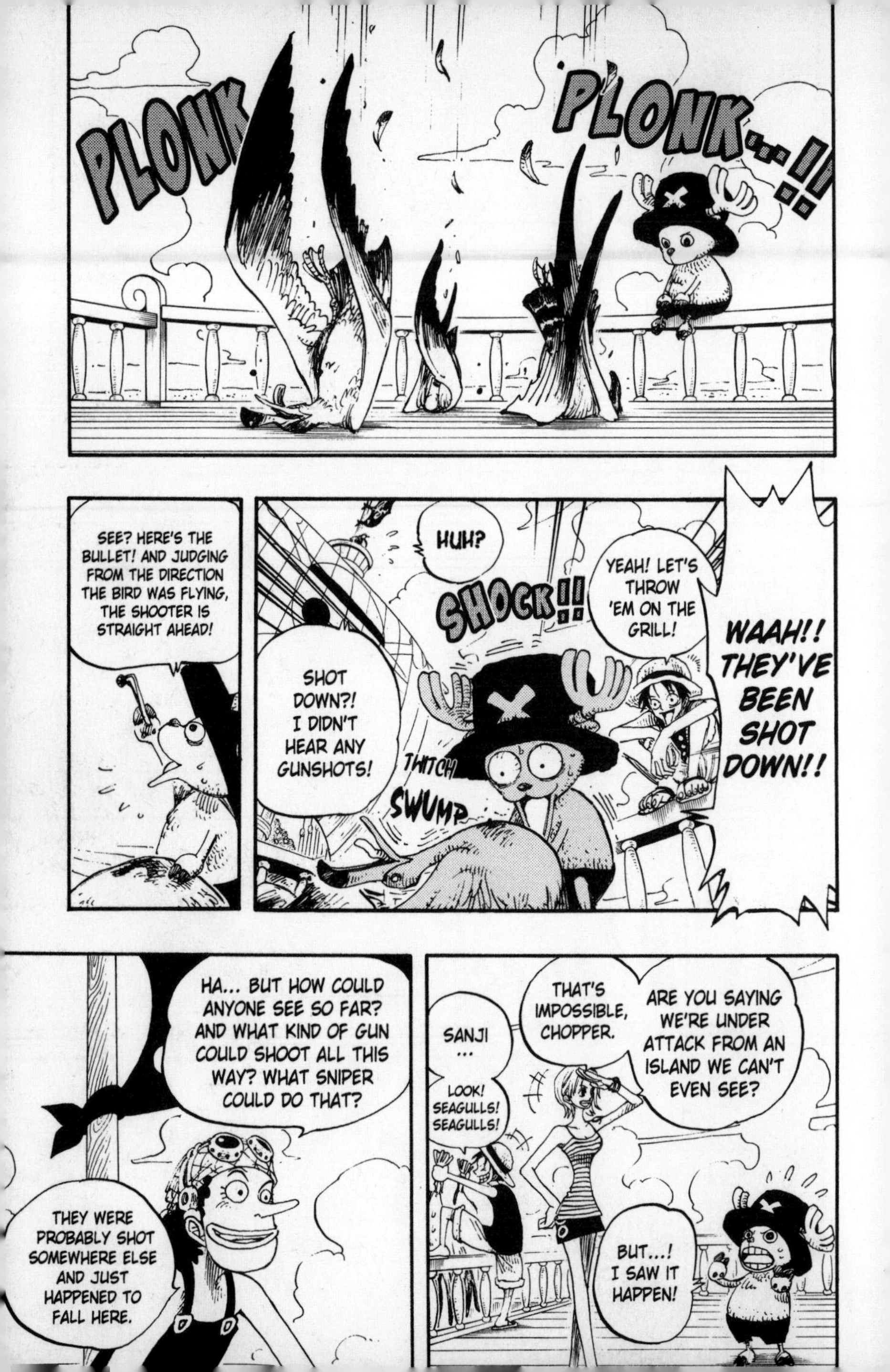

PLONK...!!
PLONK
WAAH!! THEY'VE BEEN SHOT DOWN!!
YEAH! LET'S THROW 'EM ON THE GRILL!
HUH?
SHOCK!!
SHOT DOWN?! I DIDN'T HEAR ANY GUNSHOTS!
TWITCH
SWUMP
SEE? HERE'S THE BULLET! AND JUDGING FROM THE DIRECTION THE BIRD WAS FLYING, THE SHOOTER IS STRAIGHT AHEAD!
ARE YOU SAYING WE'RE UNDER ATTACK FROM AN ISLAND WE CAN'T EVEN SEE?
THAT'S IMPOSSIBLE, CHOPPER.
SANJI ...
LOOK! SEAGULLS! SEAGULLS!
BUT...! I SAW IT HAPPEN!
HA... BUT HOW COULD ANYONE SEE SO FAR? AND WHAT KIND OF GUN COULD SHOOT ALL THIS WAY? WHAT SNIPER COULD DO THAT?
THEY WERE PROBABLY SHOT SOMEWHERE ELSE AND JUST HAPPENED TO FALL HERE.

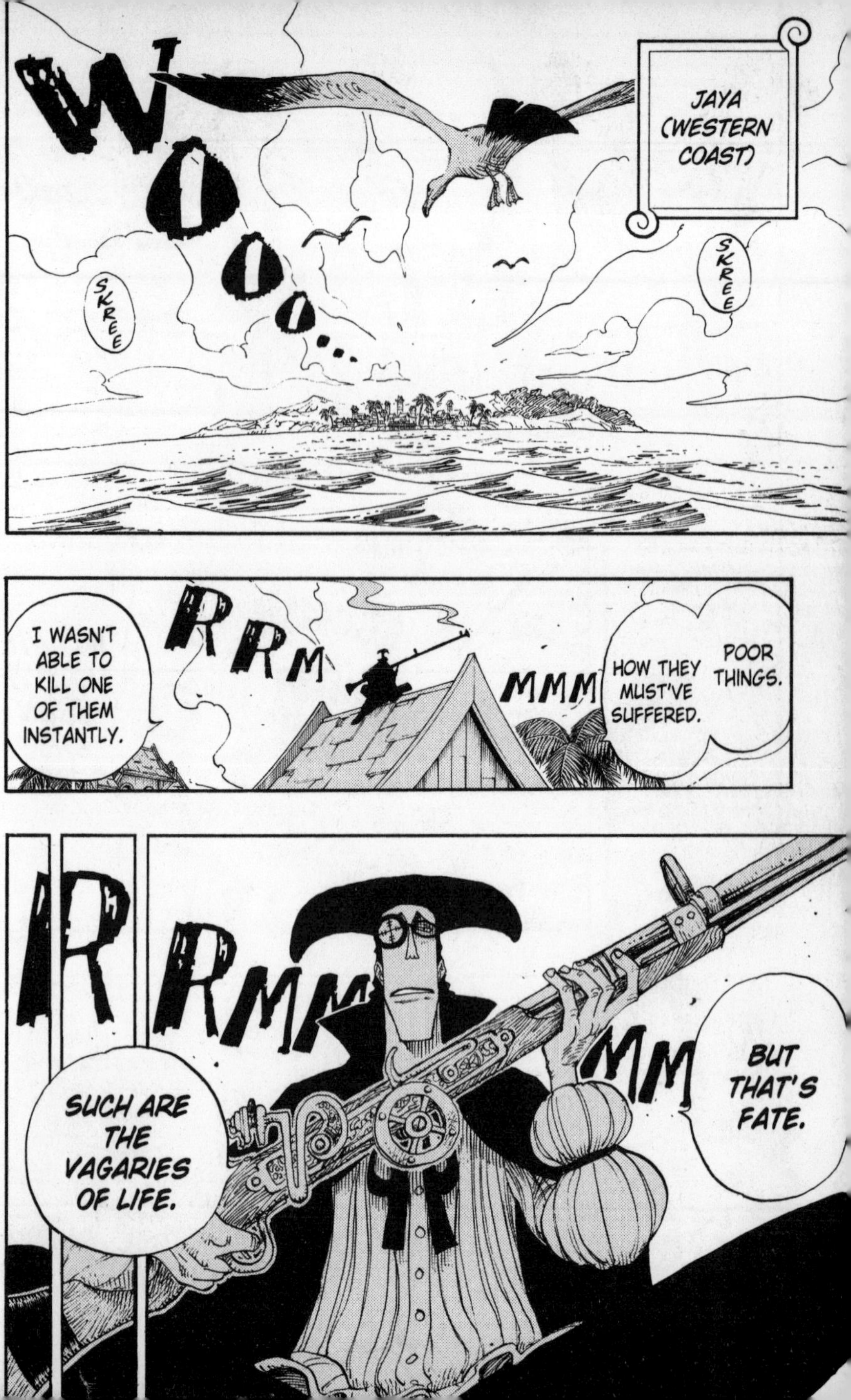
JAYA (WESTERN COAST)
SKREE
WOOOO...
SKREE
POOR THINGS.
HOW THEY MUST'VE SUFFERED.
RRMMMM
I WASN'T ABLE TO KILL ONE OF THEM INSTANTLY.
BUT THAT'S FATE.
RRRMMMM
SUCH ARE THE VAGARIES OF LIFE.

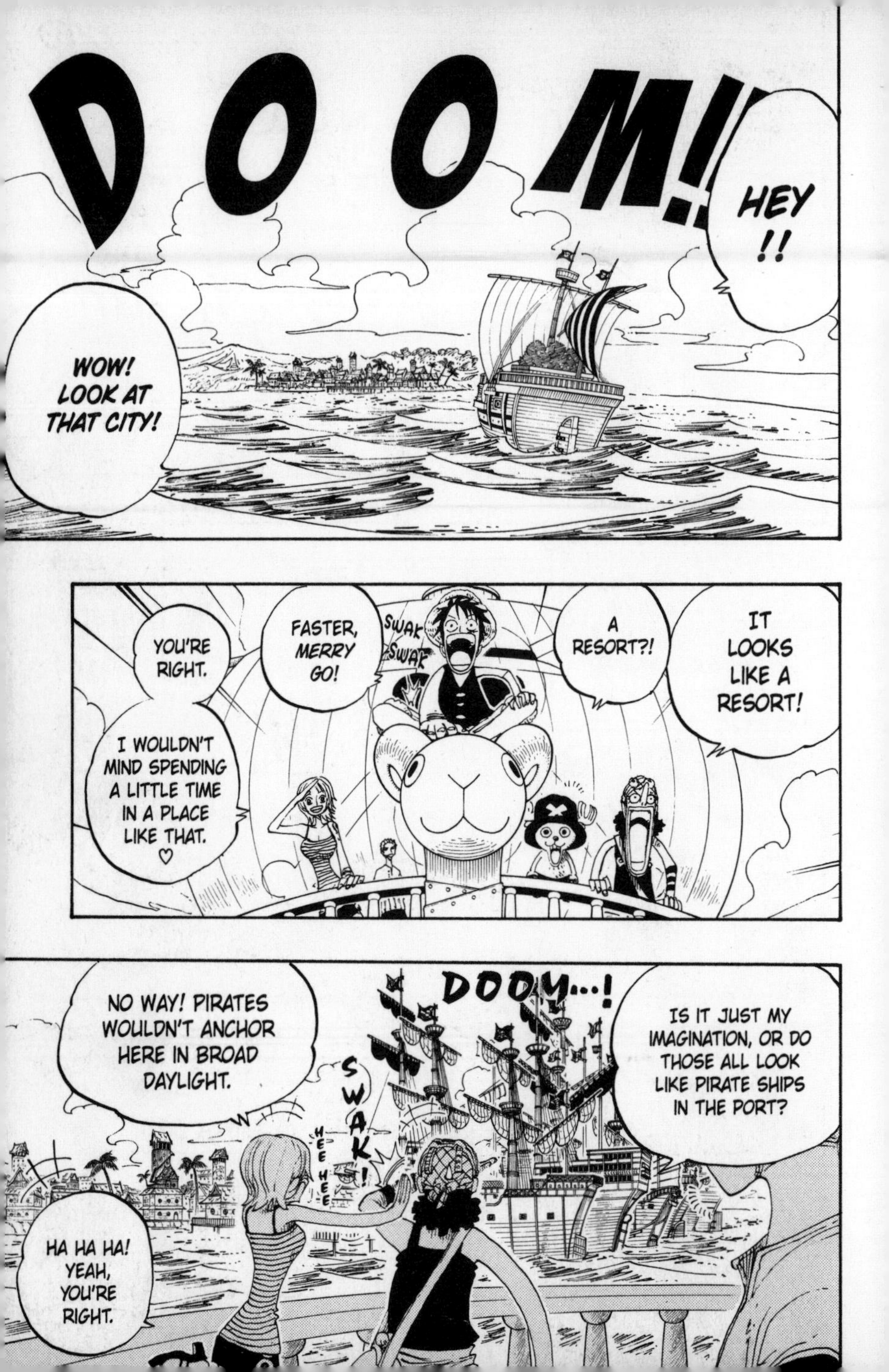
DOOM!!
HEY !!
WOW! LOOK AT THAT CITY!
IT LOOKS LIKE A RESORT!
A RESORT?!
SWAK SWAK
FASTER, MERRY GO!
YOU'RE RIGHT.
I WOULDN'T MIND SPENDING A LITTLE TIME IN A PLACE LIKE THAT. ♡
IS IT JUST MY IMAGINATION, OR DO THOSE ALL LOOK LIKE PIRATE SHIPS IN THE PORT?
DOOY...!
SWAK!
HEE HEE
NO WAY! PIRATES WOULDN'T ANCHOR HERE IN BROAD DAYLIGHT.
HA HA HA! YEAH, YOU'RE RIGHT.

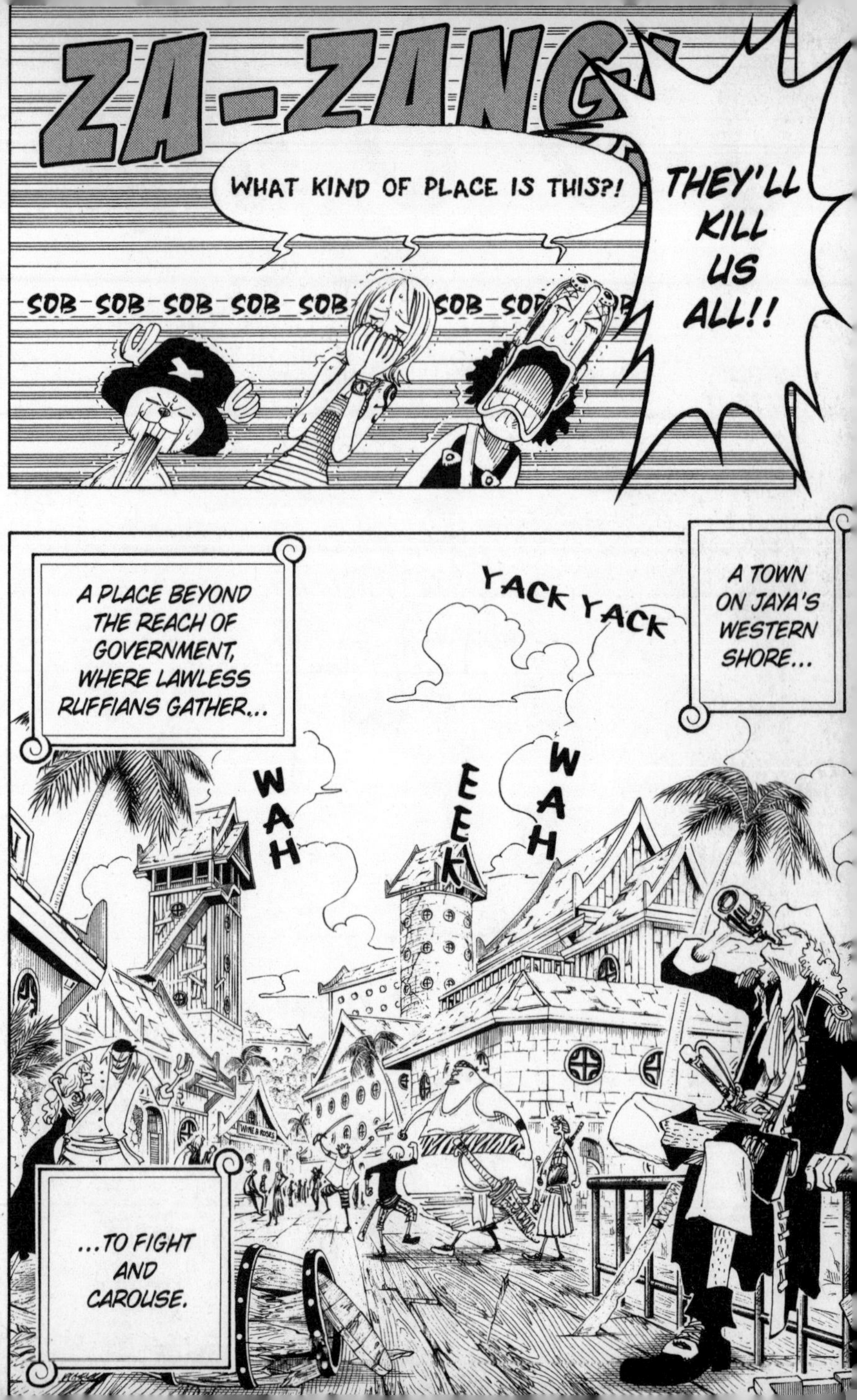
ZA-ZANG
THEY'LL KILL US ALL!!
WHAT KIND OF PLACE IS THIS?!
SOB SOB SOB SOB SOB SOB SOB
A TOWN ON JAYA'S WESTERN SHORE...
YACK YACK
A PLACE BEYOND THE REACH OF GOVERNMENT, WHERE LAWLESS RUFFIANS GATHER...
WAH
EEEK
WAH
WINE & ROSES
...TO FIGHT AND CAROUSE.

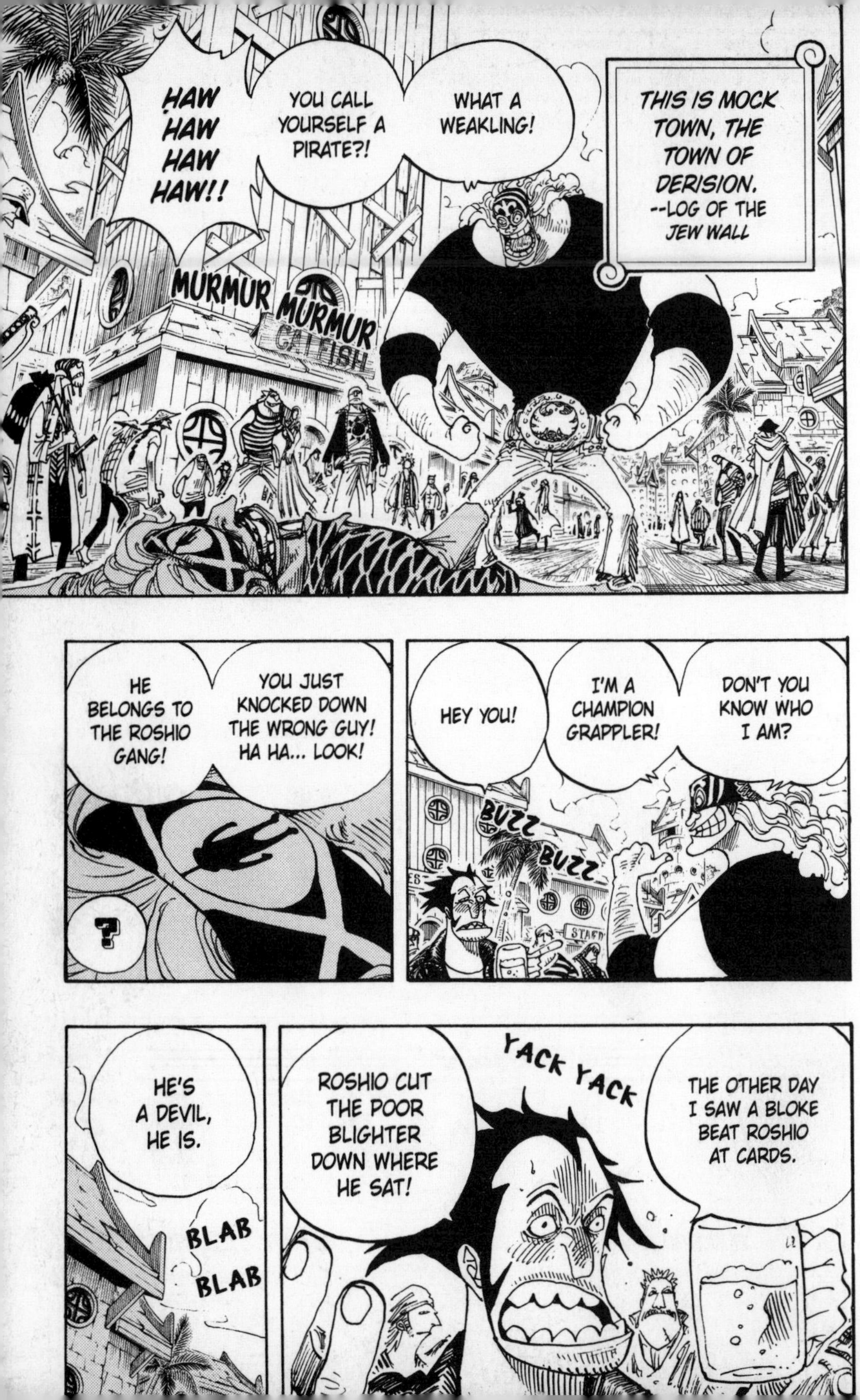
THIS IS MOCK TOWN, THE TOWN OF DERISION. --LOG OF THE JEW WALL
WHAT A WEAKLING!
YOU CALL YOURSELF A PIRATE?!
HAW HAW HAW HAW!!
MURMUR
MURMUR
DON'T YOU KNOW WHO I AM?
I'M A CHAMPION GRAPPLER!
HEY YOU!
BUZZ
BUZZ
YOU JUST KNOCKED DOWN THE WRONG GUY! HA HA... LOOK!
HE BELONGS TO THE ROSHIO GANG!
?
THE OTHER DAY I SAW A BLOKE BEAT ROSHIO AT CARDS.
YACK YACK
ROSHIO CUT THE POOR BLIGHTER DOWN WHERE HE SAT!
HE'S A DEVIL, HE IS.
BLAB
BLAB

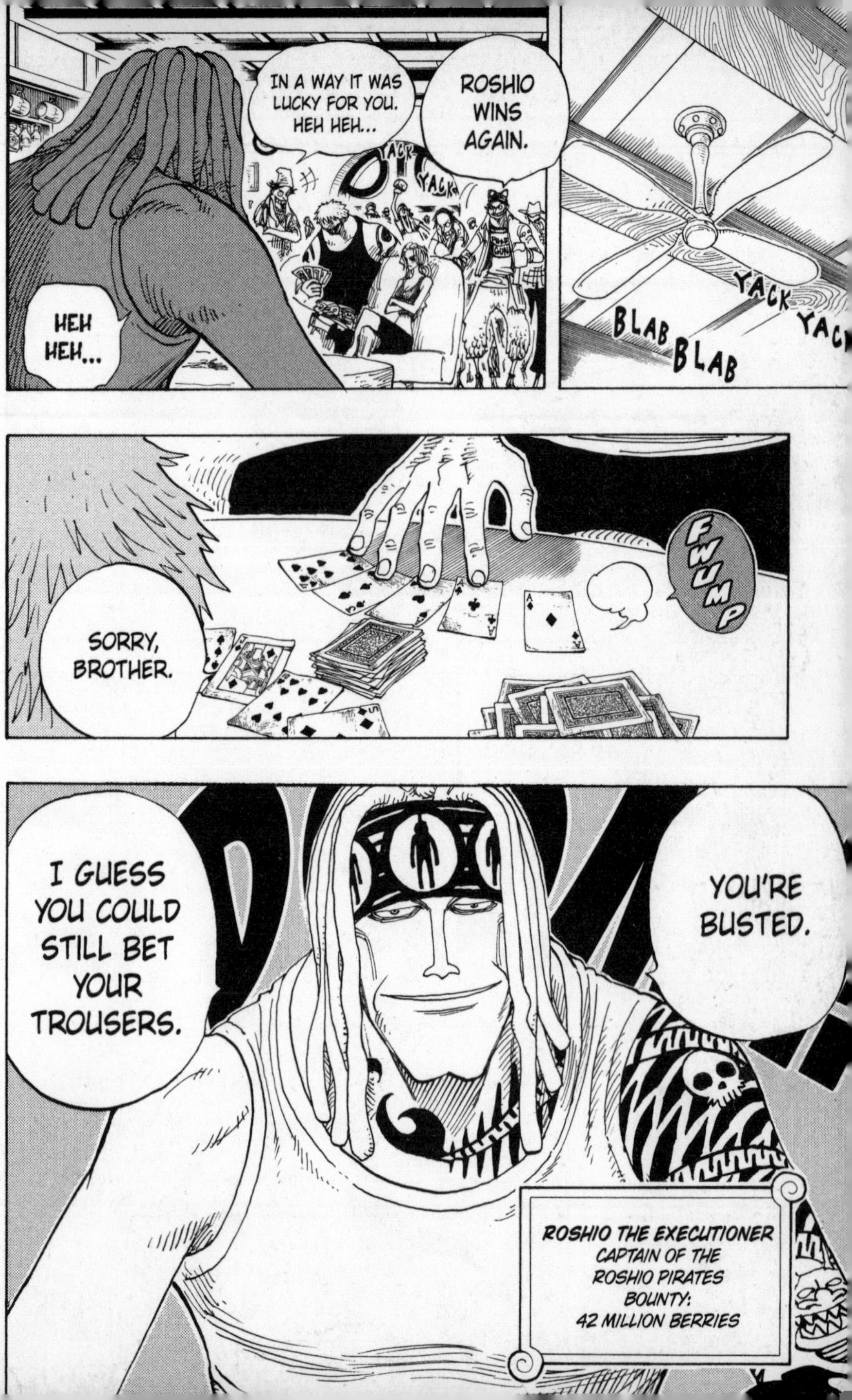
YACK YACK
BLAB BLAB
ROSHIO WINS AGAIN.
IN A WAY IT WAS LUCKY FOR YOU. HEH HEH...
YACK
YACK
HEH HEH...
FWUMP
SORRY, BROTHER.
YOU'RE BUSTED.
I GUESS YOU COULD STILL BET YOUR TROUSERS.
ROSHIO THE EXECUTIONER
CAPTAIN OF THE ROSHIO PIRATES
BOUNTY:
42 MILLION BERRIES

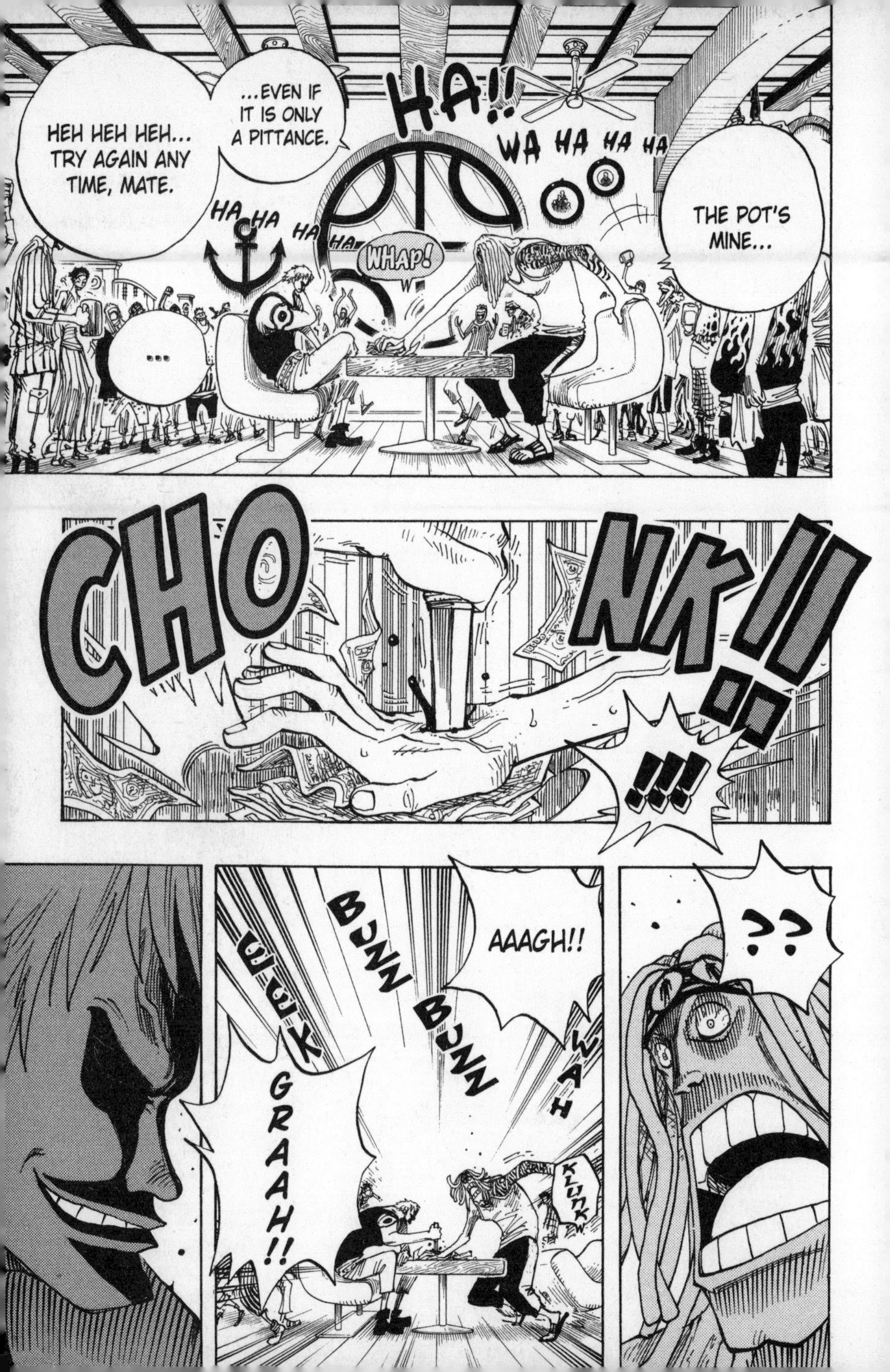
THE POT'S MINE...
WA HA HA HA
HA!!
...EVEN IF IT IS ONLY A PITTANCE.
HEH HEH HEH... TRY AGAIN ANY TIME, MATE.
WHAP!
HA HA HA HA
...
CHONK!!
!!!
??
AAAGH!!
BUNN BUNN
WAH
KLUNK
EEK
GRAAAH!!

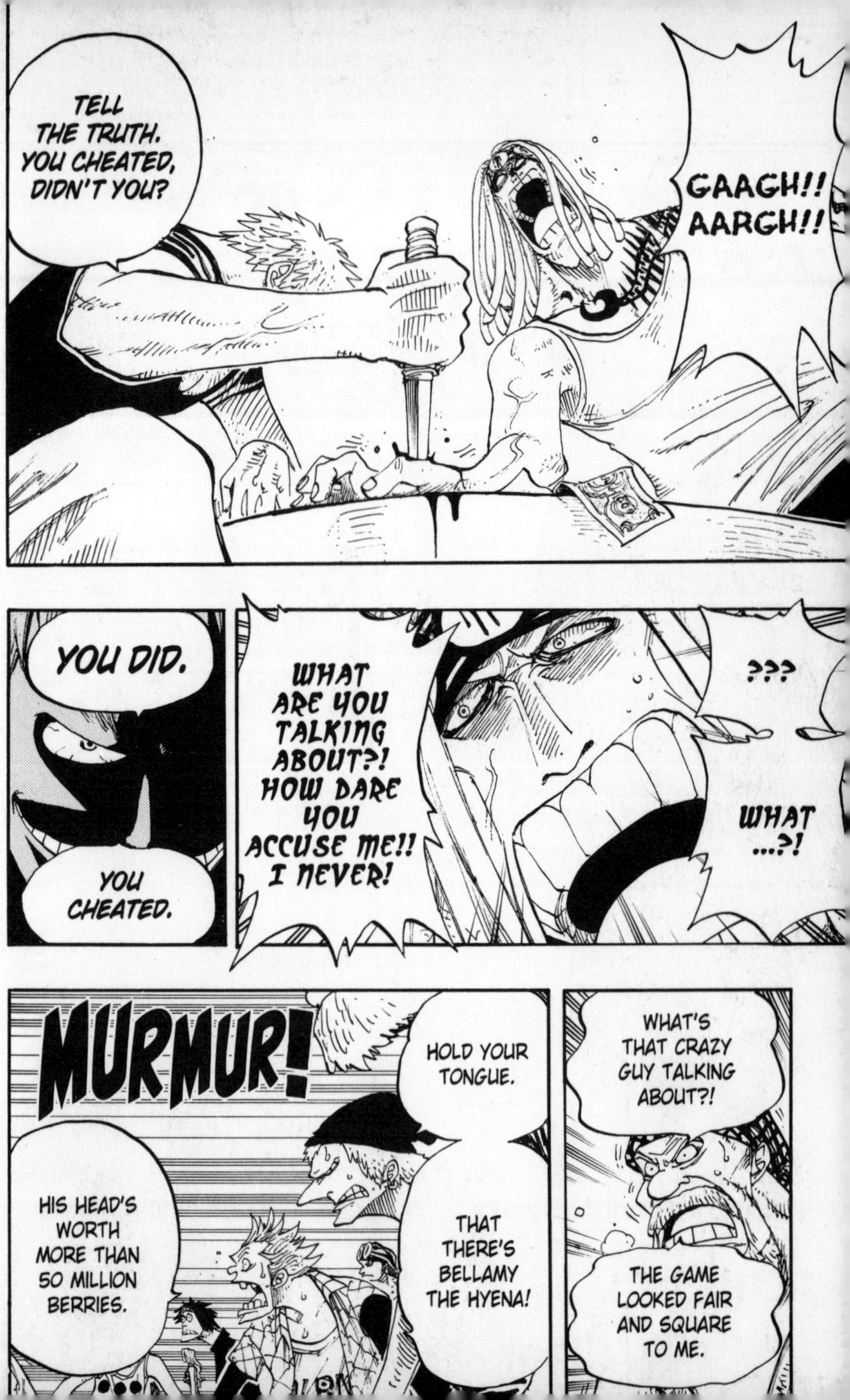
GAAGH!! AARGH!!
TELL THE TRUTH. YOU CHEATED, DIDN'T YOU?
???
WHAT ...?!
WHAT ARE YOU TALKING ABOUT?! HOW DARE YOU ACCUSE ME!! I NEVER!
YOU DID.
YOU CHEATED.
WHAT'S THAT CRAZY GUY TALKING ABOUT?!
THE GAME LOOKED FAIR AND SQUARE TO ME.
MURMUR!
HOLD YOUR TONGUE.
THAT THERE'S BELLAMY THE HYENA!
HIS HEAD'S WORTH MORE THAN 50 MILLION BERRIES.

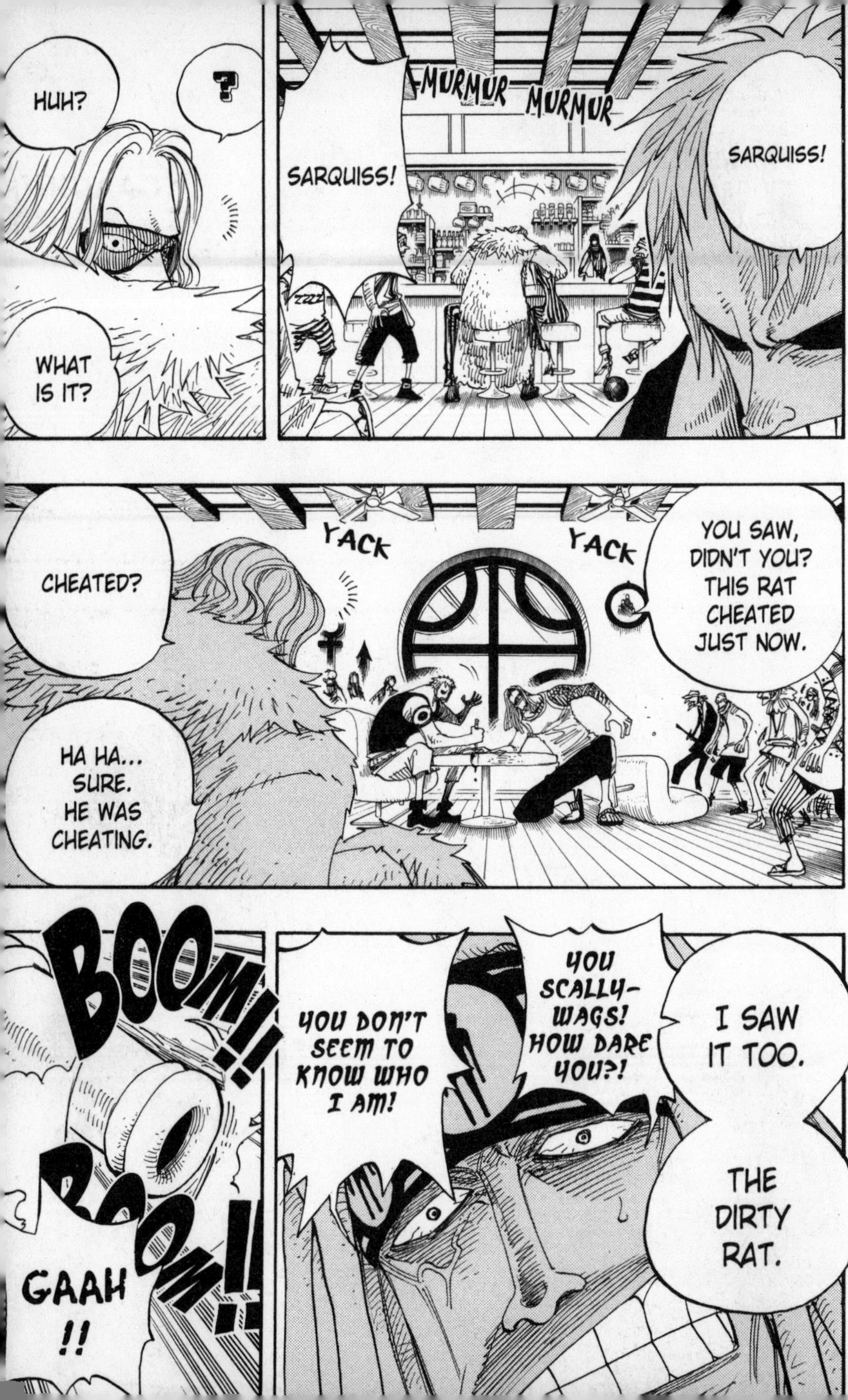
SARQUISS!
MURMUR MURMUR
SARQUISS!
?
HUH?
WHAT IS IT?
YOU SAW, DIDN'T YOU? THIS RAT CHEATED JUST NOW.
YACK YACK
CHEATED?
HA HA... SURE. HE WAS CHEATING.
I SAW IT TOO.
THE DIRTY RAT.
YOU SCALLY-WAGS! HOW DARE YOU?!
YOU DON'T SEEM TO KNOW WHO I AM!
BOOM!!
BOOM!!
GAAH !!

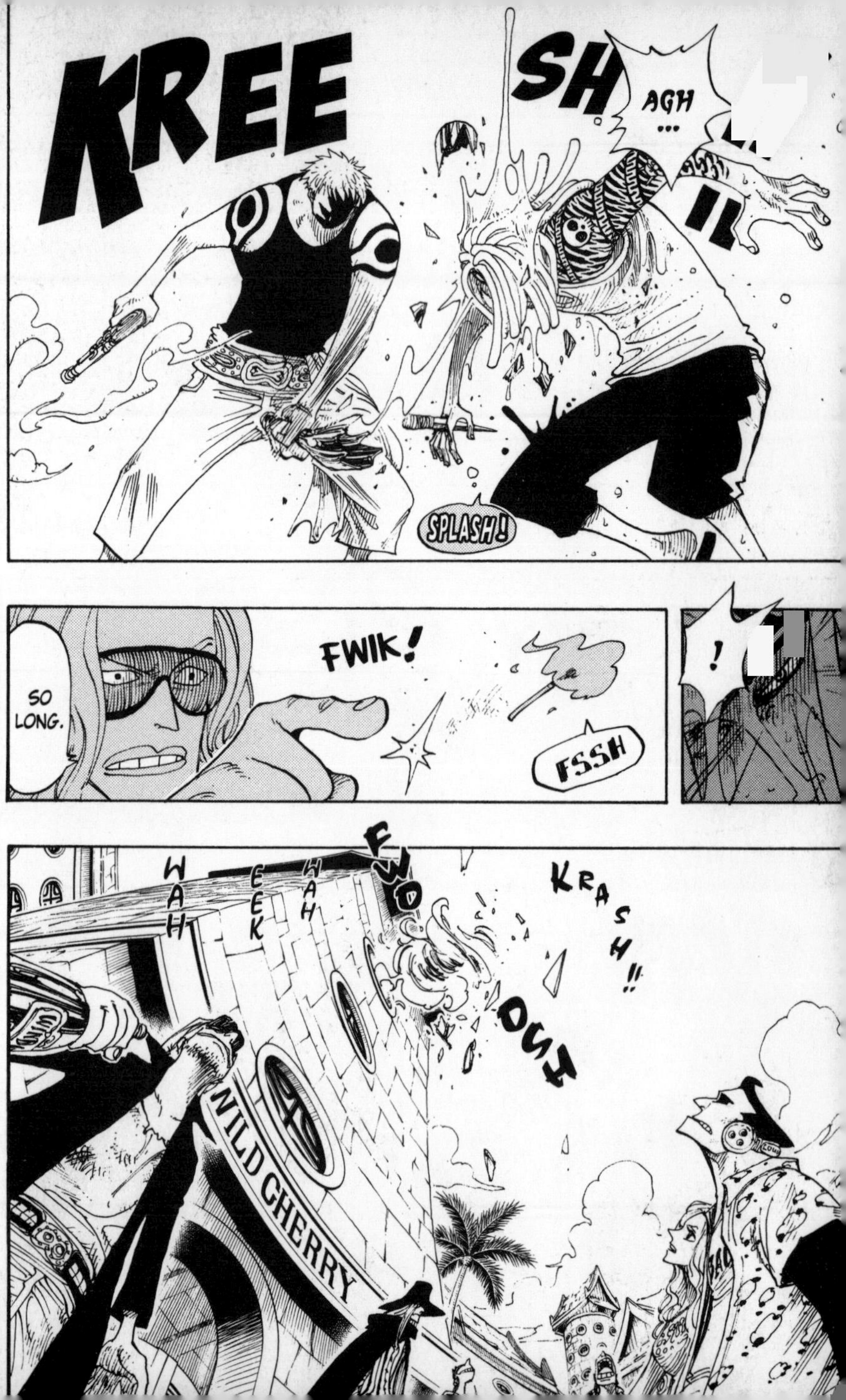

AGH ...
KREESH
SPLASH!
!
FWIK!
FSSH
SO LONG.
KRASH!!
OUCH
FWOO
WAH
EEK
WAH
WILD CHERRY

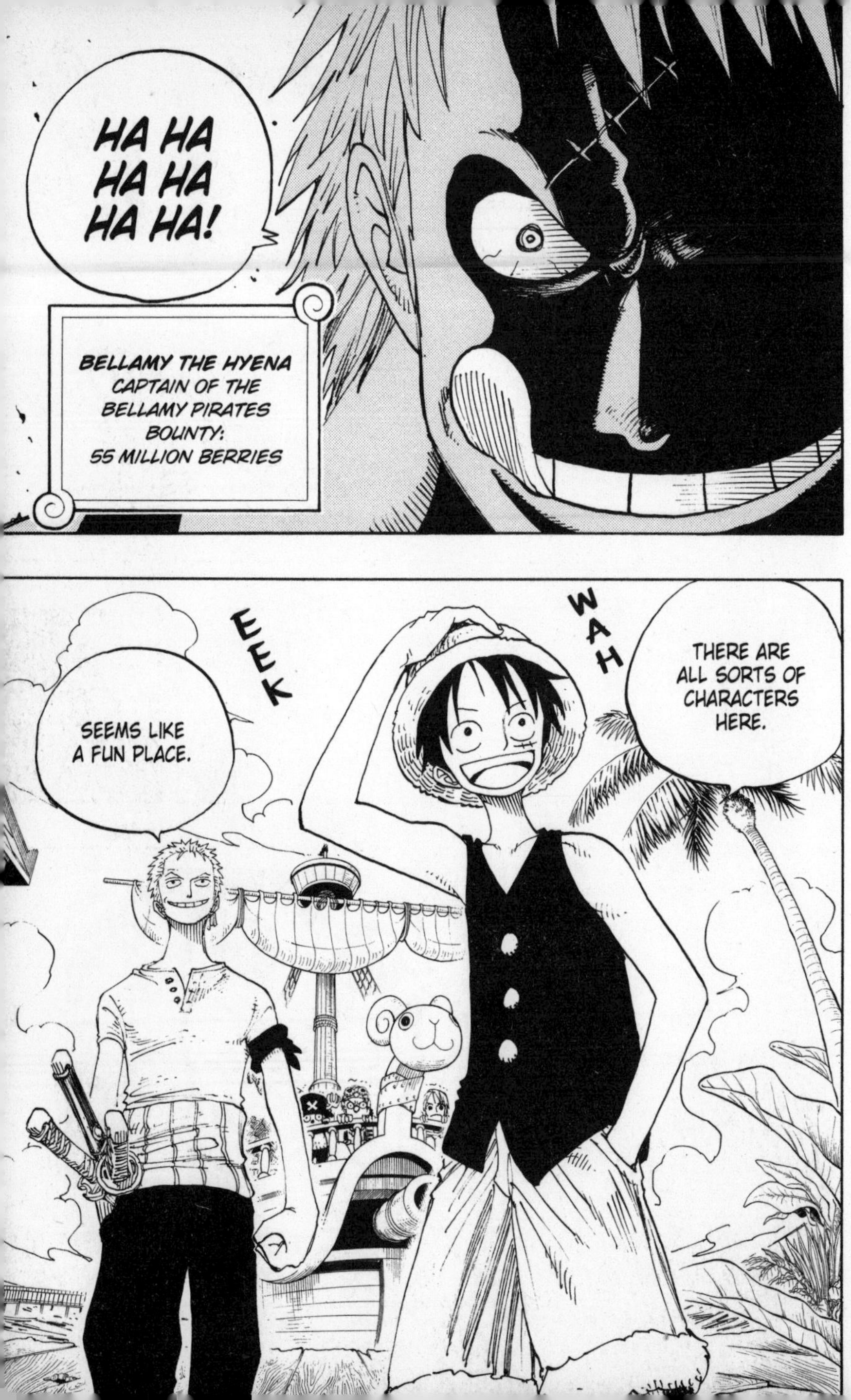
HA HA HA HA HA HA!
BELLAMY THE HYENA CAPTAIN OF THE BELLAMY PIRATES BOUNTY: 55 MILLION BERRIES
WAH
THERE ARE ALL SORTS OF CHARACTERS HERE.
EEK
SEEMS LIKE A FUN PLACE.

Chapter 223:

I PROMISE NEVER TO FIGHT IN THIS TOWN

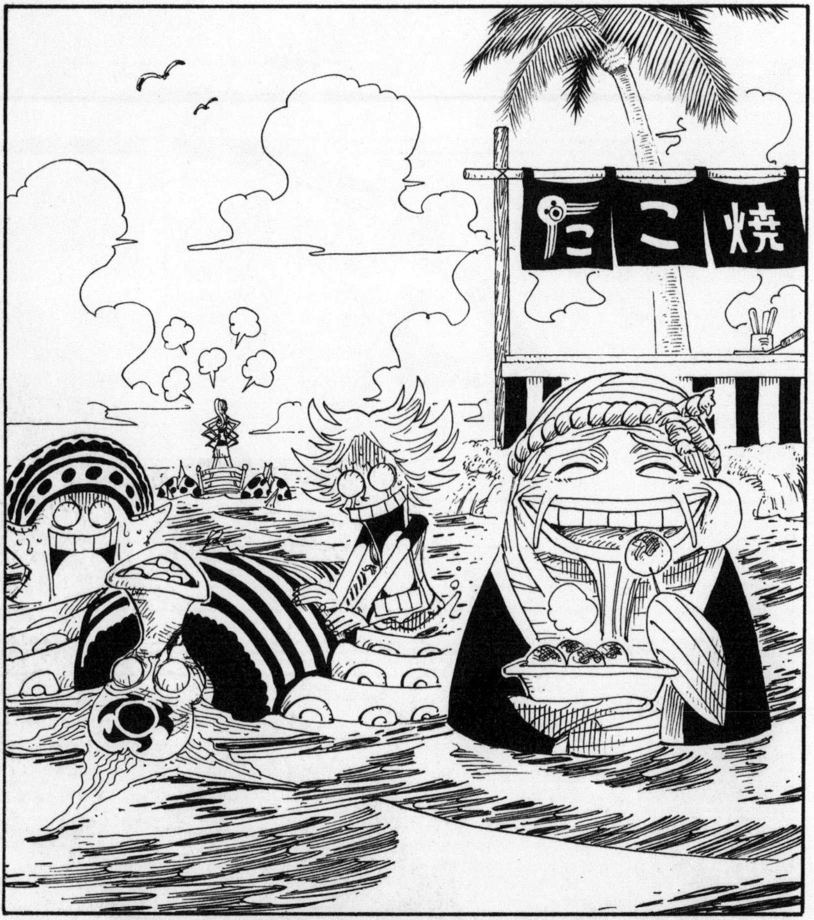
たこ焼

HACHI'S WALK ON THE SEAFLOOR, VOL. 36:
"OCTOPUNCH AND THE SMILING ELDER"

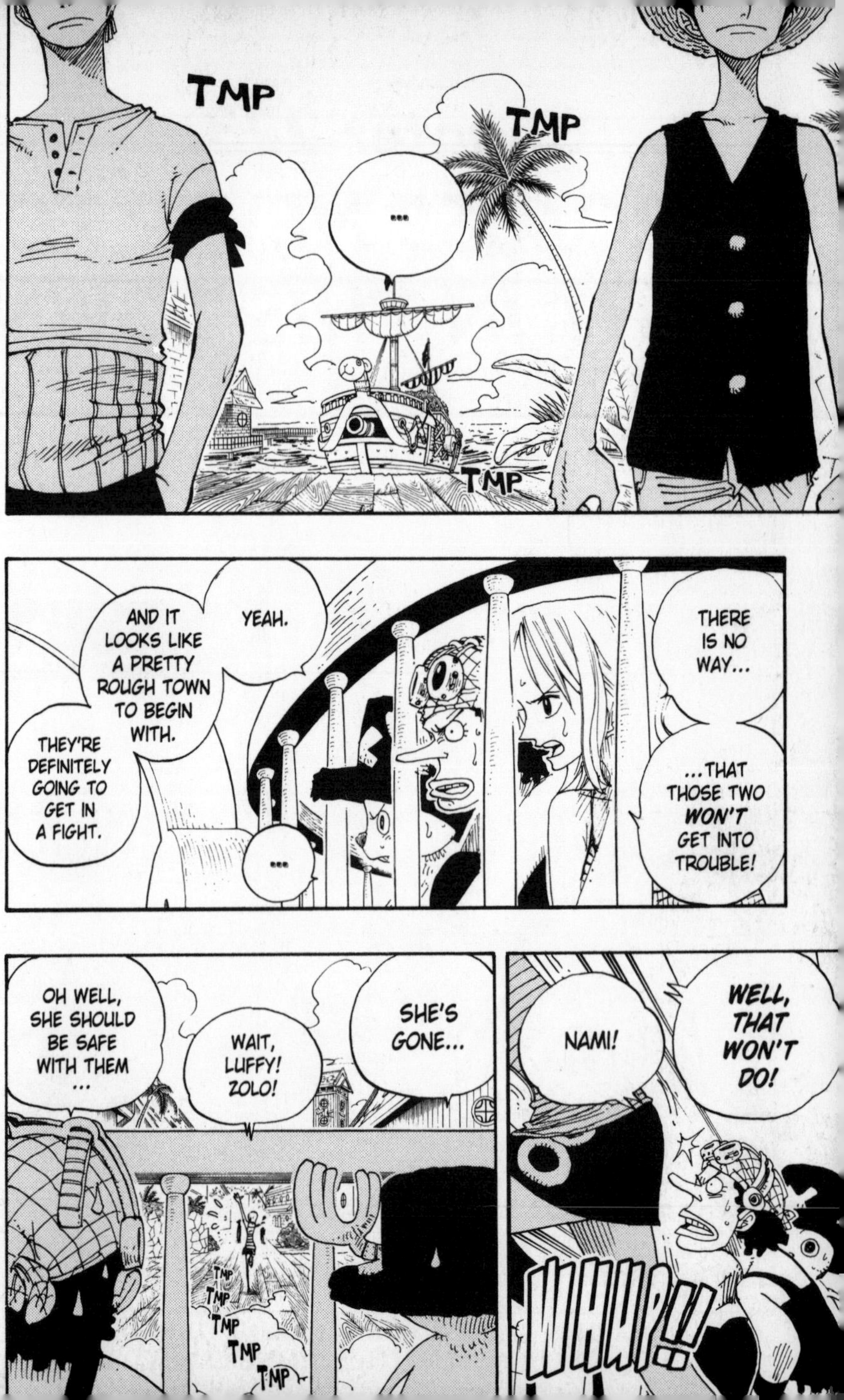
TMP
TMP
...
TMP
THERE IS NO WAY...
...THAT THOSE TWO *WON'T* GET INTO TROUBLE!
YEAH.
AND IT LOOKS LIKE A PRETTY ROUGH TOWN TO BEGIN WITH.
THEY'RE DEFINITELY GOING TO GET IN A FIGHT.
...
WELL, THAT WON'T DO!
NAMI!
WHAP!!
SHE'S GONE...
WAIT, LUFFY! ZOLO!
OH WELL, SHE SHOULD BE SAFE WITH THEM ...
TMP
TMP
TMP
TMP
TMP

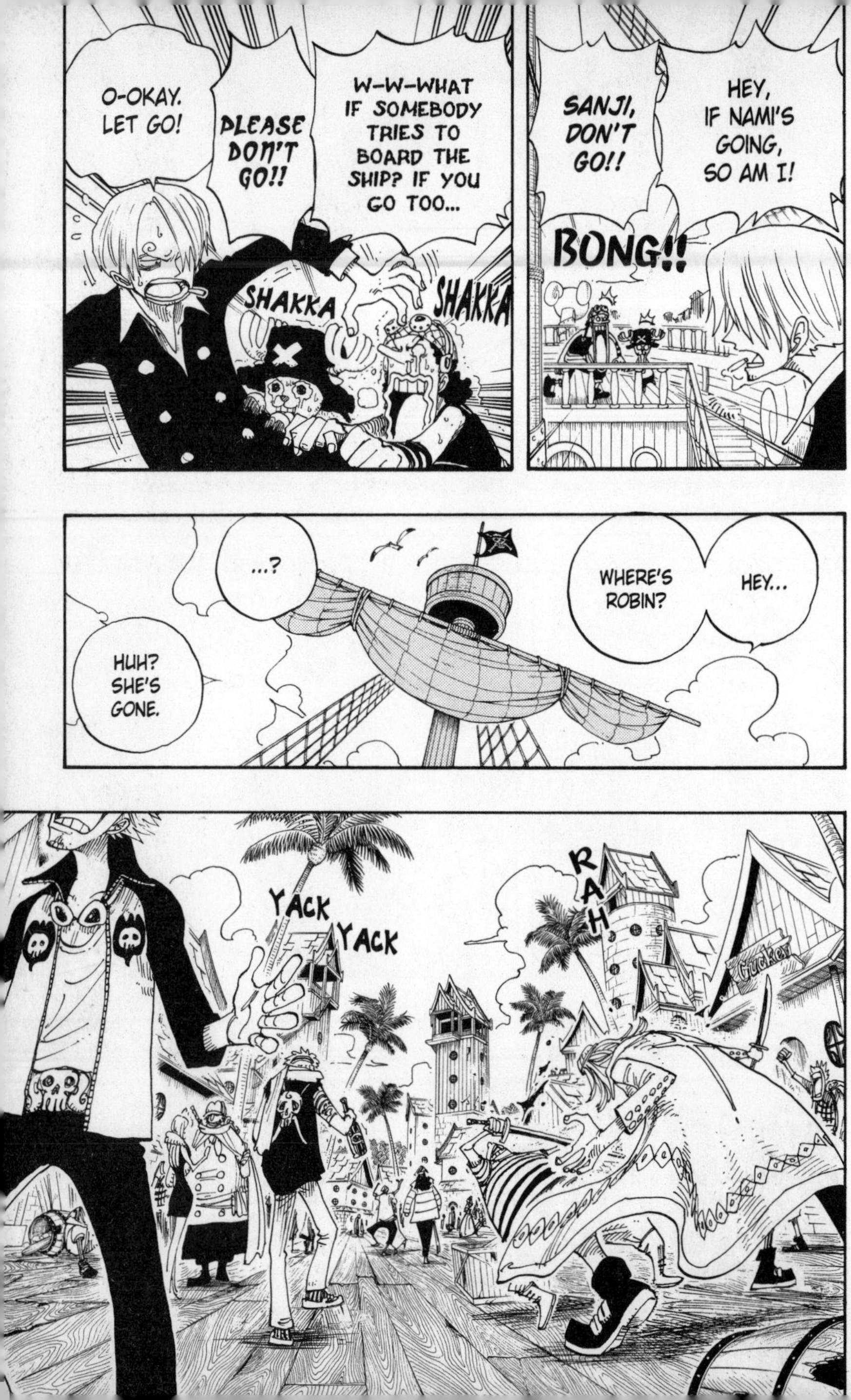
HEY, IF NAMI'S GOING, SO AM I!
SANJI, DON'T GO!!
BONG!!
W-W-WHAT IF SOMEBODY TRIES TO BOARD THE SHIP? IF YOU GO TOO...
SHAKKA
PLEASE DON'T GO!!
SHAKKA
O-OKAY. LET GO!
HEY...
WHERE'S ROBIN?
...?
HUH? SHE'S GONE.
RAH
YACK YACK

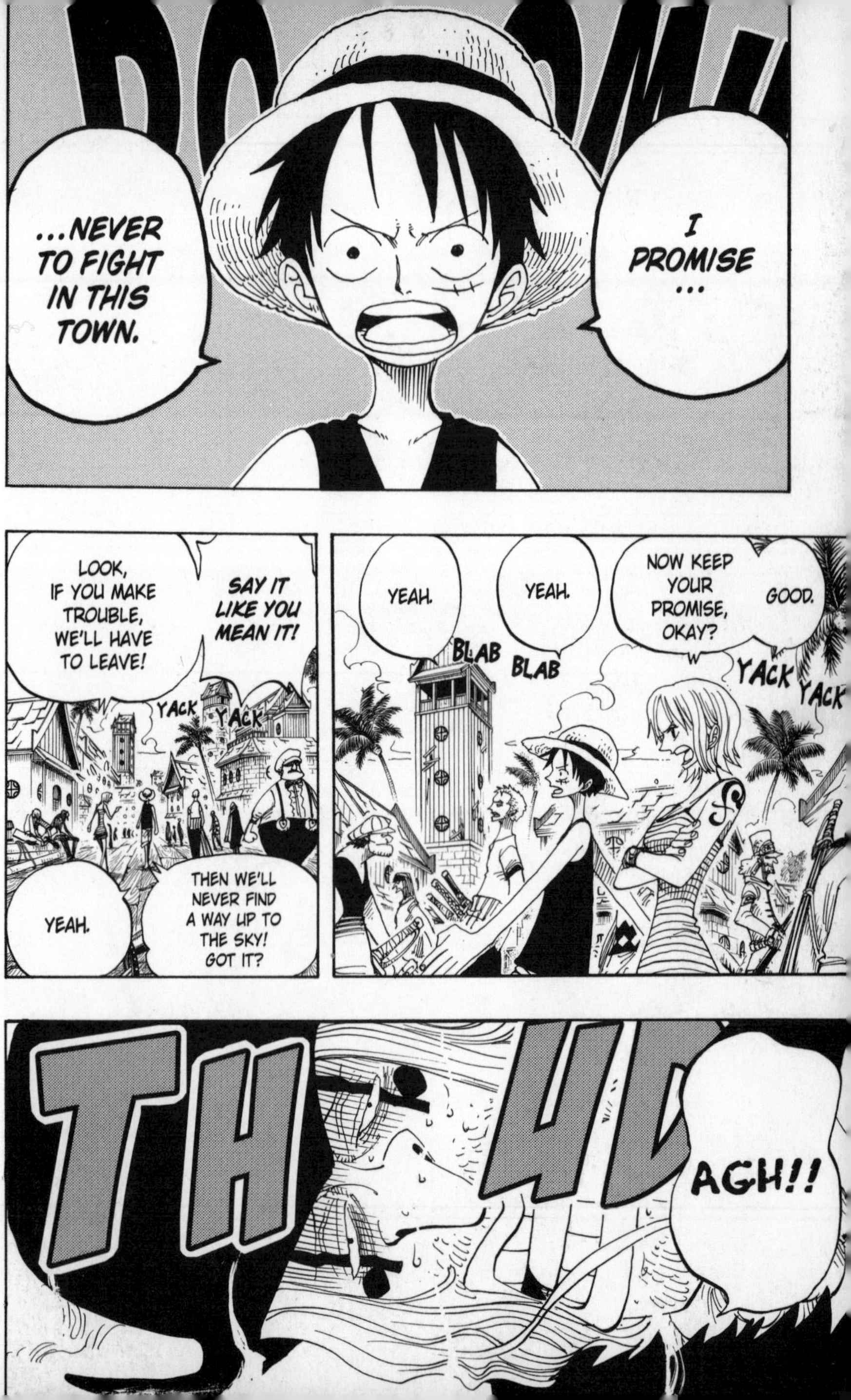
I PROMISE ...
...NEVER TO FIGHT IN THIS TOWN.
GOOD.
NOW KEEP YOUR PROMISE, OKAY?
YACK YACK
YEAH.
YEAH.
BLAB BLAB
SAY IT LIKE YOU MEAN IT!
LOOK, IF YOU MAKE TROUBLE, WE'LL HAVE TO LEAVE!
YACK YACK
THEN WE'LL NEVER FIND A WAY UP TO THE SKY! GOT IT?
YEAH.
AGH!!

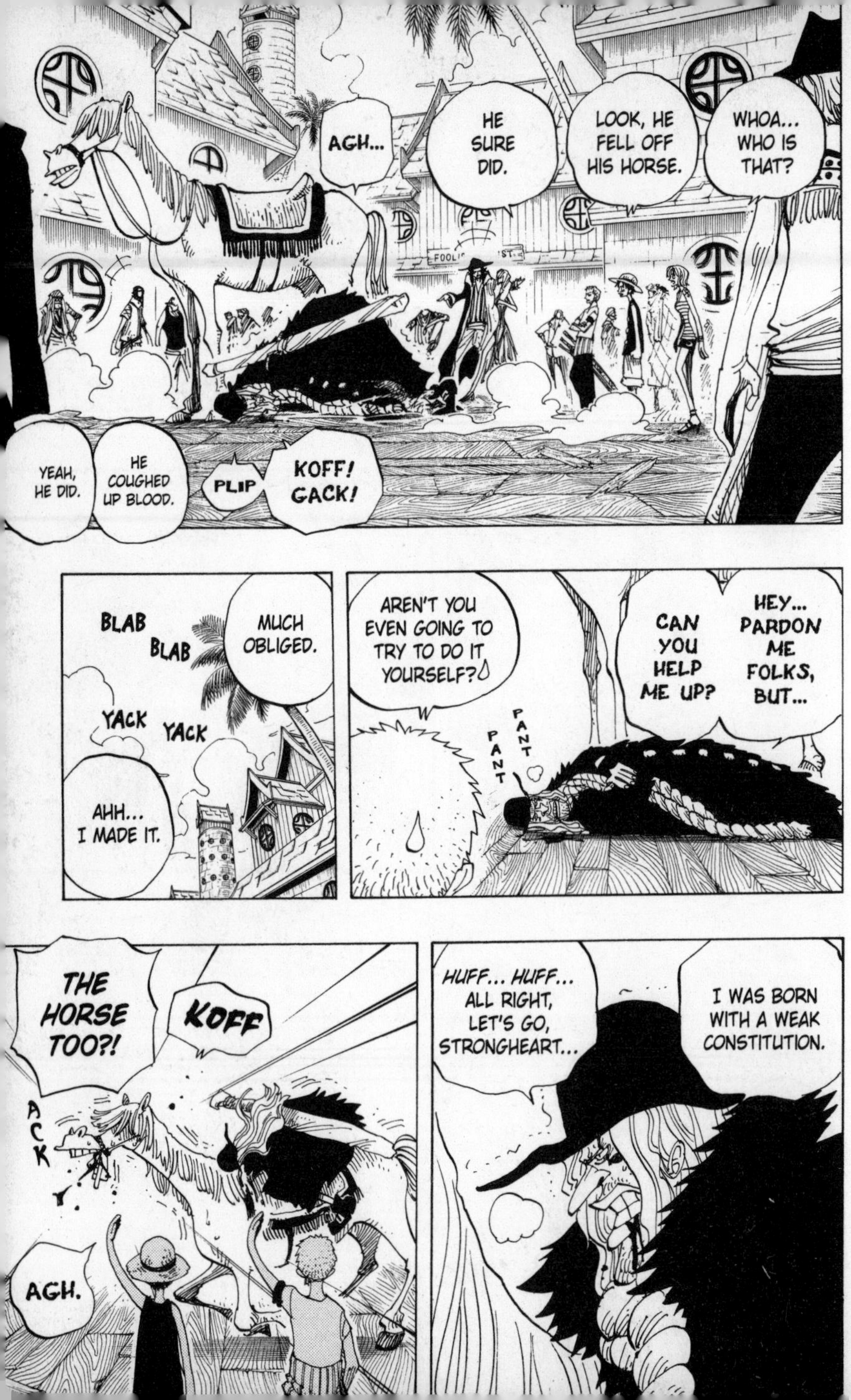
WHOA... WHO IS THAT?
LOOK, HE FELL OFF HIS HORSE.
HE SURE DID.
AGH...
KOFF! GACK!
PLIP
HE COUGHED UP BLOOD.
YEAH, HE DID.
HEY... PARDON ME FOLKS, BUT...
CAN YOU HELP ME UP?
PANT PANT
AREN'T YOU EVEN GOING TO TRY TO DO IT YOURSELF?
MUCH OBLIGED.
BLAB BLAB
YACK YACK
AHH... I MADE IT.
I WAS BORN WITH A WEAK CONSTITUTION.
HUFF... HUFF... ALL RIGHT, LET'S GO, STRONGHEART...
KOFF
THE HORSE TOO?!
ACK
AGH.

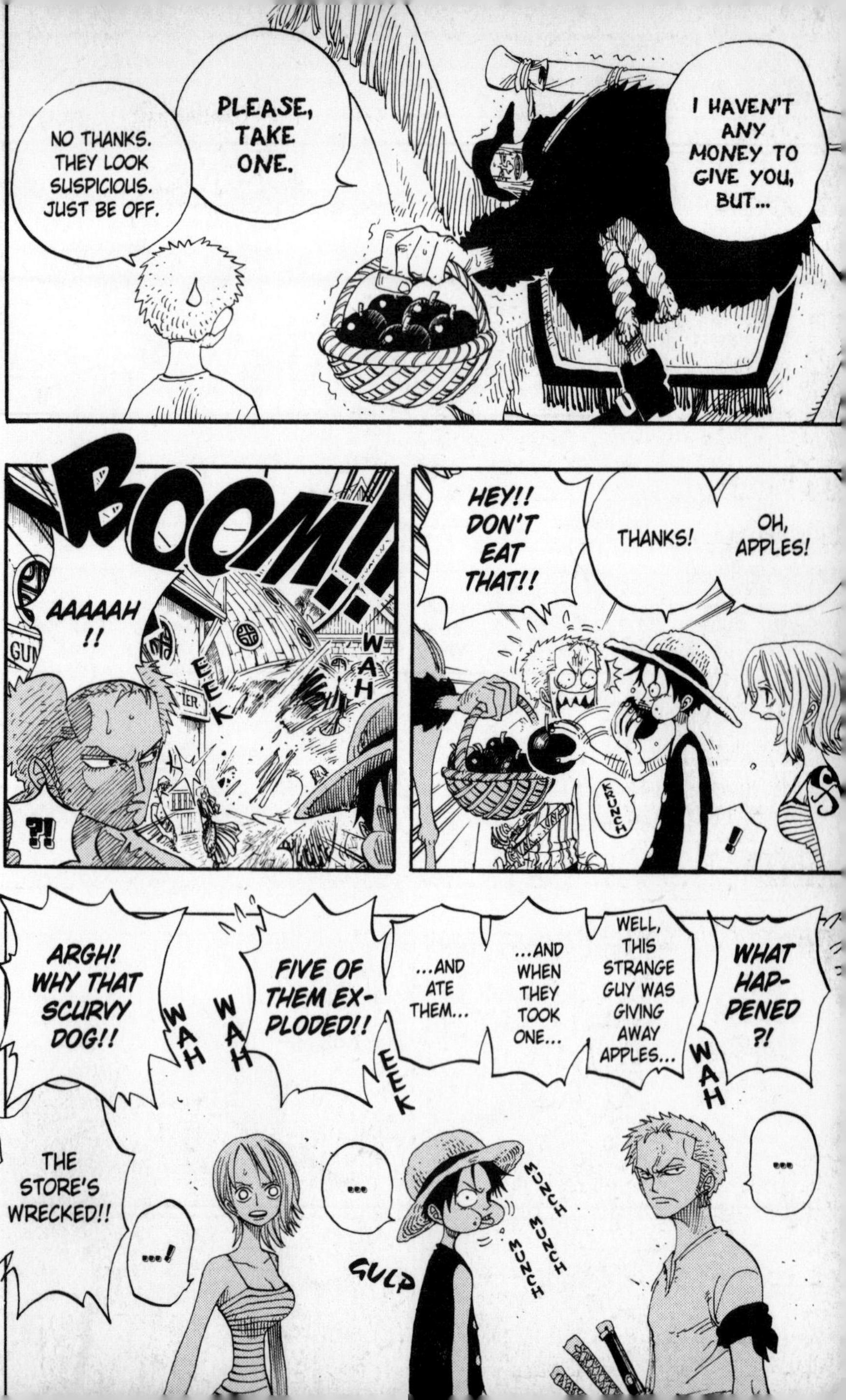
I HAVEN'T ANY MONEY TO GIVE YOU, BUT...
PLEASE, TAKE ONE.
NO THANKS. THEY LOOK SUSPICIOUS. JUST BE OFF.
OH, APPLES!
THANKS!
HEY!! DON'T EAT THAT!!
KRUNCH
!
BOOM!!
WAH
EEK
AAAAAH !!
?!
WHAT HAP-PENED ?!
WAH
WELL, THIS STRANGE GUY WAS GIVING AWAY APPLES...
...AND WHEN THEY TOOK ONE...
...AND ATE THEM...
EEK
FIVE OF THEM EX-PLODED!!
WAH
WAH
ARGH! WHY THAT SCURVY DOG!!
...
MUNCH
MUNCH
MUNCH
GULP
...
...!
THE STORE'S WRECKED!!

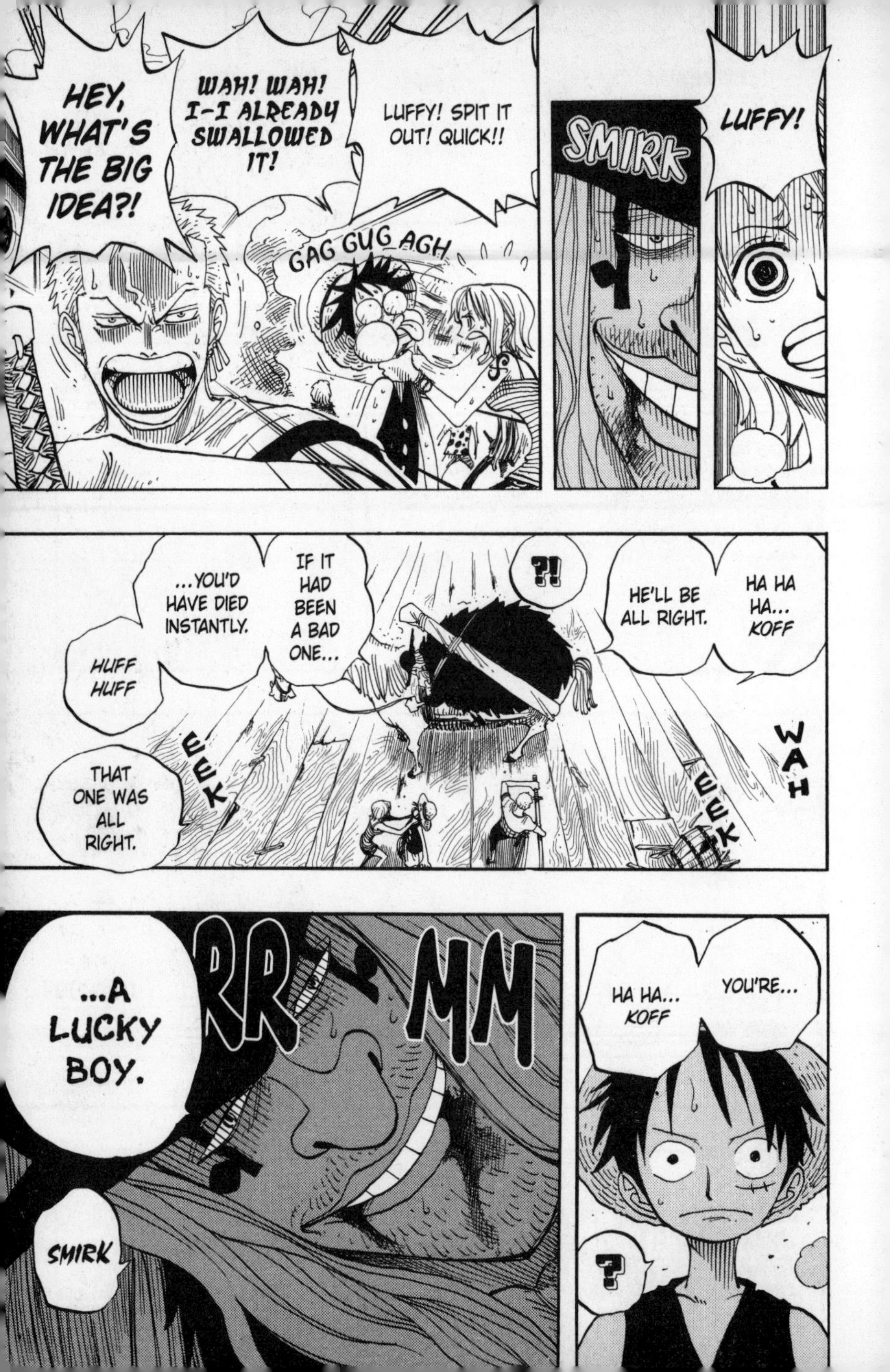

LUFFY!
SMIRK
LUFFY! SPIT IT OUT! QUICK!!
WAH! WAH! I-I ALREADY SWALLOWED IT!
HEY, WHAT'S THE BIG IDEA?!
GAG GUG AGH
HA HA HA... KOFF
HE'LL BE ALL RIGHT.
?!
WAH
EEEK
IF IT HAD BEEN A BAD ONE...
...YOU'D HAVE DIED INSTANTLY.
HUFF HUFF
EEK
THAT ONE WAS ALL RIGHT.
YOU'RE...
HA HA... KOFF
?
MM
RR
...A LUCKY BOY.
SMIRK

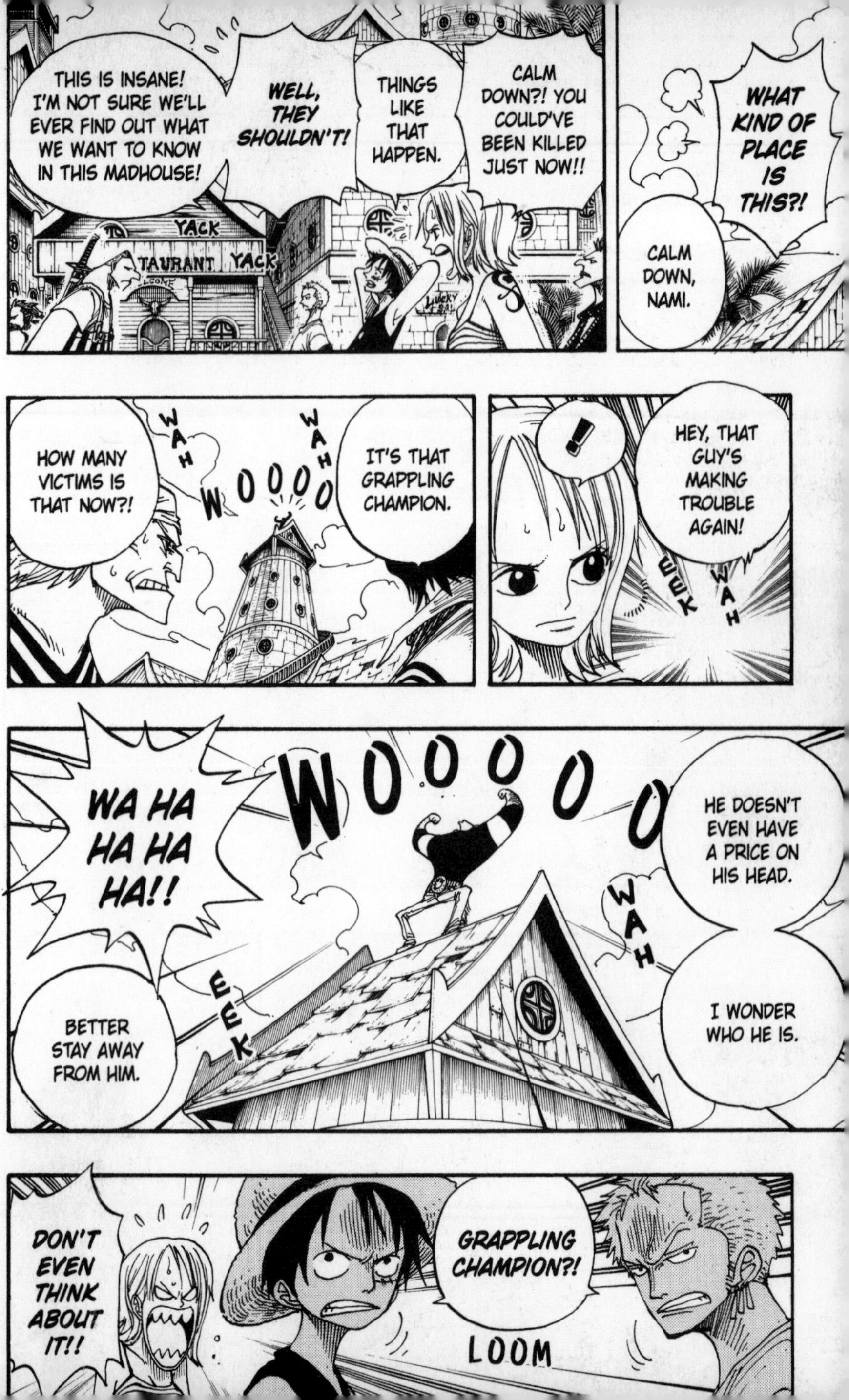
WHAT KIND OF PLACE IS THIS?!
CALM DOWN, NAMI.
CALM DOWN?! YOU COULD'VE BEEN KILLED JUST NOW!!
THINGS LIKE THAT HAPPEN.
WELL, THEY SHOULDN'T!
THIS IS INSANE! I'M NOT SURE WE'LL EVER FIND OUT WHAT WE WANT TO KNOW IN THIS MADHOUSE!
YACK
TAURANT YACK
!
HEY, THAT GUY'S MAKING TROUBLE AGAIN!
WAH
EEK
IT'S THAT GRAPPLING CHAMPION.
WAHOO
WOOOO
WAH
HOW MANY VICTIMS IS THAT NOW?!
HE DOESN'T EVEN HAVE A PRICE ON HIS HEAD.
I WONDER WHO HE IS.
WAH
WOOOOO
WA HA HA HA HA!!
EEK
BETTER STAY AWAY FROM HIM.
GRAPPLING CHAMPION?!
LOOM
DON'T EVEN THINK ABOUT IT!!

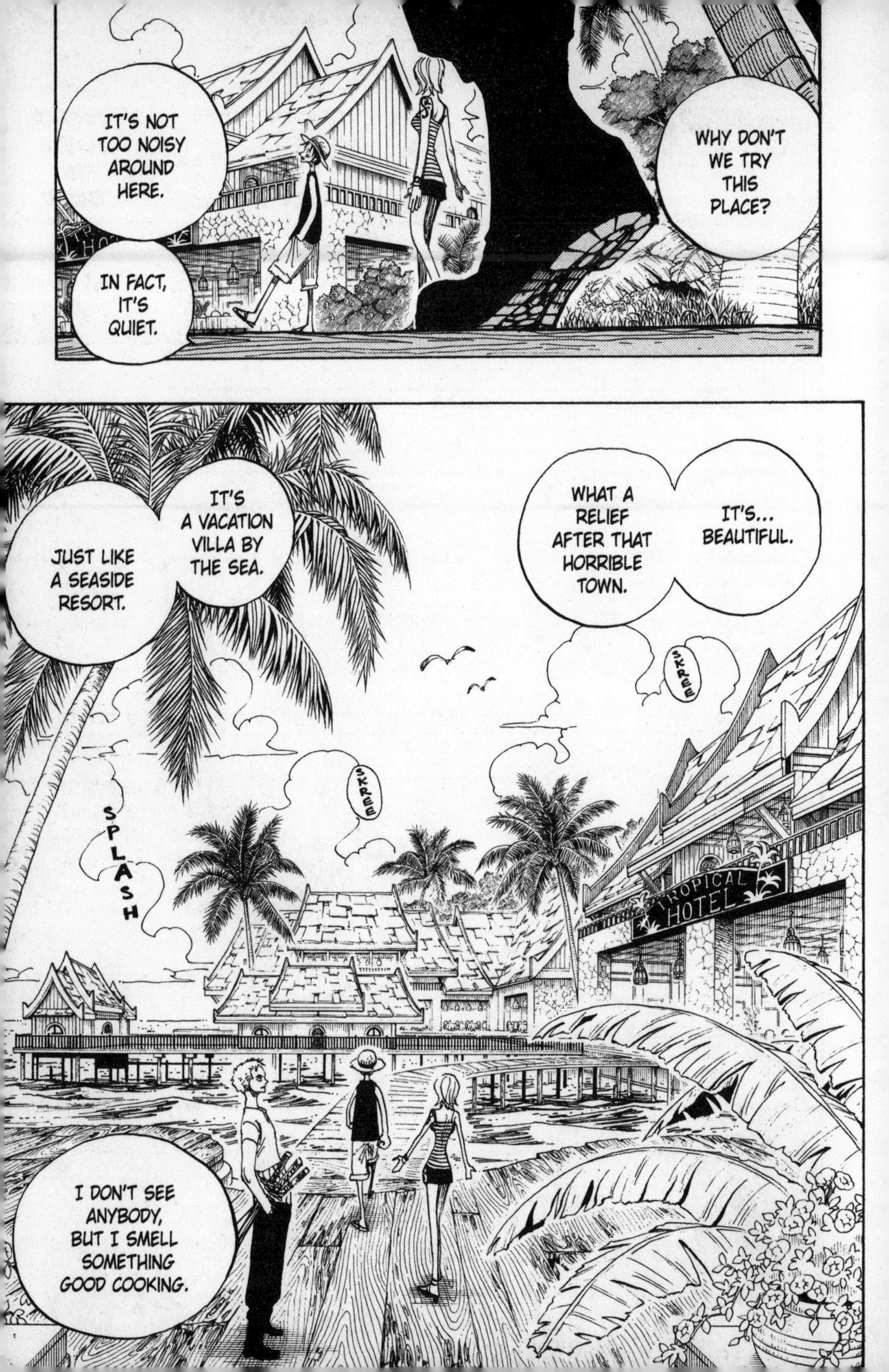
WHY DON'T WE TRY THIS PLACE?
IT'S NOT TOO NOISY AROUND HERE.
IN FACT, IT'S QUIET.
IT'S... BEAUTIFUL.
WHAT A RELIEF AFTER THAT HORRIBLE TOWN.
IT'S A VACATION VILLA BY THE SEA.
JUST LIKE A SEASIDE RESORT.
SKREE
SKREE
SPLASH
TROPICAL HOTEL
I DON'T SEE ANYBODY, BUT I SMELL SOMETHING GOOD COOKING.

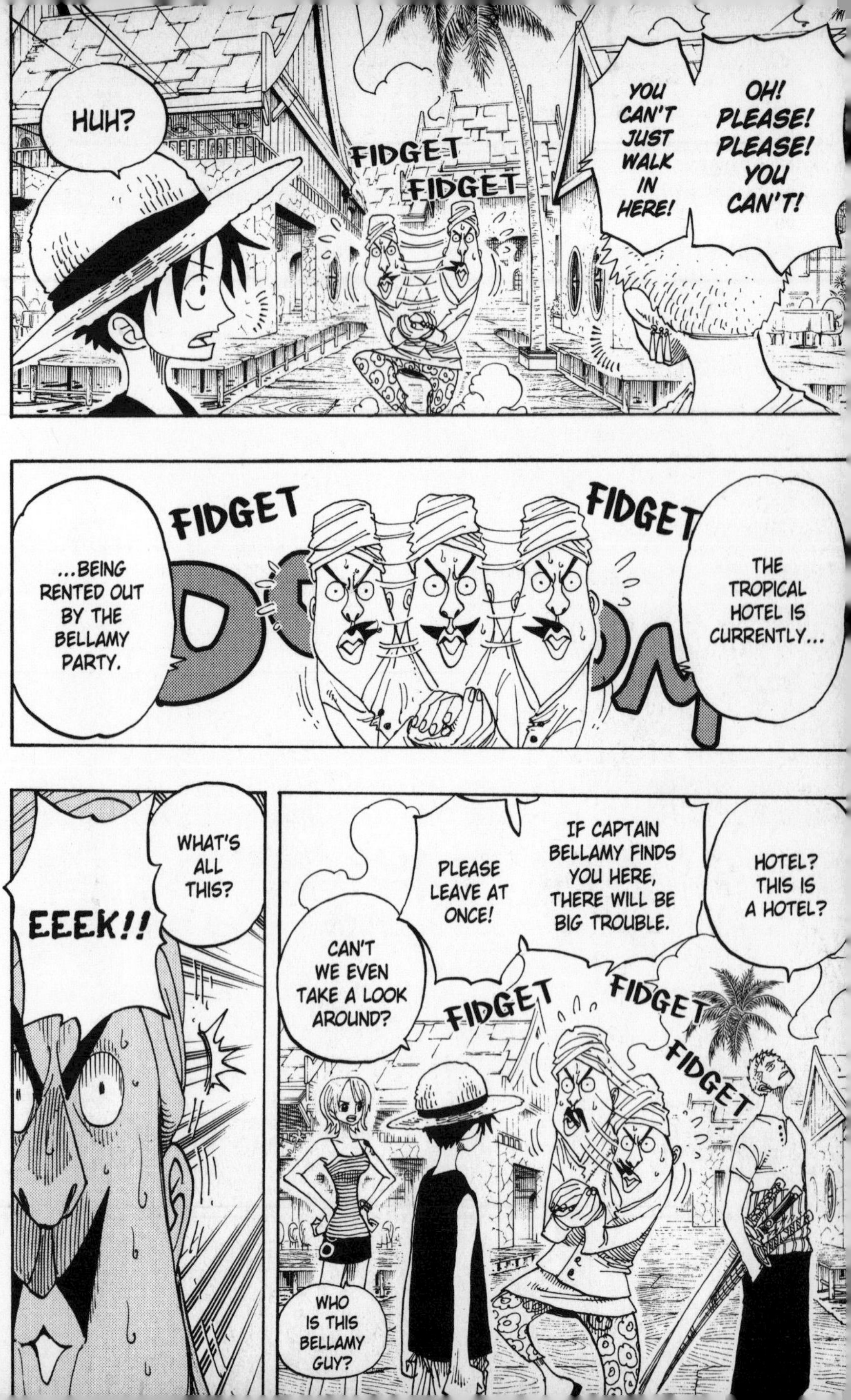
OH! PLEASE! PLEASE! YOU CAN'T!
YOU CAN'T JUST WALK IN HERE!
FIDGET
FIDGET
HUH?
THE TROPICAL HOTEL IS CURRENTLY...
FIDGET
FIDGET
...BEING RENTED OUT BY THE BELLAMY PARTY.
HOTEL? THIS IS A HOTEL?
IF CAPTAIN BELLAMY FINDS YOU HERE, THERE WILL BE BIG TROUBLE.
PLEASE LEAVE AT ONCE!
CAN'T WE EVEN TAKE A LOOK AROUND?
FIDGET
FIDGET
FIDGET
FIDGET
WHO IS THIS BELLAMY GUY?
WHAT'S ALL THIS?
EEEK!!

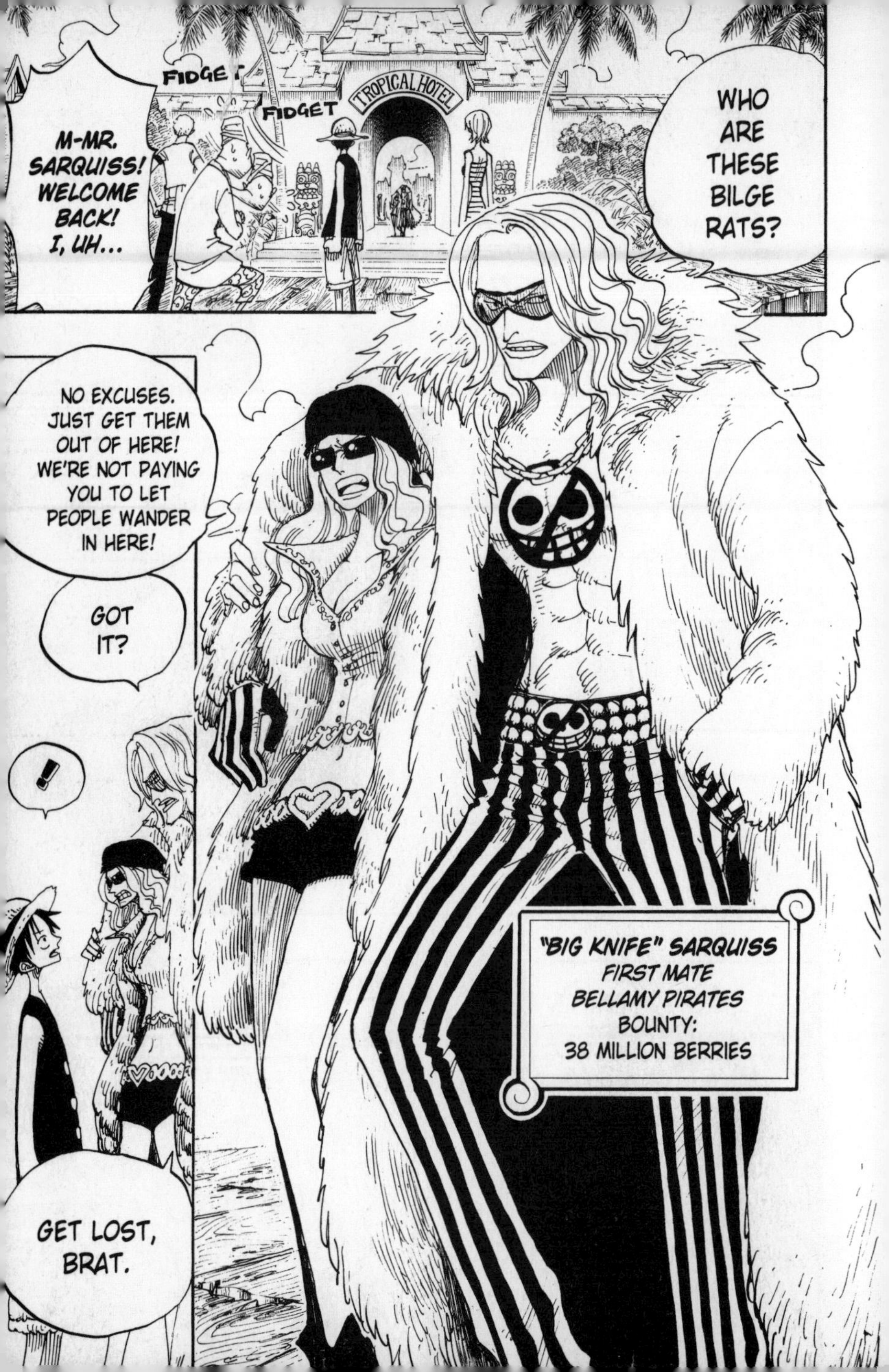
WHO ARE THESE BILGE RATS?
FIDGET
FIDGET
TROPICAL HOTEL
M-MR. SARQUISS! WELCOME BACK! I, UH...
"BIG KNIFE" SARQUISS
FIRST MATE
BELLAMY PIRATES
BOUNTY:
38 MILLION BERRIES
NO EXCUSES. JUST GET THEM OUT OF HERE! WE'RE NOT PAYING YOU TO LET PEOPLE WANDER IN HERE!
GOT IT?
!
GET LOST, BRAT.

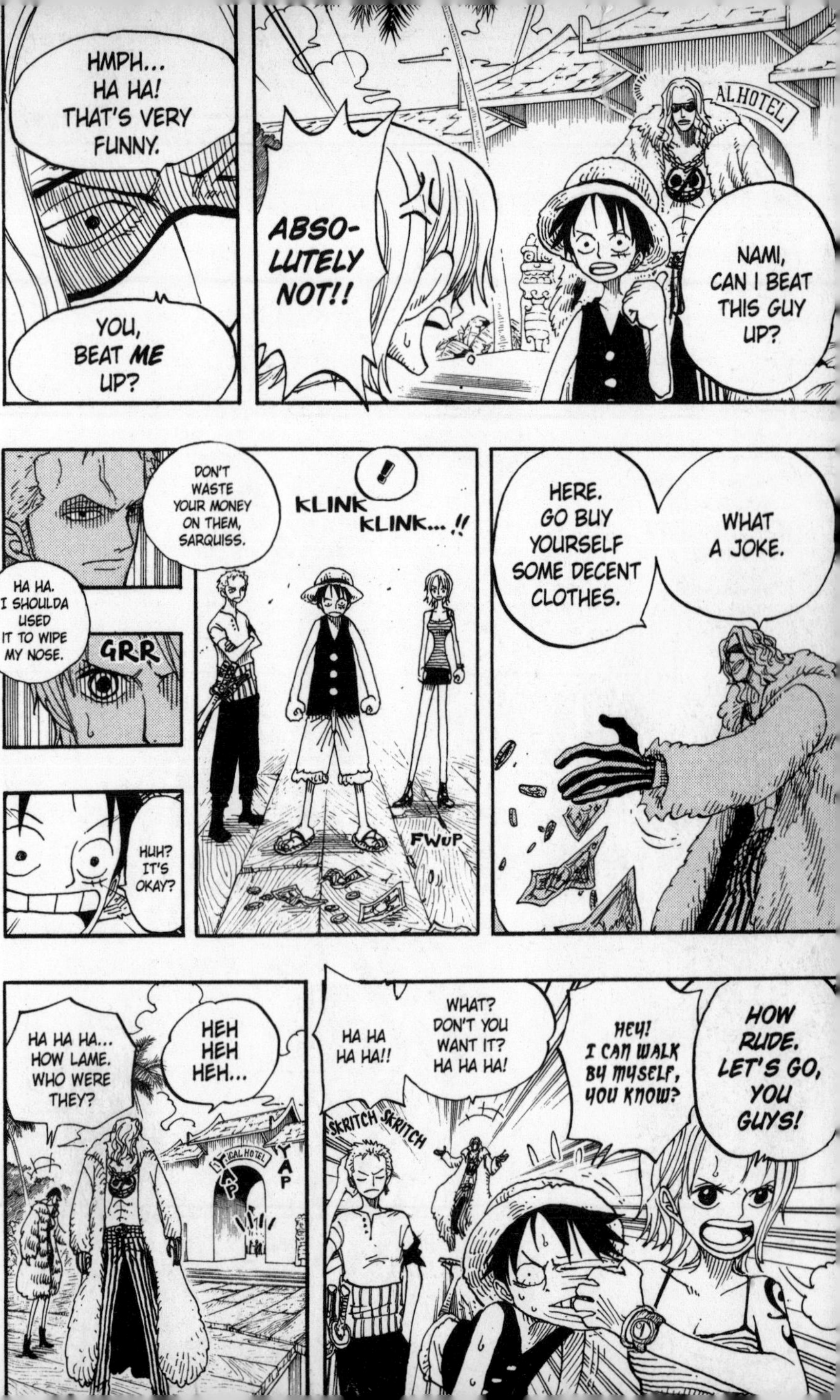
AL HOTEL
NAMI, CAN I BEAT THIS GUY UP?
ABSO-LUTELY NOT!!
HMPH... HA HA! THAT'S VERY FUNNY.
YOU, BEAT ME UP?
WHAT A JOKE.
HERE. GO BUY YOURSELF SOME DECENT CLOTHES.
!
KLINK KLINK...!!
FWUP
DON'T WASTE YOUR MONEY ON THEM, SARQUISS.
HA HA. I SHOULDA USED IT TO WIPE MY NOSE.
GRR
HUH? IT'S OKAY?
HOW RUDE. LET'S GO, YOU GUYS!
HEY! I CAN WALK BY MYSELF, YOU KNOW?
WHAT? DON'T YOU WANT IT? HA HA HA!
HA HA HA HA!!
SKRITCH SKRITCH
HEH HEH HEH...
HA HA HA... HOW LAME. WHO WERE THEY?

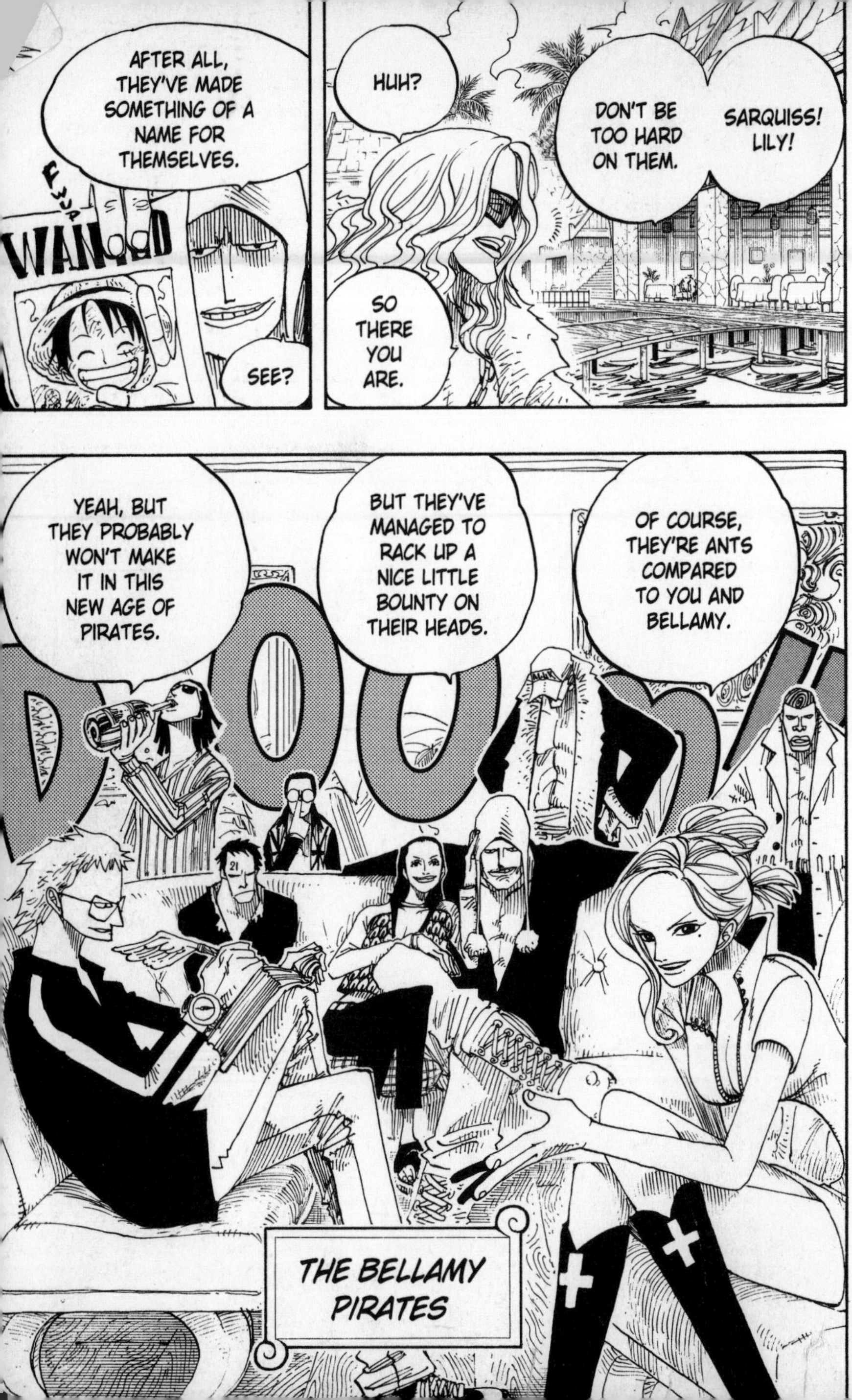
SARQUISS! LILY!
DON'T BE TOO HARD ON THEM.
HUH?
SO THERE YOU ARE.
AFTER ALL, THEY'VE MADE SOMETHING OF A NAME FOR THEMSELVES.
FWUP
WANTED
SEE?
OF COURSE, THEY'RE ANTS COMPARED TO YOU AND BELLAMY.
BUT THEY'VE MANAGED TO RACK UP A NICE LITTLE BOUNTY ON THEIR HEADS.
YEAH, BUT THEY PROBABLY WON'T MAKE IT IN THIS NEW AGE OF PIRATES.
THE BELLAMY PIRATES

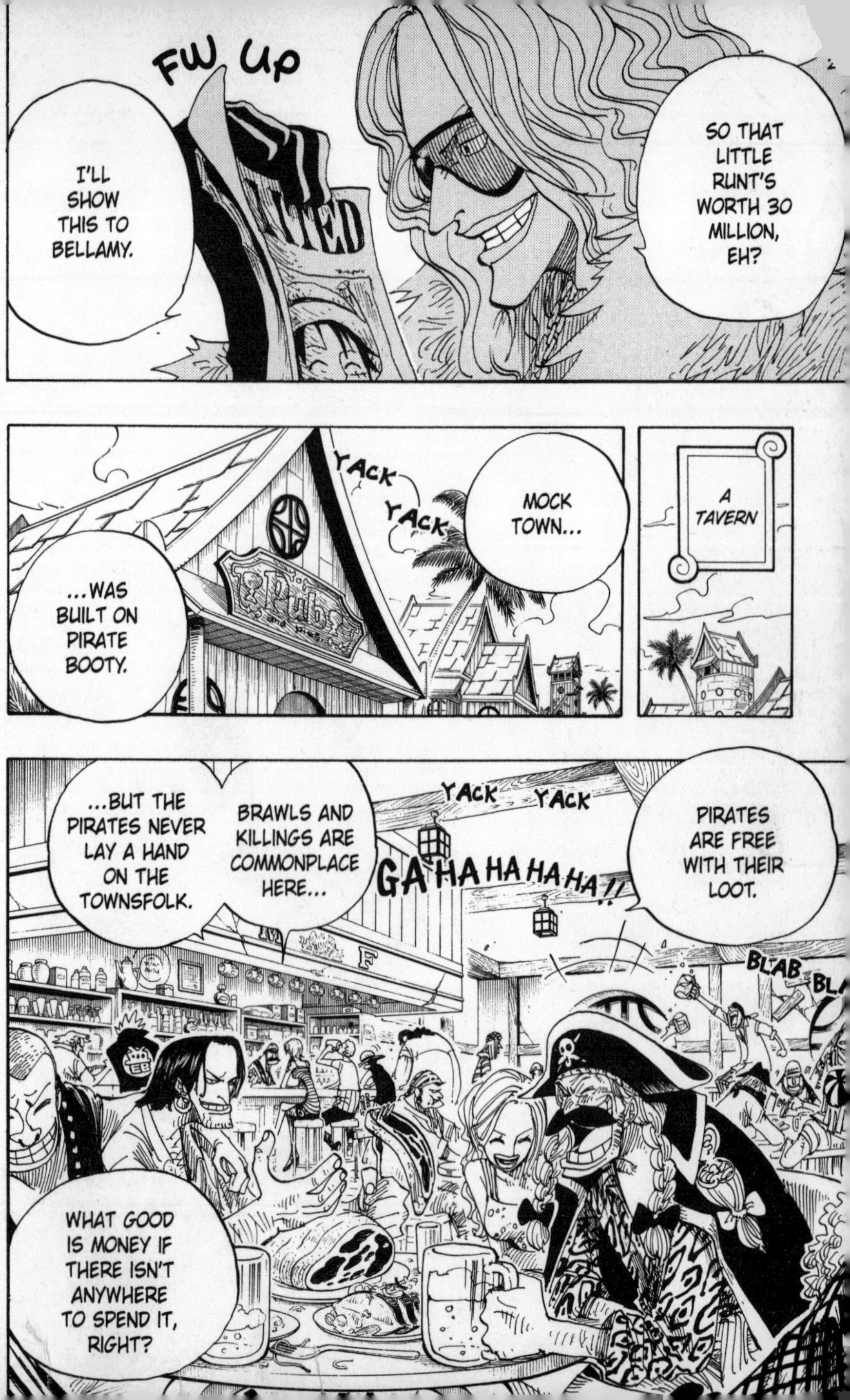
SO THAT LITTLE RUNT'S WORTH 30 MILLION, EH?
FW UP
I'LL SHOW THIS TO BELLAMY.
A TAVERN
MOCK TOWN...
YACK
YACK
...WAS BUILT ON PIRATE BOOTY.
PIRATES ARE FREE WITH THEIR LOOT.
YACK YACK
GAHAHAHAHA!!
BRAWLS AND KILLINGS ARE COMMONPLACE HERE...
...BUT THE PIRATES NEVER LAY A HAND ON THE TOWNSFOLK.
BLAB
WHAT GOOD IS MONEY IF THERE ISN'T ANYWHERE TO SPEND IT, RIGHT?

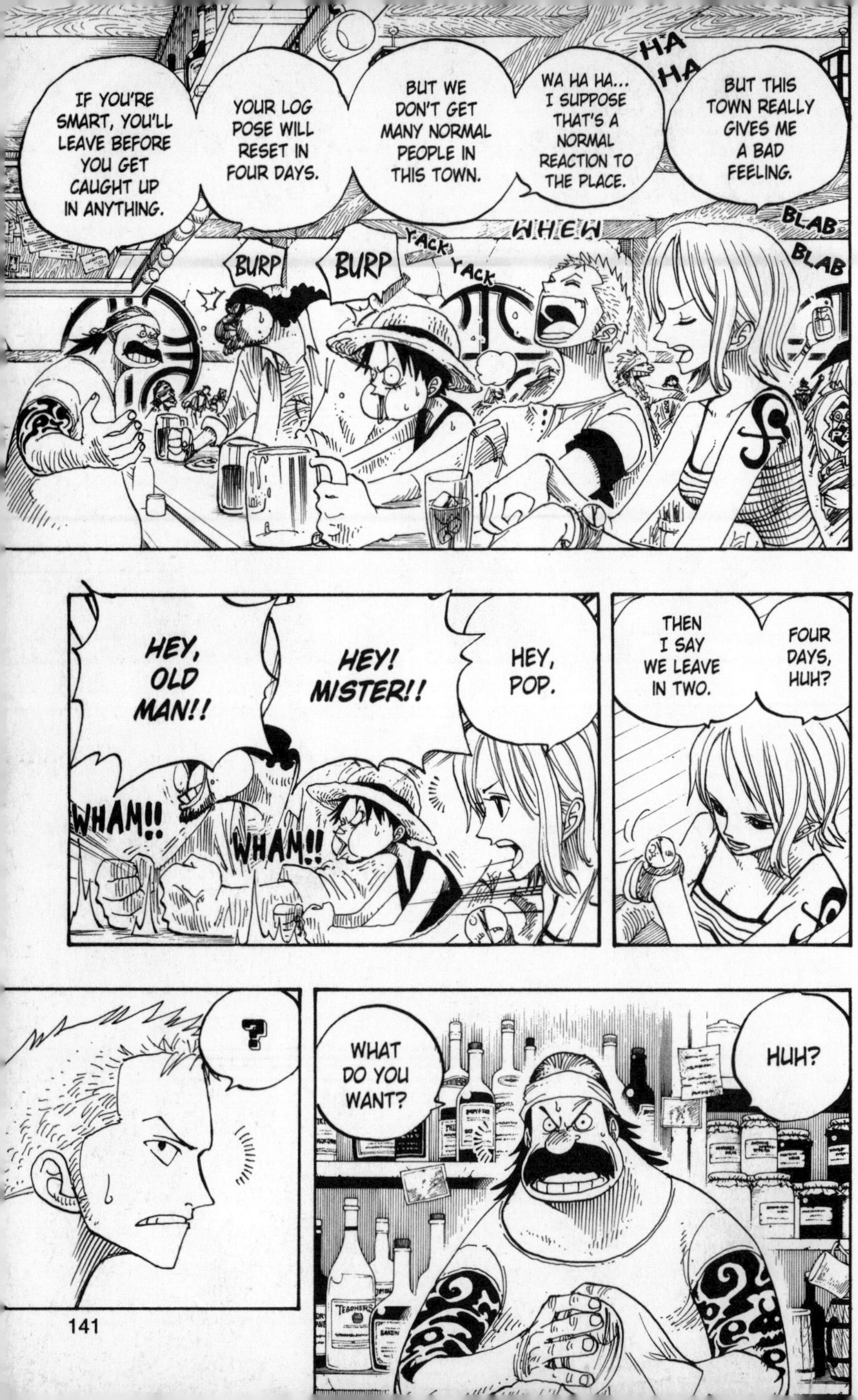
BUT THIS TOWN REALLY GIVES ME A BAD FEELING.
BLAB BLAB
HA HA
WA HA HA... I SUPPOSE THAT'S A NORMAL REACTION TO THE PLACE.
WHEW
BUT WE DON'T GET MANY NORMAL PEOPLE IN THIS TOWN.
YACK YACK
BURP
YOUR LOG POSE WILL RESET IN FOUR DAYS.
BURP
IF YOU'RE SMART, YOU'LL LEAVE BEFORE YOU GET CAUGHT UP IN ANYTHING.
FOUR DAYS, HUH?
THEN I SAY WE LEAVE IN TWO.
HEY, POP.
HEY! MISTER!!
HEY, OLD MAN!!
WHAM!!
WHAM!!
HUH?
WHAT DO YOU WANT?
?

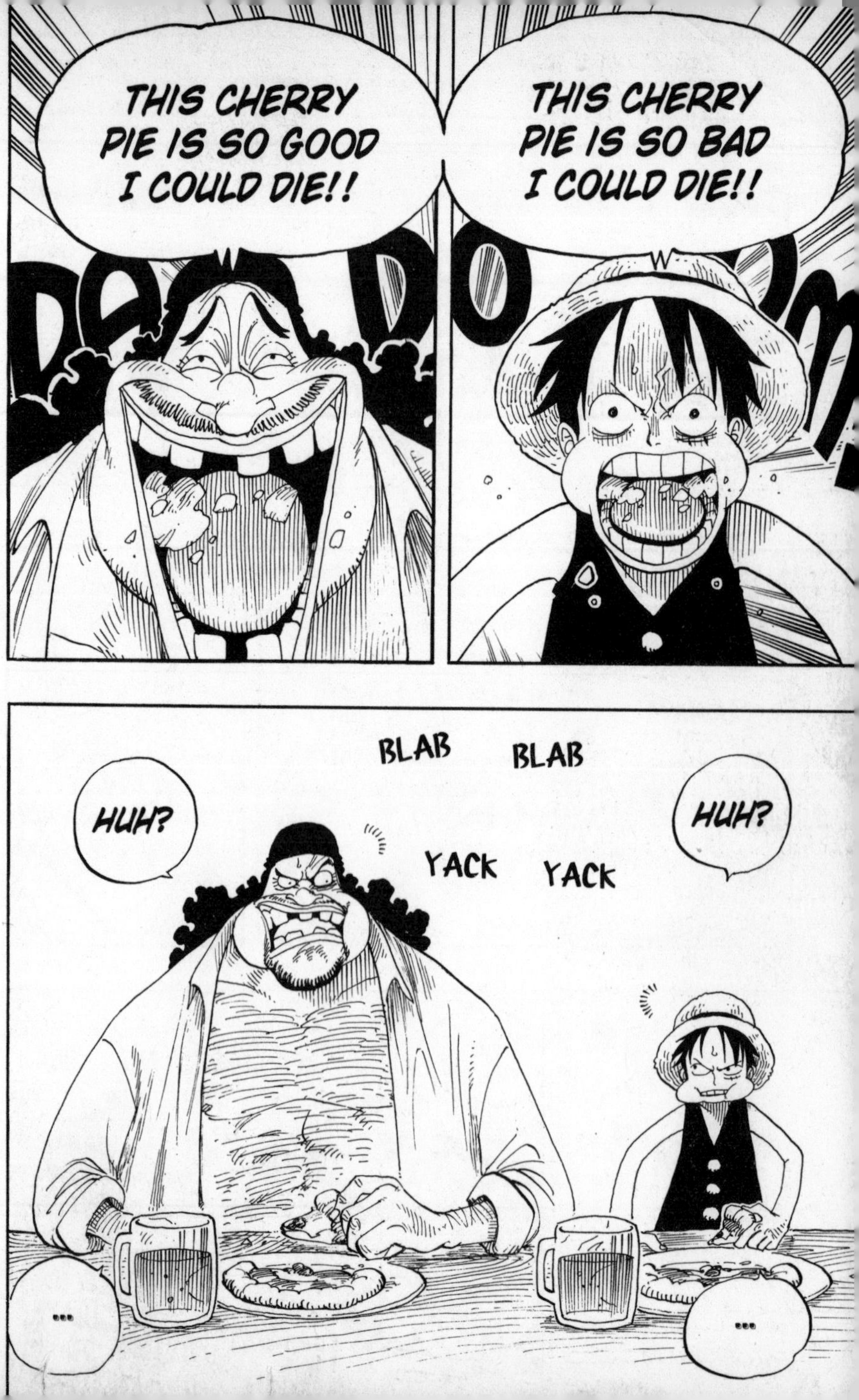
THIS CHERRY PIE IS SO BAD I COULD DIE!!
THIS CHERRY PIE IS SO GOOD I COULD DIE!!
HUH?
BLAB BLAB
YACK YACK
HUH?
...
...

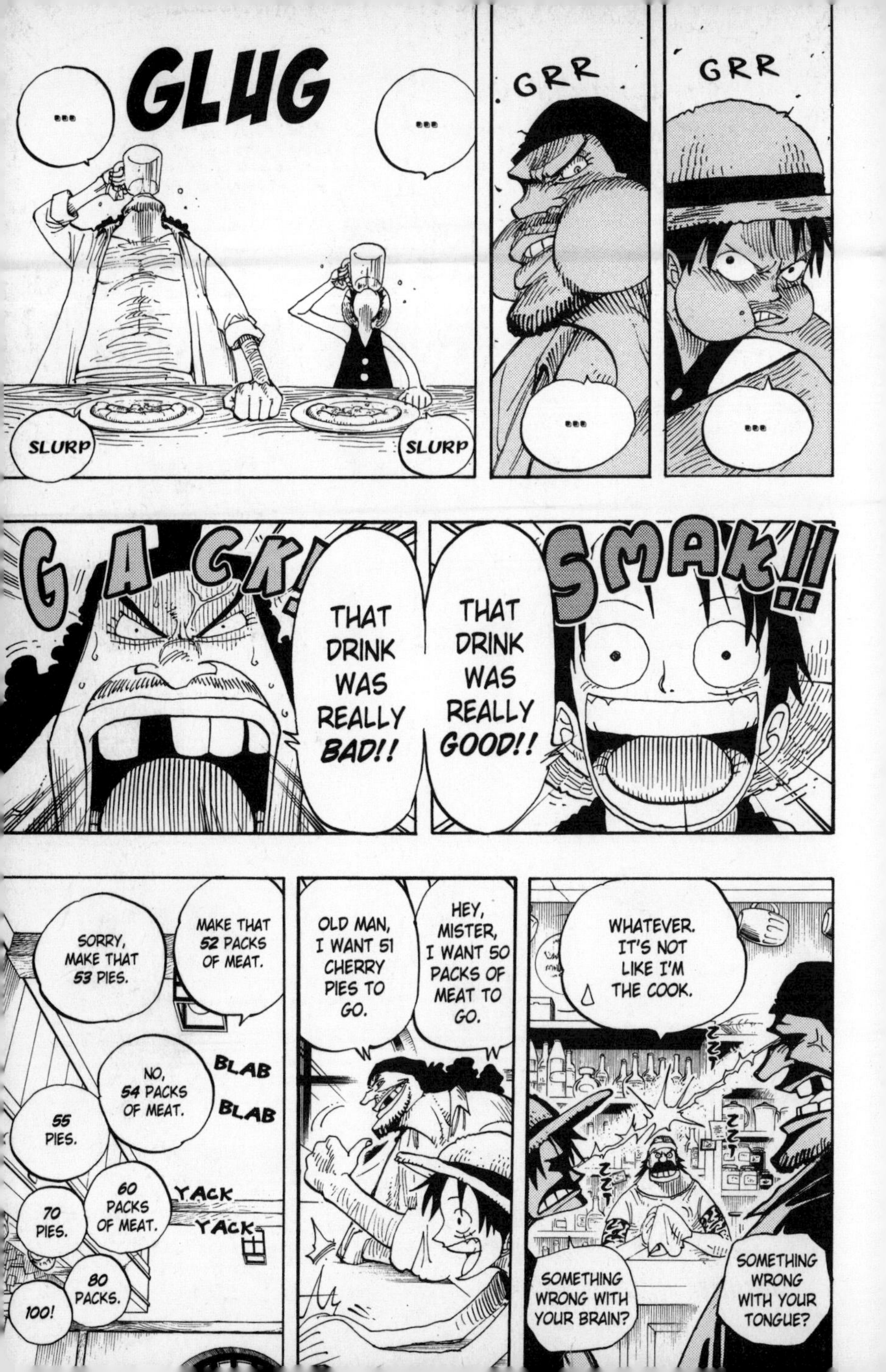
GRR
...
GRR
...
...
GLUG
...
SLURP
SLURP
SMAK!!
THAT DRINK WAS REALLY GOOD!!
GACK!
THAT DRINK WAS REALLY BAD!!
WHATEVER. IT'S NOT LIKE I'M THE COOK.
SOMETHING WRONG WITH YOUR TONGUE?
SOMETHING WRONG WITH YOUR BRAIN?
HEY, MISTER, I WANT 50 PACKS OF MEAT TO GO.
OLD MAN, I WANT 51 CHERRY PIES TO GO.
MAKE THAT 52 PACKS OF MEAT.
SORRY, MAKE THAT 53 PIES.
BLAB
BLAB
NO, 54 PACKS OF MEAT.
55 PIES.
YACK
YACK
60 PACKS OF MEAT.
70 PIES.
80 PACKS.
100!

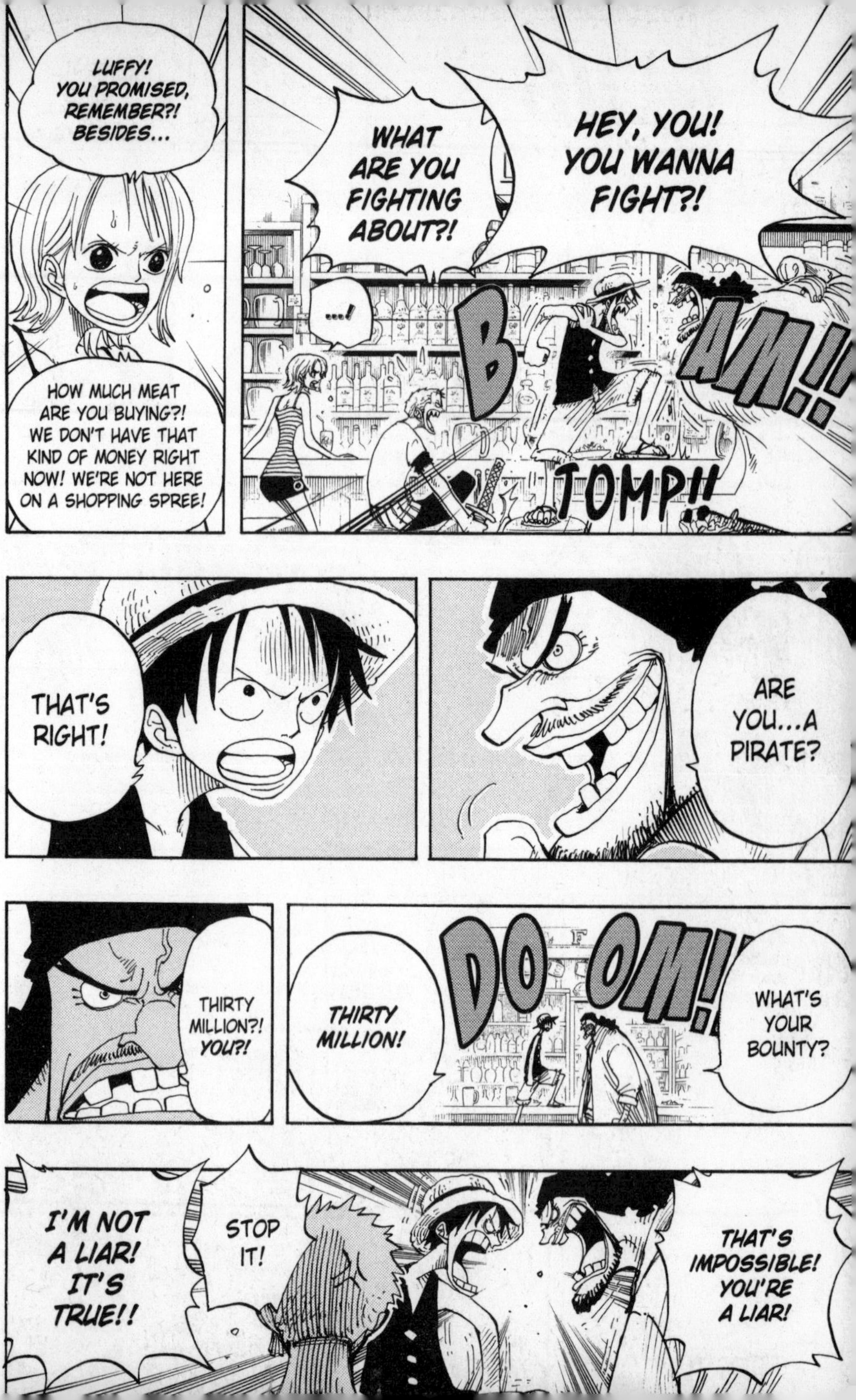
HEY, YOU! YOU WANNA FIGHT?!
WHAT ARE YOU FIGHTING ABOUT?!
...!
BAM!!
TOMP!!
LUFFY! YOU PROMISED, REMEMBER?! BESIDES...
HOW MUCH MEAT ARE YOU BUYING?! WE DON'T HAVE THAT KIND OF MONEY RIGHT NOW! WE'RE NOT HERE ON A SHOPPING SPREE!
ARE YOU...A PIRATE?
THAT'S RIGHT!
WHAT'S YOUR BOUNTY?
DOOM!!
THIRTY MILLION!
THIRTY MILLION?! YOU?!
THAT'S IMPOSSIBLE! YOU'RE A LIAR!
STOP IT!
I'M NOT A LIAR! IT'S TRUE!!

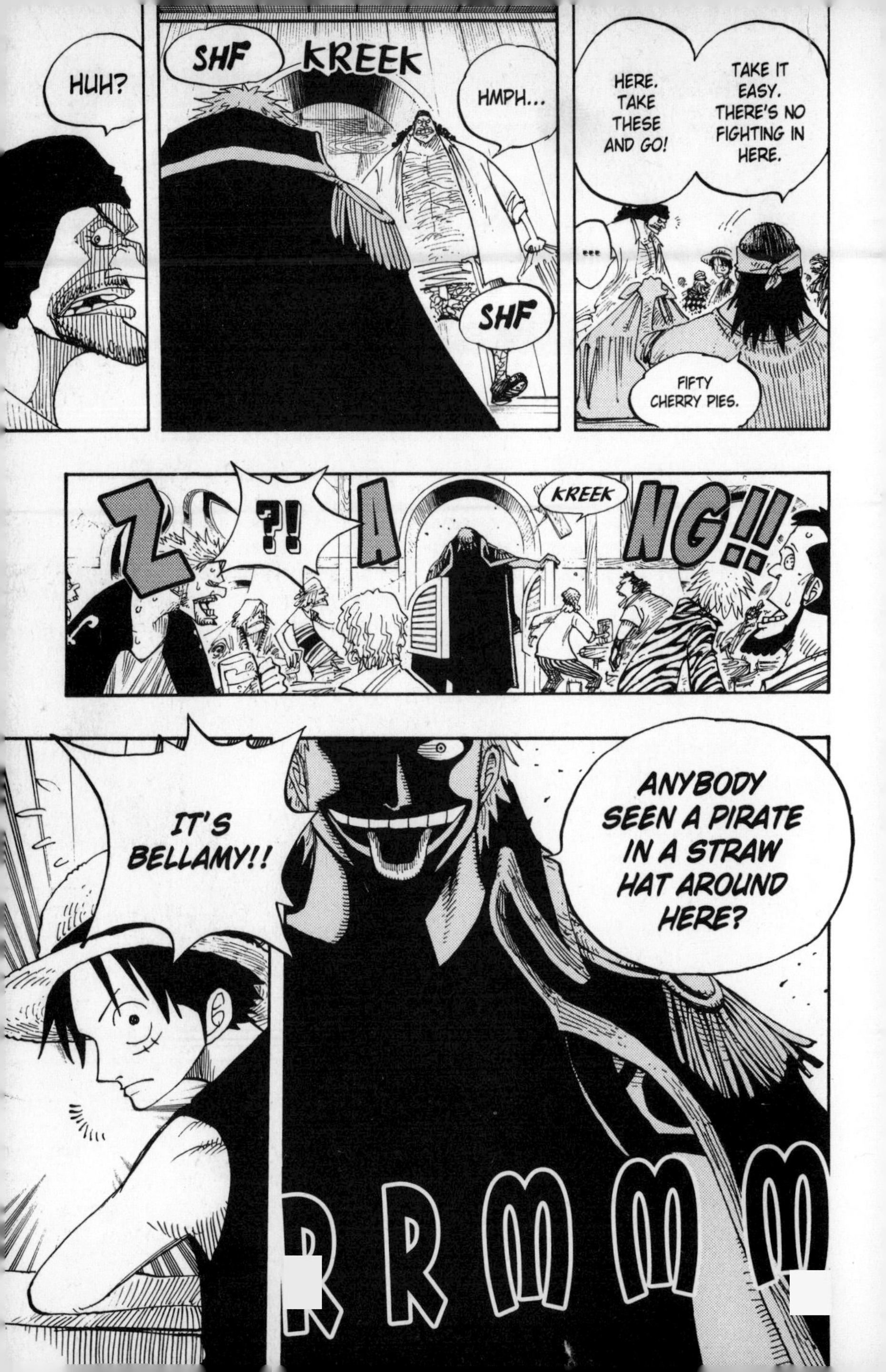
TAKE IT EASY. THERE'S NO FIGHTING IN HERE.
HERE. TAKE THESE AND GO!
...
FIFTY CHERRY PIES.
HMPH...
SHF
KREEK
SHF
HUH?
Z
?!
A
KREEK
NG!!
ANYBODY SEEN A PIRATE IN A STRAW HAT AROUND HERE?
IT'S BELLAMY!!
RRMMMM

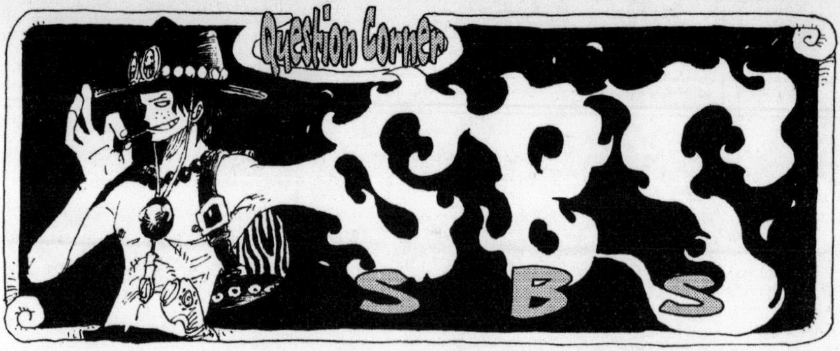
Question Corner
SBS

Q. Oda-chan! How are you? I have a question. ♡ In *One Piece* volume 18 (chapter 157) Luffy and the crew are hungry and crying for food. But just behind them is a tree full of tangerines. So why didn't they just eat them?

A. Tangerines... Yes, there are tangerines, but if they took a bite, it would mean instant death. Definitely certain death. A man can live without food for a week. He can be strong and live with hope for the future, or he can eat the tangerine and battle with the navigator. But that would be taking a big risk with his life... I'm sure if it were a life-or-death situation, she wouldn't be so mean as to let them die. (Shiver shiver)

Q. Oda Sensei!
Your phone is ringing.

--Souda ☆

A. Oh, let it ring. It's just my editor.

Q. Oda Sensei, may I ask you something? I want to send a letter to you personally, but I don't know your address. Can you give it to me?

A. My address? For a letter?
Oh, I do get letters...! (BONG!!)
Uh... I have two addresses. You can send your letter to the editorial department of Jump magazine, or you can send it to the special Question Corner mailbox Either way, I'll get it, rest assured.

FOR NON-JAPANESE READERS, YOU CAN SEND YOUR LETTERS TO THE *ONE PIECE* EDITOR AT VIZ MEDIA.

Chapter 224:
DO NOT DREAM

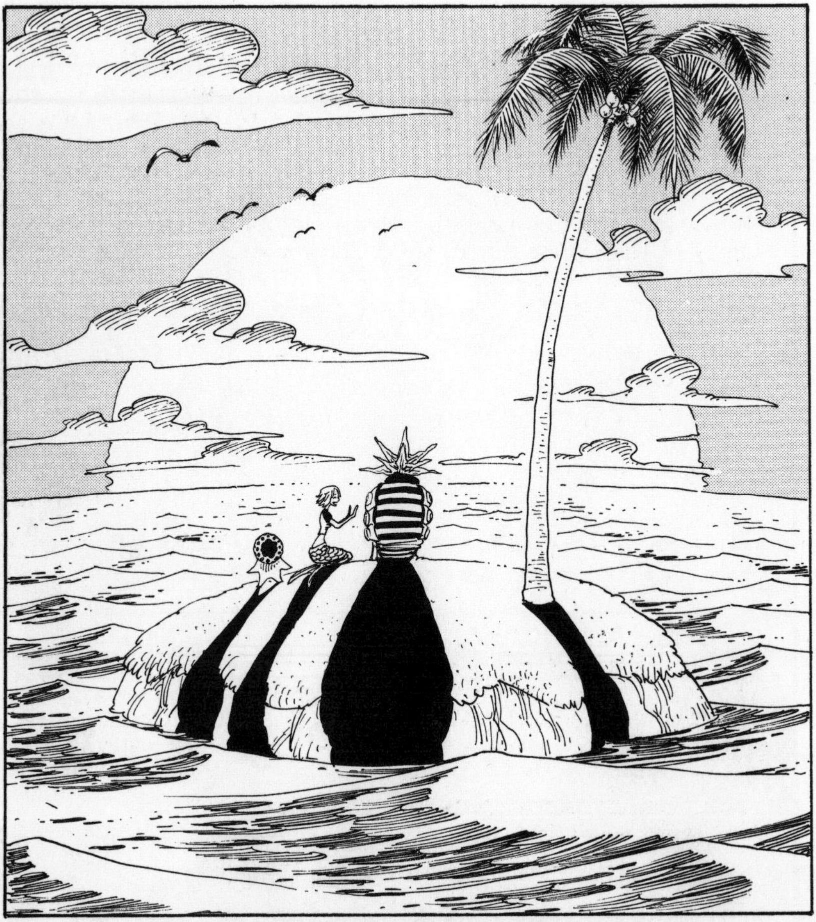

HACHI'S WALK ON THE SEAFLOOR, VOL. 37:
"HACHI AND THE SUNSET"

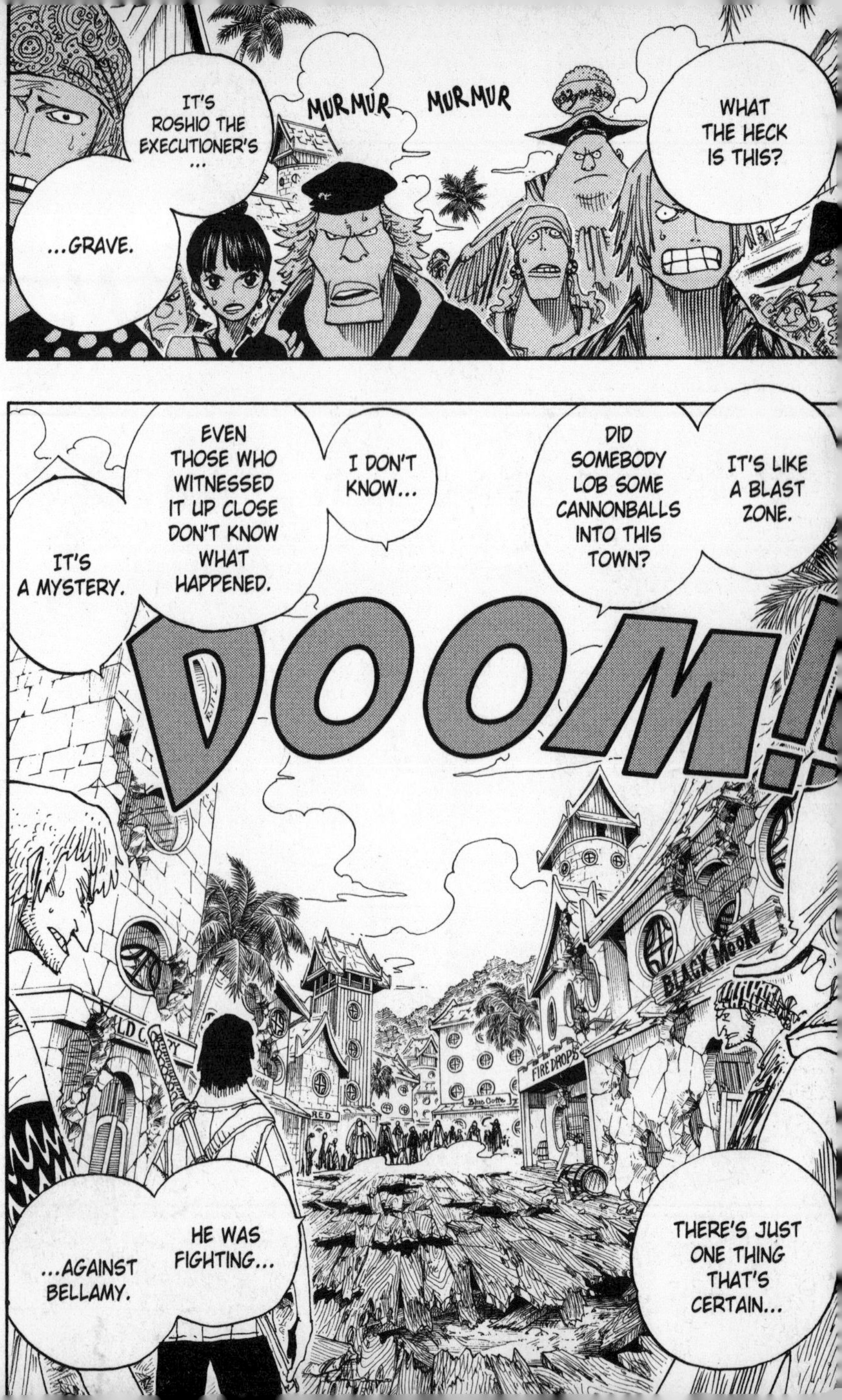
WHAT THE HECK IS THIS?
MURMUR MURMUR
IT'S ROSHIO THE EXECUTIONER'S ...
...GRAVE.
IT'S LIKE A BLAST ZONE.
DID SOMEBODY LOB SOME CANNONBALLS INTO THIS TOWN?
I DON'T KNOW...
EVEN THOSE WHO WITNESSED IT UP CLOSE DON'T KNOW WHAT HAPPENED.
IT'S A MYSTERY.
DOOM!!
BLACK MOON
FIRE DROPS
THERE'S JUST ONE THING THAT'S CERTAIN...
HE WAS FIGHTING...
...AGAINST BELLAMY.

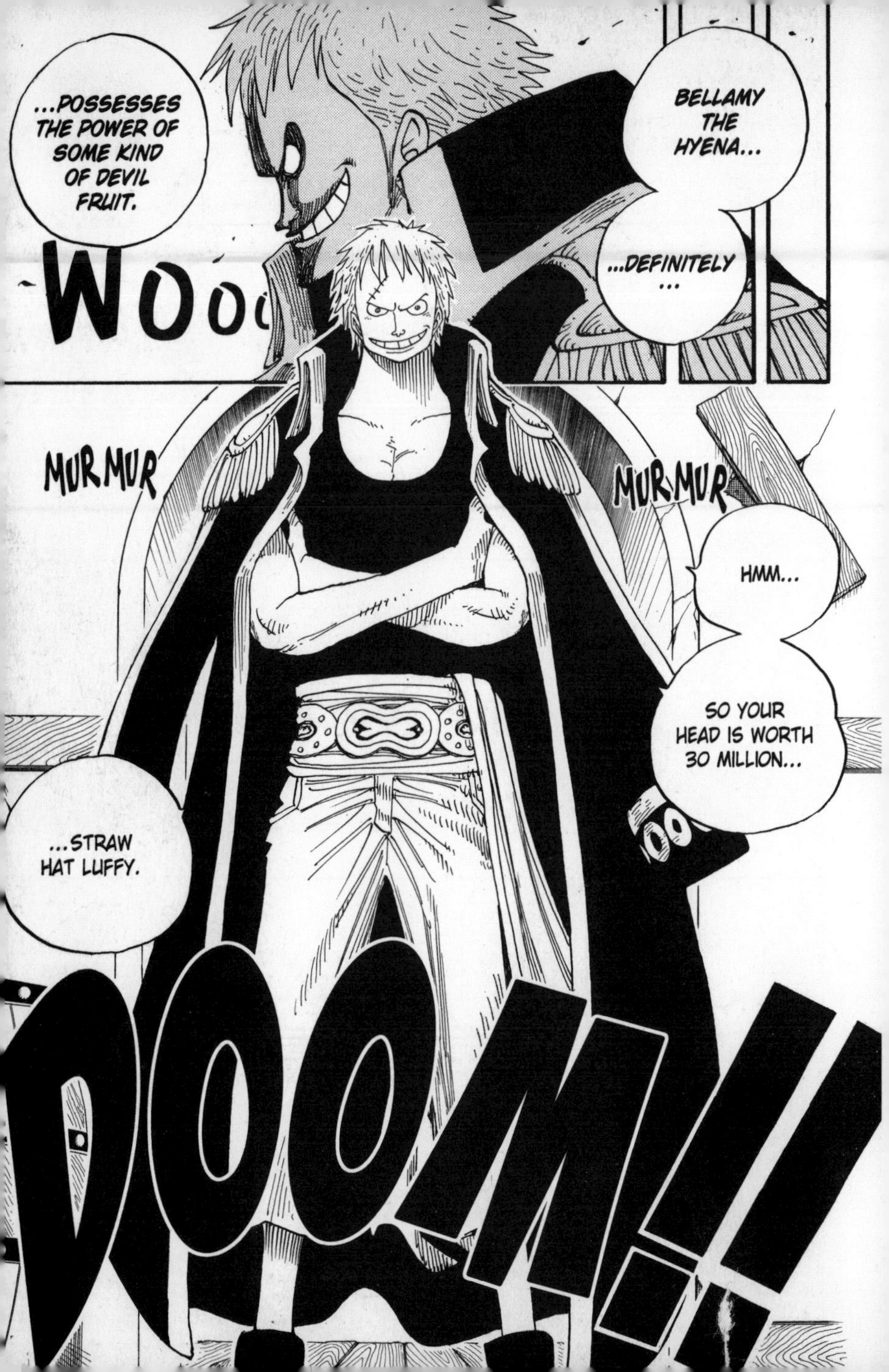
BELLAMY THE HYENA...
...DEFINITELY...
...POSSESSES THE POWER OF SOME KIND OF DEVIL FRUIT.
WOO
MUR MUR
MUR MUR
HMM...
SO YOUR HEAD IS WORTH 30 MILLION...
...STRAW HAT LUFFY.
DOOM!!

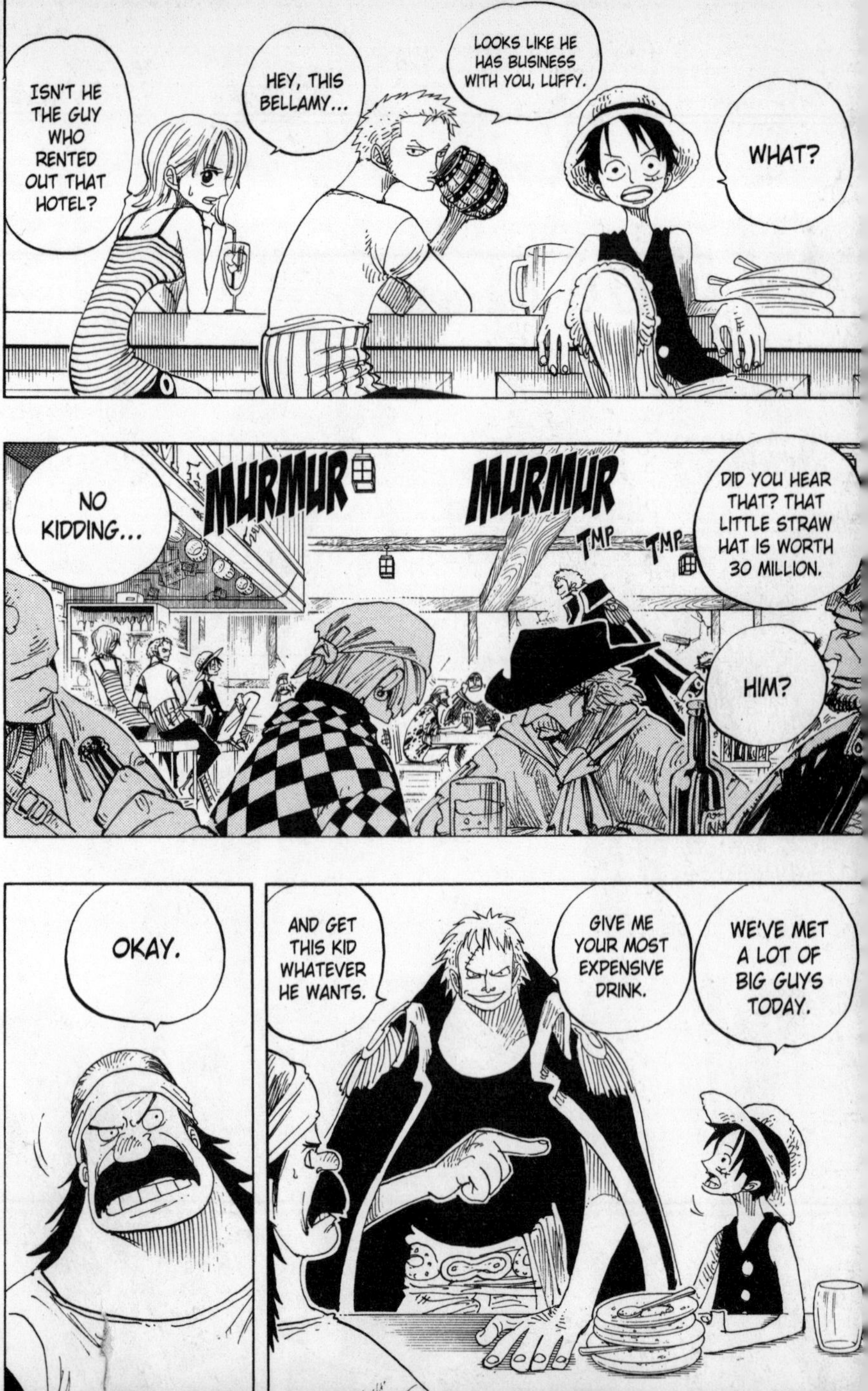
LOOKS LIKE HE HAS BUSINESS WITH YOU, LUFFY.
WHAT?
HEY, THIS BELLAMY...
ISN'T HE THE GUY WHO RENTED OUT THAT HOTEL?
DID YOU HEAR THAT? THAT LITTLE STRAW HAT IS WORTH 30 MILLION.
HIM?
TMP
TMP
MURMUR
MURMUR
NO KIDDING...
WE'VE MET A LOT OF BIG GUYS TODAY.
GIVE ME YOUR MOST EXPENSIVE DRINK.
AND GET THIS KID WHATEVER HE WANTS.
OKAY.

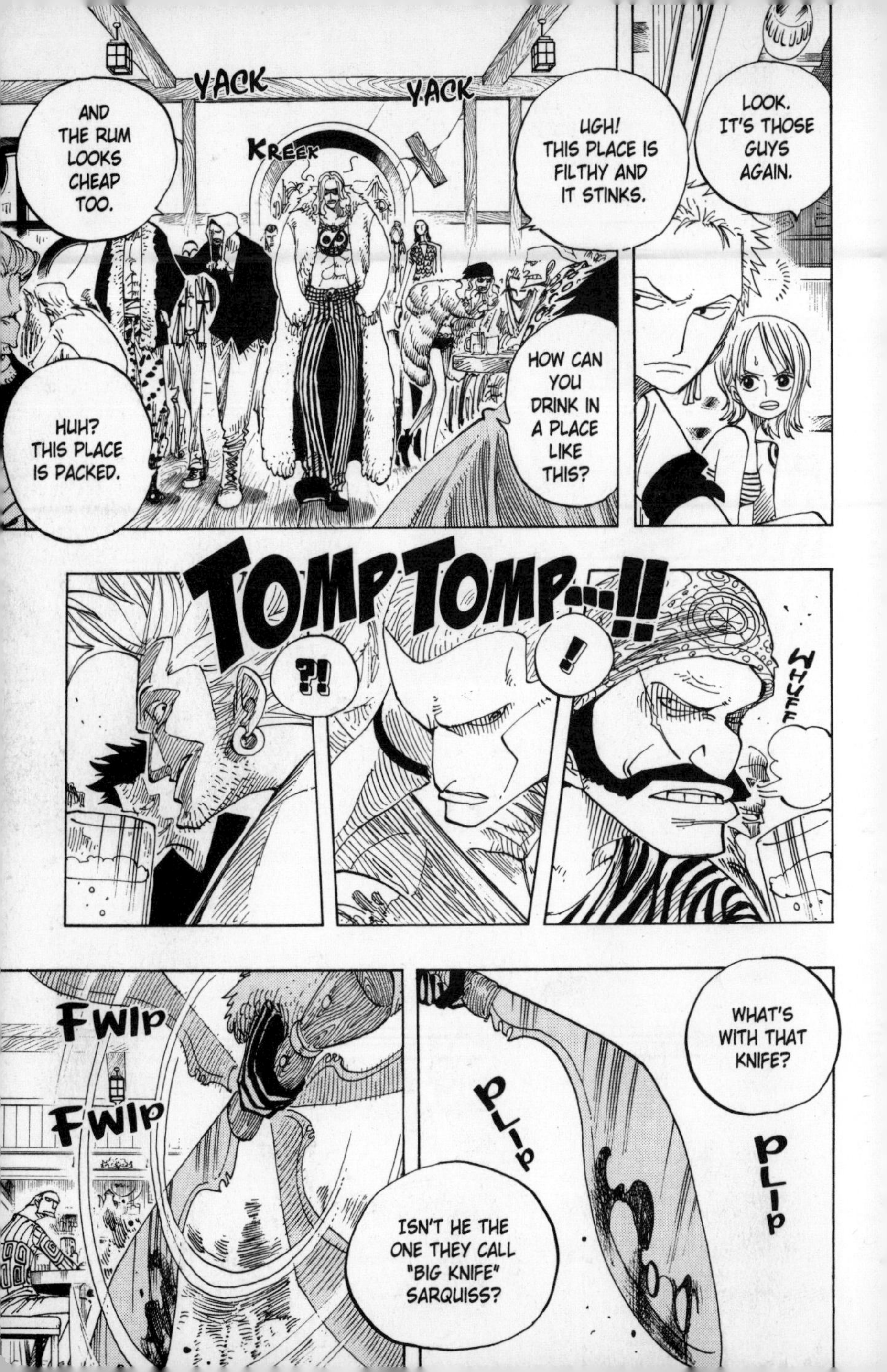

LOOK. IT'S THOSE GUYS AGAIN.
UGH! THIS PLACE IS FILTHY AND IT STINKS.
YACK
YACK
KREEK
AND THE RUM LOOKS CHEAP TOO.
HOW CAN YOU DRINK IN A PLACE LIKE THIS?
HUH? THIS PLACE IS PACKED.
TOMP TOMP...!!
WHUFF
!
?!
WHAT'S WITH THAT KNIFE?
PLIP
PLIP
ISN'T HE THE ONE THEY CALL "BIG KNIFE" SARQUISS?
FWIP
FWIP

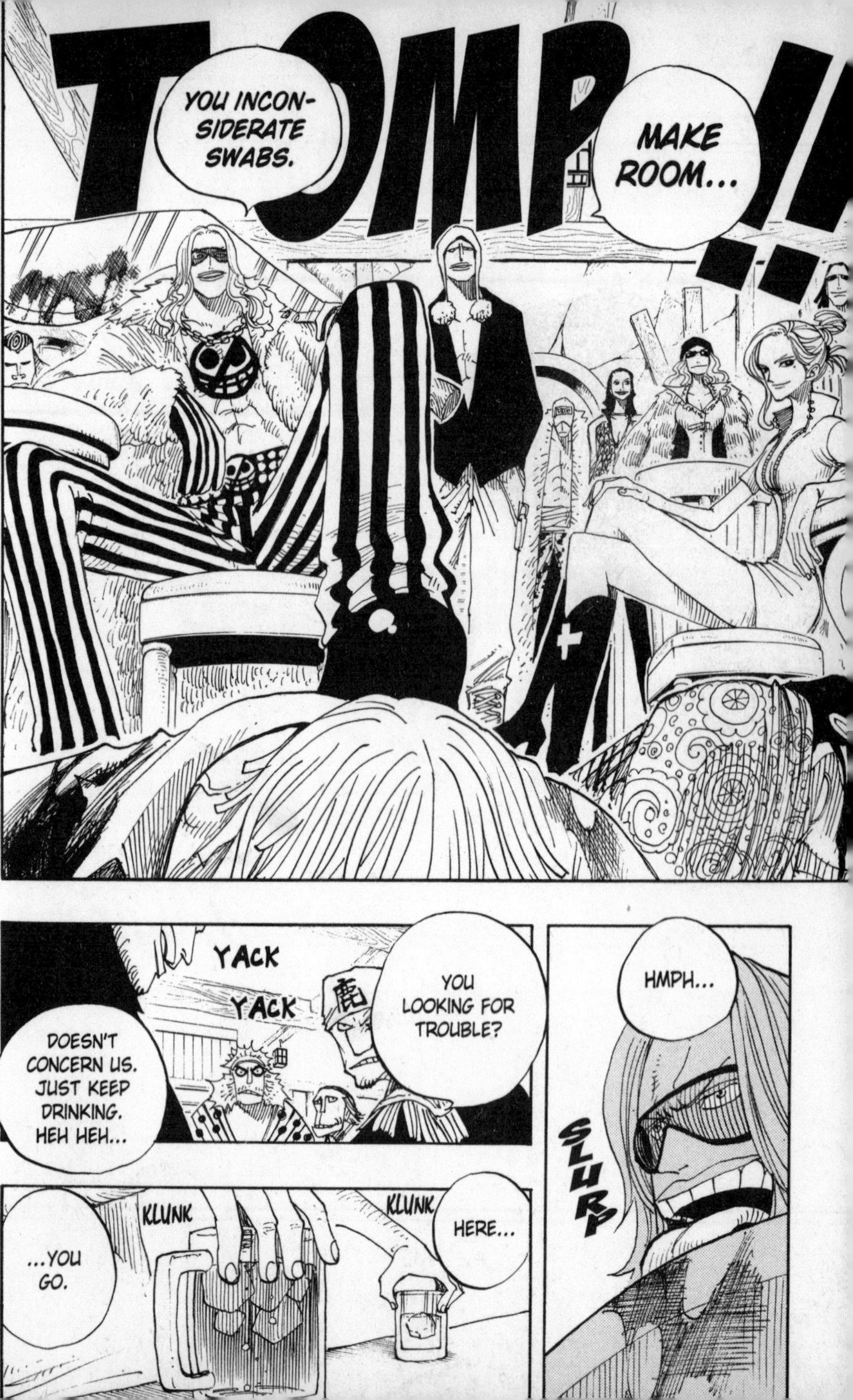
TOMP!!
MAKE ROOM...
YOU INCON-SIDERATE SWABS.
HMPH...
SLURP
YOU LOOKING FOR TROUBLE?
YACK
YACK
DOESN'T CONCERN US. JUST KEEP DRINKING. HEH HEH...
KLUNK
HERE...
KLUNK
...YOU GO.

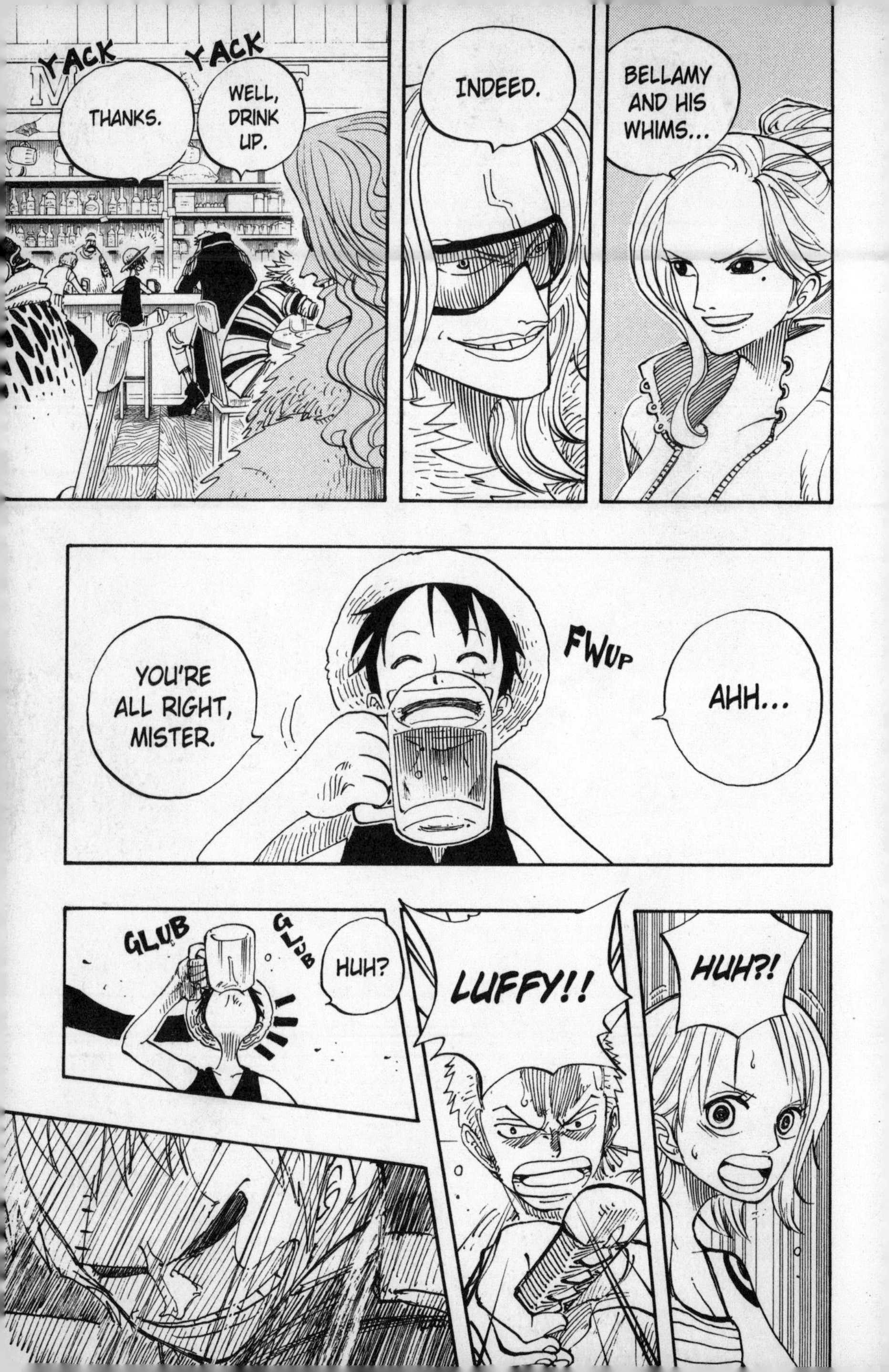
BELLAMY AND HIS WHIMS...
INDEED.
YACK
WELL, DRINK UP.
YACK
THANKS.
AHH...
FWUP
YOU'RE ALL RIGHT, MISTER.
HUH?!
LUFFY!!
HUH?
GLUB
GLUB

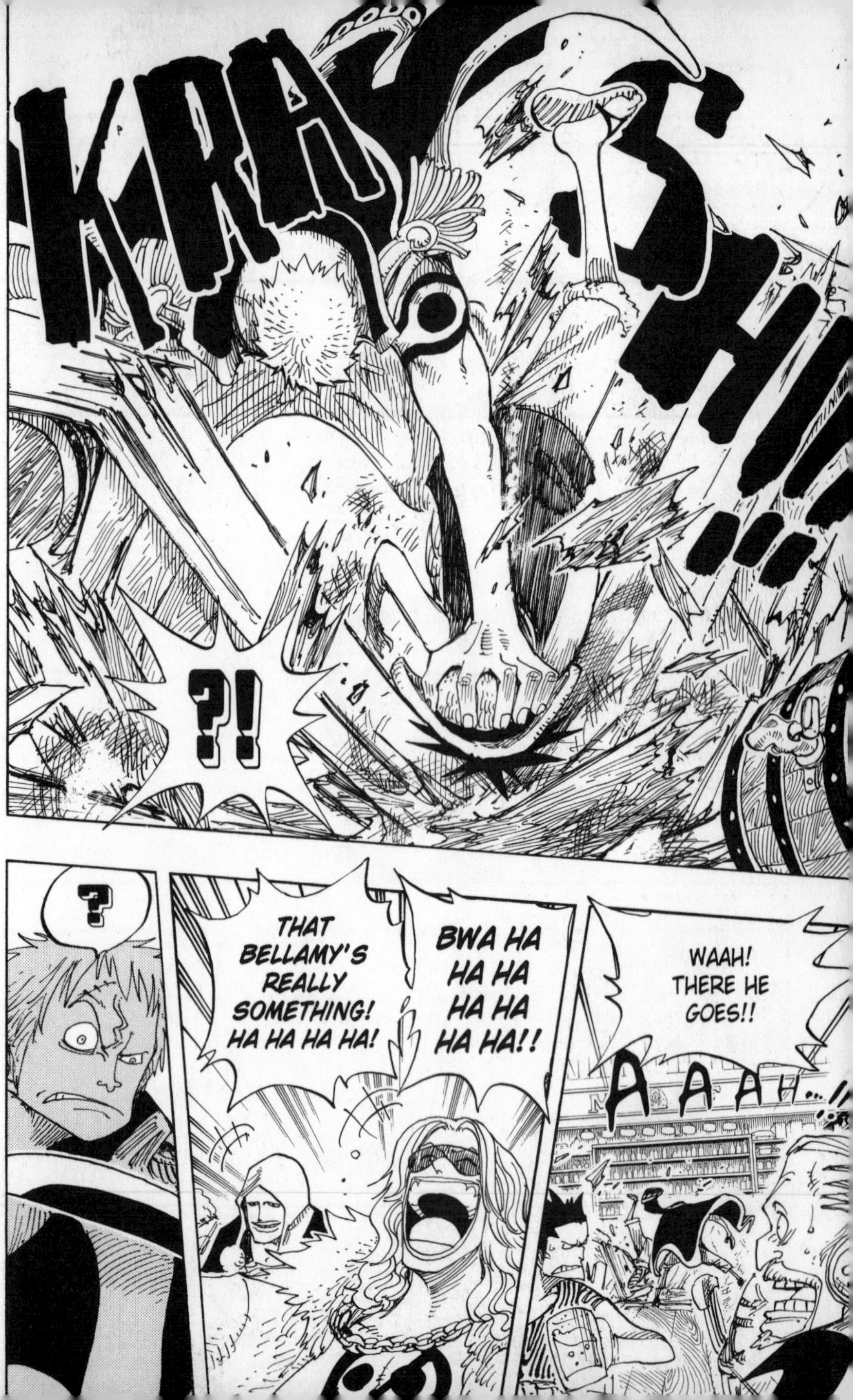
KRASH!!
?!
WAAH! THERE HE GOES!!
AAAH...!!
BWA HA HA HA HA HA HA HA!!
THAT BELLAMY'S REALLY SOMETHING! HA HA HA HA!
?

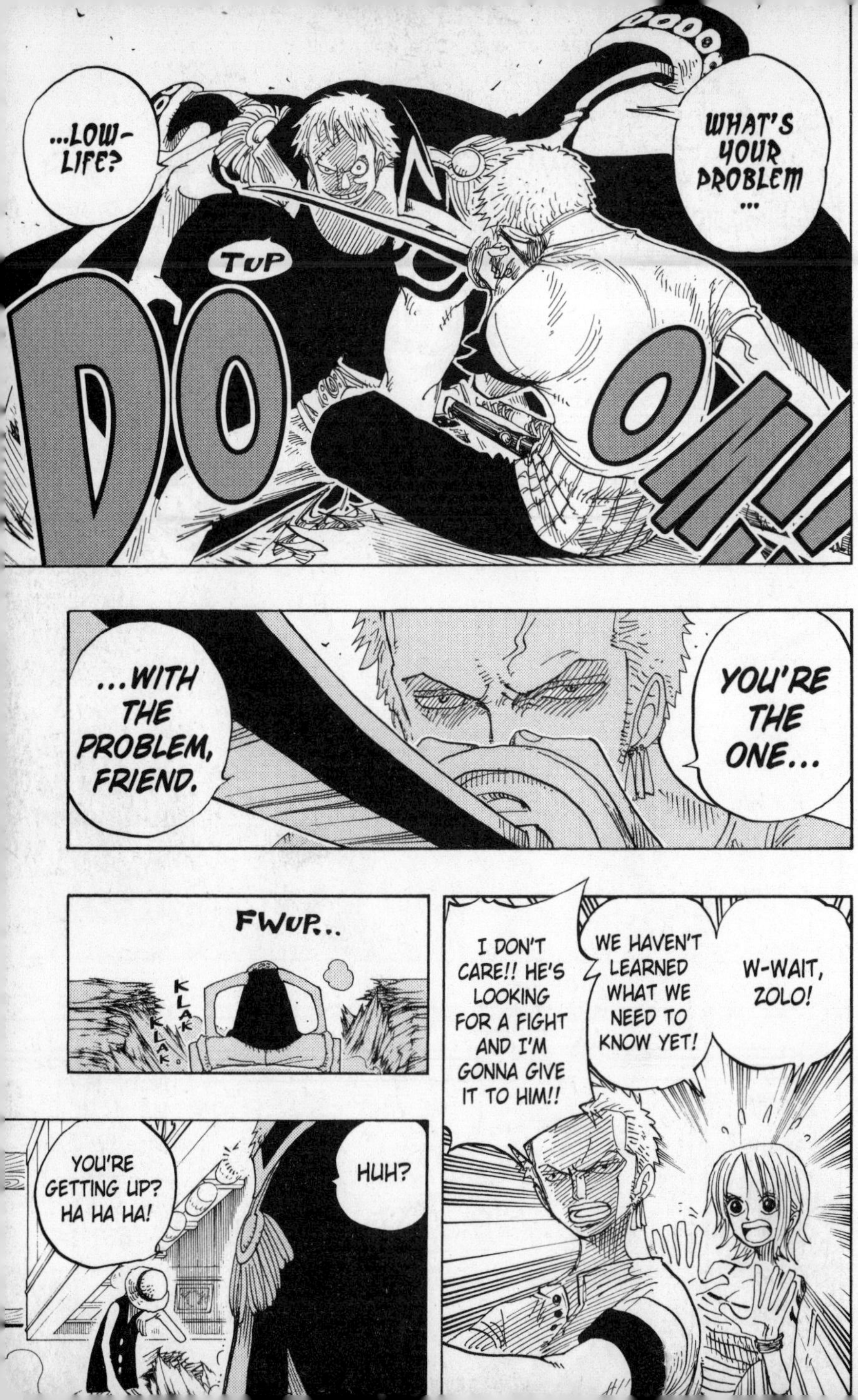
WHAT'S YOUR PROBLEM ...
...LOW-LIFE?
TUP
DO
ON
YOU'RE THE ONE...
...WITH THE PROBLEM, FRIEND.
W-WAIT, ZOLO!
WE HAVEN'T LEARNED WHAT WE NEED TO KNOW YET!
I DON'T CARE!! HE'S LOOKING FOR A FIGHT AND I'M GONNA GIVE IT TO HIM!!
FWUP...
KLAK
KLAK
HUH?
YOU'RE GETTING UP? HA HA HA!

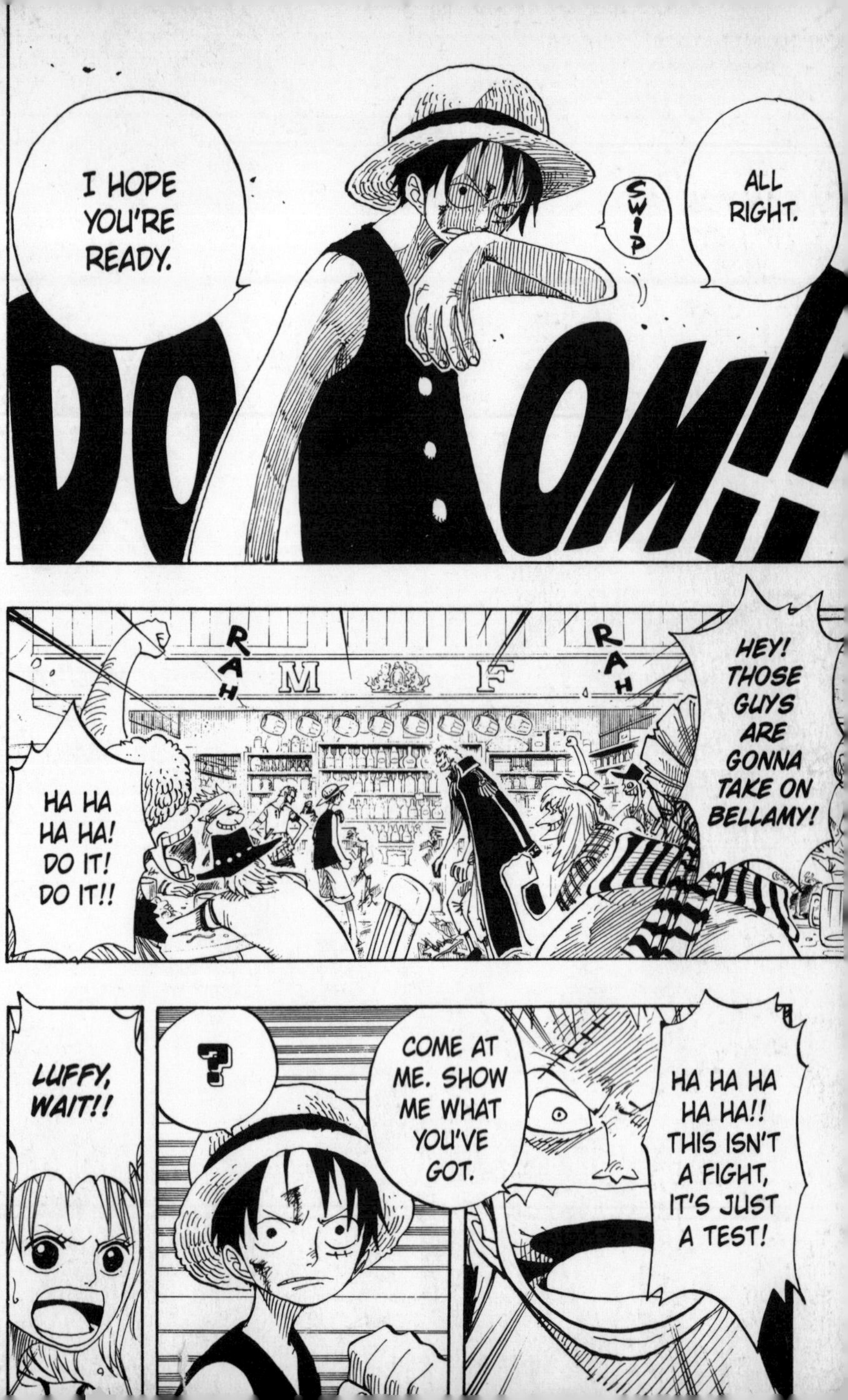
ALL RIGHT.
SWIP
I HOPE YOU'RE READY.
DO OM!!
HEY! THOSE GUYS ARE GONNA TAKE ON BELLAMY!
RAH
RAH
HA HA HA HA! DO IT! DO IT!!
HA HA HA HA HA!! THIS ISN'T A FIGHT, IT'S JUST A TEST!
COME AT ME. SHOW ME WHAT YOU'VE GOT.
?
LUFFY, WAIT!!

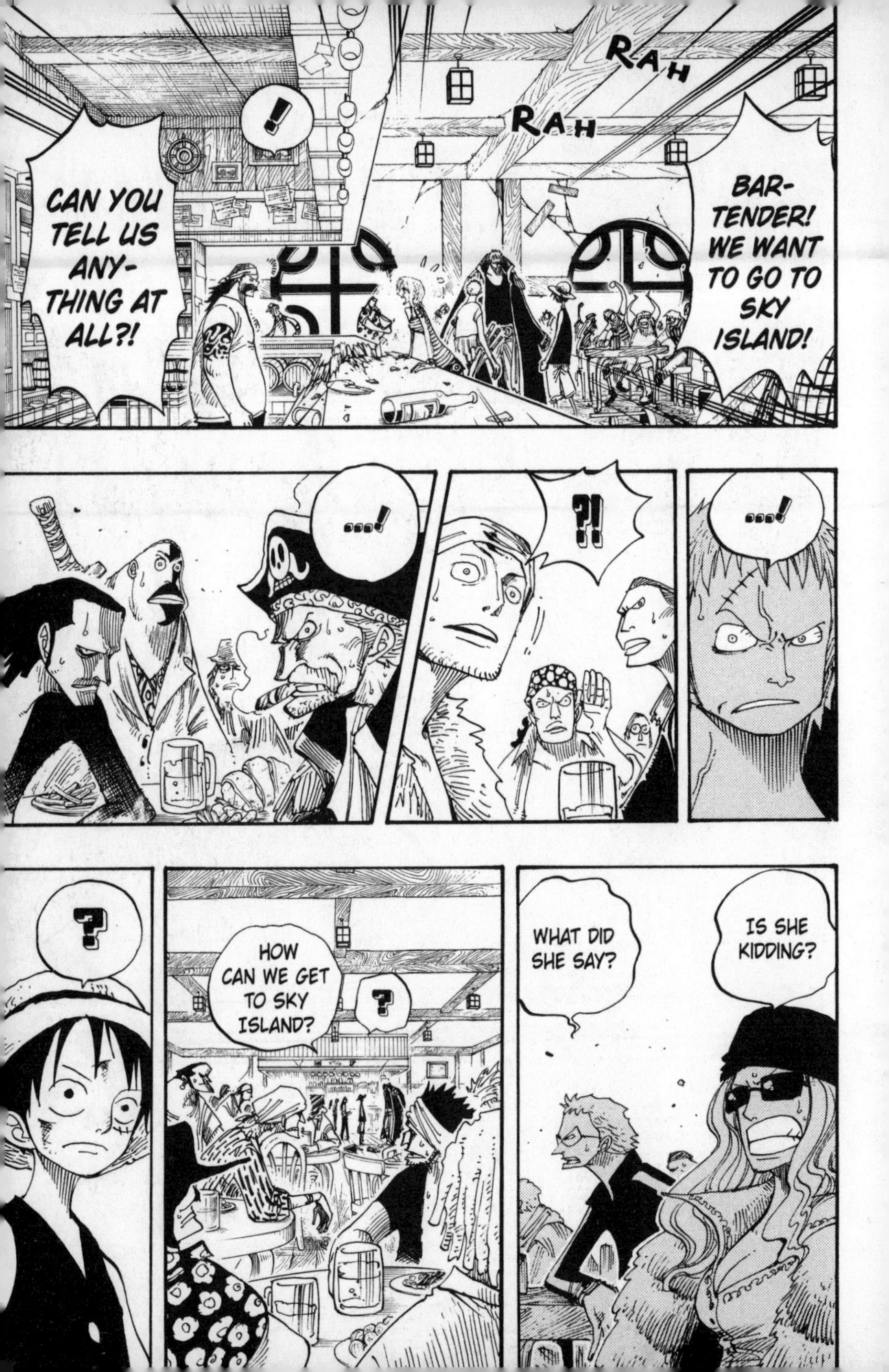
BAR-TENDER! WE WANT TO GO TO SKY ISLAND!
RAH
RAH
!
CAN YOU TELL US ANY-THING AT ALL?!
...!
?!
...!
IS SHE KIDDING?
WHAT DID SHE SAY?
HOW CAN WE GET TO SKY ISLAND?
?
?

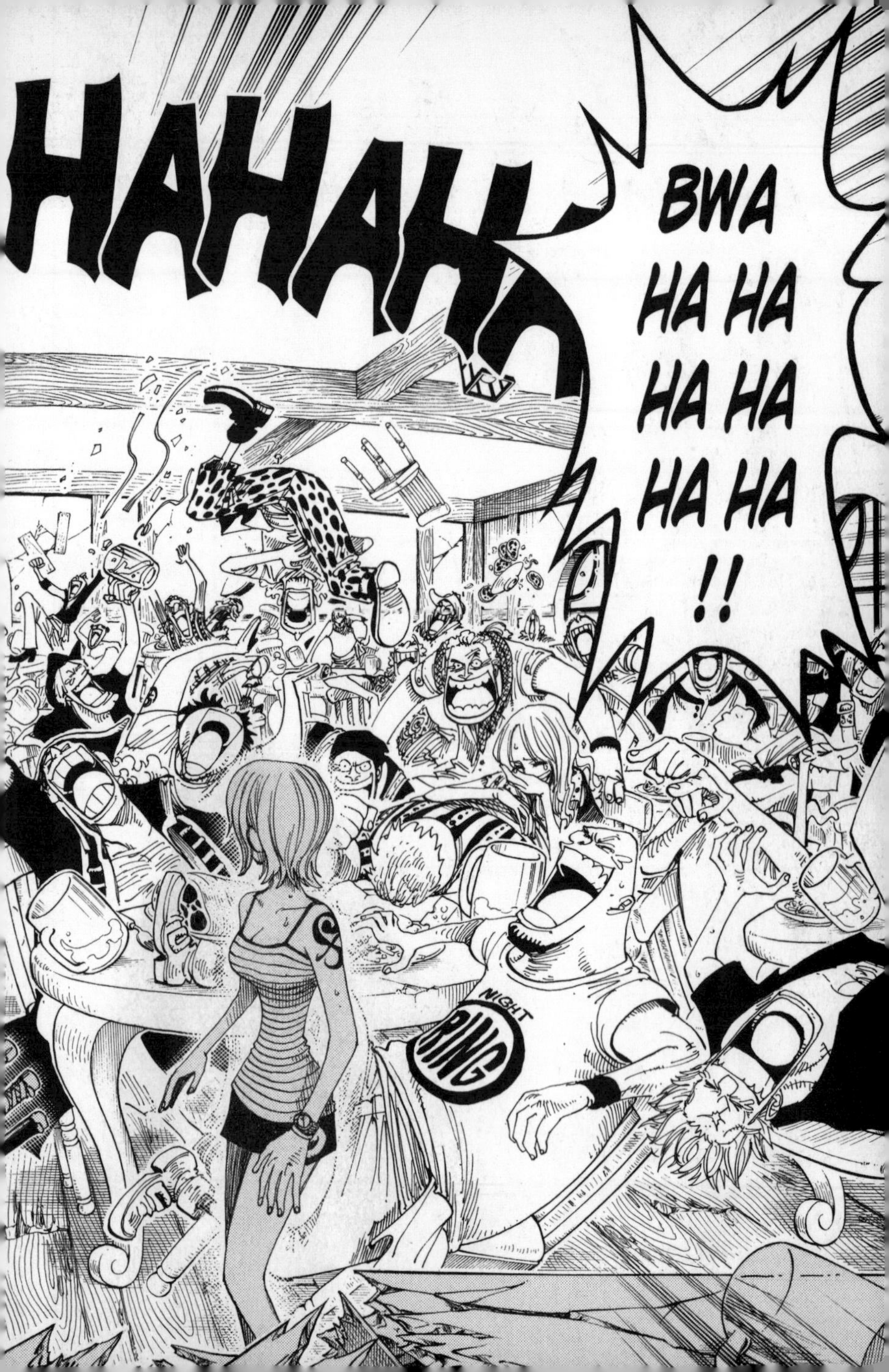
BWA HA HA HA HA HA HA!!
HAHAH
NIGHT
RING

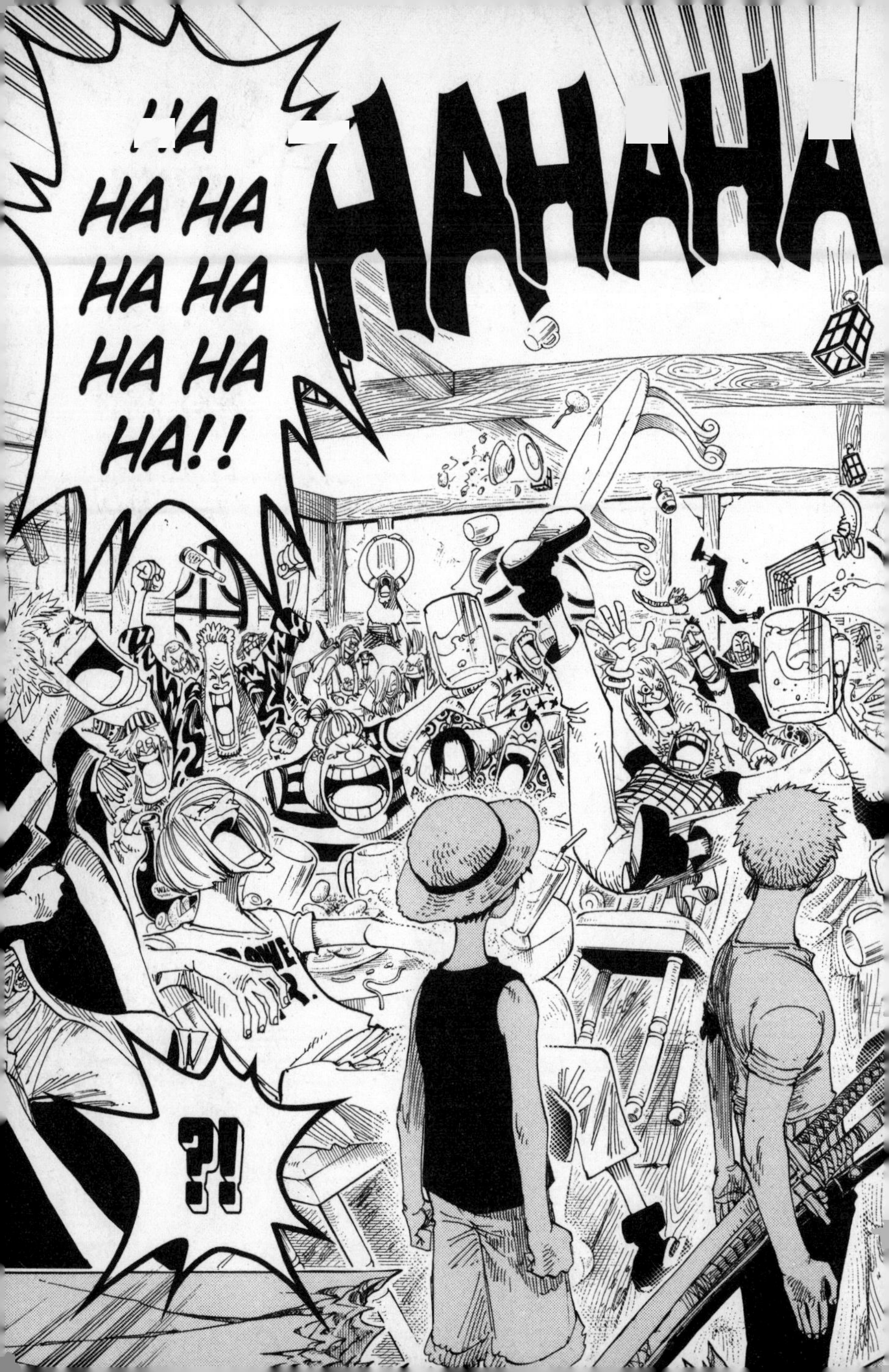
HAHAHA
HA HA HA HA HA HA HA HA HA!!
?!

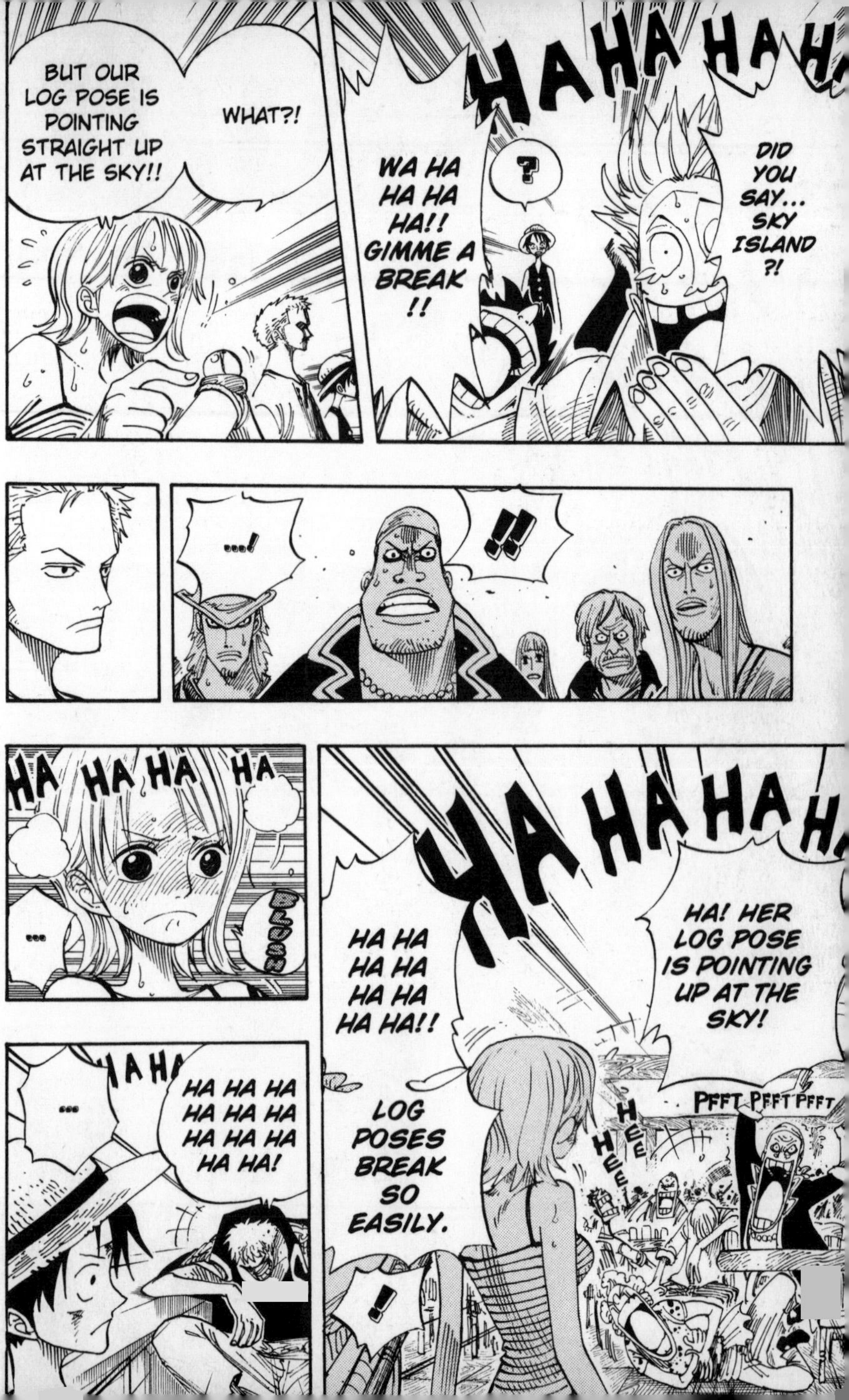
HA HA HA HA HA!
DID YOU SAY... SKY ISLAND?!
?
WA HA HA HA HA!! GIMME A BREAK!!
WHAT?!
BUT OUR LOG POSE IS POINTING STRAIGHT UP AT THE SKY!!
!!
...!
HA HA HA HA HA
HA! HER LOG POSE IS POINTING UP AT THE SKY!
HA HA HA HA HA HA HA HA!!
PFFT PFFT PFFT
HEE HEE!
LOG POSES BREAK SO EASILY.
!
HA HA HA HA
BLUSH
...
HA HA HA HA HA HA HA HA HA HA HA!
HA HA
...

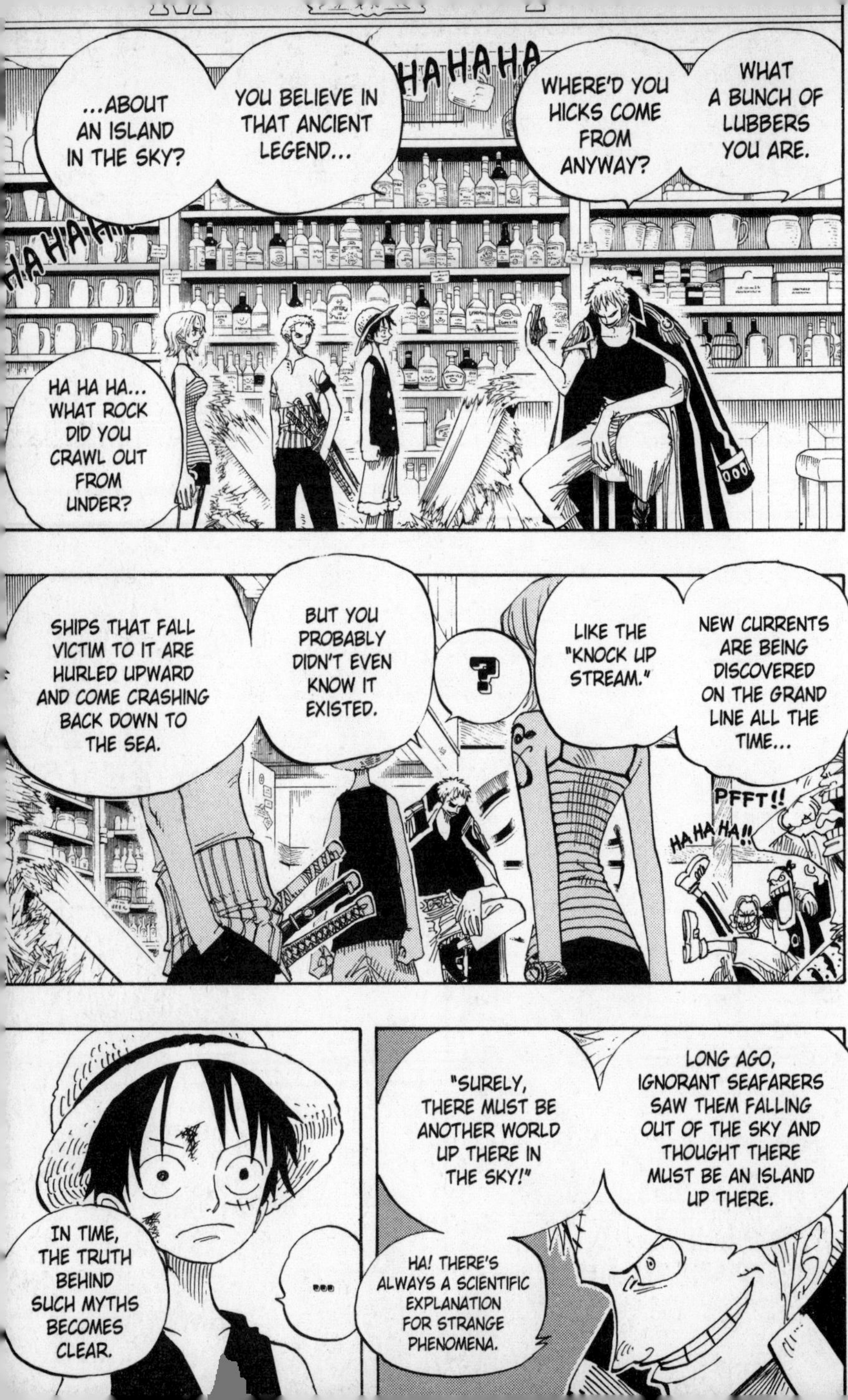
WHAT A BUNCH OF LUBBERS YOU ARE.
WHERE'D YOU HICKS COME FROM ANYWAY?
HAHAHA
YOU BELIEVE IN THAT ANCIENT LEGEND...
...ABOUT AN ISLAND IN THE SKY?
HAHAHA
HA HA HA... WHAT ROCK DID YOU CRAWL OUT FROM UNDER?
NEW CURRENTS ARE BEING DISCOVERED ON THE GRAND LINE ALL THE TIME...
LIKE THE "KNOCK UP STREAM."
?
BUT YOU PROBABLY DIDN'T EVEN KNOW IT EXISTED.
SHIPS THAT FALL VICTIM TO IT ARE HURLED UPWARD AND COME CRASHING BACK DOWN TO THE SEA.
PFFT!!
HA HA HA!!
LONG AGO, IGNORANT SEAFARERS SAW THEM FALLING OUT OF THE SKY AND THOUGHT THERE MUST BE AN ISLAND UP THERE.
"SURELY, THERE MUST BE ANOTHER WORLD UP THERE IN THE SKY!"
HA! THERE'S ALWAYS A SCIENTIFIC EXPLANATION FOR STRANGE PHENOMENA.
...
IN TIME, THE TRUTH BEHIND SUCH MYTHS BECOMES CLEAR.

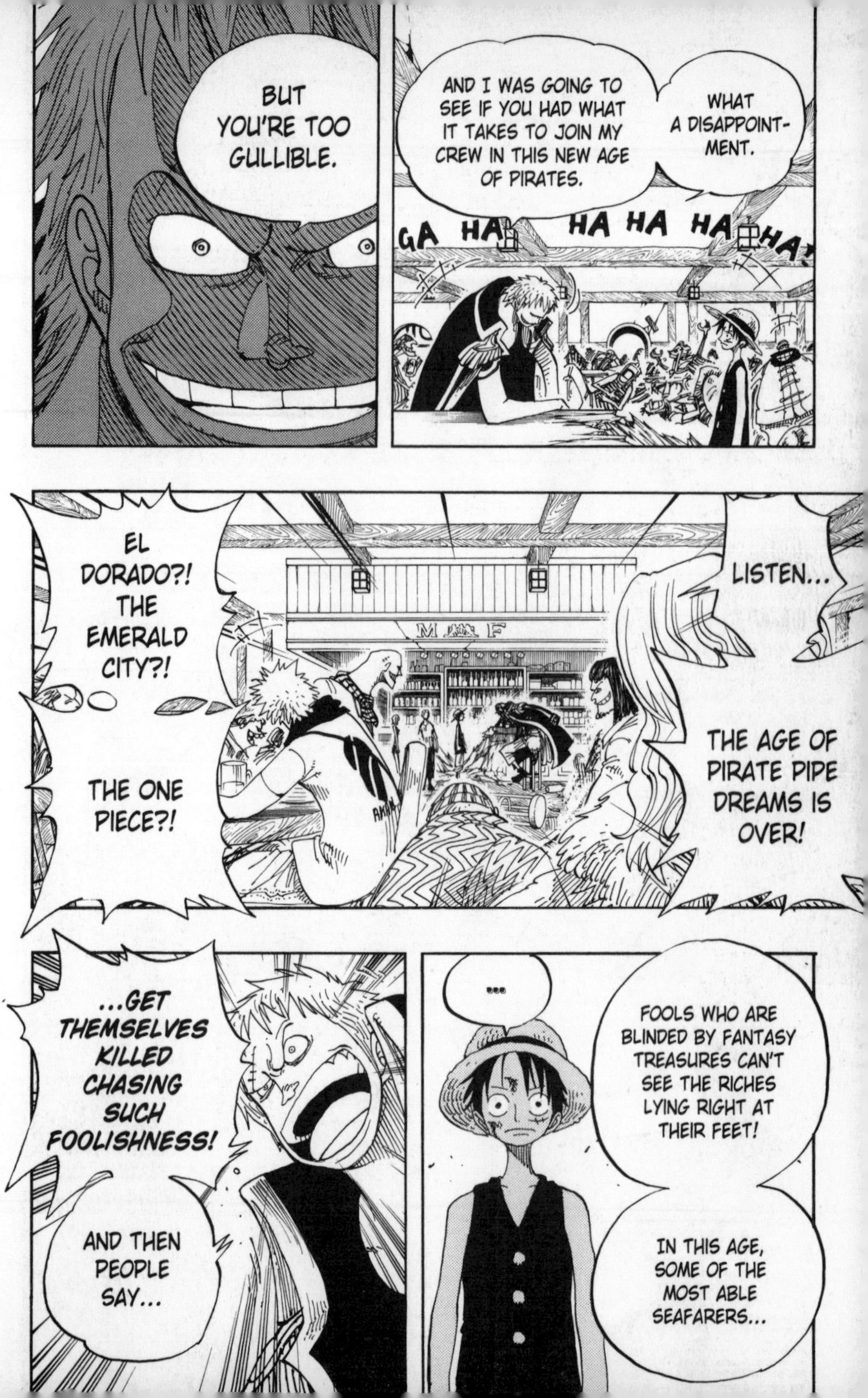
WHAT A DISAPPOINTMENT.
AND I WAS GOING TO SEE IF YOU HAD WHAT IT TAKES TO JOIN MY CREW IN THIS NEW AGE OF PIRATES.
GA HA HA HA HA HA HA
BUT YOU'RE TOO GULLIBLE.
LISTEN...
THE AGE OF PIRATE PIPE DREAMS IS OVER!
EL DORADO?! THE EMERALD CITY?!
THE ONE PIECE?!
...
FOOLS WHO ARE BLINDED BY FANTASY TREASURES CAN'T SEE THE RICHES LYING RIGHT AT THEIR FEET!
IN THIS AGE, SOME OF THE MOST ABLE SEAFARERS...
...GET THEMSELVES KILLED CHASING SUCH FOOLISHNESS!
AND THEN PEOPLE SAY...

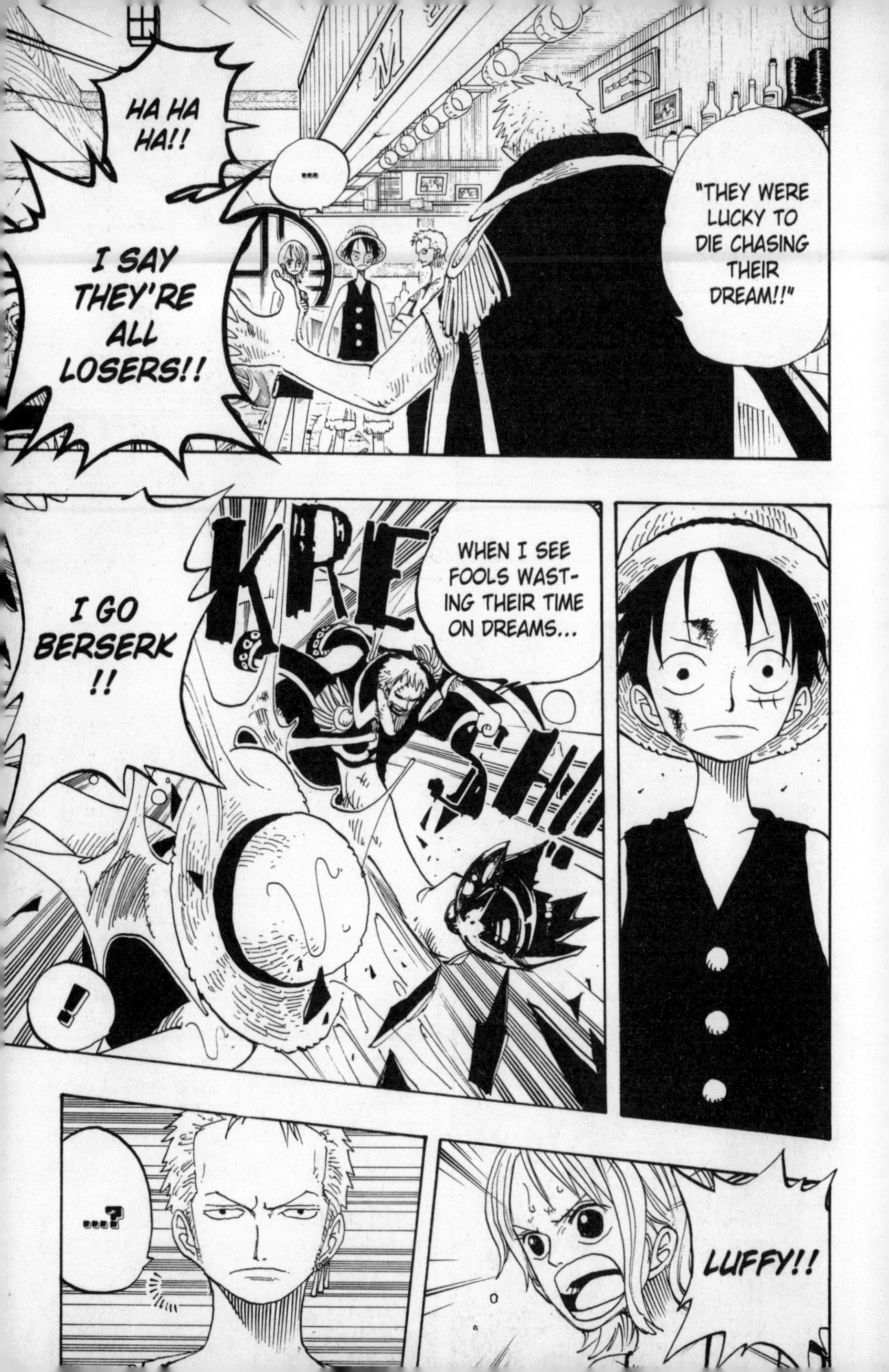

"THEY WERE LUCKY TO DIE CHASING THEIR DREAM!!"
HA HA HA!!
...
I SAY THEY'RE ALL LOSERS!!
WHEN I SEE FOOLS WASTING THEIR TIME ON DREAMS...
I GO BERSERK!!
KRESH!!
!
LUFFY!!
...?

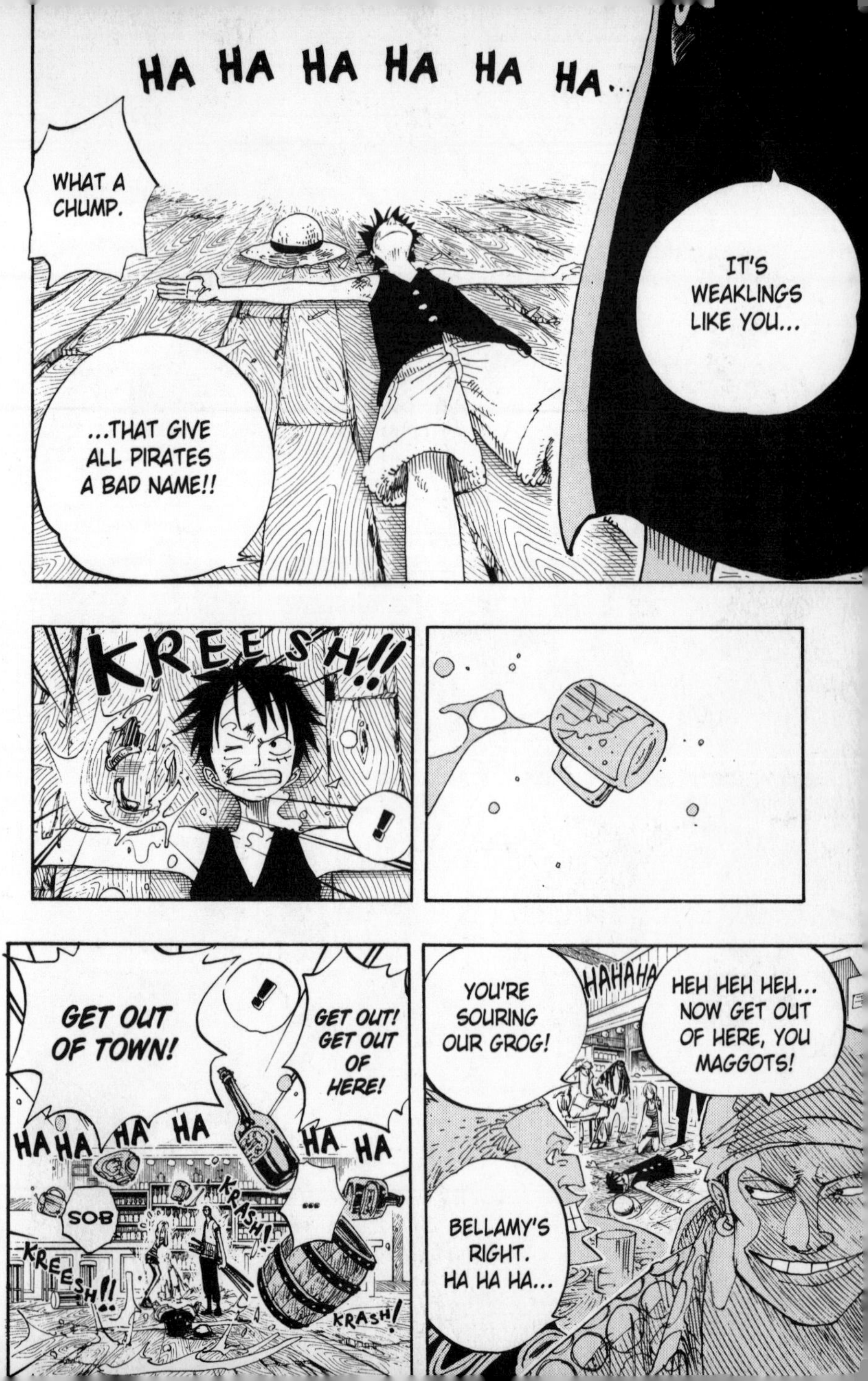
HA HA HA HA HA HA...
IT'S WEAKLINGS LIKE YOU...
WHAT A CHUMP.
...THAT GIVE ALL PIRATES A BAD NAME!!
KREESH!!
!
HEH HEH HEH... NOW GET OUT OF HERE, YOU MAGGOTS!
HAHAHA
YOU'RE SOURING OUR GROG!
BELLAMY'S RIGHT. HA HA HA...
!
GET OUT! GET OUT OF HERE!
GET OUT OF TOWN!
HA HA
HA HA HA HA HA HA
...
KRASH!
SOB
KREESH!!
KRASH!

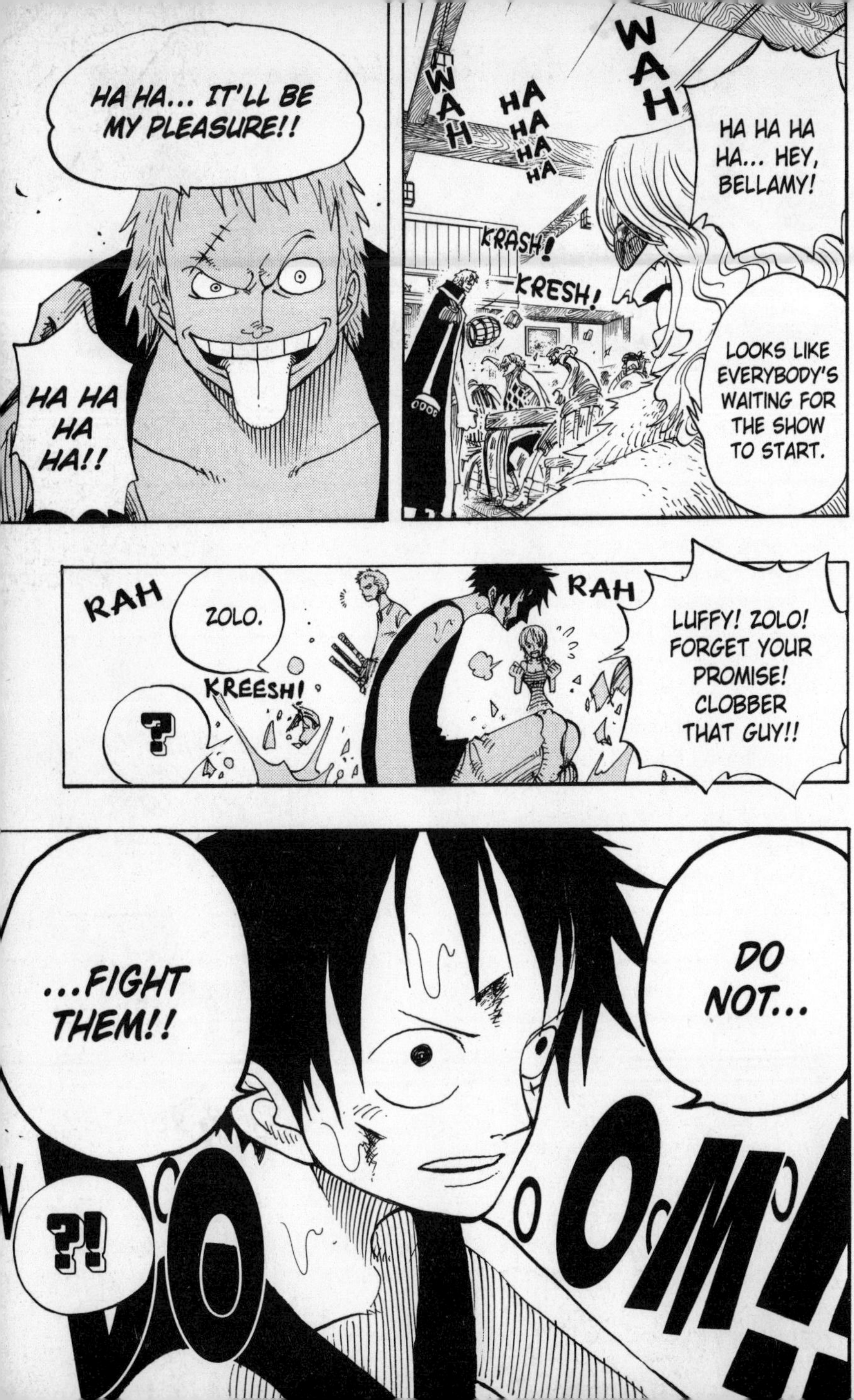
WAH
WAH
HA HA HA HA HA
HA HA HA HA... HEY, BELLAMY!
LOOKS LIKE EVERYBODY'S WAITING FOR THE SHOW TO START.
KRASH!
KRESH!
HA HA... IT'LL BE MY PLEASURE!!
HA HA HA HA!!
LUFFY! ZOLO! FORGET YOUR PROMISE! CLOBBER THAT GUY!!
RAH
ZOLO.
RAH
KREESH!
?
DO NOT...
...FIGHT THEM!!
?!

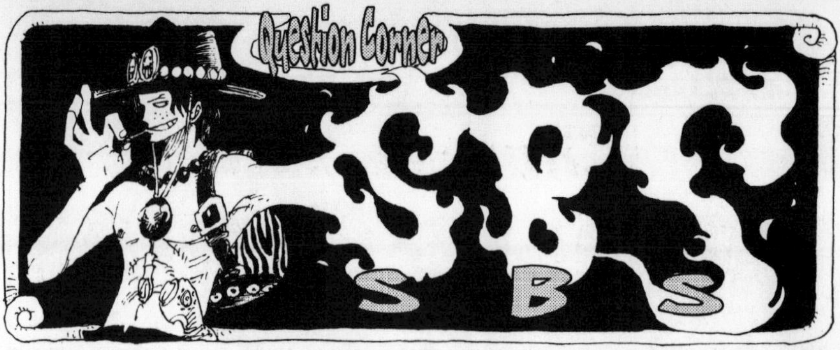
Question Corner
SBS

Q : When Ms. Doublefinger uses her Spike-Spike Fruit powers, how come it doesn't rip her clothing to pieces?

A : What? Are you suggesting she shred her outfit with her spikes? Sorry, but this isn't that kind of manga! And if I were to draw that, you know I'd put it on the cover. Can you imagine how embarrassed people would be if they saw something like that on the cover?! Should I do it?!

Q : Hello. I'm Sam's daughter. Oda Sensei! I have a complaint! In volume 23, when Django and Fullbody bring flowers to Hina, don't you think Django's flowers looked a bit shabby? But you took the time to make Fullbody's flowers look like roses! What's going on?!

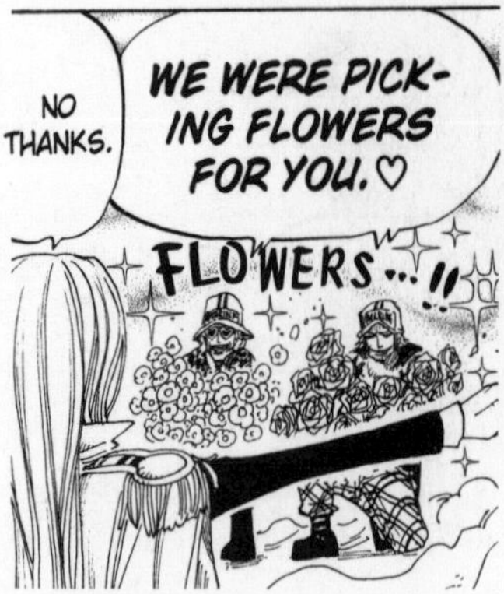
WE WERE PICK-ING FLOWERS FOR YOU. ♡
NO THANKS.
FLOWERS...!!

A : Don't nitpick! I put equal (minimal) effort into both of those bouquets! (Ta dah!) All right, let me show you an easy way to draw a rose.

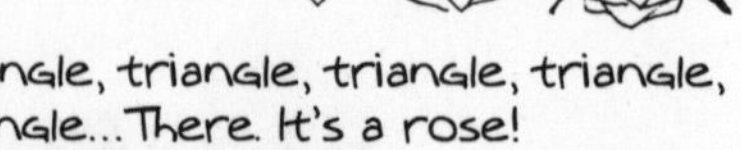

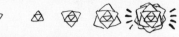

Triangle, triangle, triangle, triangle, triangle... There. It's a rose!

Q : Oda Sensei, you're very mischievous, aren't you? You like to draw things like Panda Man a lot. Then let me have a little fun too. The Question Corner is over! Nyah!

A : It...It ended. See you in the next volume.

Chapter 225:
PEOPLE'S DREAMS

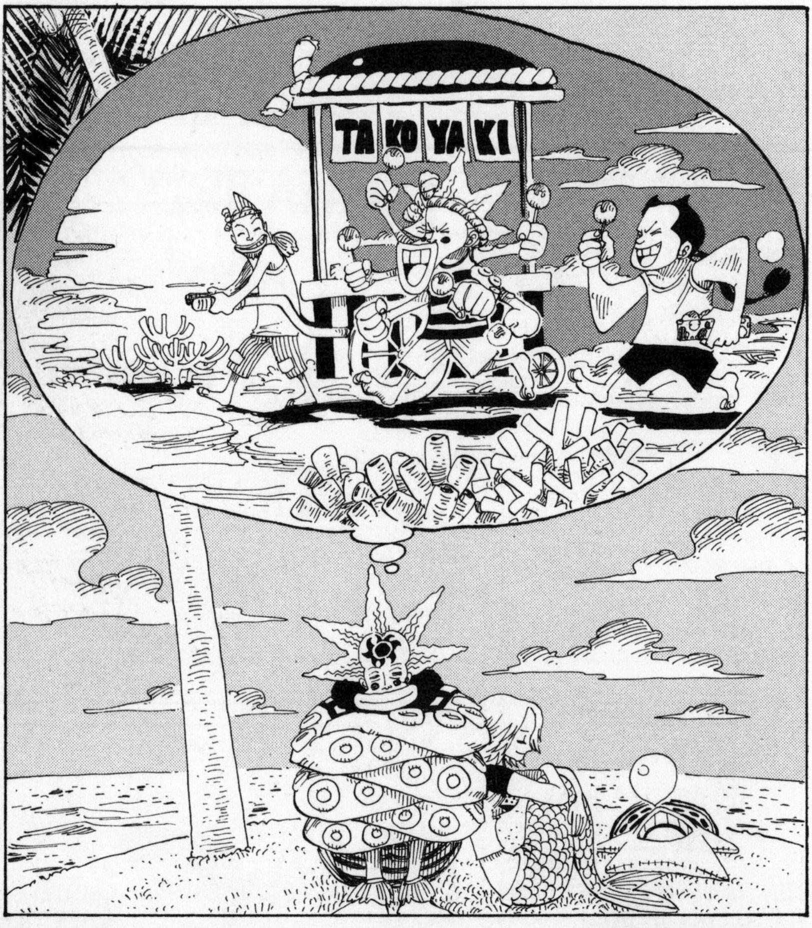
TAKOYAKI

HACHI'S WALK ON THE SEAFLOOR, VOL. 38:
"SUNSET DREAMING—REMEMBERING A CHILDHOOD DREAM TO HAVE AN OCTOPUS FRITTER CART"

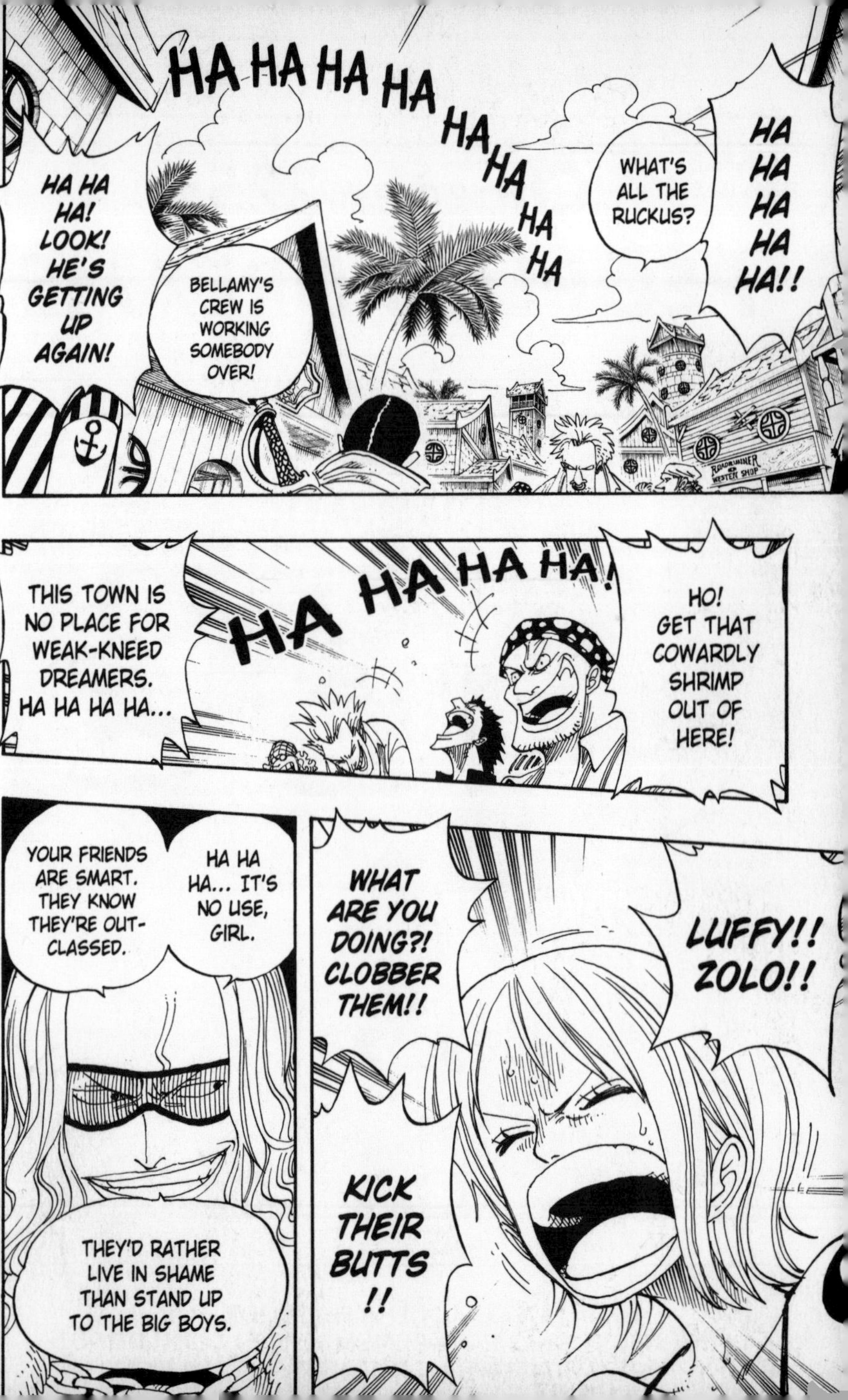

HA HA HA HA HA!!
WHAT'S ALL THE RUCKUS?
HA HA HA HA HA HA HA HA HA
BELLAMY'S CREW IS WORKING SOMEBODY OVER!
HA HA HA! LOOK! HE'S GETTING UP AGAIN!
HO! GET THAT COWARDLY SHRIMP OUT OF HERE!
HA HA HA HA!
THIS TOWN IS NO PLACE FOR WEAK-KNEED DREAMERS. HA HA HA HA...
LUFFY!! ZOLO!!
WHAT ARE YOU DOING?! CLOBBER THEM!!
KICK THEIR BUTTS !!
HA HA HA... IT'S NO USE, GIRL.
YOUR FRIENDS ARE SMART. THEY KNOW THEY'RE OUT-CLASSED.
THEY'D RATHER LIVE IN SHAME THAN STAND UP TO THE BIG BOYS.

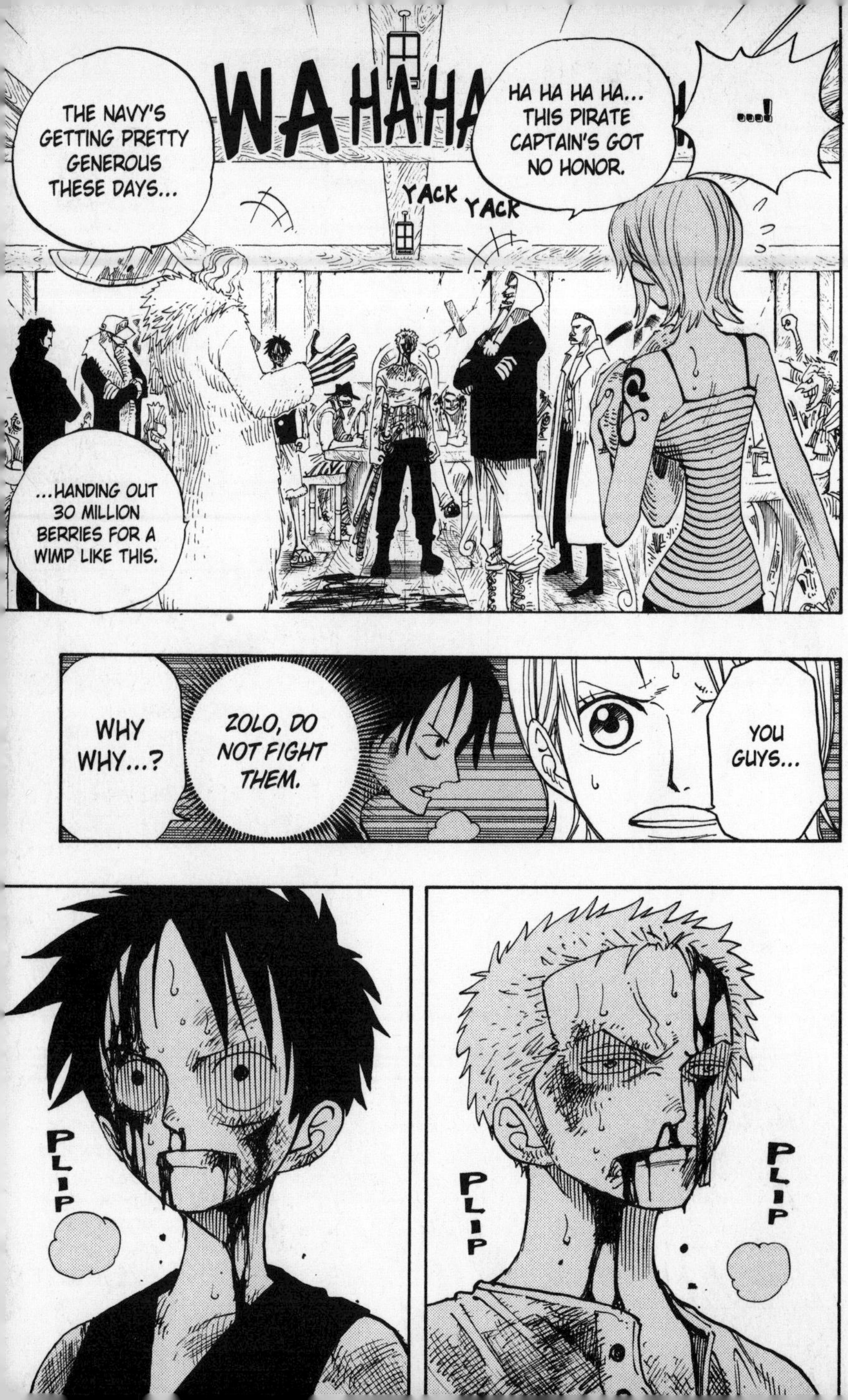
...!
HA HA HA HA... THIS PIRATE CAPTAIN'S GOT NO HONOR.
WA HAHA
YACK YACK
THE NAVY'S GETTING PRETTY GENEROUS THESE DAYS...
...HANDING OUT 30 MILLION BERRIES FOR A WIMP LIKE THIS.
YOU GUYS...
ZOLO, DO NOT FIGHT THEM.
WHY WHY...?
PLIP
PLIP
PLIP

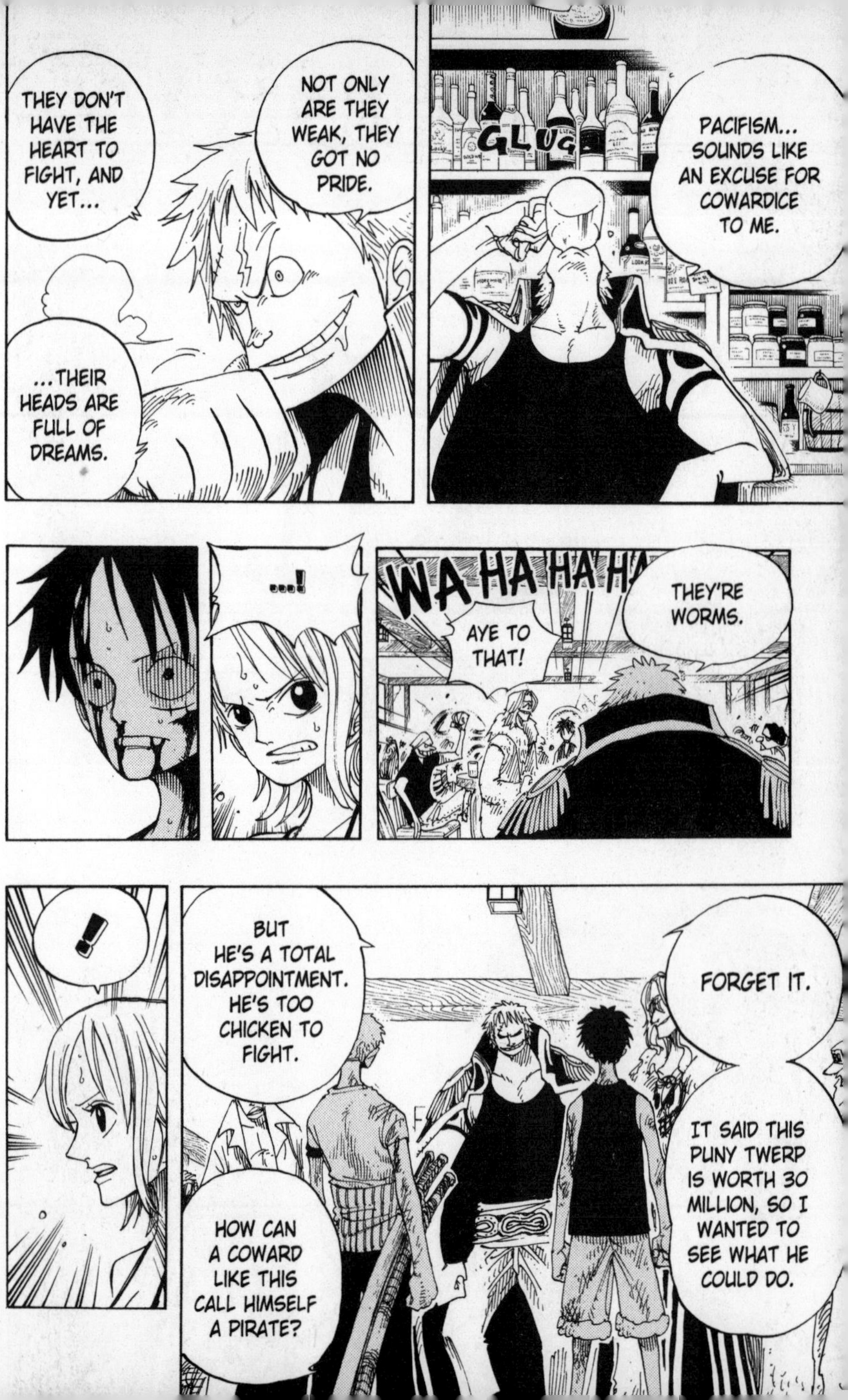
PACIFISM... SOUNDS LIKE AN EXCUSE FOR COWARDICE TO ME.
GLUG
NOT ONLY ARE THEY WEAK, THEY GOT NO PRIDE.
THEY DON'T HAVE THE HEART TO FIGHT, AND YET...
...THEIR HEADS ARE FULL OF DREAMS.
WA HA HA HA
THEY'RE WORMS.
AYE TO THAT!
...!
FORGET IT.
IT SAID THIS PUNY TWERP IS WORTH 30 MILLION, SO I WANTED TO SEE WHAT HE COULD DO.
BUT HE'S A TOTAL DISAPPOINTMENT. HE'S TOO CHICKEN TO FIGHT.
HOW CAN A COWARD LIKE THIS CALL HIMSELF A PIRATE?
!

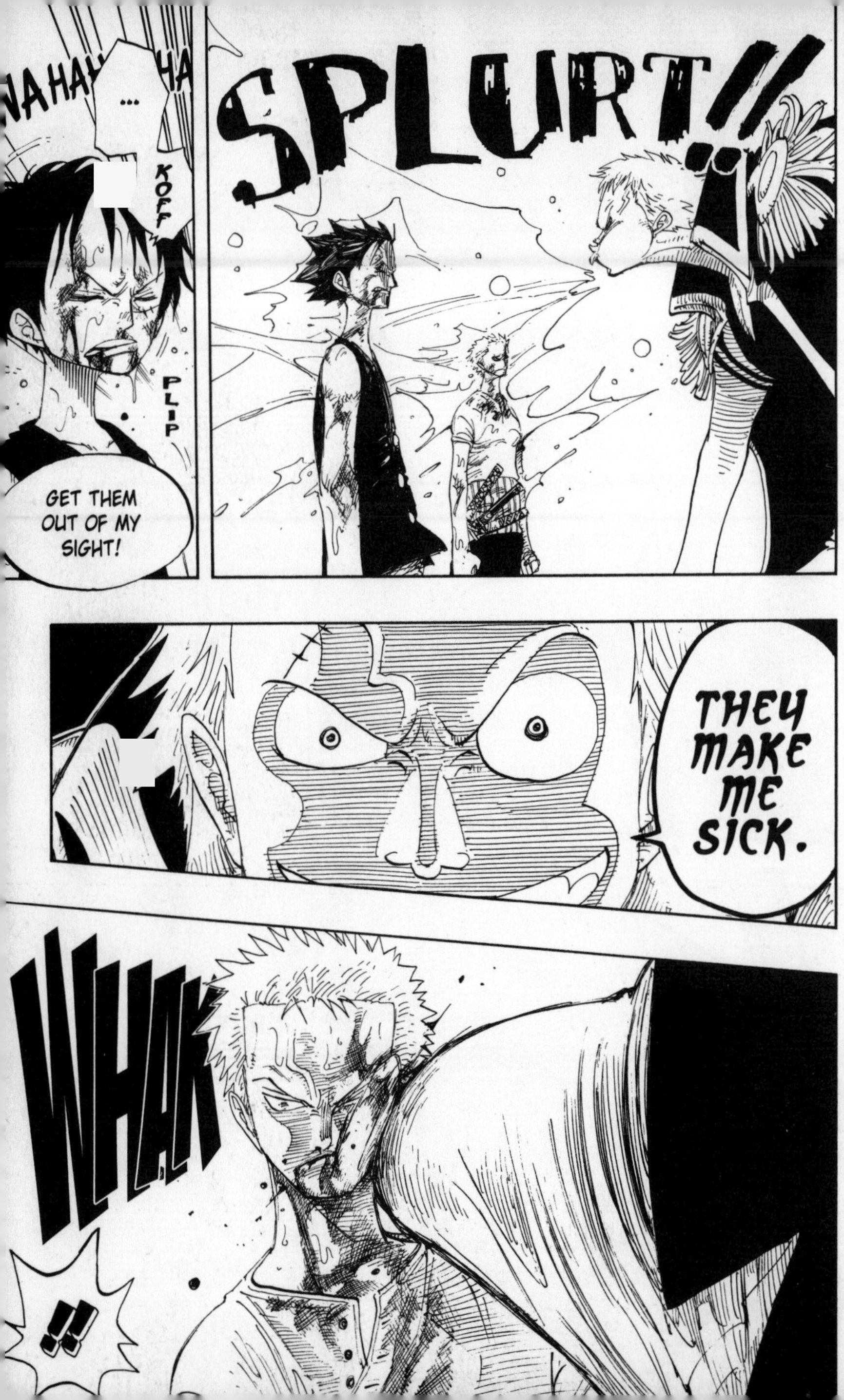
SPLURT!!
HA HAH
HA
...
KOFF
PLIP
GET THEM OUT OF MY SIGHT!
THEY MAKE ME SICK.
WHAK
!!

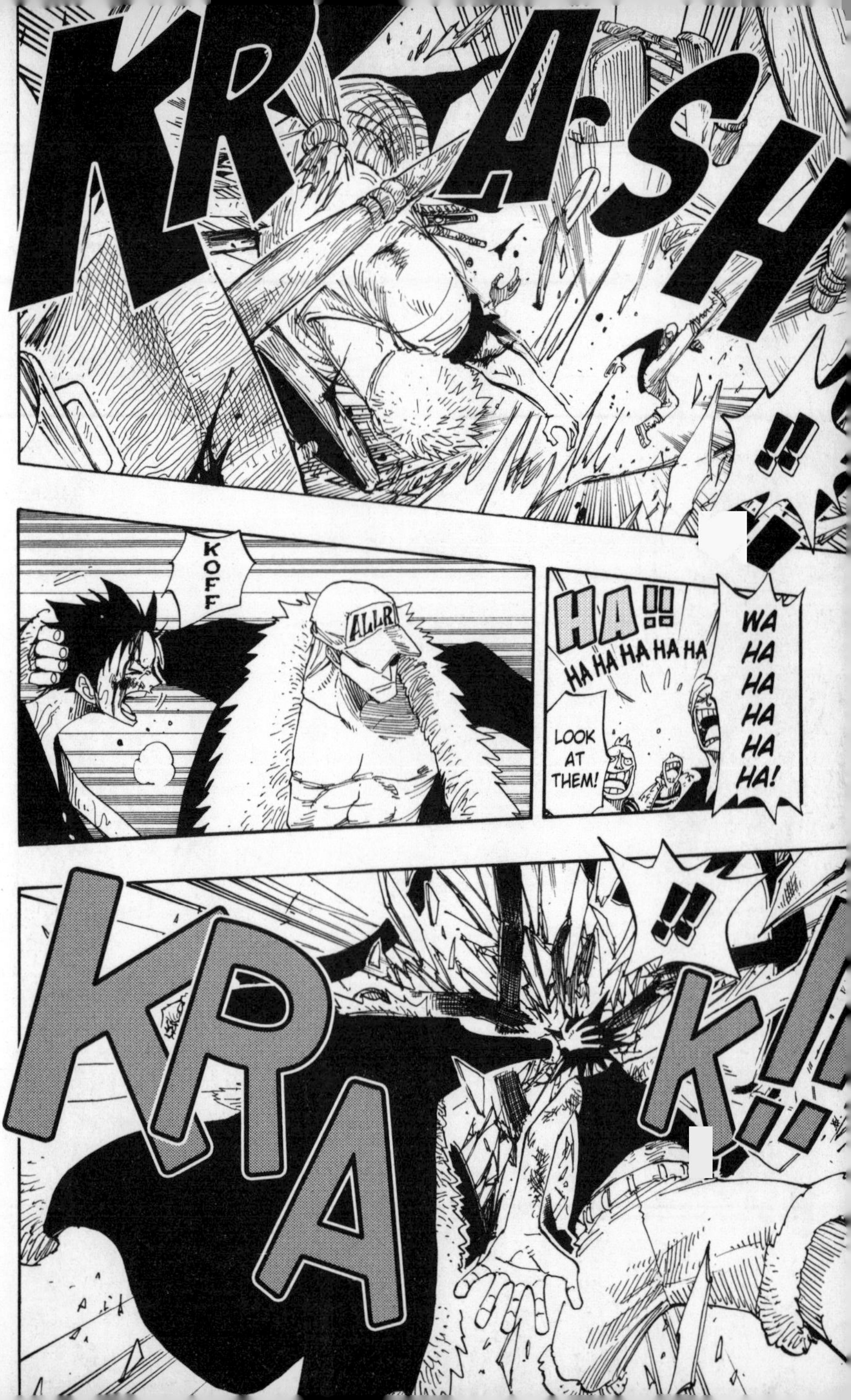
KRASH!!
WA HA HA HA HA HA!
HA!! HA HA HA HA HA
LOOK AT THEM!
KOFF
KRAK!!

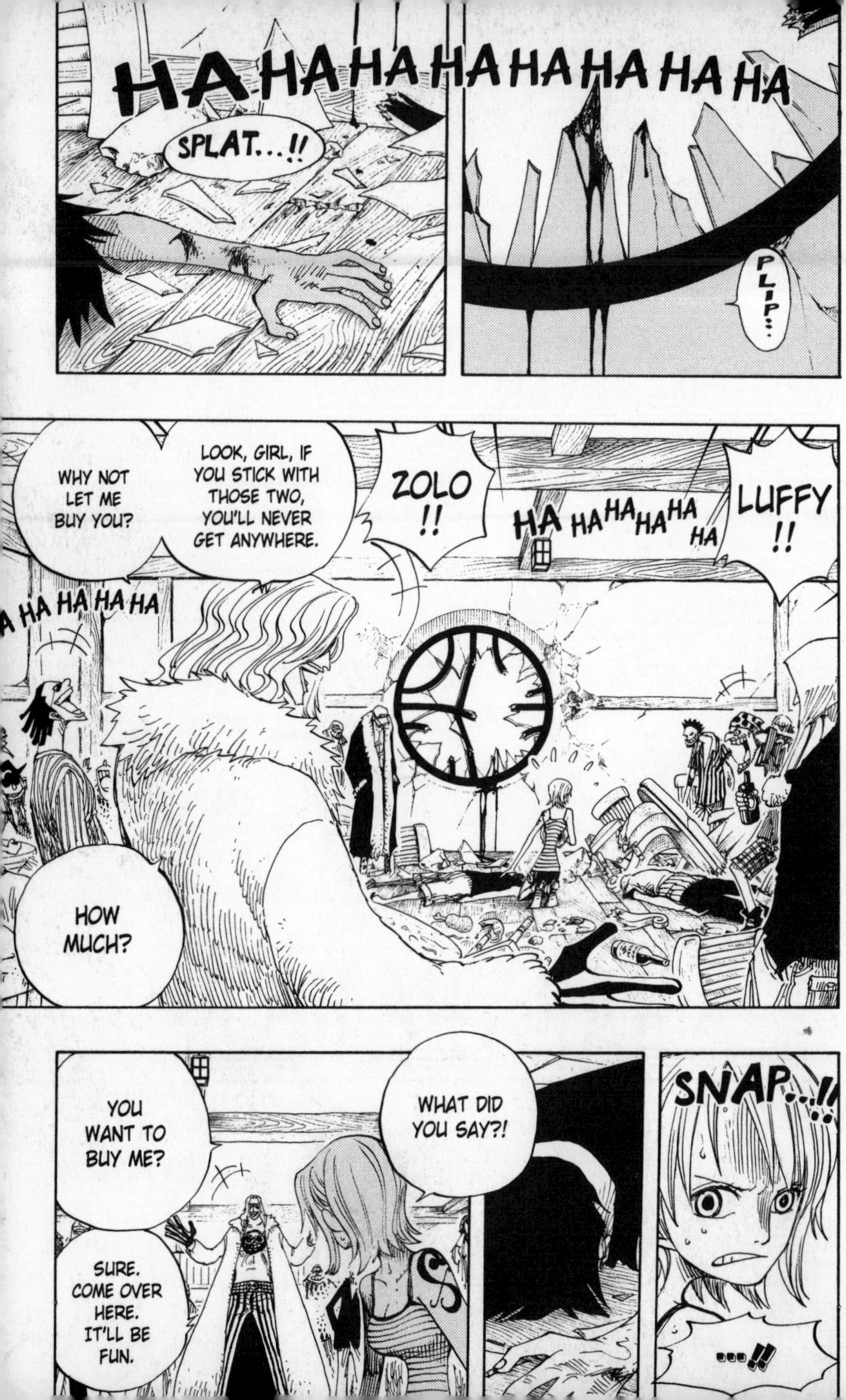
HA HA HA HA HA HA HA HA HA
PLIP...
SPLAT...!!
LUFFY!!
HA HA HA HA HA HA
ZOLO!!
LOOK, GIRL, IF YOU STICK WITH THOSE TWO, YOU'LL NEVER GET ANYWHERE.
WHY NOT LET ME BUY YOU?
HA HA HA HA HA
HOW MUCH?
SNAP...!!
...!!
WHAT DID YOU SAY?!
YOU WANT TO BUY ME?
SURE. COME OVER HERE. IT'LL BE FUN.

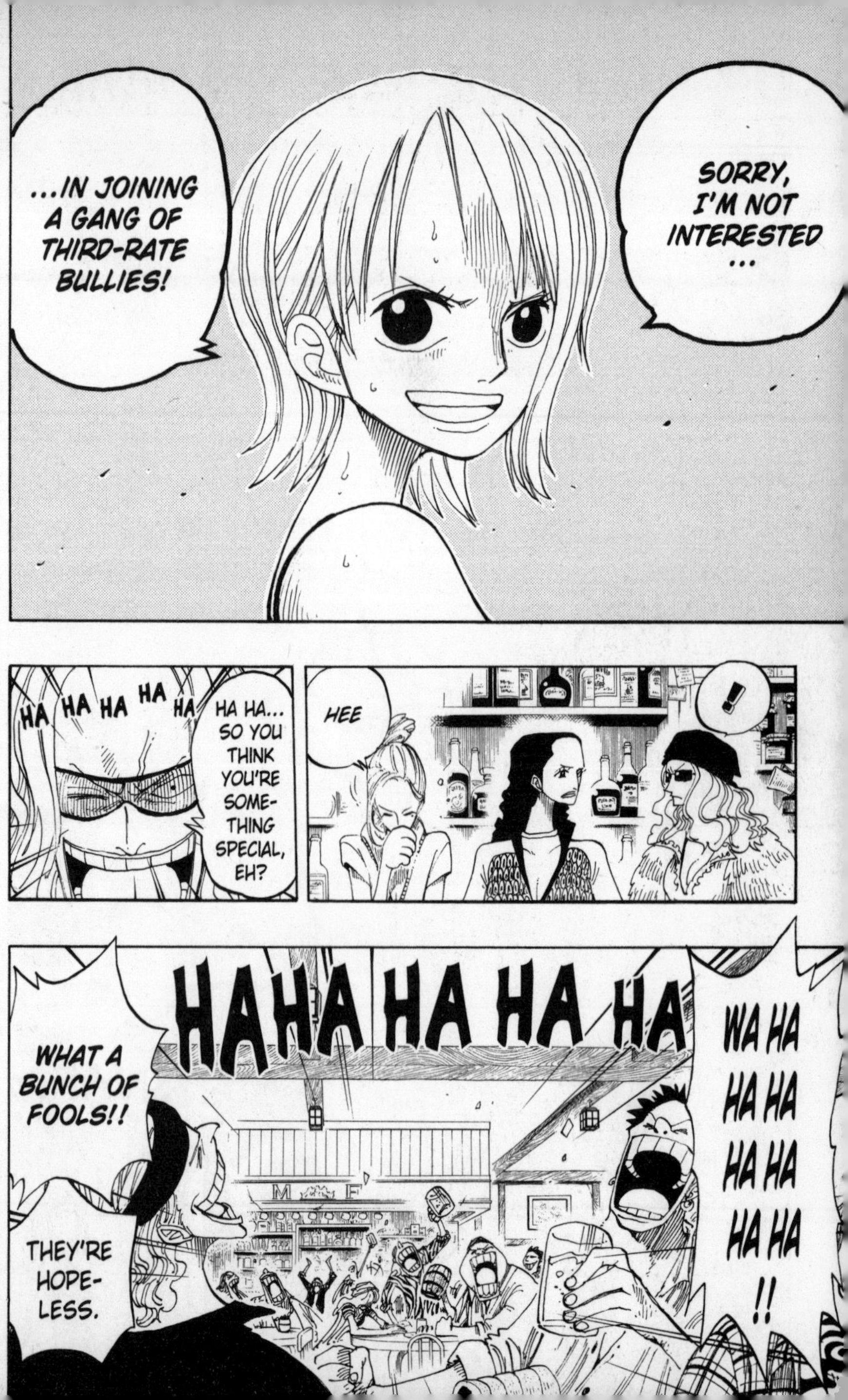
SORRY, I'M NOT INTERESTED ...
...IN JOINING A GANG OF THIRD-RATE BULLIES!
!
HEE
HA HA HA HA HA
HA HA... SO YOU THINK YOU'RE SOME-THING SPECIAL, EH?
WA HA HA HA HA HA HA HA HA HA !!
HAHA HA HA HA HA
WHAT A BUNCH OF FOOLS!!
THEY'RE HOPE-LESS.

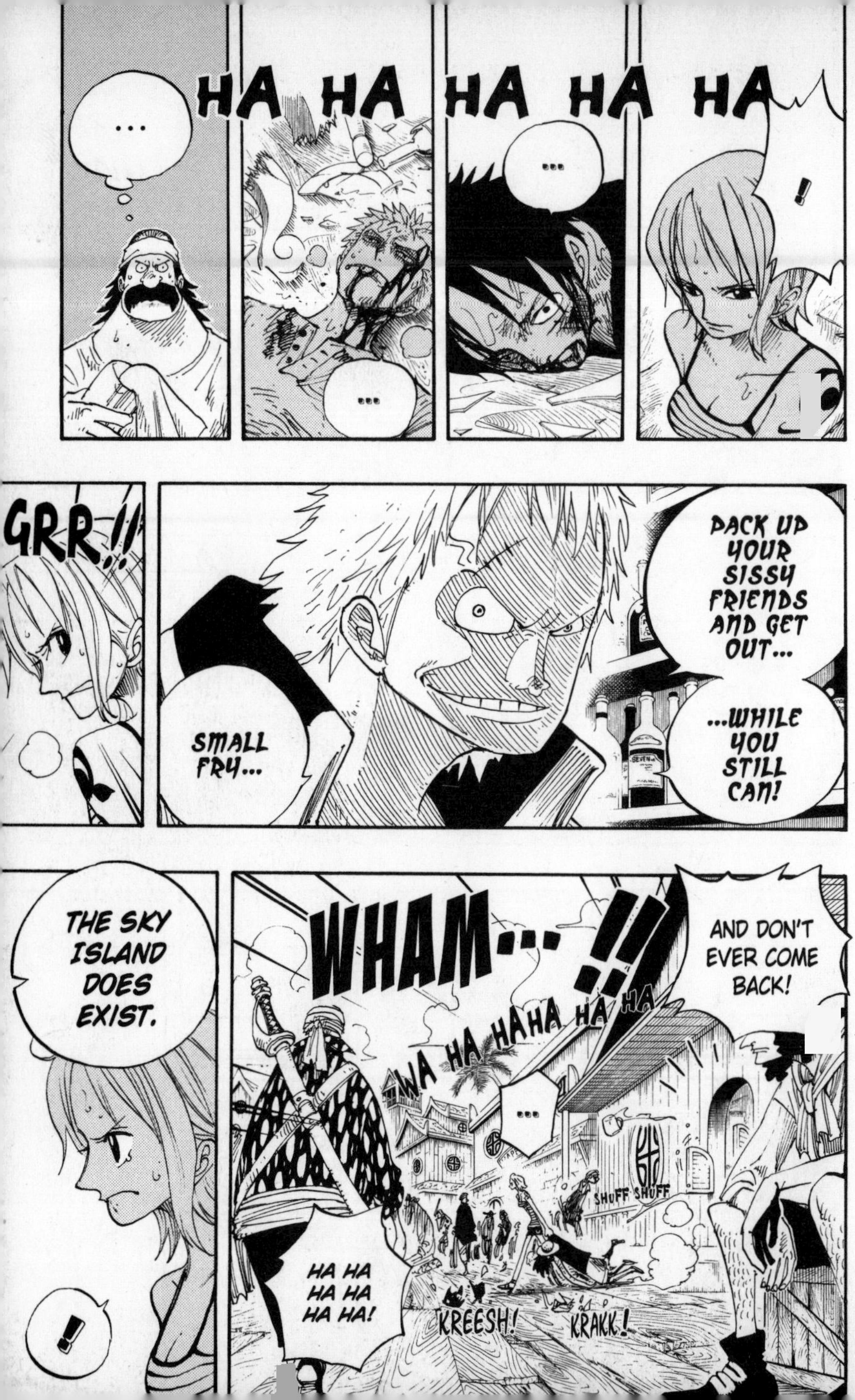
HA HA HA HA HA
!
...
...
...
PACK UP YOUR SISSY FRIENDS AND GET OUT...
...WHILE YOU STILL CAN!
SMALL FRY...
GRR!!
AND DON'T EVER COME BACK!
WHAM...!!
WA HA HA HAHA HA HA
...
SHUFF SHUFF
HA HA HA HA HA HA!
KREESH!
KRAKK!
THE SKY ISLAND DOES EXIST.
!

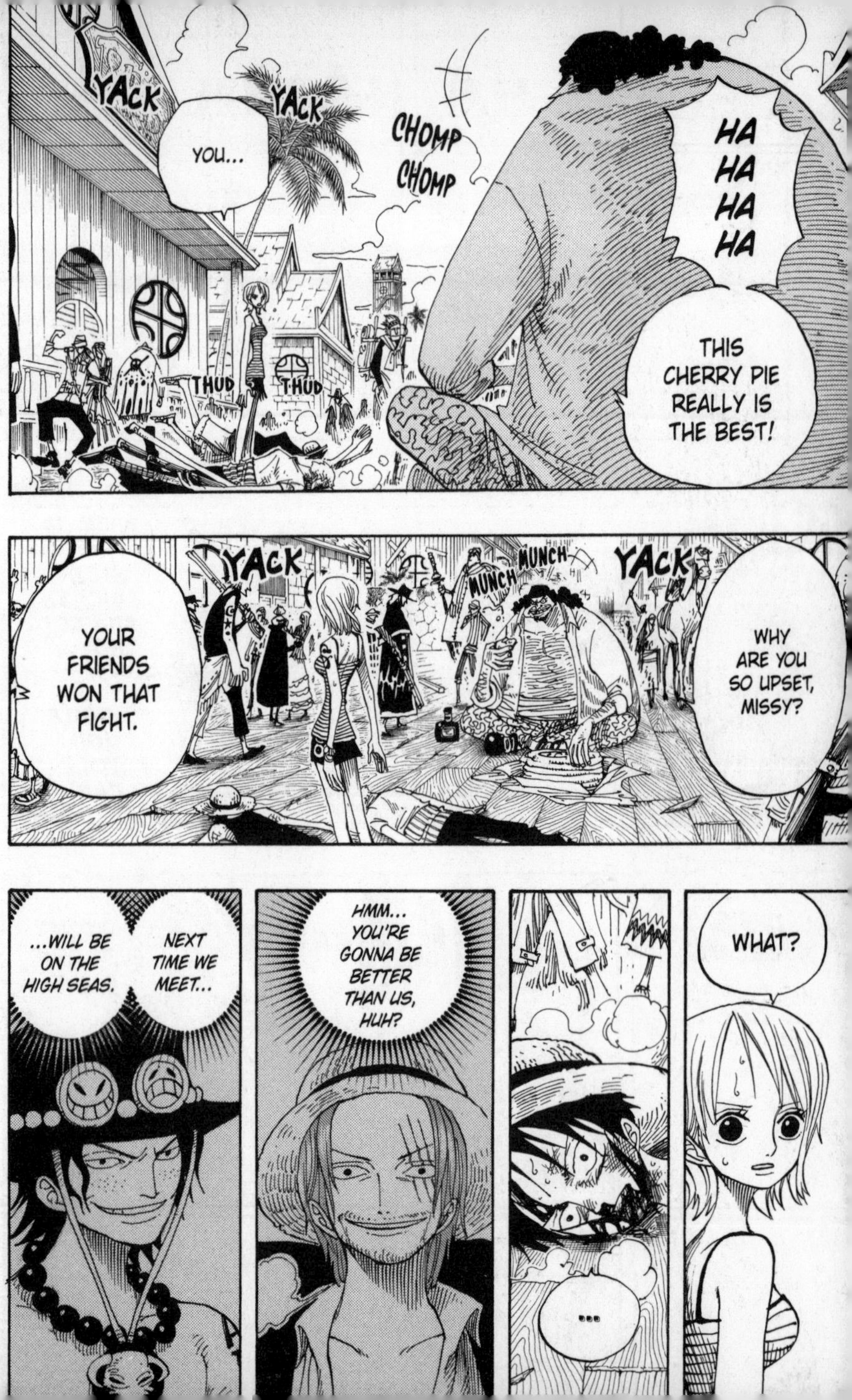
HA HA HA HA
THIS CHERRY PIE REALLY IS THE BEST!
CHOMP CHOMP
YACK
YACK
YOU...
THUD
THUD
WHY ARE YOU SO UPSET, MISSY?
YACK
MUNCH MUNCH
YACK
YOUR FRIENDS WON THAT FIGHT.
WHAT?
...
HMM... YOU'RE GONNA BE BETTER THAN US, HUH?
NEXT TIME WE MEET...
...WILL BE ON THE HIGH SEAS.

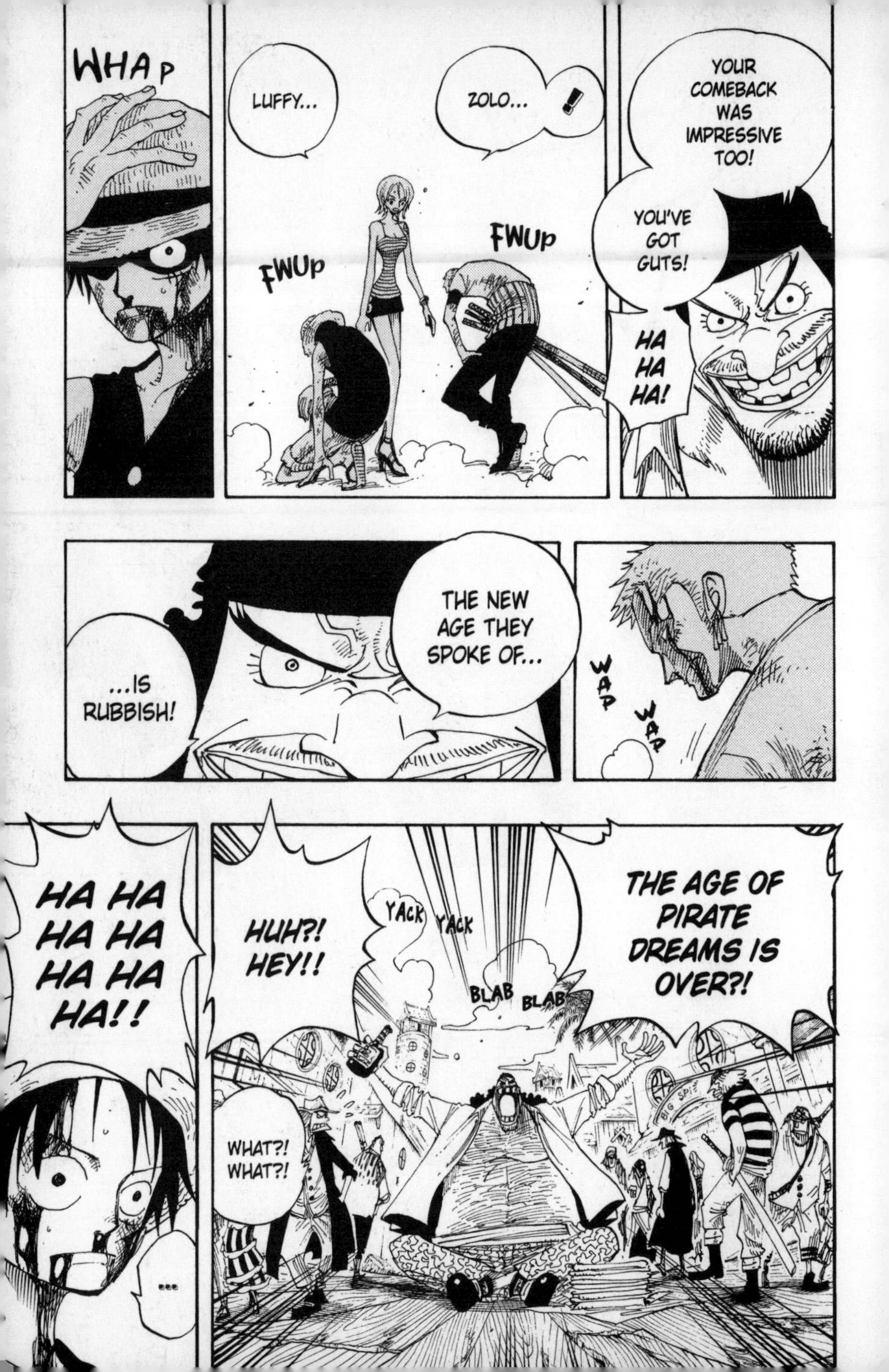
YOUR COMEBACK WAS IMPRESSIVE TOO!
YOU'VE GOT GUTS!
HA HA HA!
ZOLO...
!
LUFFY...
FWUp
FWUp
WHAp
WAP
WAP
THE NEW AGE THEY SPOKE OF...
...IS RUBBISH!
THE AGE OF PIRATE DREAMS IS OVER?!
YACK YACK
HUH?! HEY!!
BLAB BLAB
WHAT?! WHAT?!
HA HA HA HA HA HA HA!!
...

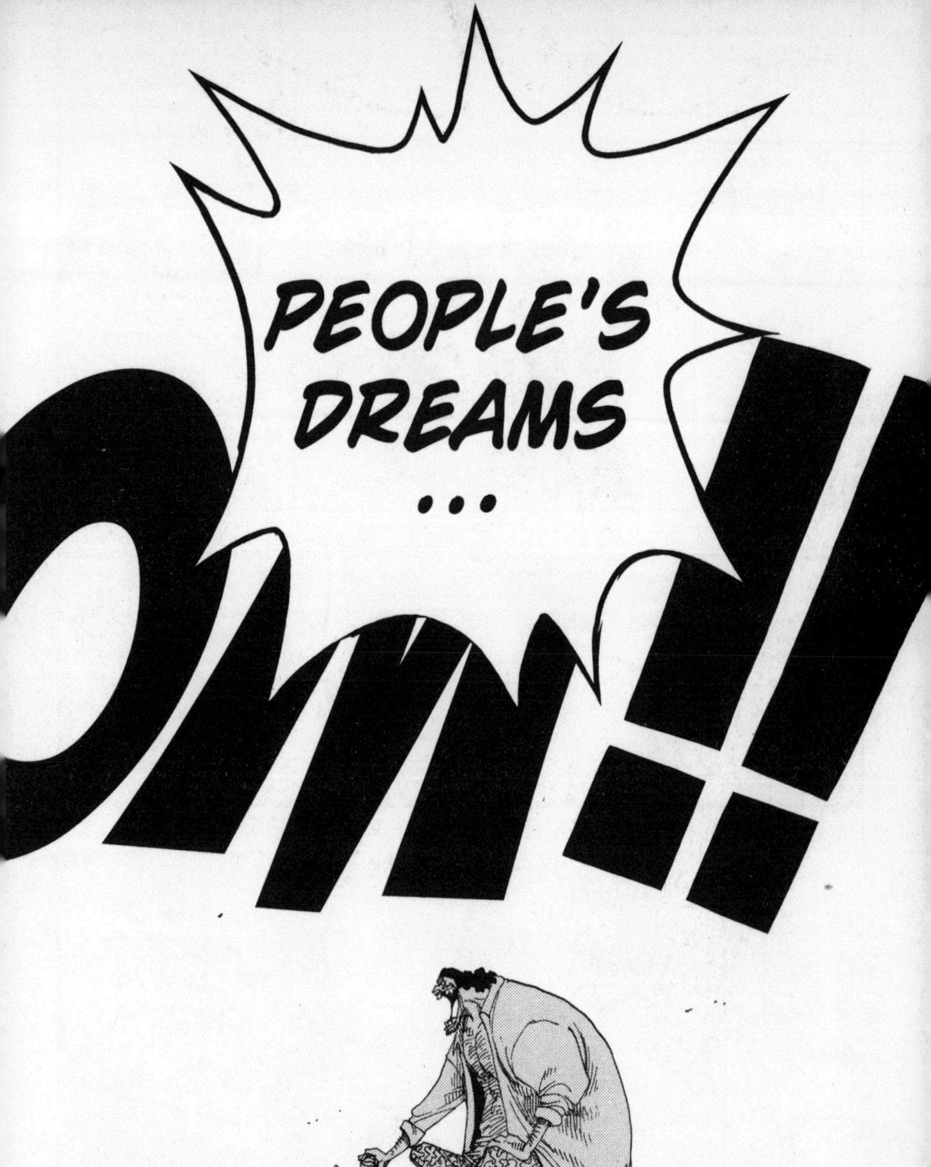
PEOPLE'S DREAMS ...

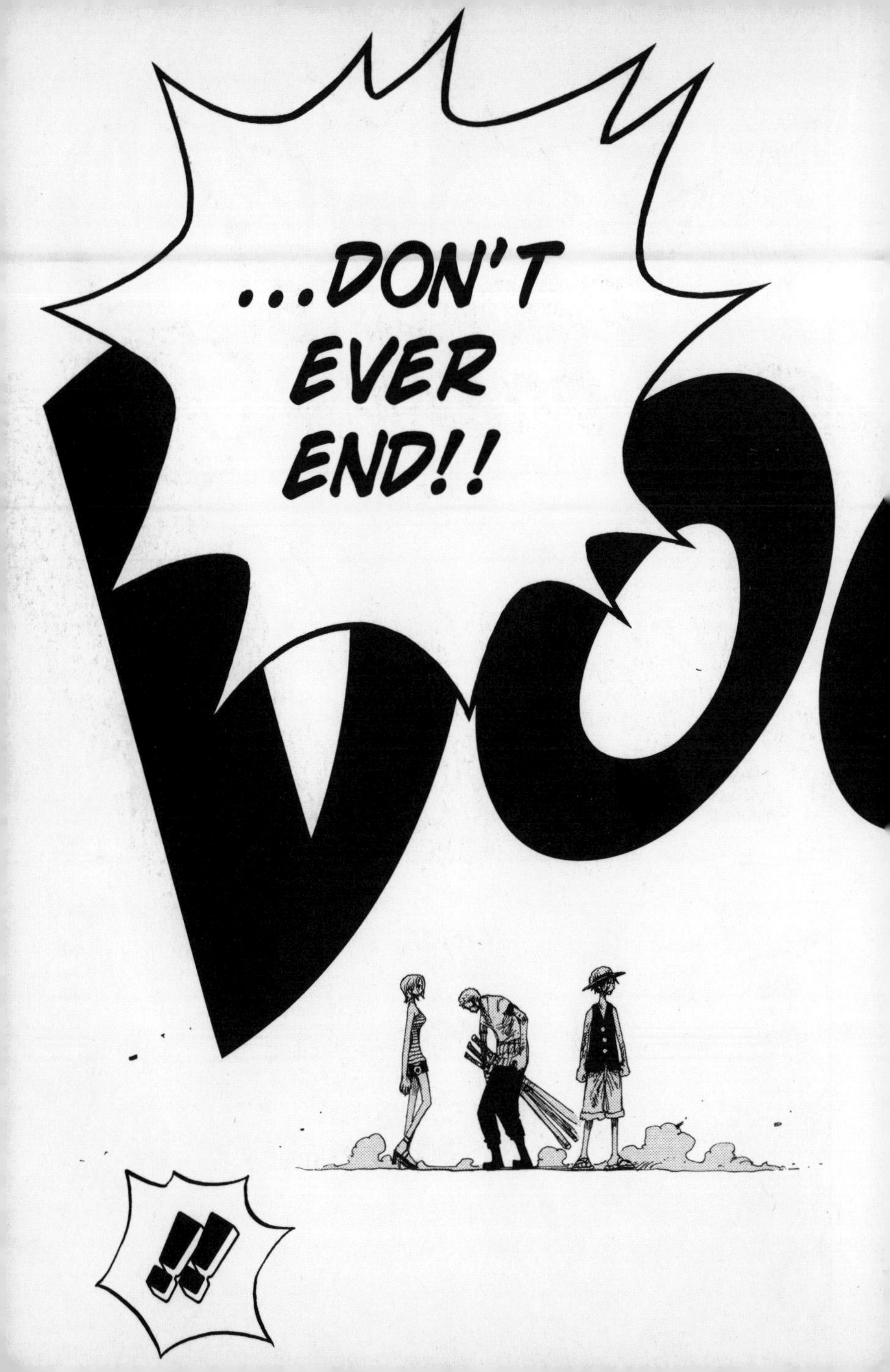
...DON'T EVER END!!
!!

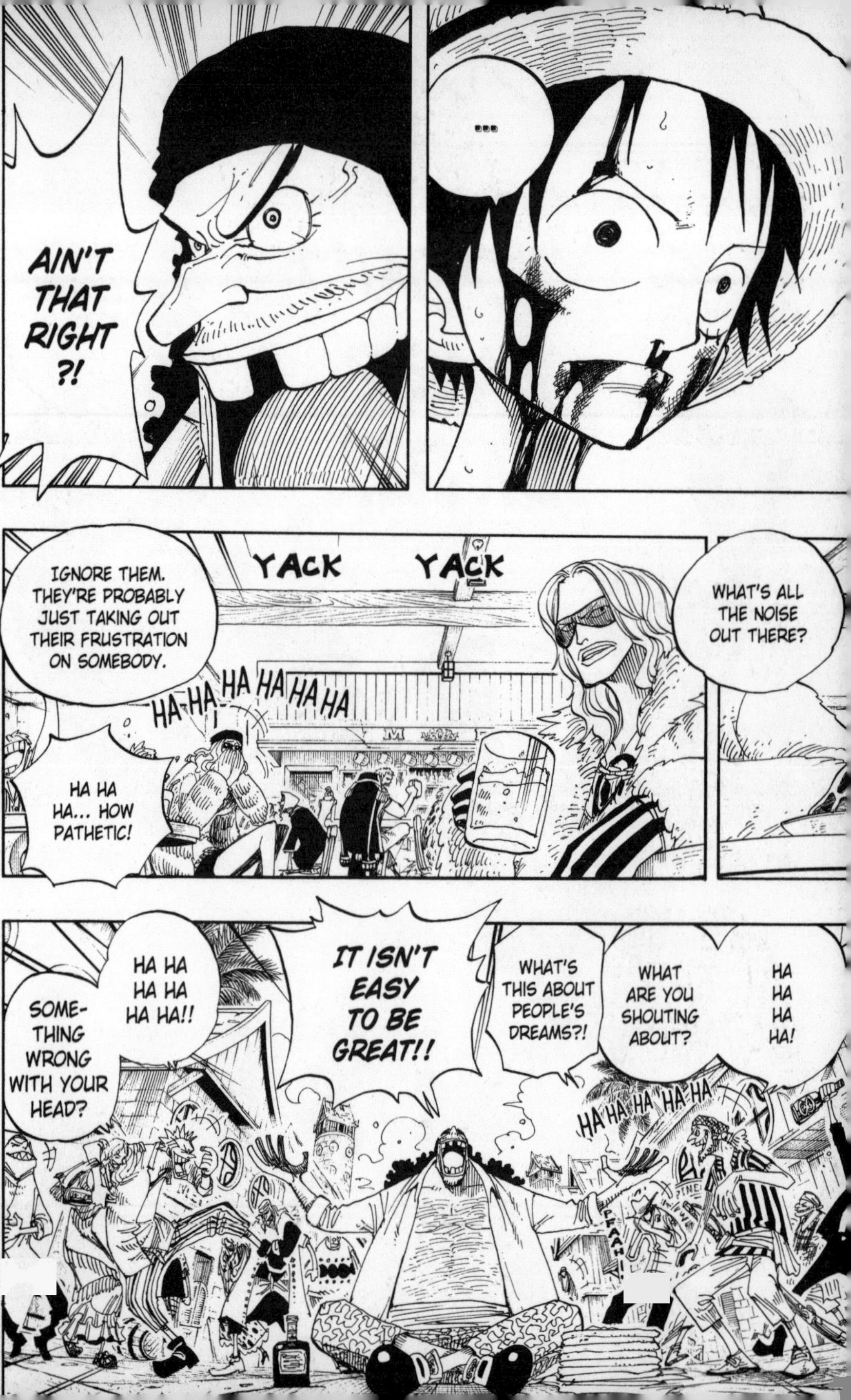
...
AIN'T THAT RIGHT?!
WHAT'S ALL THE NOISE OUT THERE?
YACK YACK
IGNORE THEM. THEY'RE PROBABLY JUST TAKING OUT THEIR FRUSTRATION ON SOMEBODY.
HA-HA HA HA HA HA
HA HA HA... HOW PATHETIC!
HA HA HA HA!
WHAT ARE YOU SHOUTING ABOUT?
WHAT'S THIS ABOUT PEOPLE'S DREAMS?!
HA HA HA HA HA
IT ISN'T EASY TO BE GREAT!!
HA HA HA HA HA HA!!
SOME-THING WRONG WITH YOUR HEAD?

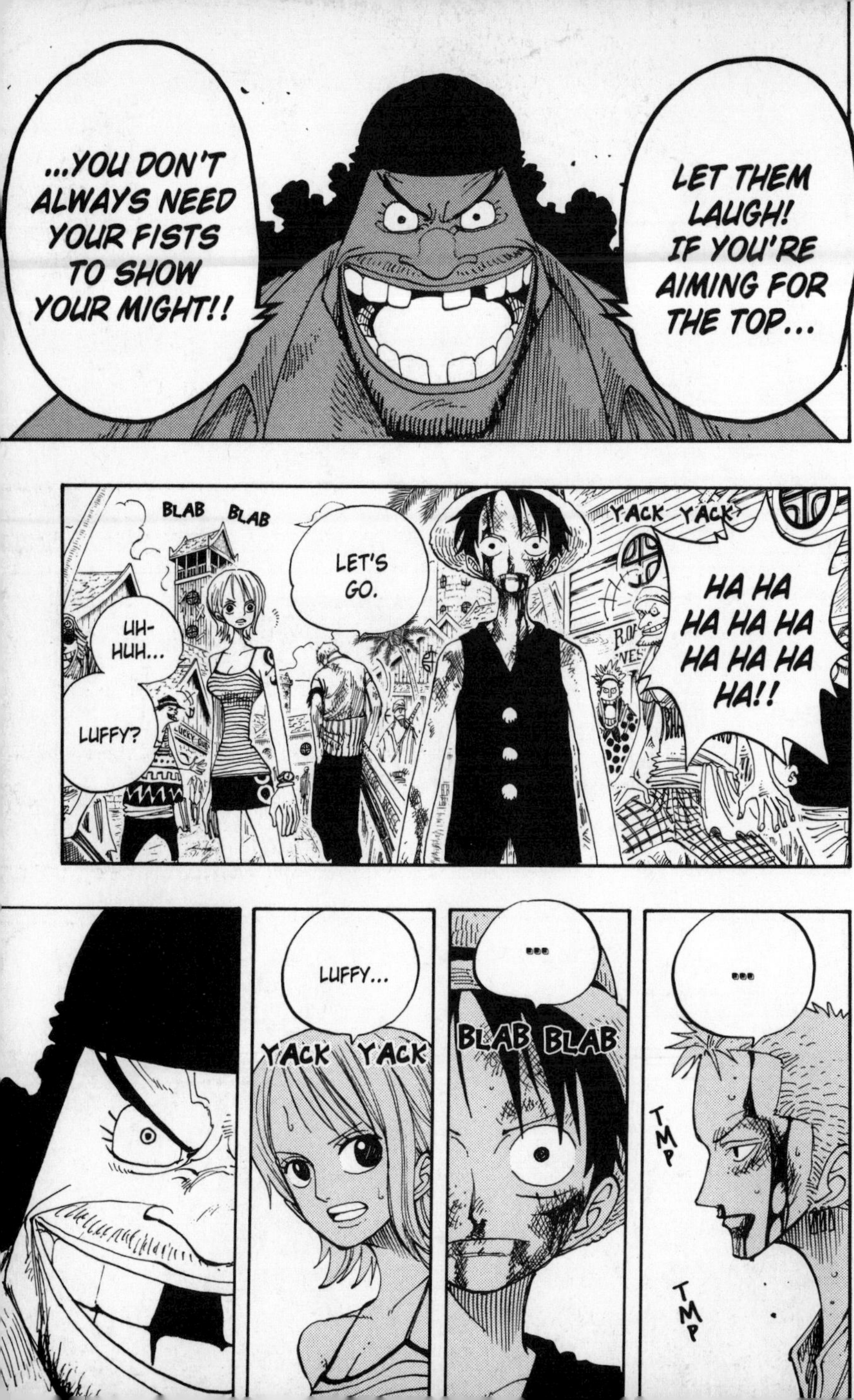
LET THEM LAUGH! IF YOU'RE AIMING FOR THE TOP...
...YOU DON'T ALWAYS NEED YOUR FISTS TO SHOW YOUR MIGHT!!
YACK YACK
HA HA HA HA HA HA HA HA HA!!
LET'S GO.
BLAB BLAB
UH-HUH...
LUFFY?
...
TMP
TMP
...
BLAB BLAB
LUFFY...
YACK YACK

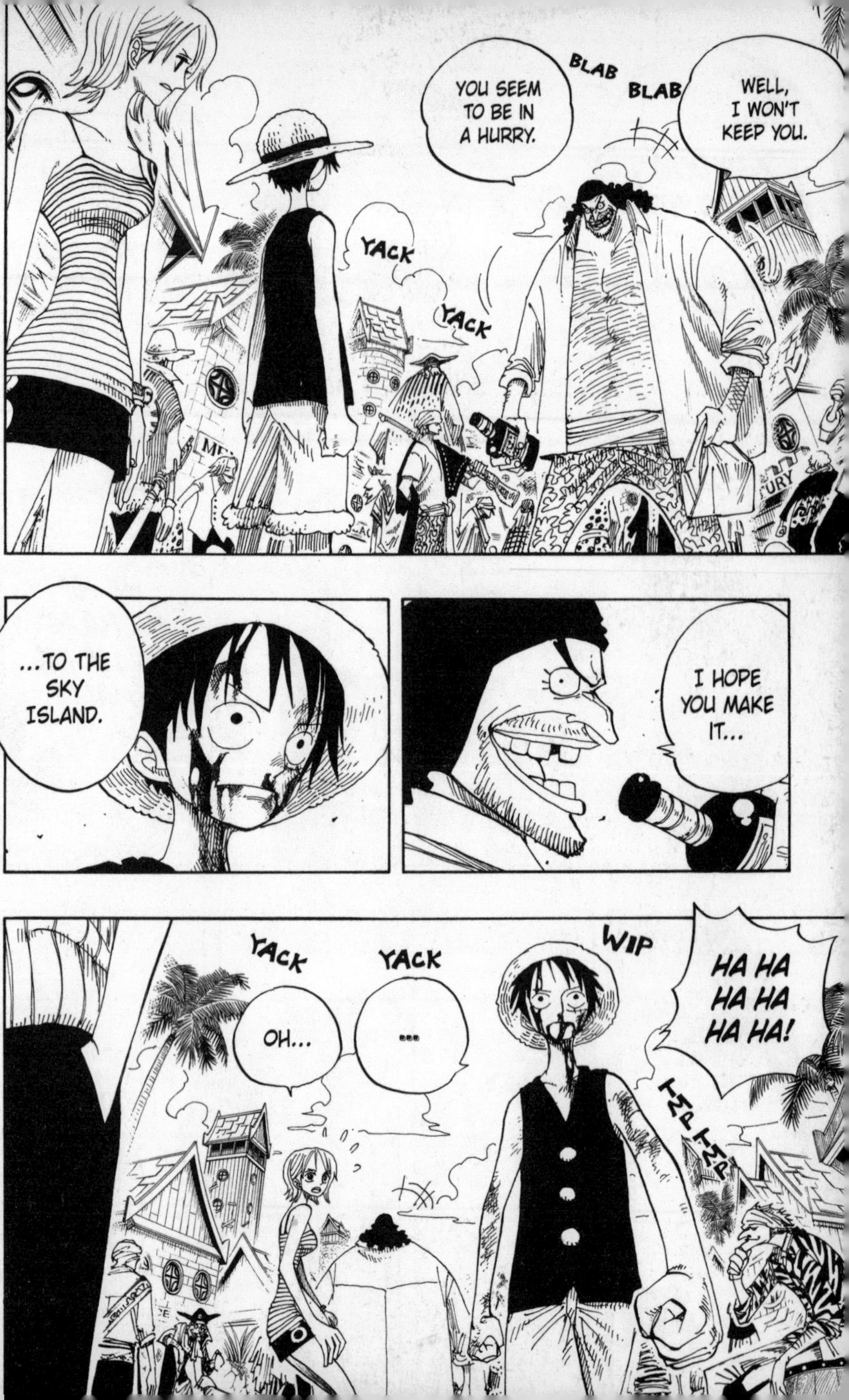
WELL, I WON'T KEEP YOU.
BLAB BLAB
YOU SEEM TO BE IN A HURRY.
YACK
YACK
I HOPE YOU MAKE IT...
...TO THE SKY ISLAND.
HA HA HA HA HA HA!
WIP
YACK
...
YACK
OH...

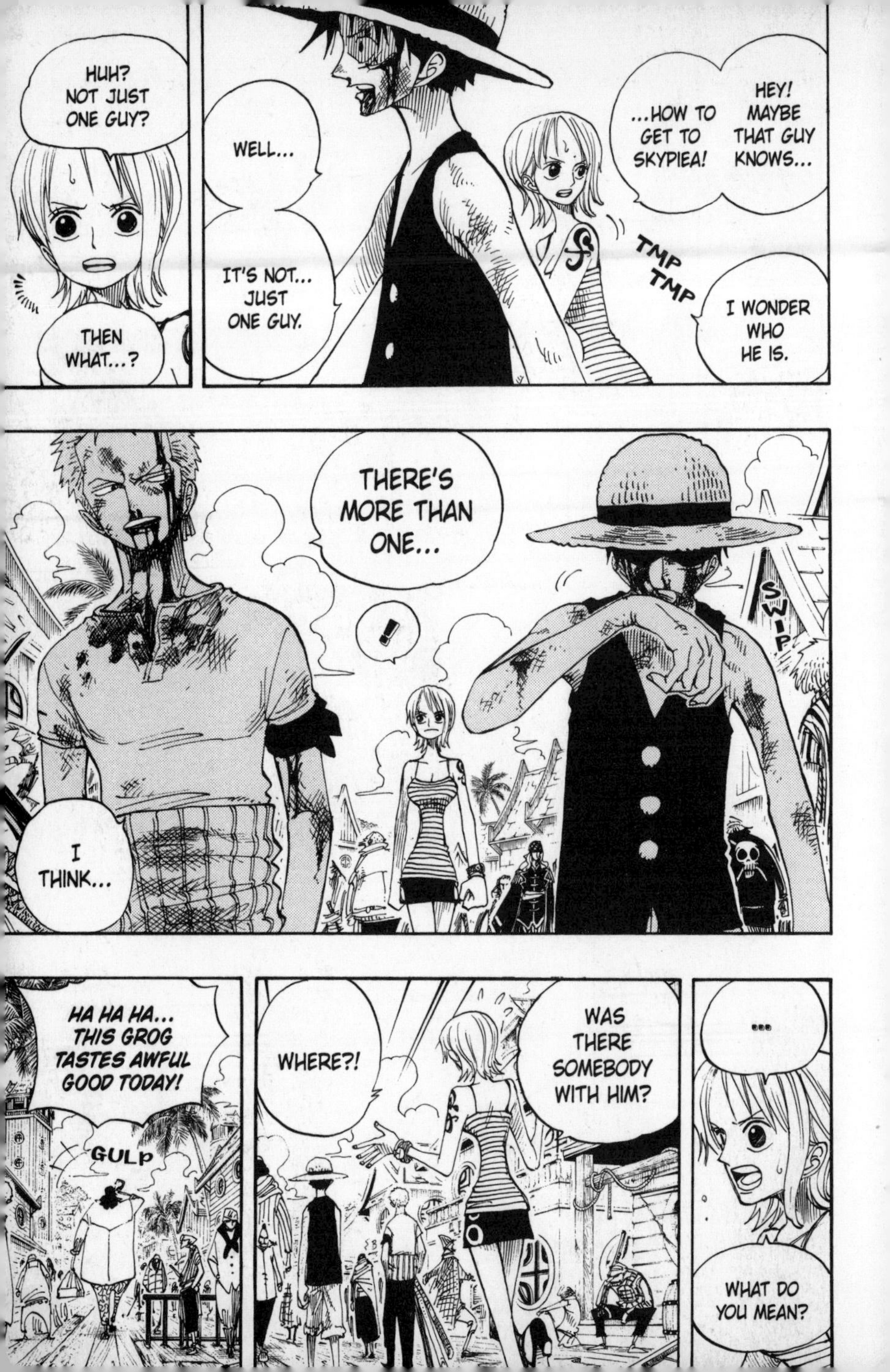
HEY! MAYBE THAT GUY KNOWS...
...HOW TO GET TO SKYPIEA!
TMP TMP
I WONDER WHO HE IS.
WELL...
IT'S NOT... JUST ONE GUY.
HUH? NOT JUST ONE GUY?
THEN WHAT...?
THERE'S MORE THAN ONE...
SWIP
!
I THINK...
...
WHAT DO YOU MEAN?
WAS THERE SOMEBODY WITH HIM?
WHERE?!
HA HA HA... THIS GROG TASTES AWFUL GOOD TODAY!
GULP

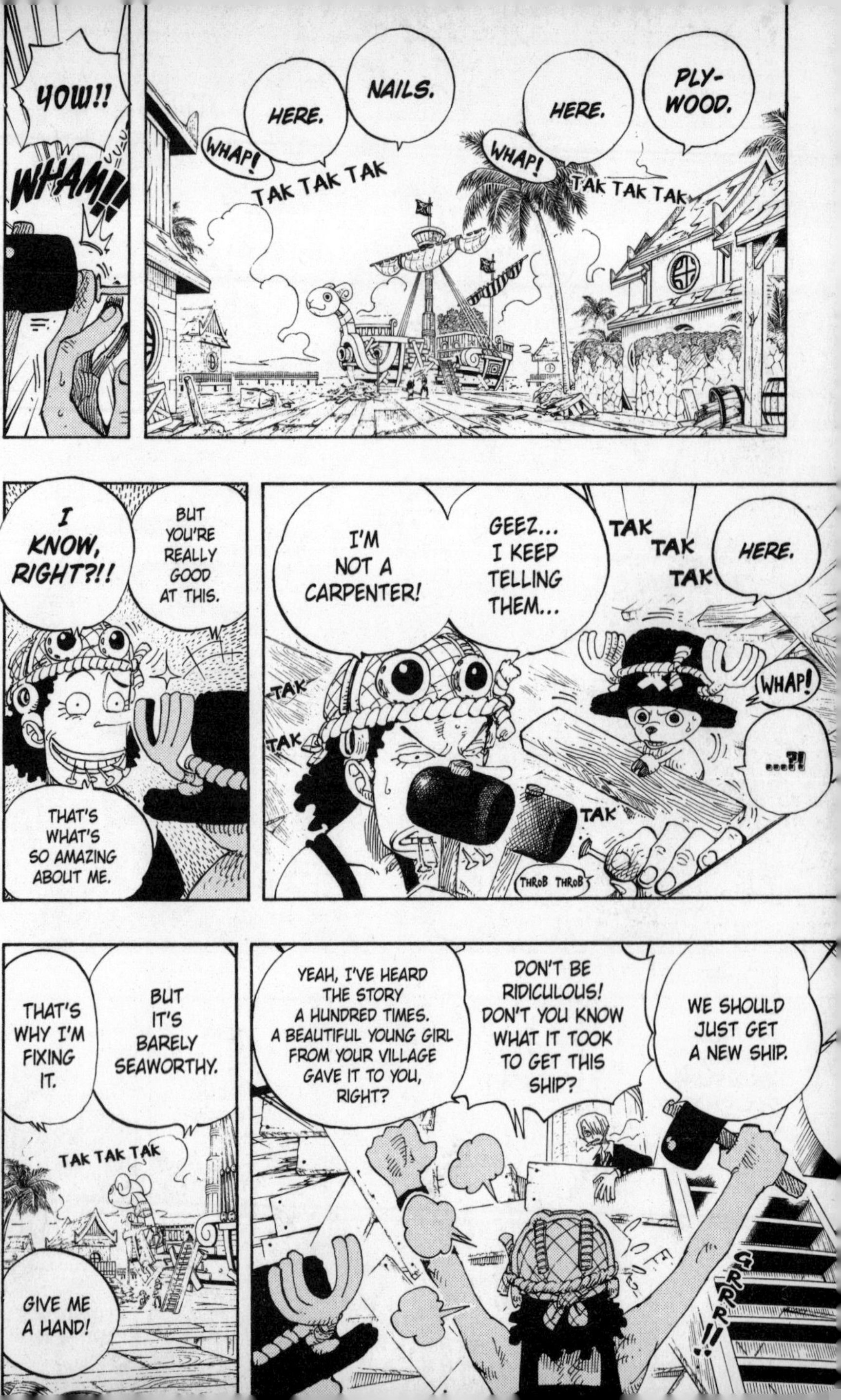
PLY-WOOD.
HERE.
WHAP!
TAK TAK TAK
NAILS.
HERE.
WHAP!
TAK TAK TAK
YOW!!
WHAM!!
HERE.
TAK TAK TAK
GEEZ... I KEEP TELLING THEM...
I'M NOT A CARPENTER!
WHAP!
...?!
TAK TAK
TAK
THROB THROB
BUT YOU'RE REALLY GOOD AT THIS.
I KNOW, RIGHT?!!
THAT'S WHAT'S SO AMAZING ABOUT ME.
WE SHOULD JUST GET A NEW SHIP.
DON'T BE RIDICULOUS! DON'T YOU KNOW WHAT IT TOOK TO GET THIS SHIP?
YEAH, I'VE HEARD THE STORY A HUNDRED TIMES. A BEAUTIFUL YOUNG GIRL FROM YOUR VILLAGE GAVE IT TO YOU, RIGHT?
GRRR!!
BUT IT'S BARELY SEAWORTHY.
THAT'S WHY I'M FIXING IT.
TAK TAK TAK
GIVE ME A HAND!

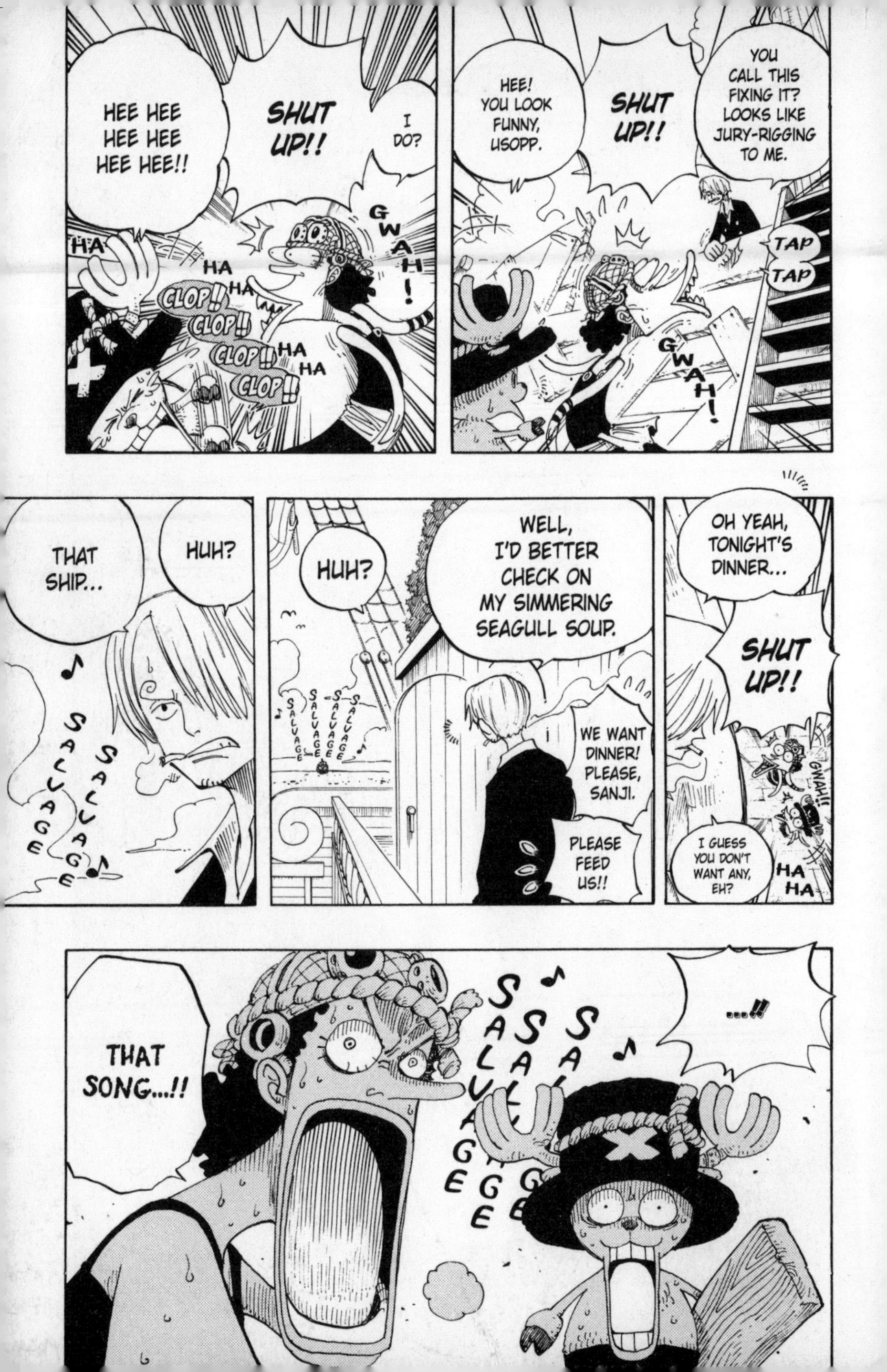

YOU CALL THIS FIXING IT? LOOKS LIKE JURY-RIGGING TO ME.
SHUT UP!!
HEE! YOU LOOK FUNNY, USOPP.
TAP
TAP
GWAH!
I DO?
SHUT UP!!
HEE HEE HEE HEE HEE HEE!!
GWAH!
HA
HA
HA
HA
HA
CLOP!!
CLOP!!
CLOP!!
CLOP!!
OH YEAH, TONIGHT'S DINNER...
SHUT UP!!
GWAH!!
I GUESS YOU DON'T WANT ANY, EH?
HA
HA
WELL, I'D BETTER CHECK ON MY SIMMERING SEAGULL SOUP.
WE WANT DINNER! PLEASE, SANJI.
PLEASE FEED US!!
HUH?
SALVAGE
SALVAGE
SALVAGE
SALVAGE
HUH?
THAT SHIP...
SALVAGE
SALVAGE
...!!
SALVAGE
SALVAGE
SALVAGE
THAT SONG...!!

KING OF THE SEAFLOOR

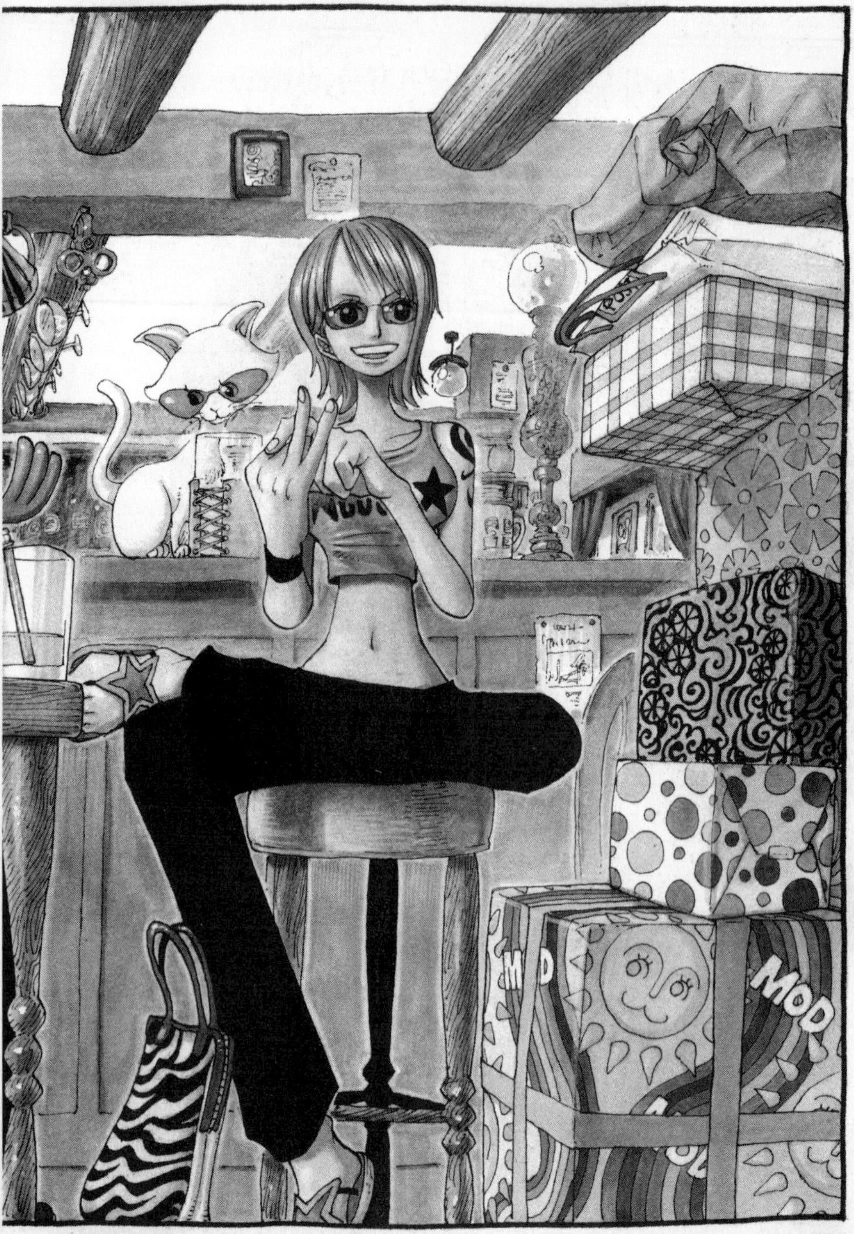
MOD

Chapter 226: SHOUJOU, THE SALVAGE

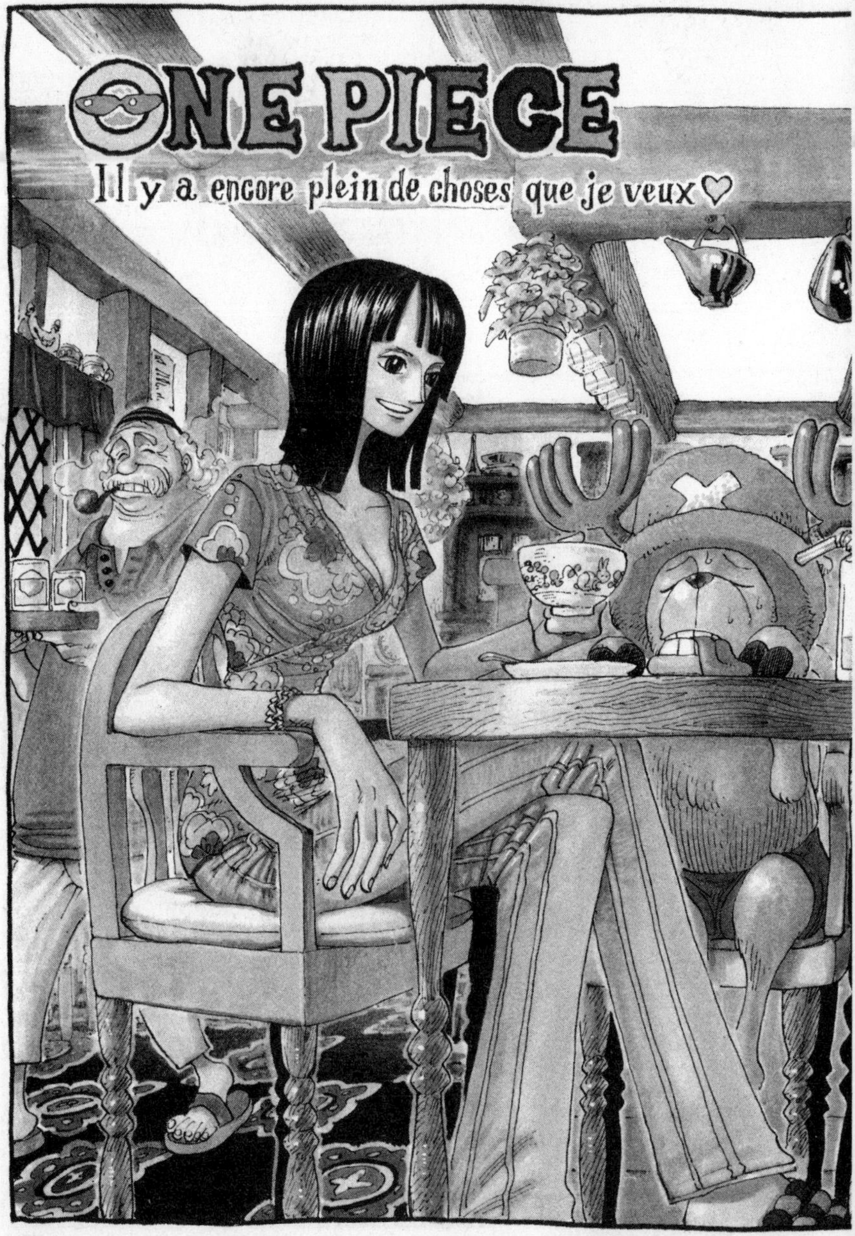
ONE PIECE
Il y a encore plein de choses que je veux♡

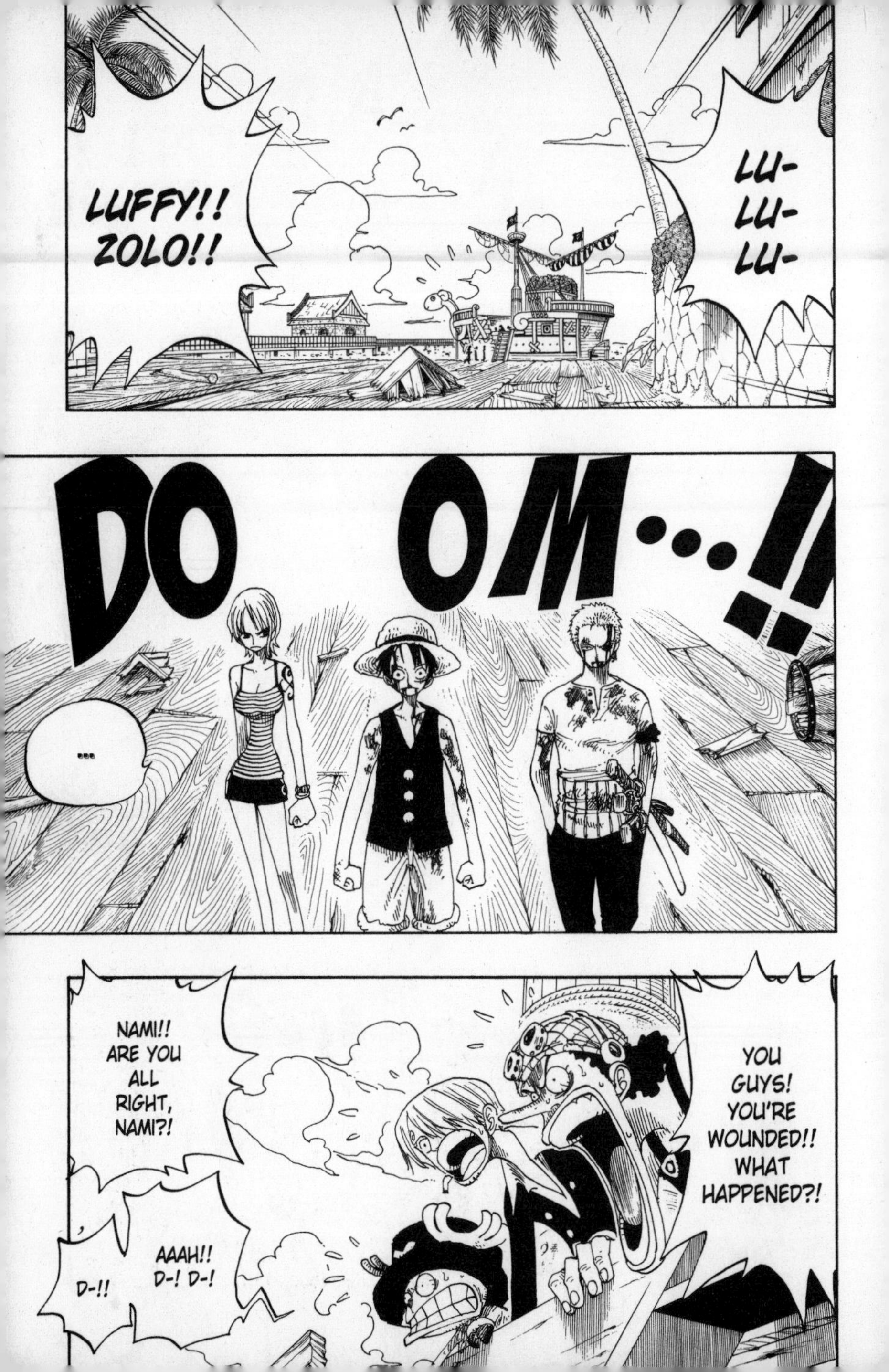
LU-
LU-
LU-
LUFFY!!
ZOLO!!
DO OM...!!
...
YOU GUYS! YOU'RE WOUNDED!! WHAT HAPPENED?!
NAMI!! ARE YOU ALL RIGHT, NAMI?!
AAAH!! D-! D-!
D-!!

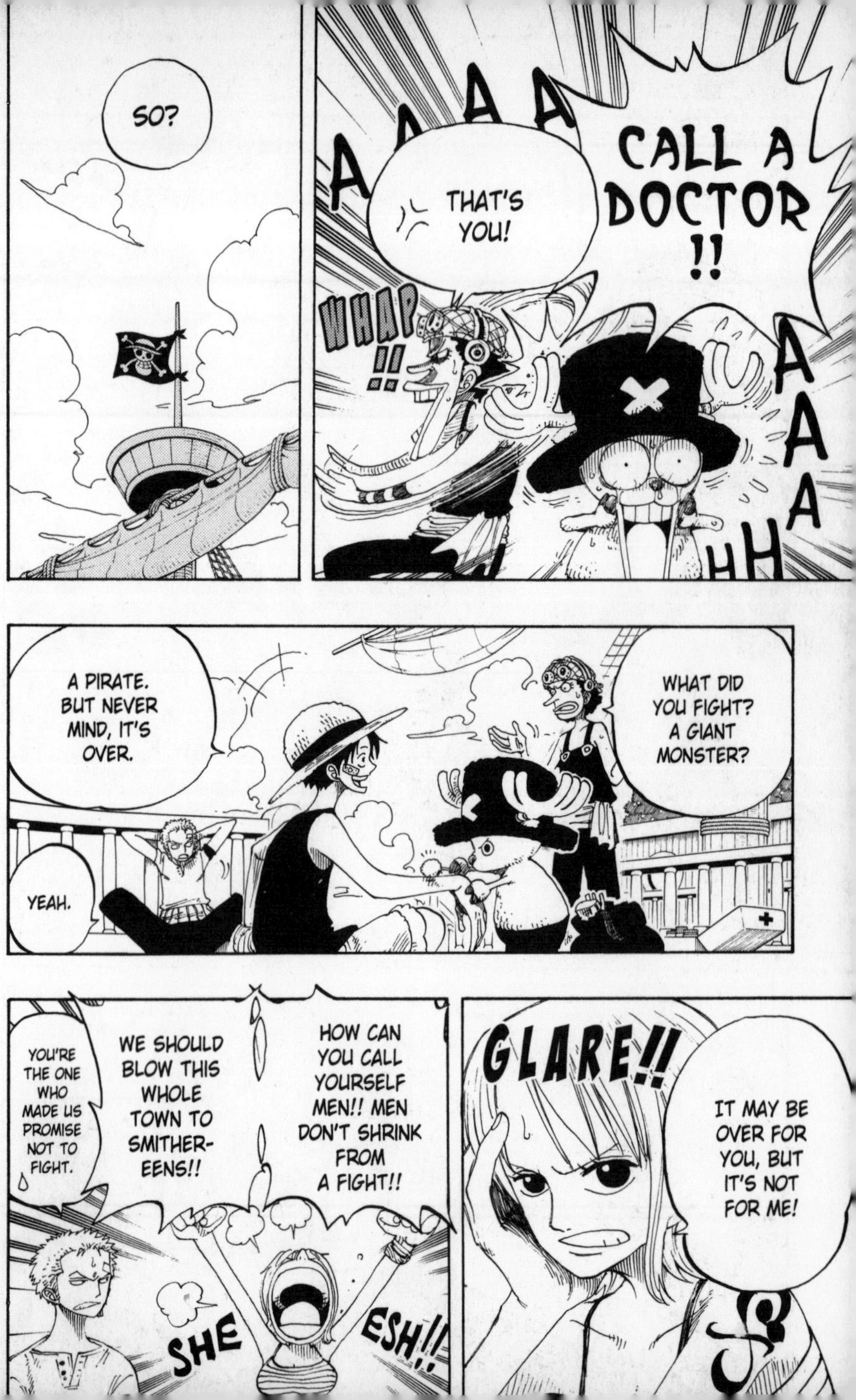
CALL A DOCTOR !!
AAAAAAAAHH
THAT'S YOU!
WHAP !!
SO?
WHAT DID YOU FIGHT? A GIANT MONSTER?
A PIRATE. BUT NEVER MIND, IT'S OVER.
YEAH.
GLARE!!
IT MAY BE OVER FOR YOU, BUT IT'S NOT FOR ME!
HOW CAN YOU CALL YOURSELF MEN!! MEN DON'T SHRINK FROM A FIGHT!!
WE SHOULD BLOW THIS WHOLE TOWN TO SMITHER-EENS!!
YOU'RE THE ONE WHO MADE US PROMISE NOT TO FIGHT.
SHEESH!!

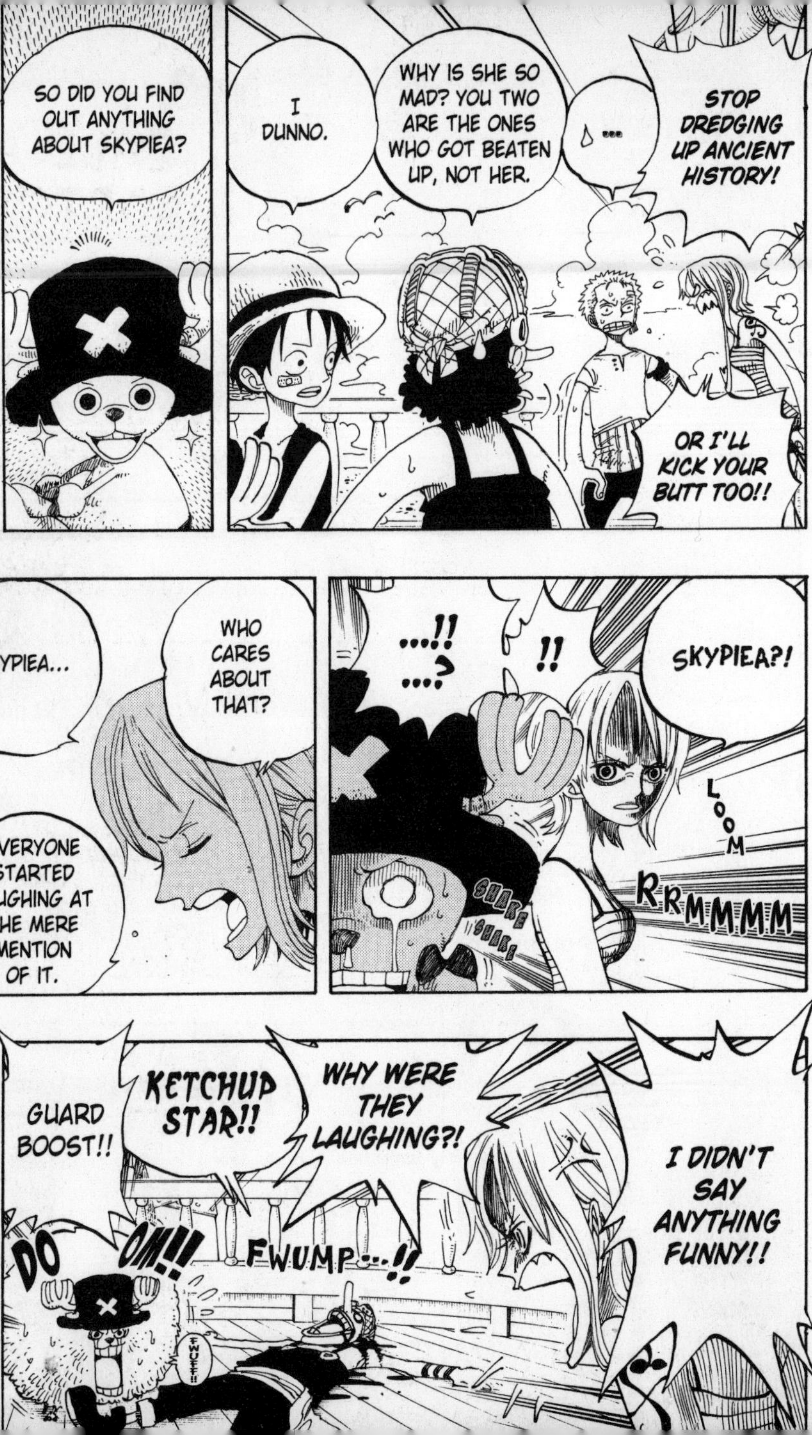
STOP DREDGING UP ANCIENT HISTORY!
OR I'LL KICK YOUR BUTT TOO!!
...
WHY IS SHE SO MAD? YOU TWO ARE THE ONES WHO GOT BEATEN UP, NOT HER.
I DUNNO.
SO DID YOU FIND OUT ANYTHING ABOUT SKYPIEA?
SKYPIEA?!
!!
...!!
...?
LOOM
RRMMMMM
SHAKE
SHAKE
WHO CARES ABOUT THAT?
SKYPIEA...
EVERYONE STARTED LAUGHING AT THE MERE MENTION OF IT.
I DIDN'T SAY ANYTHING FUNNY!!
WHY WERE THEY LAUGHING?!
KETCHUP STAR!!
GUARD BOOST!!
FWUMP...!!
DOOM!!
FWUFF!!

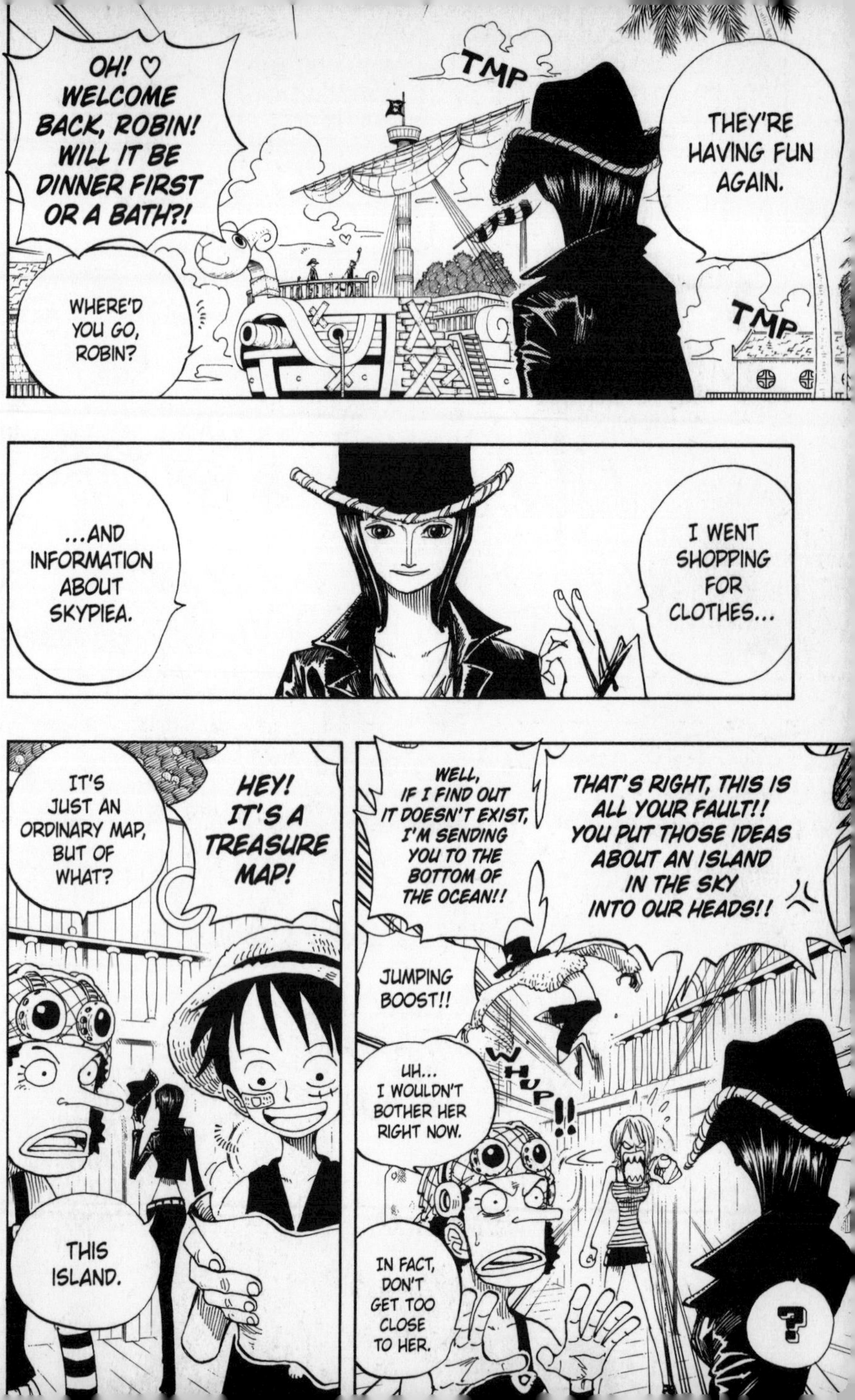
TMP
THEY'RE HAVING FUN AGAIN.
TMP
OH! ♡ WELCOME BACK, ROBIN! WILL IT BE DINNER FIRST OR A BATH?!
WHERE'D YOU GO, ROBIN?
I WENT SHOPPING FOR CLOTHES...
...AND INFORMATION ABOUT SKYPIEA.
THAT'S RIGHT, THIS IS ALL YOUR FAULT!! YOU PUT THOSE IDEAS ABOUT AN ISLAND IN THE SKY INTO OUR HEADS!!
WELL, IF I FIND OUT IT DOESN'T EXIST, I'M SENDING YOU TO THE BOTTOM OF THE OCEAN!!
JUMPING BOOST!!
WHUP!!
UH... I WOULDN'T BOTHER HER RIGHT NOW.
?
IN FACT, DON'T GET TOO CLOSE TO HER.
HEY! IT'S A TREASURE MAP!
IT'S JUST AN ORDINARY MAP, BUT OF WHAT?
THIS ISLAND.

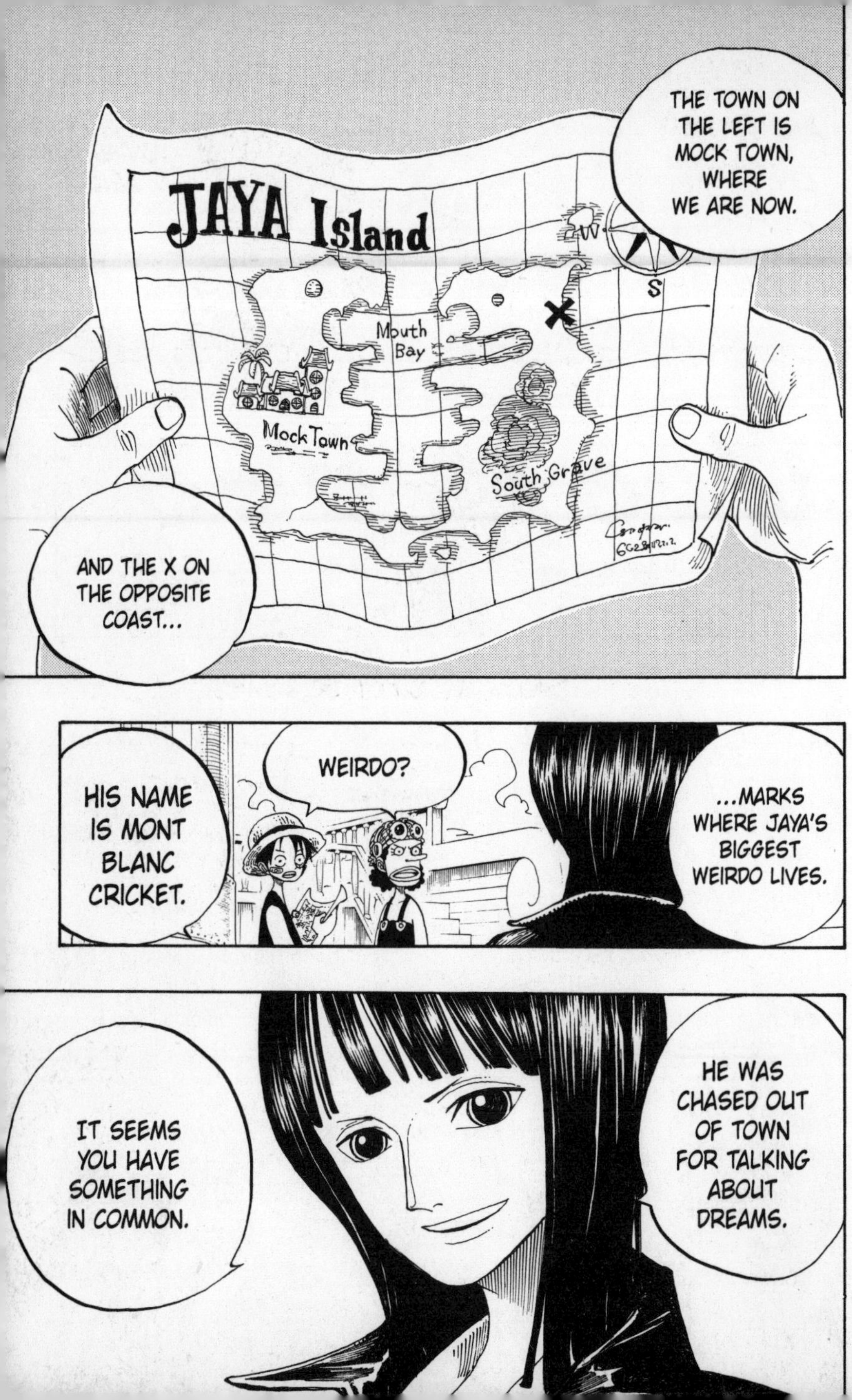
THE TOWN ON THE LEFT IS MOCK TOWN, WHERE WE ARE NOW.
JAYA Island
Mouth Bay
Mock Town
South Grave
AND THE X ON THE OPPOSITE COAST...
...MARKS WHERE JAYA'S BIGGEST WEIRDO LIVES.
WEIRDO?
HIS NAME IS MONT BLANC CRICKET.
HE WAS CHASED OUT OF TOWN FOR TALKING ABOUT DREAMS.
IT SEEMS YOU HAVE SOMETHING IN COMMON.

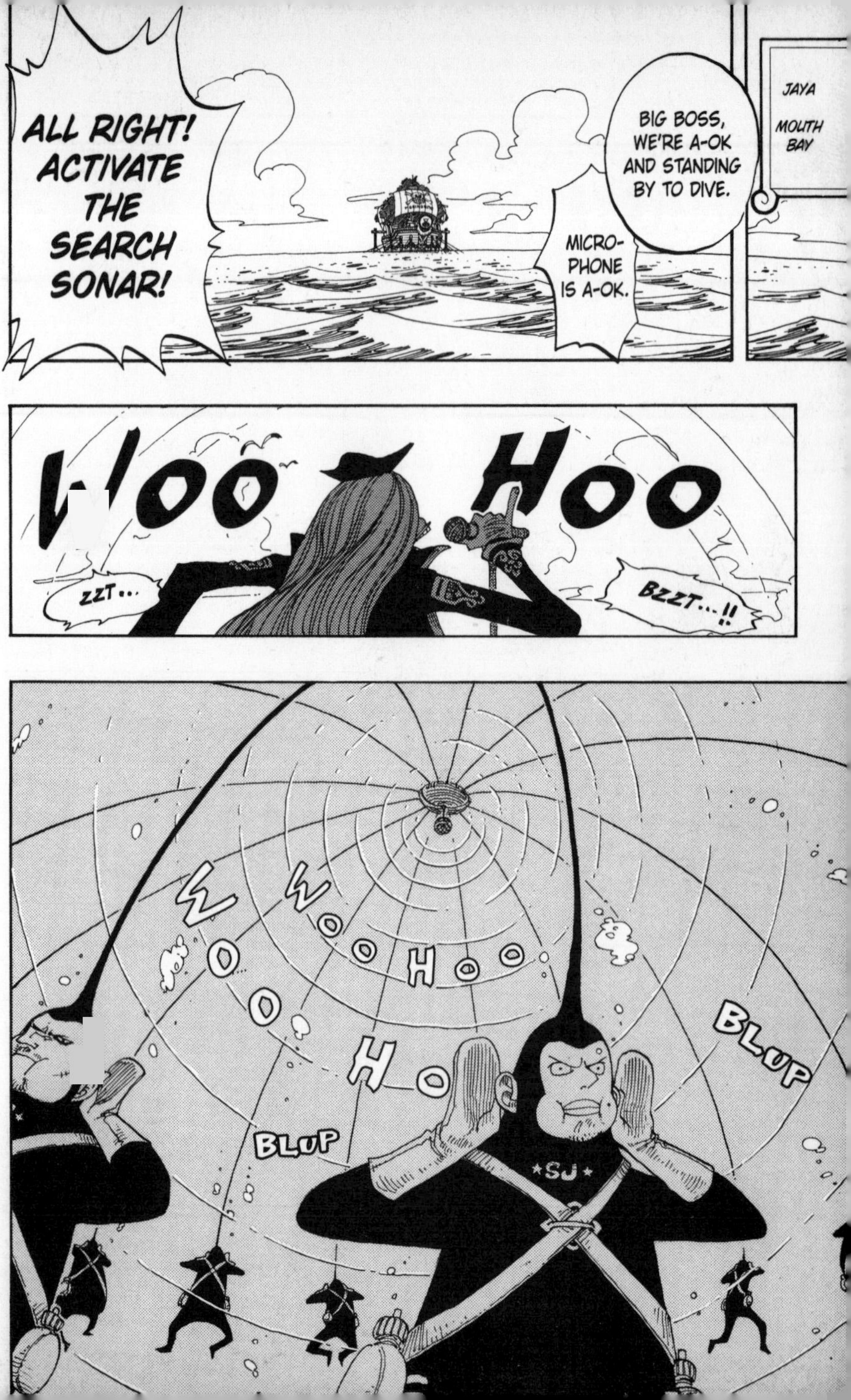
JAYA MOUTH BAY
BIG BOSS, WE'RE A-OK AND STANDING BY TO DIVE.
MICRO-PHONE IS A-OK.
ALL RIGHT! ACTIVATE THE SEARCH SONAR!
WOO HOO
BZZT...!!
ZZT...
WOOHOO
WOOHO
BLUP
BLUP

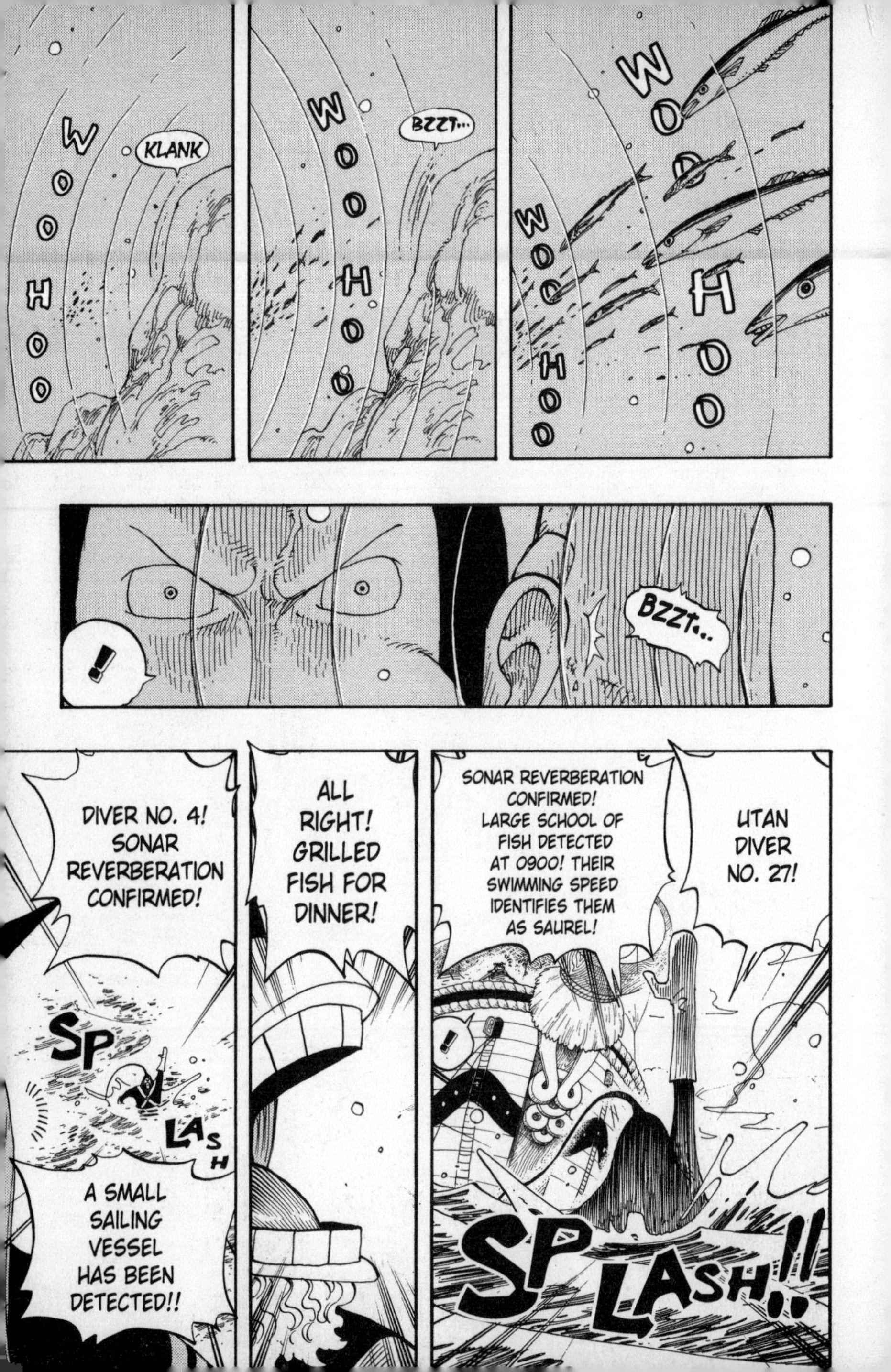
WOOOHOOO
WOOOHOO
BZZT...
WOOOHOOO
KLANK
WOOOHOOO
BZZT..
!
UTAN DIVER NO. 27!
SONAR REVERBERATION CONFIRMED! LARGE SCHOOL OF FISH DETECTED AT 0900! THEIR SWIMMING SPEED IDENTIFIES THEM AS SAUREL!
!
SPLASH!!
ALL RIGHT! GRILLED FISH FOR DINNER!
DIVER NO. 4! SONAR REVERBERATION CONFIRMED!
SPLASH
A SMALL SAILING VESSEL HAS BEEN DETECTED!!

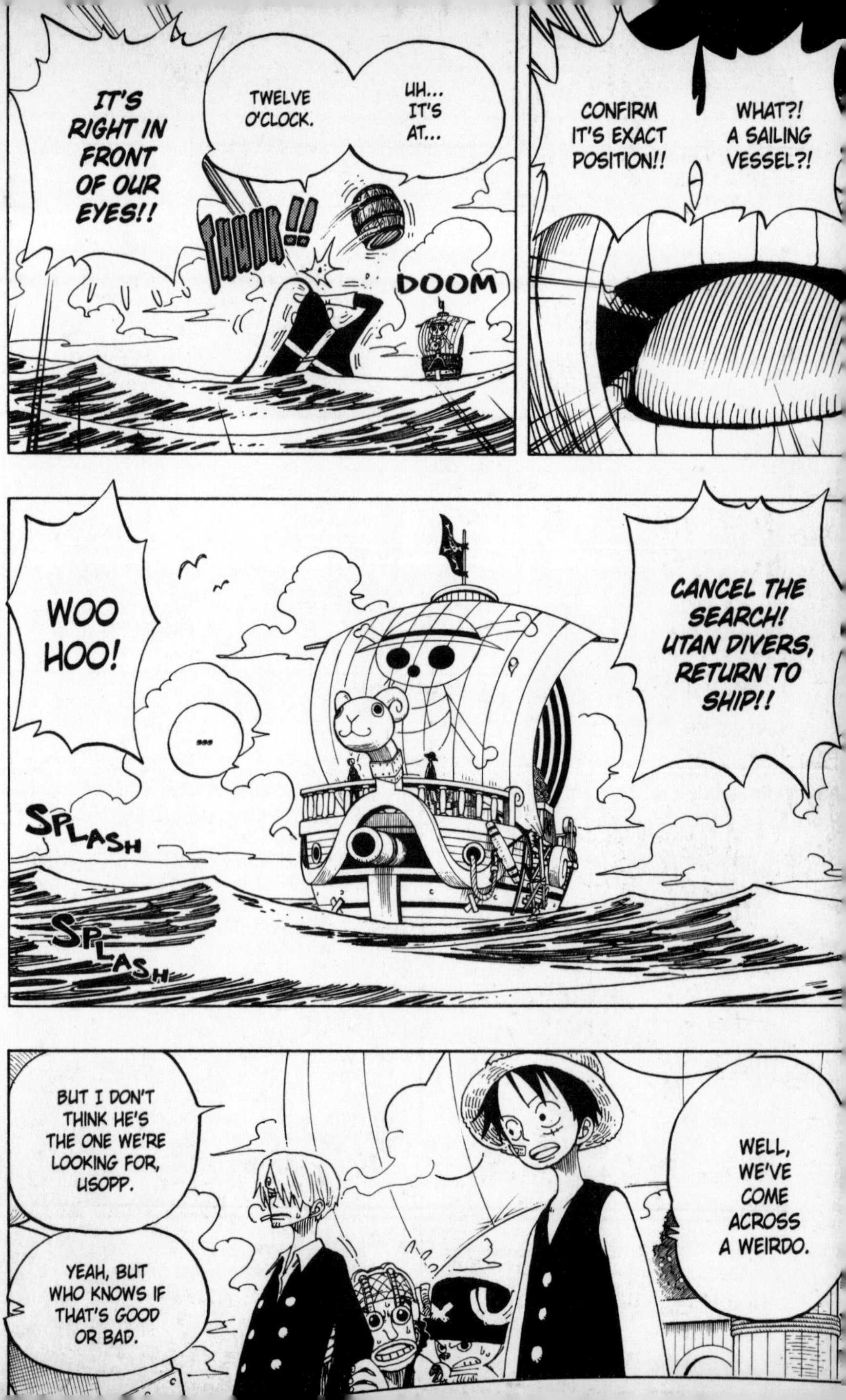
WHAT?! A SAILING VESSEL?!
CONFIRM IT'S EXACT POSITION!!
UH... IT'S AT...
TWELVE O'CLOCK.
DOOM
IT'S RIGHT IN FRONT OF OUR EYES!!
CANCEL THE SEARCH! UTAN DIVERS, RETURN TO SHIP!!
...
WOO HOO!
SPLASH
SPLASH
WELL, WE'VE COME ACROSS A WEIRDO.
BUT I DON'T THINK HE'S THE ONE WE'RE LOOKING FOR, USOPP.
YEAH, BUT WHO KNOWS IF THAT'S GOOD OR BAD.

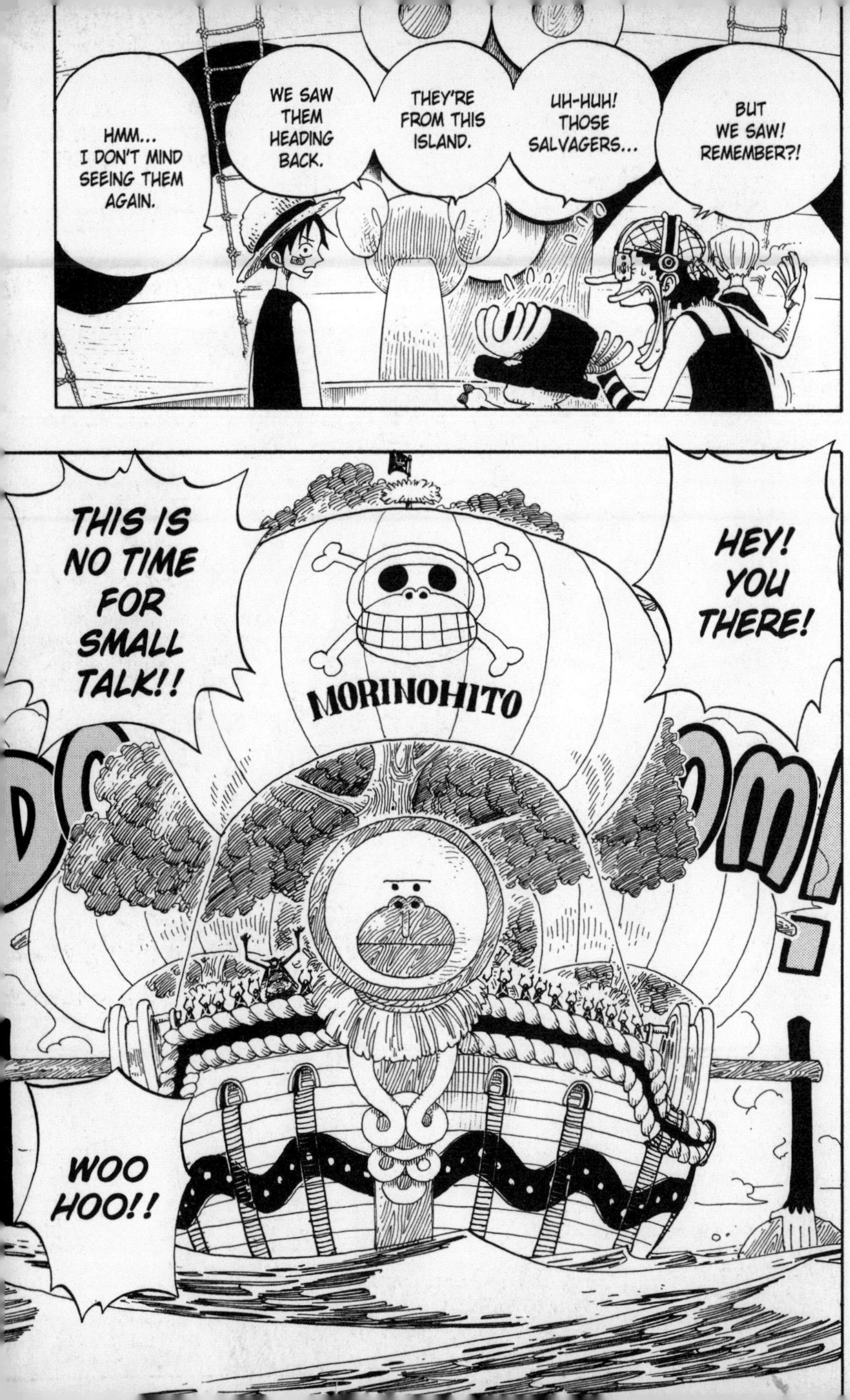
BUT WE SAW! REMEMBER?!
UH-HUH! THOSE SALVAGERS...
THEY'RE FROM THIS ISLAND.
WE SAW THEM HEADING BACK.
HMM... I DON'T MIND SEEING THEM AGAIN.
HEY! YOU THERE!
THIS IS NO TIME FOR SMALL TALK!!
MORINOHITO
DOOM!
WOO HOO!!

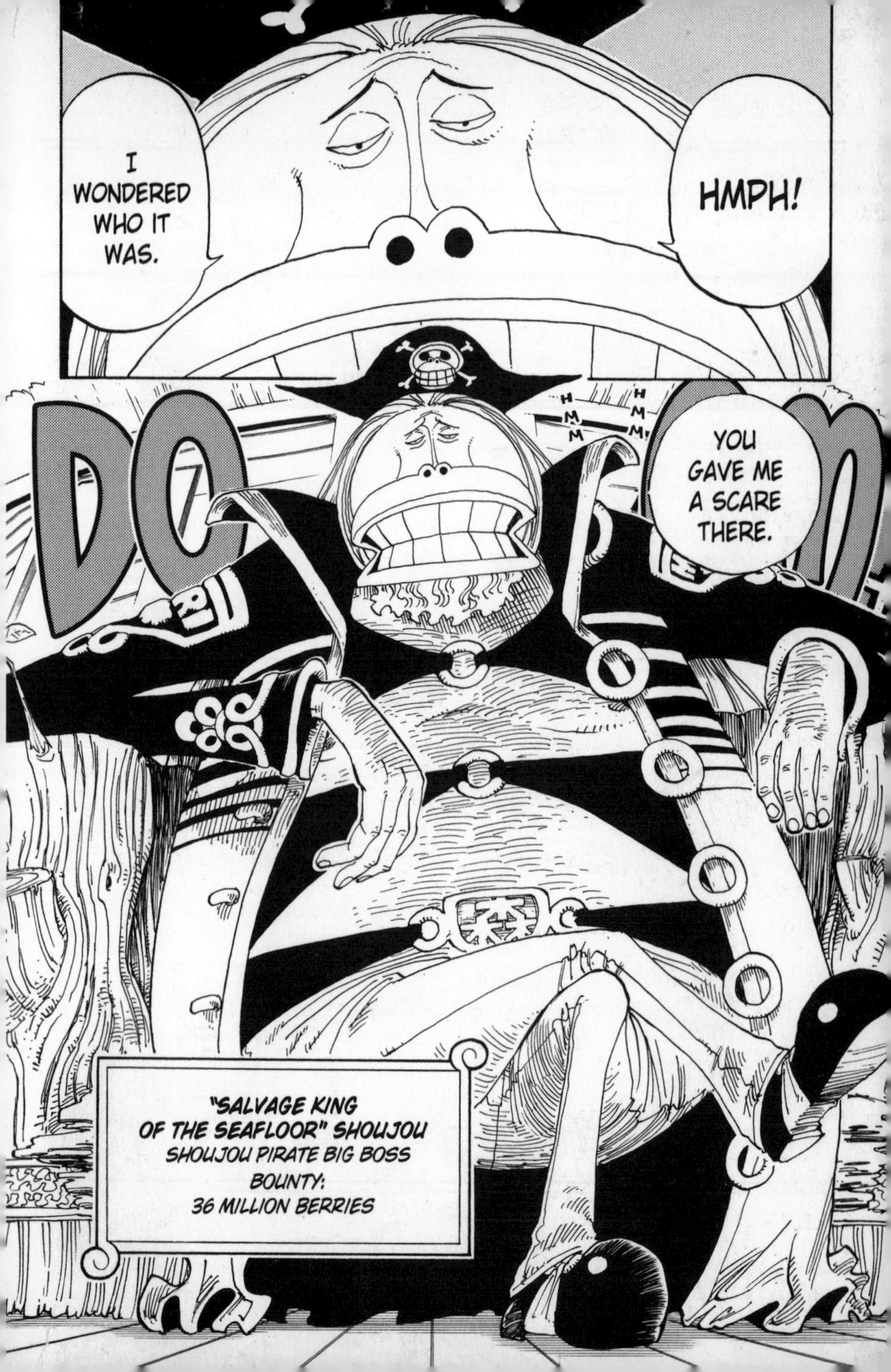
HMPH!
I WONDERED WHO IT WAS.
DOM
HMMM
YOU GAVE ME A SCARE THERE.
"SALVAGE KING OF THE SEAFLOOR" SHOUJOU
SHOUJOU PIRATE BIG BOSS
BOUNTY:
36 MILLION BERRIES

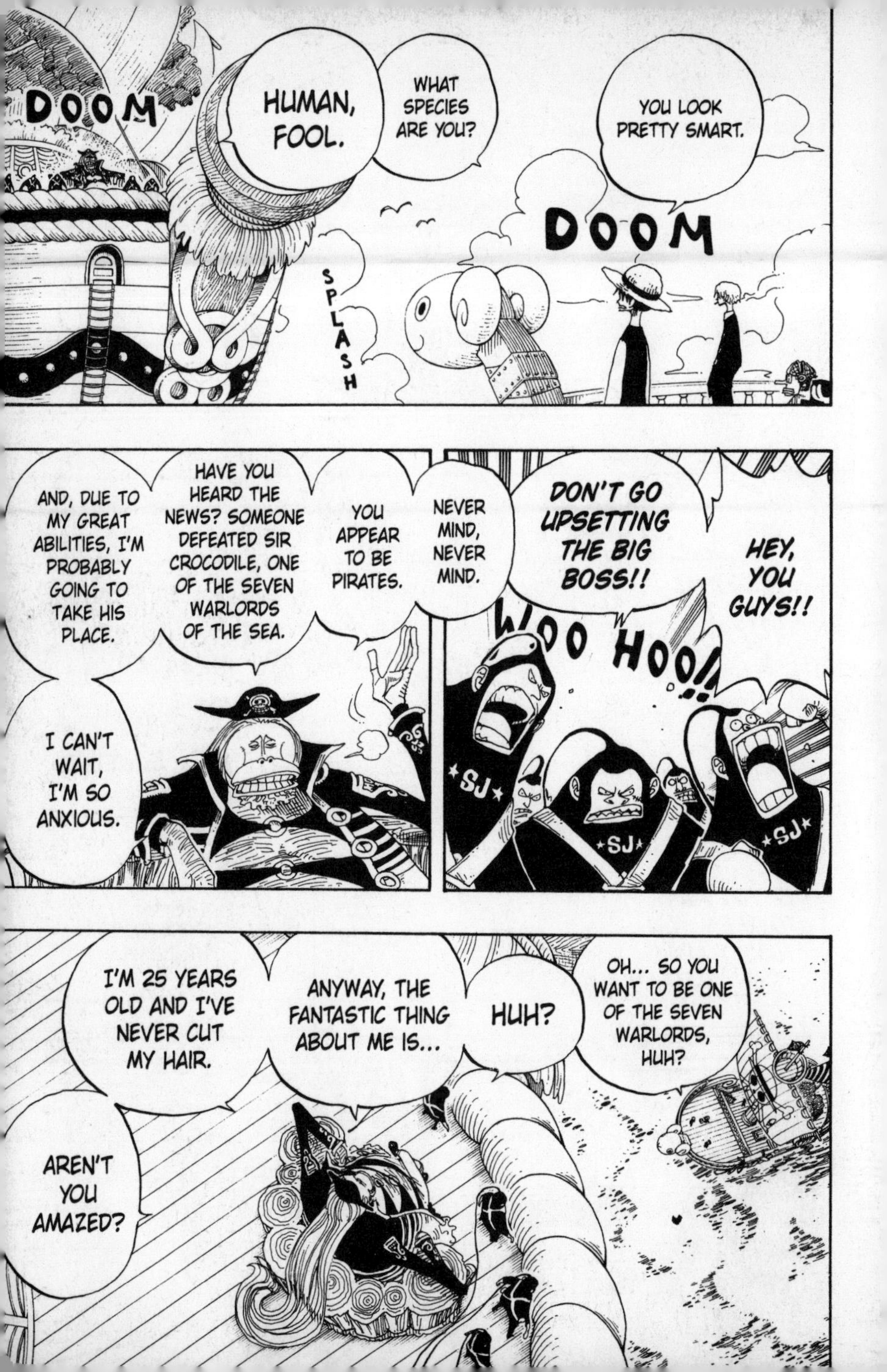
YOU LOOK PRETTY SMART.
DOOM
WHAT SPECIES ARE YOU?
HUMAN, FOOL.
SPLASH
DOOM
HEY, YOU GUYS!!
DON'T GO UPSETTING THE BIG BOSS!!
WOO HOO!!
NEVER MIND, NEVER MIND.
YOU APPEAR TO BE PIRATES.
HAVE YOU HEARD THE NEWS? SOMEONE DEFEATED SIR CROCODILE, ONE OF THE SEVEN WARLORDS OF THE SEA.
AND, DUE TO MY GREAT ABILITIES, I'M PROBABLY GOING TO TAKE HIS PLACE.
I CAN'T WAIT, I'M SO ANXIOUS.
OH... SO YOU WANT TO BE ONE OF THE SEVEN WARLORDS, HUH?
HUH?
ANYWAY, THE FANTASTIC THING ABOUT ME IS...
I'M 25 YEARS OLD AND I'VE NEVER CUT MY HAIR.
AREN'T YOU AMAZED?

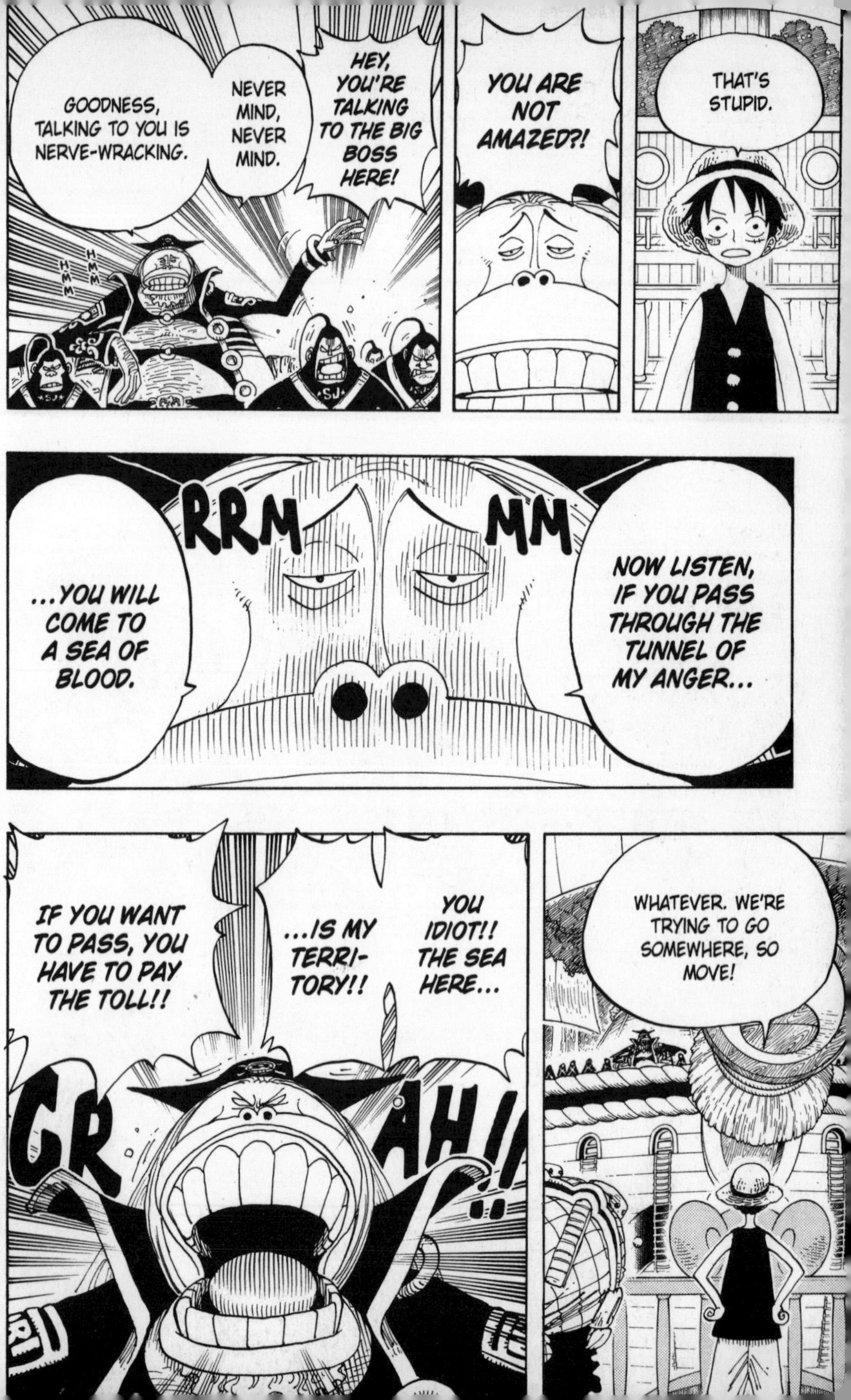
THAT'S STUPID.
YOU ARE NOT AMAZED?!
HEY, YOU'RE TALKING TO THE BIG BOSS HERE!
NEVER MIND, NEVER MIND.
GOODNESS, TALKING TO YOU IS NERVE-WRACKING.
HMM HMM
RRM MM
NOW LISTEN, IF YOU PASS THROUGH THE TUNNEL OF MY ANGER...
...YOU WILL COME TO A SEA OF BLOOD.
WHATEVER. WE'RE TRYING TO GO SOMEWHERE, SO MOVE!
YOU IDIOT!! THE SEA HERE...
...IS MY TERRI-TORY!!
IF YOU WANT TO PASS, YOU HAVE TO PAY THE TOLL!!
CR AH!!

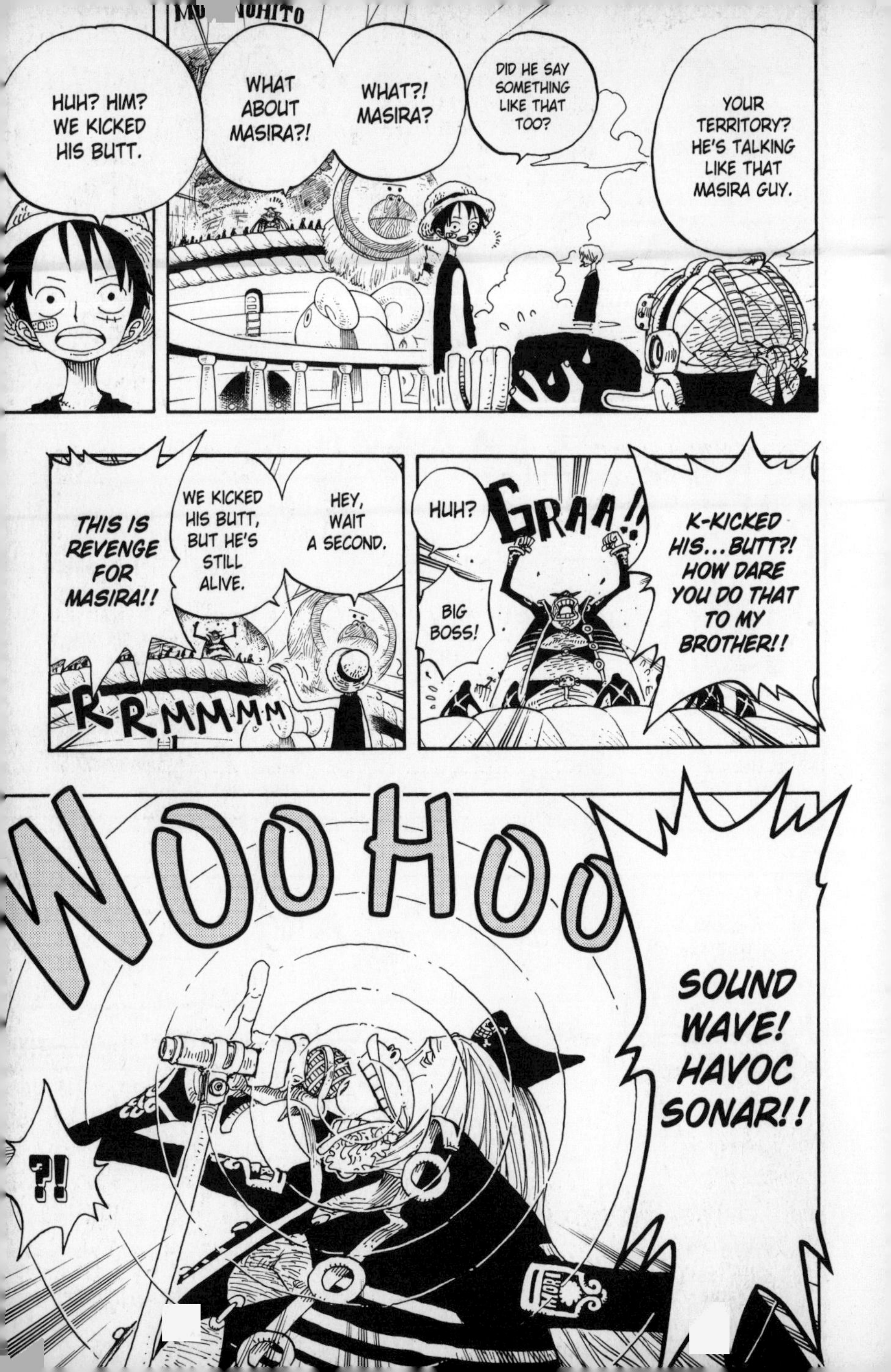

YOUR TERRITORY? HE'S TALKING LIKE THAT MASIRA GUY.
DID HE SAY SOMETHING LIKE THAT TOO?
WHAT?! MASIRA?
WHAT ABOUT MASIRA?!
HUH? HIM? WE KICKED HIS BUTT.
K-KICKED HIS...BUTT?! HOW DARE YOU DO THAT TO MY BROTHER!!
GRAA!!
HUH?
BIG BOSS!
HEY, WAIT A SECOND.
WE KICKED HIS BUTT, BUT HE'S STILL ALIVE.
THIS IS REVENGE FOR MASIRA!!
RRMMMMM
WOOHOO
SOUND WAVE! HAVOC SONAR!!
?!

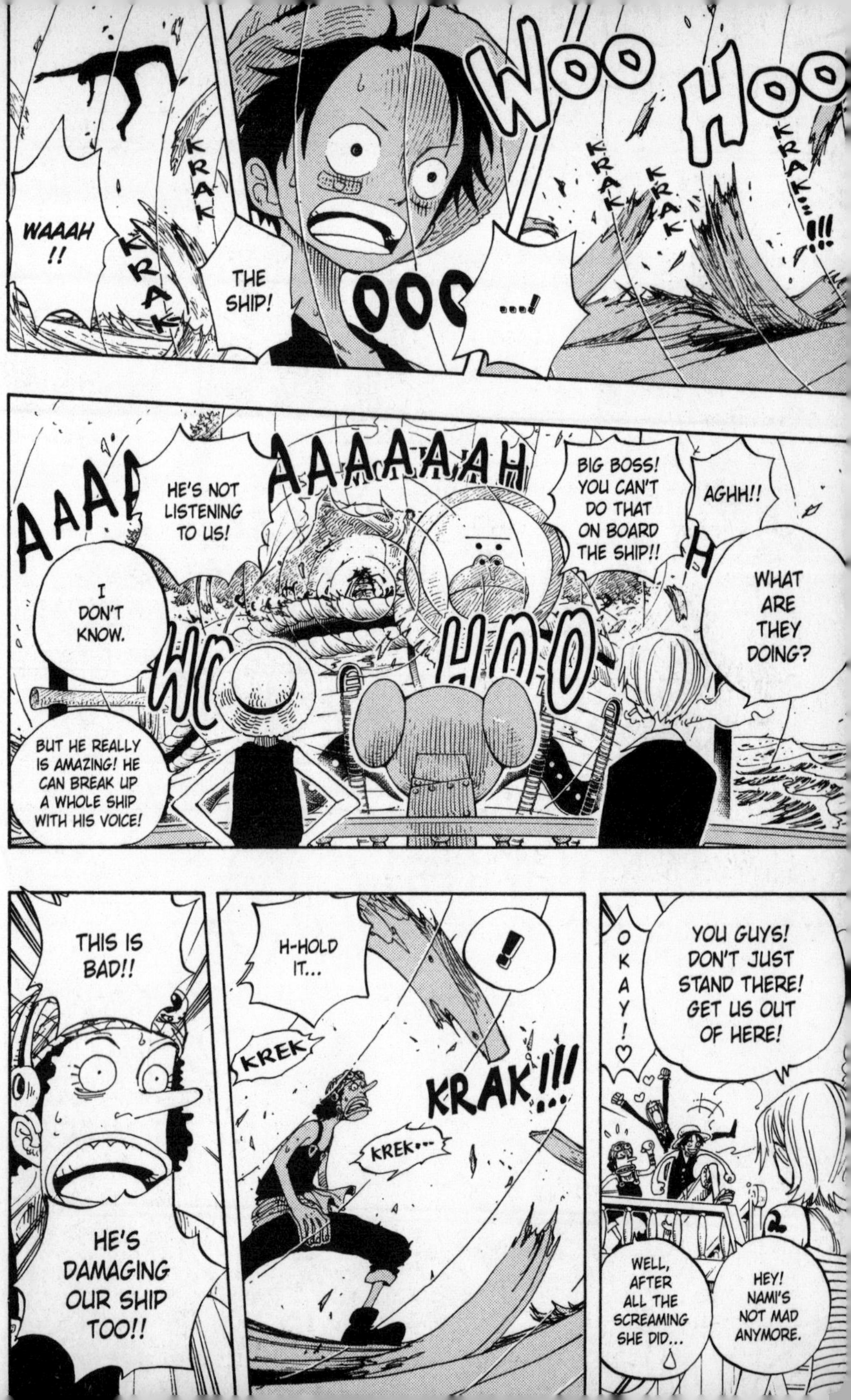
WOO HOO
KRAK KRAK KRAK KRAK...!!!
...!
OOO
THE SHIP!
KRAK KRAK
WAAAH!!
AGHH!!
WHAT ARE THEY DOING?
BIG BOSS! YOU CAN'T DO THAT ON BOARD THE SHIP!!
AAAAAAH
HE'S NOT LISTENING TO US!
AAAA
I DON'T KNOW.
WO HOO
BUT HE REALLY IS AMAZING! HE CAN BREAK UP A WHOLE SHIP WITH HIS VOICE!
YOU GUYS! DON'T JUST STAND THERE! GET US OUT OF HERE!
OKAY!♡
HEY! NAMI'S NOT MAD ANYMORE.
WELL, AFTER ALL THE SCREAMING SHE DID...
!
H-HOLD IT...
KREK
KRAK!!!...
KREK...
THIS IS BAD!!
HE'S DAMAGING OUR SHIP TOO!!

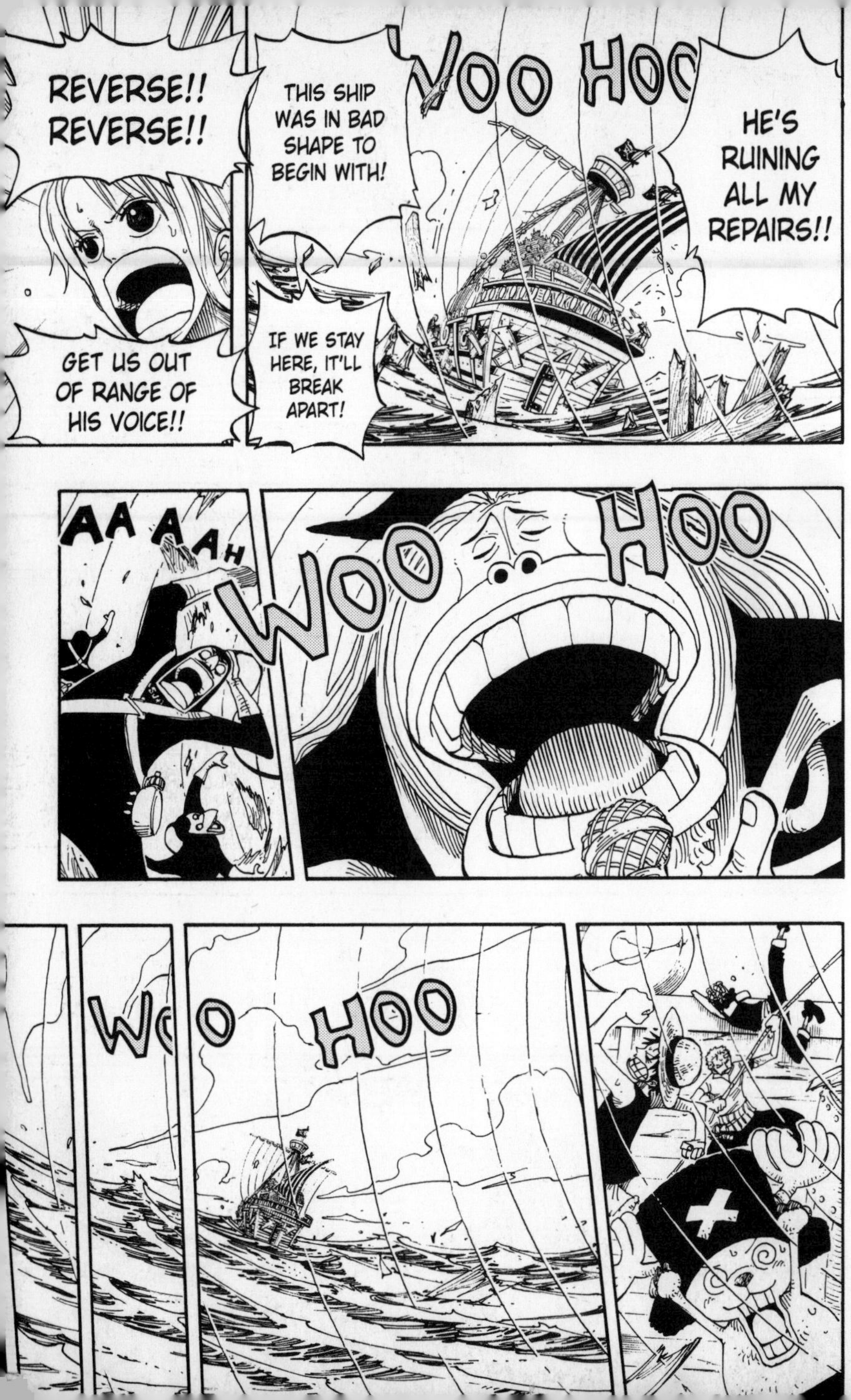
VOO HOO
HE'S RUINING ALL MY REPAIRS!!
THIS SHIP WAS IN BAD SHAPE TO BEGIN WITH!
IF WE STAY HERE, IT'LL BREAK APART!
REVERSE!! REVERSE!!
GET US OUT OF RANGE OF HIS VOICE!!
WOO HOO
AA AAAH
WOO HOO

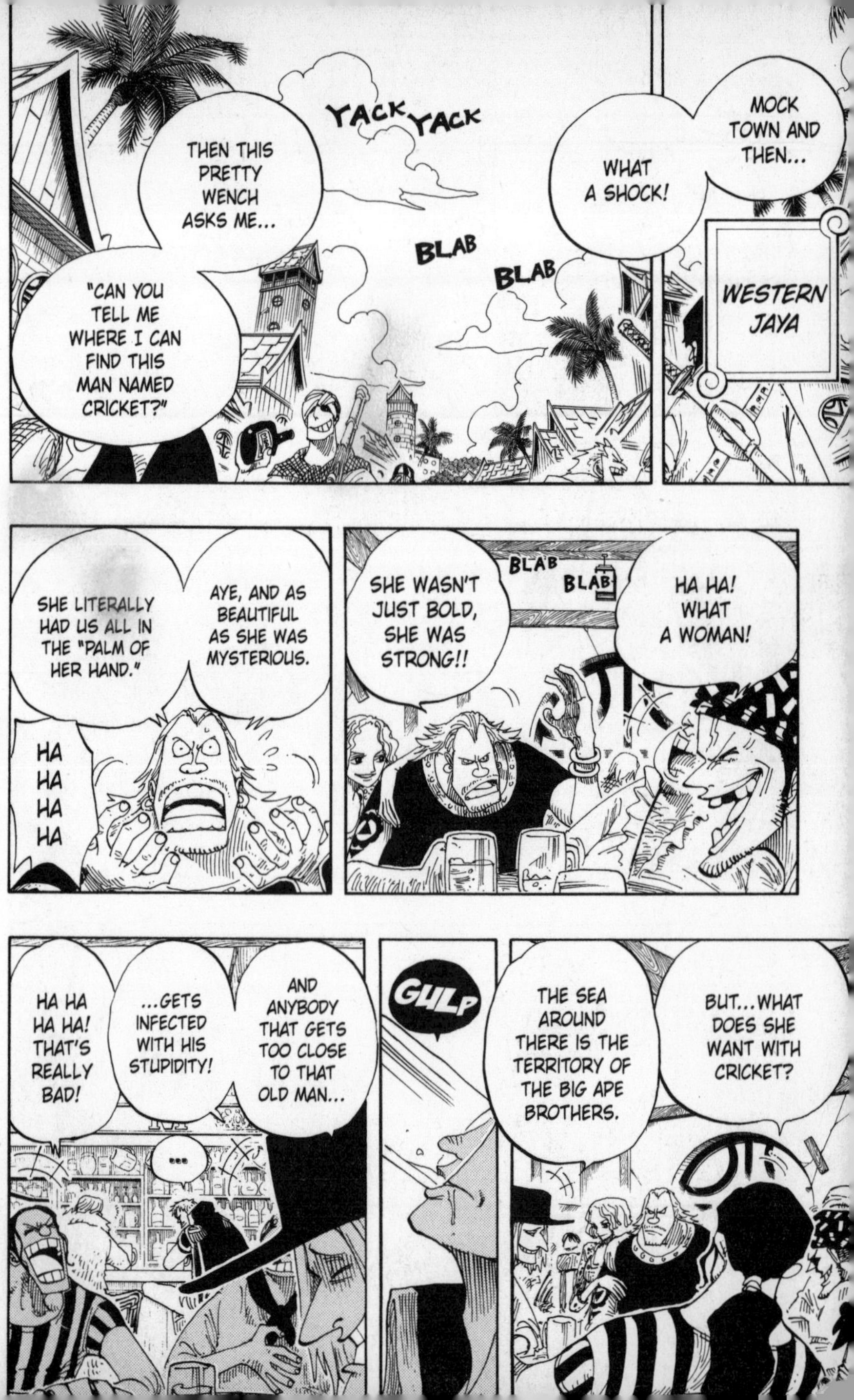

MOCK TOWN AND THEN...
WHAT A SHOCK!
WESTERN JAYA
YACK YACK
BLAB
BLAB
THEN THIS PRETTY WENCH ASKS ME...
"CAN YOU TELL ME WHERE I CAN FIND THIS MAN NAMED CRICKET?"
HA HA! WHAT A WOMAN!
BLAB
BLAB
SHE WASN'T JUST BOLD, SHE WAS STRONG!!
AYE, AND AS BEAUTIFUL AS SHE WAS MYSTERIOUS.
SHE LITERALLY HAD US ALL IN THE "PALM OF HER HAND."
HA HA HA HA
BUT...WHAT DOES SHE WANT WITH CRICKET?
THE SEA AROUND THERE IS THE TERRITORY OF THE BIG APE BROTHERS.
GULP
AND ANYBODY THAT GETS TOO CLOSE TO THAT OLD MAN...
...GETS INFECTED WITH HIS STUPIDITY!
HA HA HA HA! THAT'S REALLY BAD!
...

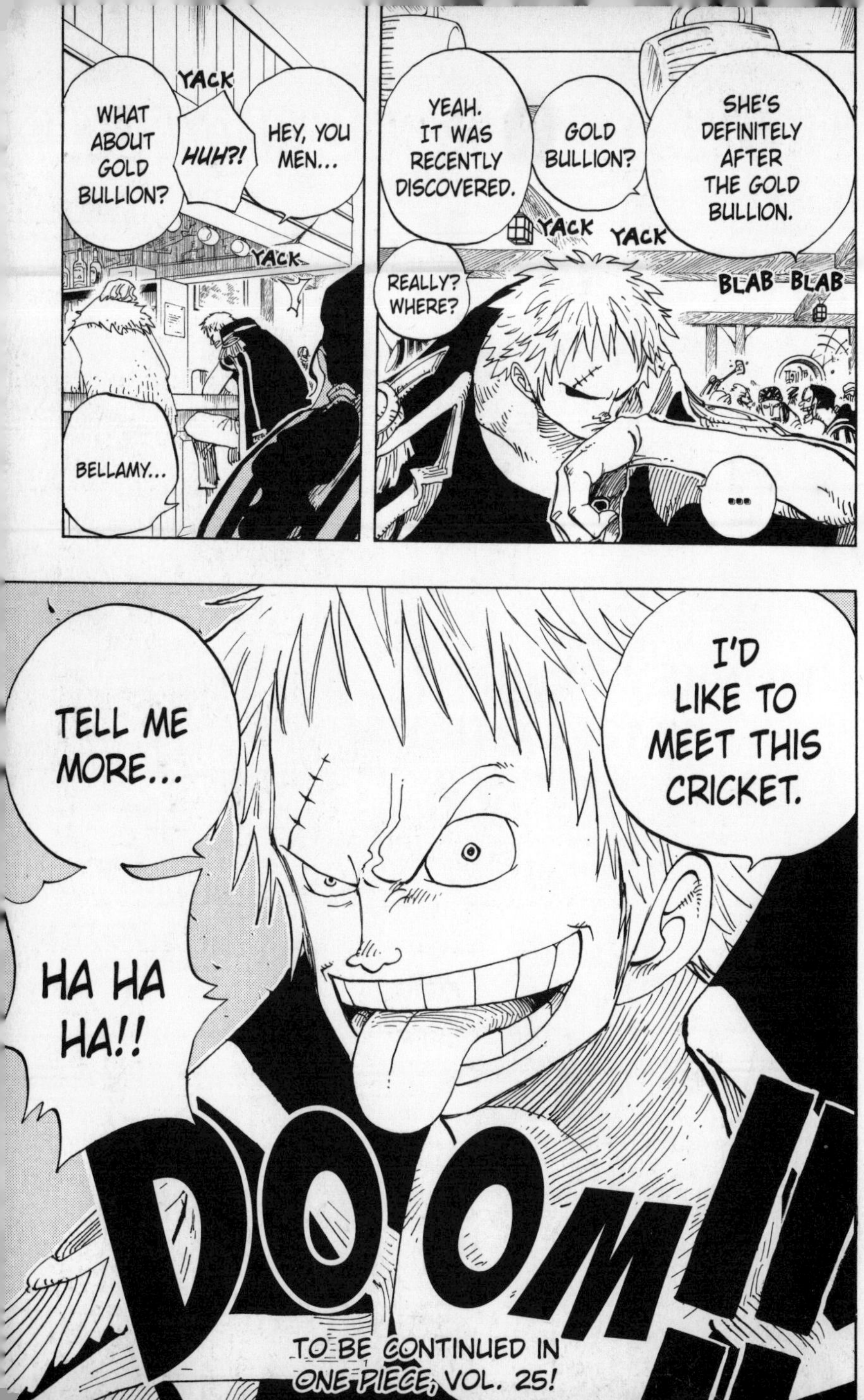
SHE'S DEFINITELY AFTER THE GOLD BULLION.
GOLD BULLION?
YEAH. IT WAS RECENTLY DISCOVERED.
YACK
YACK
BLAB BLAB
REALLY? WHERE?
...
HEY, YOU MEN...
YACK
HUH?!
WHAT ABOUT GOLD BULLION?
YACK
BELLAMY...
I'D LIKE TO MEET THIS CRICKET.
TELL ME MORE...
HA HA HA!!
DOOM!!
TO BE CONTINUED IN ONE PIECE, VOL. 25!

ECE CHARACTER POPULARITY POLL!

RITE CHARACTERS DO?!

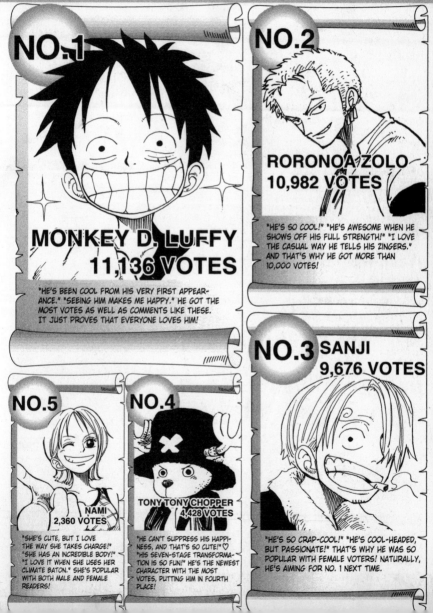

NO.1

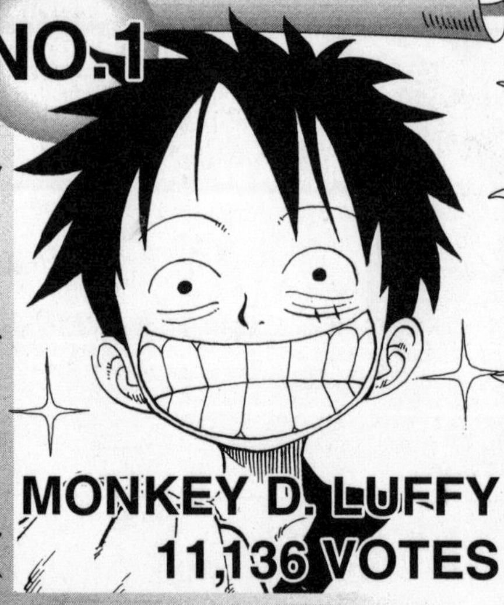

MONKEY D. LUFFY
11,136 VOTES

"HE'S BEEN COOL FROM HIS VERY FIRST APPEARANCE." "SEEING HIM MAKES ME HAPPY." HE GOT THE MOST VOTES AS WELL AS COMMENTS LIKE THESE. IT JUST PROVES THAT EVERYONE LOVES HIM!

NO.2

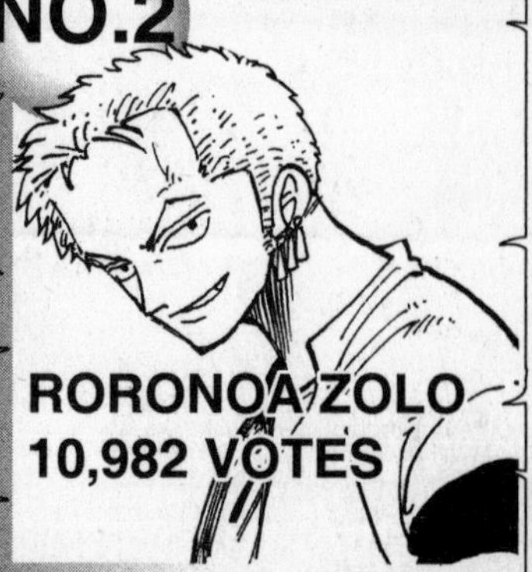

RORONOA ZOLO
10,982 VOTES

"HE'S SO COOL!" "HE'S AWESOME WHEN HE SHOWS OFF HIS FULL STRENGTH!" "I LOVE THE CASUAL WAY HE TELLS HIS ZINGERS." AND THAT'S WHY HE GOT MORE THAN 10,000 VOTES!

NO.3

SANJI
9,676 VOTES

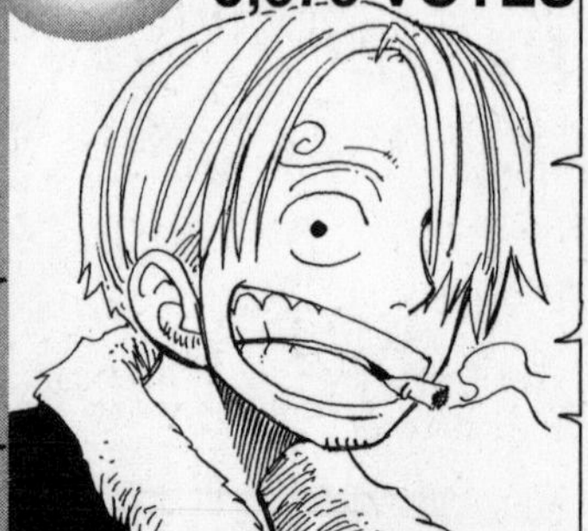

"HE'S SO CRAP-COOL!" "HE'S COOL-HEADED, BUT PASSIONATE!" THAT'S WHY HE WAS SO POPULAR WITH FEMALE VOTERS! NATURALLY, HE'S AIMING FOR NO. 1 NEXT TIME.

NO.4

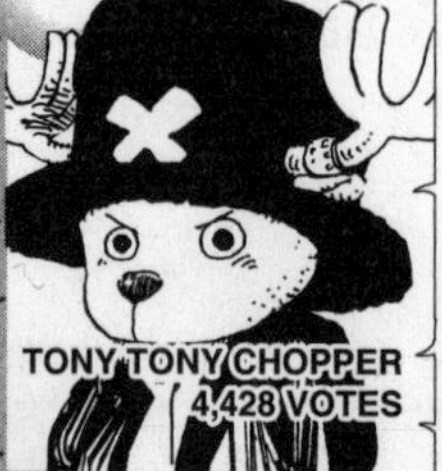

TONY TONY CHOPPER
4,428 VOTES

"HE CAN'T SUPPRESS HIS HAPPINESS, AND THAT'S SO CUTE!"♡ "HIS SEVEN-STAGE TRANSFORMATION IS SO FUN!" HE'S THE NEWEST CHARACTER WITH THE MOST VOTES, PUTTING HIM IN FOURTH PLACE!

NO.5

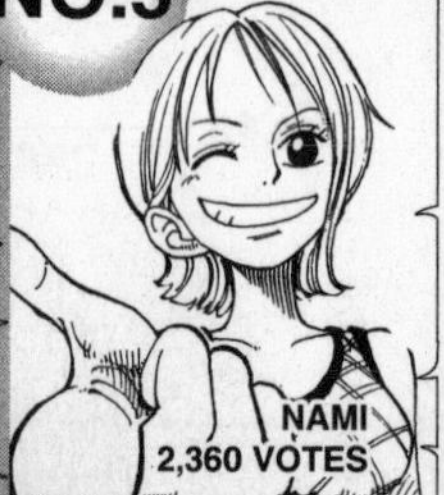

NAMI
2,360 VOTES

"SHE'S CUTE, BUT I LOVE THE WAY SHE TAKES CHARGE!" "SHE HAS AN INCREDIBLE BODY!" "I LOVE IT WHEN SHE USES HER CLIMATE BATON." SHE'S POPULAR WITH BOTH MALE AND FEMALE READERS!

51,873 TOTAL VOTES CAST

RESULTS OF THE 2ND ONE PI

THANK YOU FOR VOTING! HOW DID YOUR FAVO

No.6 1,957 VOTES
USOPP
"USOPP REALLY MAKES ME LAUGH!" "HE'S SO HAPPY-GO-LUCKY." HE WENT UP TWO RANKS HIGHER THAN THE LAST TIME!

No.7 1,880 VOTES
SHANKS
"I CAN'T WAIT TILL HE APPEARS AGAIN!" "HE'S THE GROWN-UP I ADMIRE MOST." HE'S A POPULAR CHARACTER WHO LEAVES A STRONG IMPRESSION WITH READERS.

No.8 1,735 VOTES
PORTGAZ D. ACE
"HE'S A GREAT BIG BROTHER!" "HIS FIRE FIST IS SUPER COOL!" THAT'S LUFFY'S POPULAR BIG BROTHER FOR YOU!

No.9 811 VOTES
MR. 2 BON CLAY
"HE'S SO FUNNY. REALLY, THIS AIN'T NO JOKE!" "HIS CLONE-CLONE TRICK IS TOPS!" HIS POPULARITY AIN'T NO JOKE!

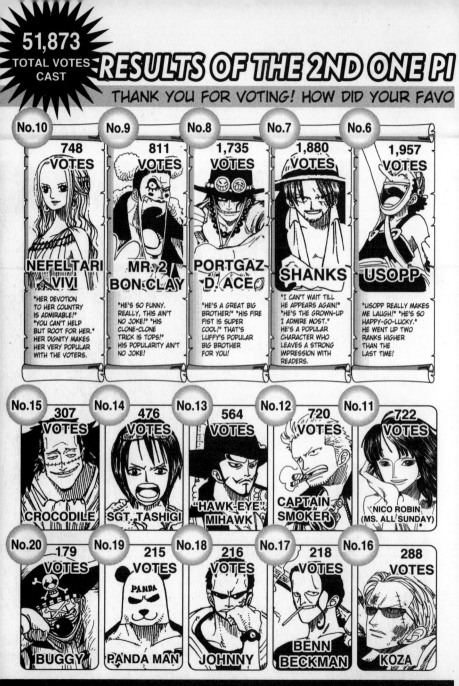

No.10 748 VOTES
NEFELTARI VIVI
"HER DEVOTION TO HER COUNTRY IS ADMIRABLE!" "YOU CAN'T HELP BUT ROOT FOR HER." HER DIGNITY MAKES HER VERY POPULAR WITH THE VOTERS.

No.11 722 VOTES
NICO ROBIN (MS. ALL SUNDAY)

No.12 720 VOTES
CAPTAIN SMOKER

No.13 564 VOTES
"HAWK-EYE" MIHAWK

No.14 476 VOTES
SGT. TASHIGI

No.15 307 VOTES
CROCODILE

No.16 288 VOTES
KOZA

No.17 218 VOTES
BENN BECKMAN

No.18 216 VOTES
JOHNNY

No.19 215 VOTES
PANDA MAN

No.20 179 VOTES
BUGGY

NO.21 CONTINUES ON THE NEXT PAGE, ALONG WITH USOPP'S OVERALL CRITIQUE.

THE SECOND ONE PIECE CHARACTER POPULARITY POLL RESULTS!! CONTINUED

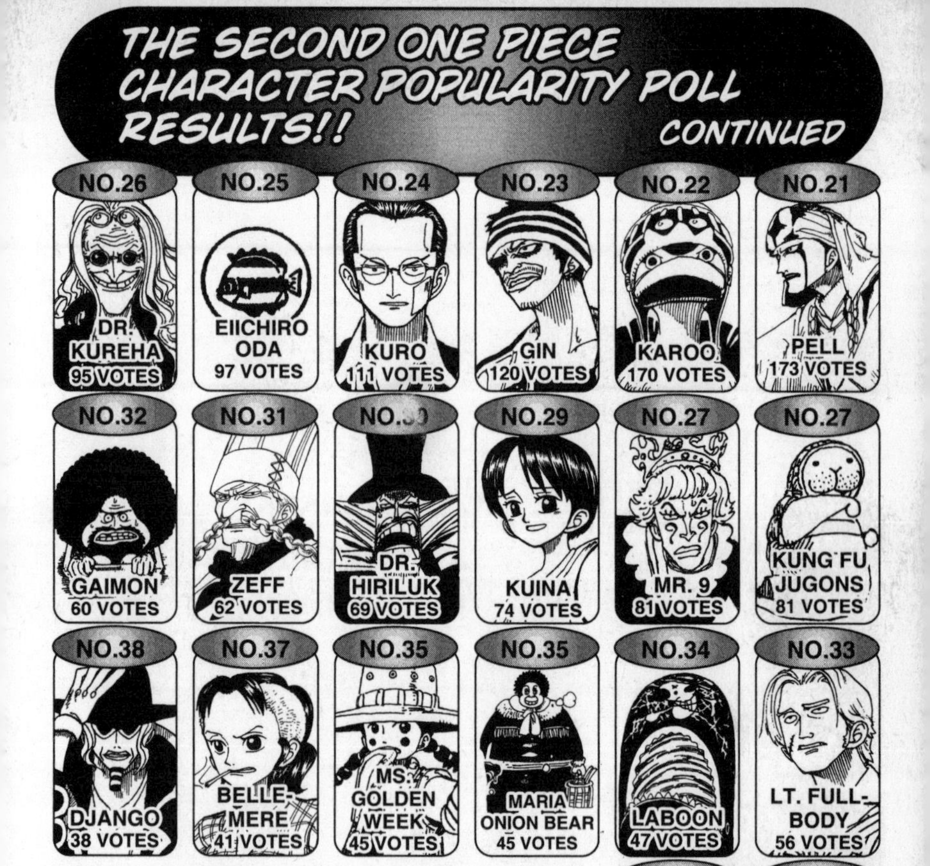

NO.21
PELL
173 VOTES
NO.22
KAROO
170 VOTES
NO.23
GIN
120 VOTES
NO.24
KURO
111 VOTES
NO.25
EIICHIRO ODA
97 VOTES
NO.26
DR. KUREHA
95 VOTES
NO.27
KUNG FU JUGONS
81 VOTES
NO.27
MR. 9
81 VOTES
NO.29
KUINA
74 VOTES
NO.3
DR. HIRILUK
69 VOTES
NO.31
ZEFF
62 VOTES
NO.32
GAIMON
60 VOTES
NO.33
LT. FULL-BODY
56 VOTES
NO.34
LABOON
47 VOTES
NO.35
MARIA ONION BEAR
45 VOTES
NO.35
MS. GOLDEN WEEK
45 VOTES
NO.37
BELLE-MERE
41 VOTES
NO.38
DJANGO
38 VOTES

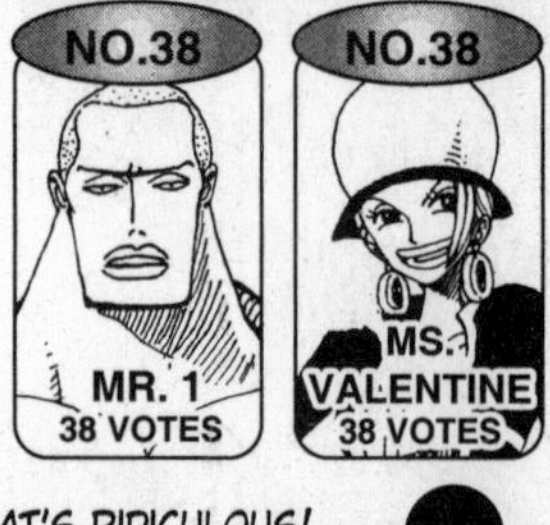

NO.38
MS. VALENTINE
38 VOTES
NO.38
MR. 1
38 VOTES

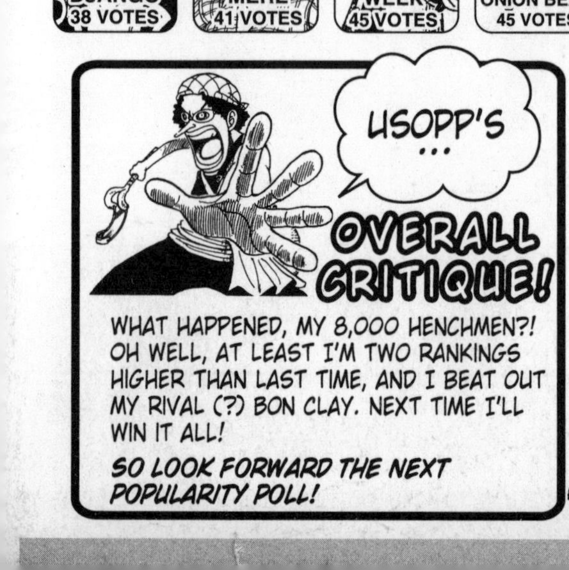

USOPP'S ...
OVERALL CRITIQUE!

WHAT HAPPENED, MY 8,000 HENCHMEN?! OH WELL, AT LEAST I'M TWO RANKINGS HIGHER THAN LAST TIME, AND I BEAT OUT MY RIVAL (?) BON CLAY. NEXT TIME I'LL WIN IT ALL!

SO LOOK FORWARD THE NEXT POPULARITY POLL!

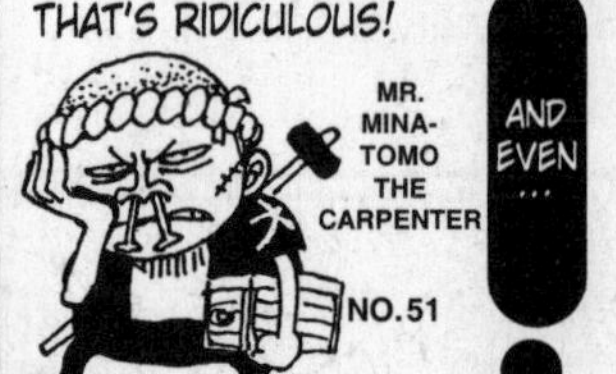

AND EVEN ...
THAT'S RIDICULOUS!
MR. MINA-TOMO THE CARPENTER
NO.51

COMING NEXT VOLUME:

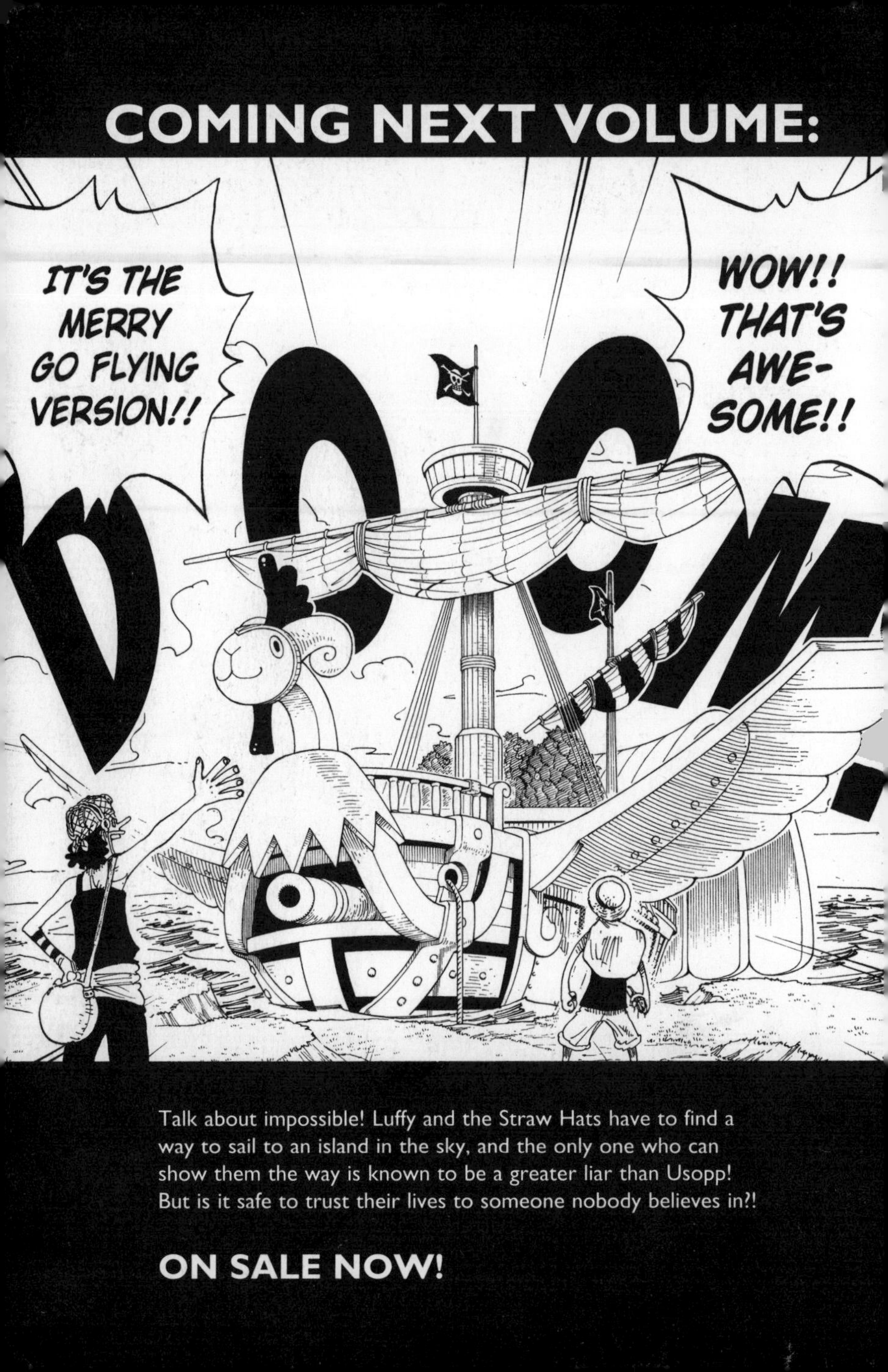
WOW!! THAT'S AWE-SOME!!
IT'S THE MERRY GO FLYING VERSION!!
DOOM!

Talk about impossible! Luffy and the Straw Hats have to find a way to sail to an island in the sky, and the only one who can show them the way is known to be a greater liar than Usopp! But is it safe to trust their lives to someone nobody believes in?!

ON SALE NOW!

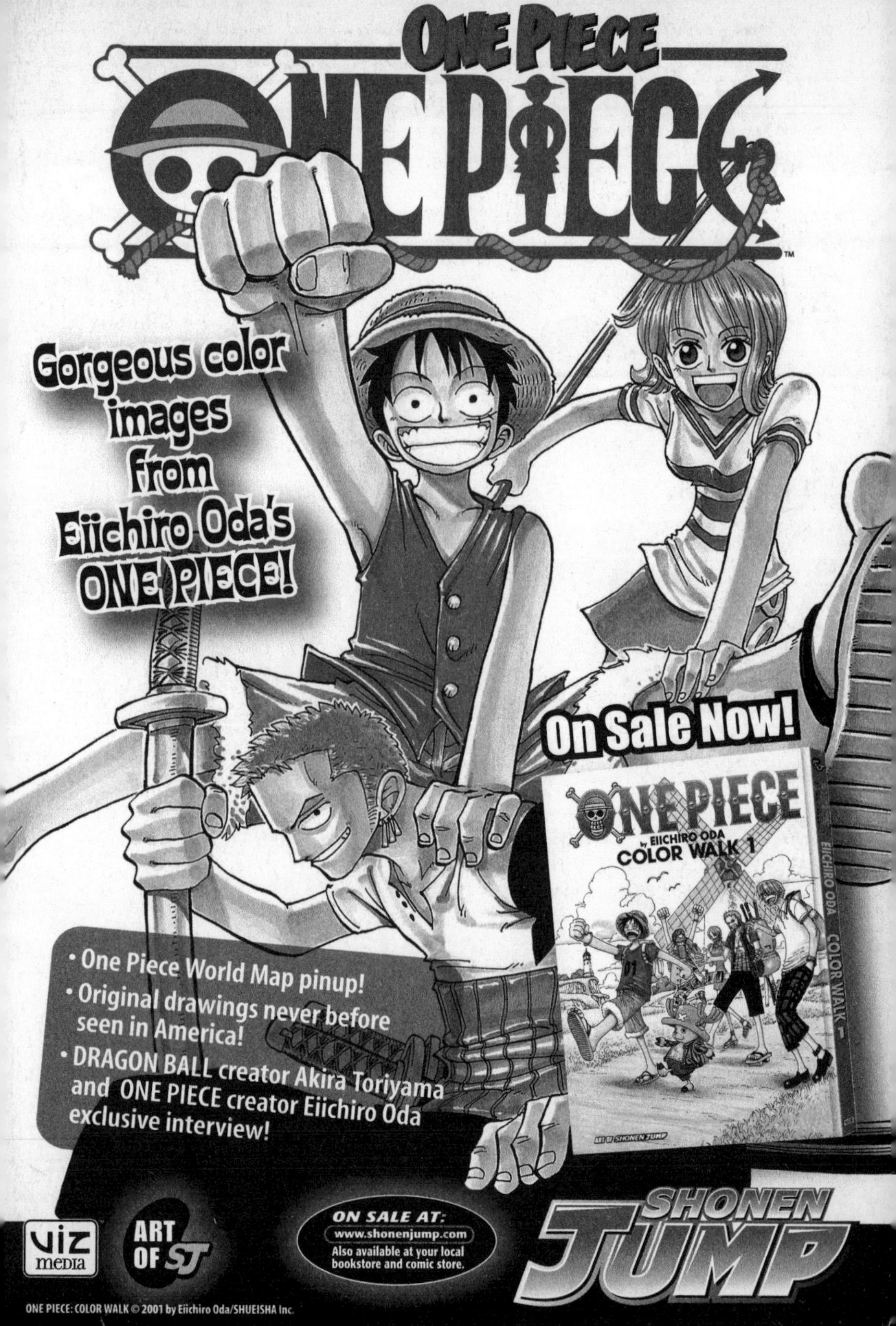

ONE PIECE
ONE PIECE™
Gorgeous color images from Eiichiro Oda's ONE PIECE!
On Sale Now!
ONE PIECE by EIICHIRO ODA COLOR WALK 1
• One Piece World Map pinup!
• Original drawings never before seen in America!
• DRAGON BALL creator Akira Toriyama and ONE PIECE creator Eiichiro Oda exclusive interview!
viz media
ART OF SJ
ON SALE AT:
www.shonenjump.com
Also available at your local bookstore and comic store.
SHONEN JUMP

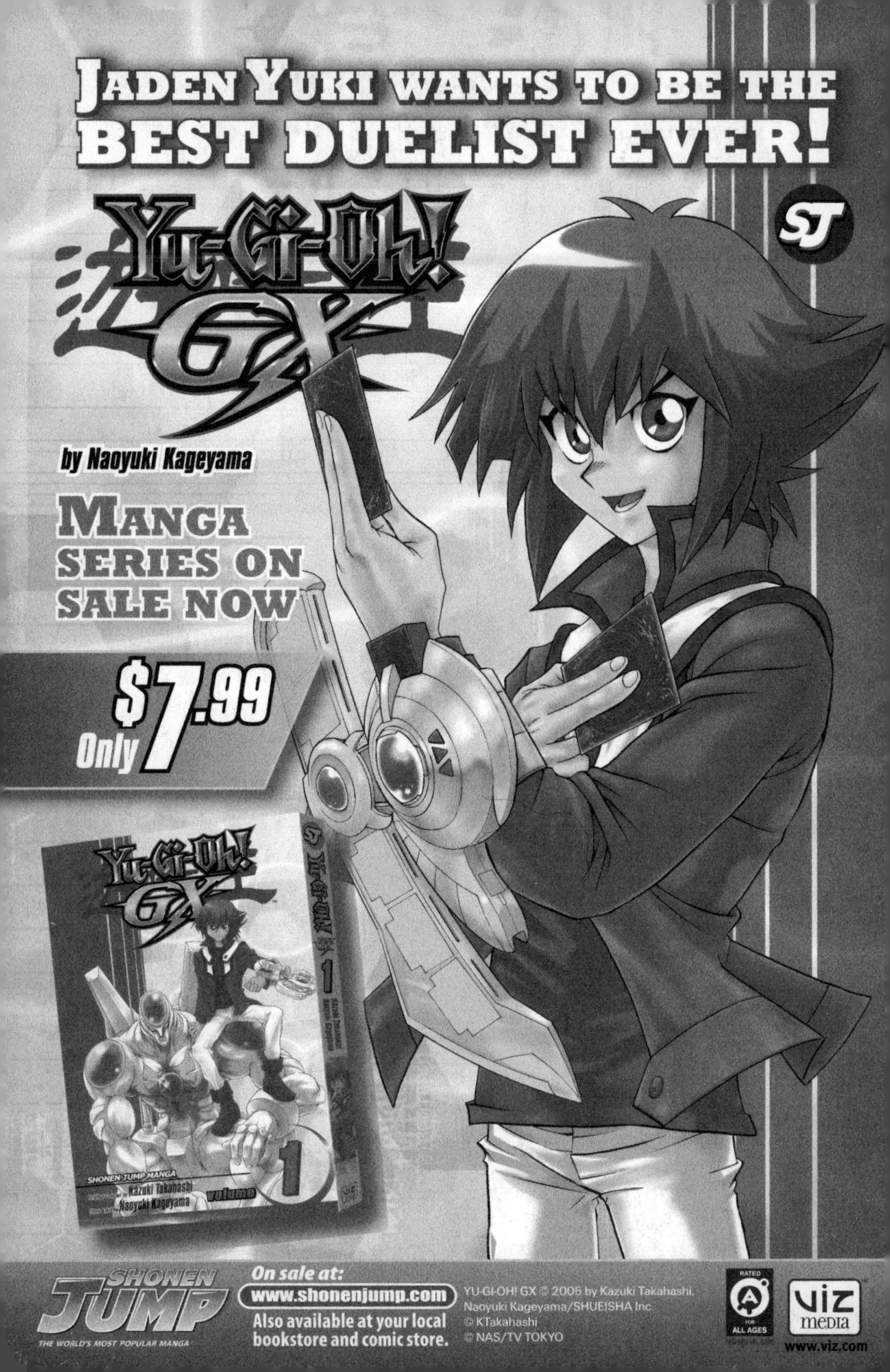
JADEN YUKI WANTS TO BE THE
BEST DUELIST EVER!
SJ
YU-GI-OH! GX
by Naoyuki Kageyama
MANGA
SERIES ON
SALE NOW
Only $7.99
YU-GI-OH! GX
SHONEN JUMP MANGA
Kazuki Takahashi
Naoyuki Kageyama
volume 1
SHONEN JUMP
THE WORLD'S MOST POPULAR MANGA
On sale at:
www.shonenjump.com
Also available at your local bookstore and comic store.
YU-GI-OH! GX © 2005 by Kazuki Takahashi, Naoyuki Kageyama/SHUEISHA Inc.
© KTakahashi
© NAS/TV TOKYO
RATED
A
FOR ALL AGES
VIZ media
www.viz.com

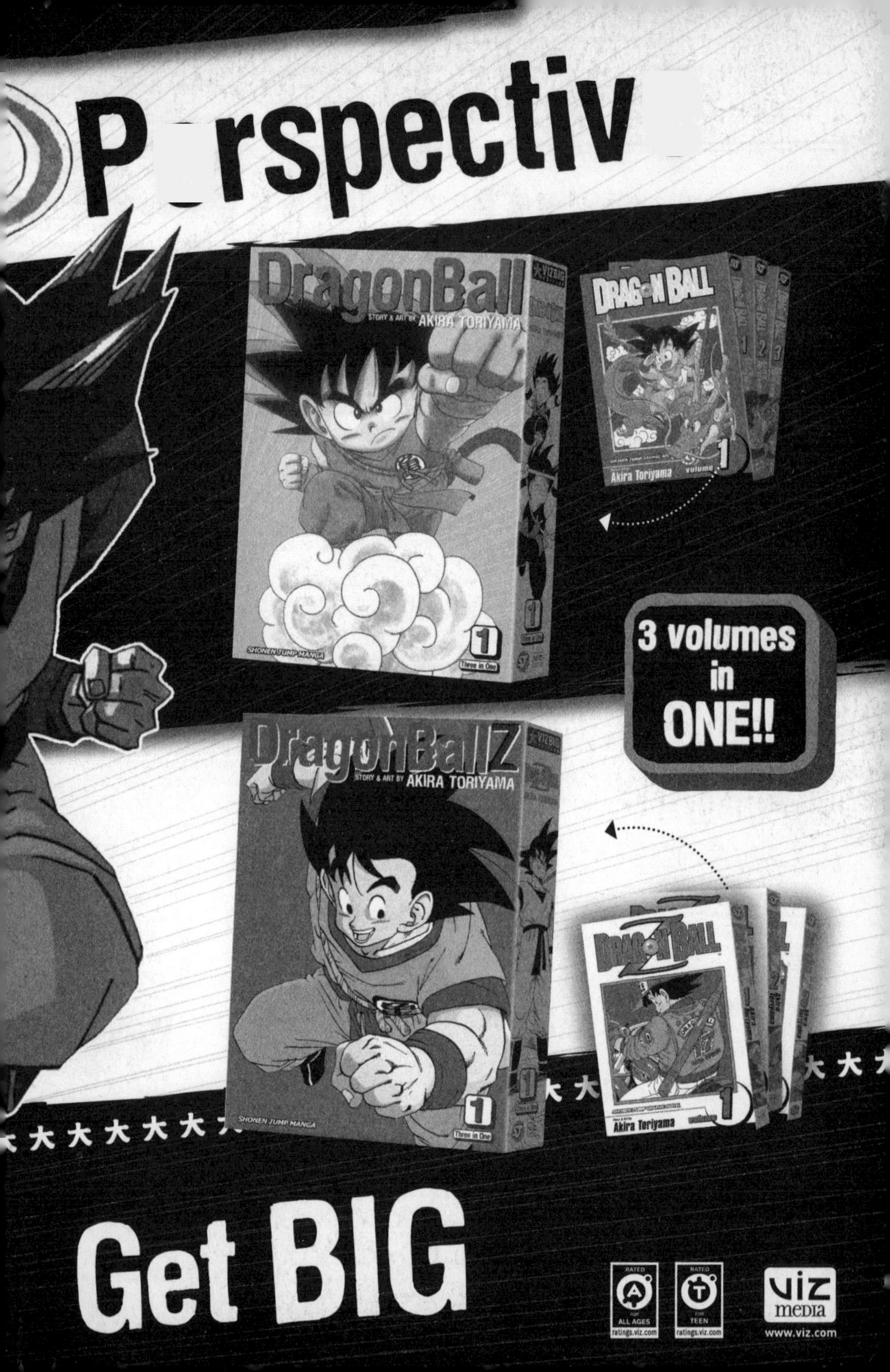
P rspectiv
DragonBall
STORY & ART BY AKIRA TORIYAMA
SHONEN JUMP MANGA
1
Three in One
DRAGON BALL
Akira Toriyama volume 1
3 volumes in ONE!!
DragonBallZ
STORY & ART BY AKIRA TORIYAMA
SHONEN JUMP MANGA
1
Three in One
DRAGON BALL Z
Akira Toriyama
Get BIG
RATED ALL AGES ratings.viz.com
RATED TEEN ratings.viz.com
VIZ MEDIA
www.viz.com

Tell us what you think about SHONEN JUMP manga!

Our survey is now available online.
Go to: **www.*SHONENJUMP*.com/*mangasurvey***

Help us make our product offering better!

THE REAL ACTION
STARTS IN...

www.shonenjump.com

SAVE 50% OFF
THE COVER PRICE!
IT'S LIKE GETTING 6 ISSUES
FREE!

OVER **350+** PAGES PER ISSUE

SHONEN JUMP
THE WORLD'S MOST POPULAR MANGA

This monthly magazine contains 7 of the coolest manga available in the U.S., PLUS anime news, and info about video & card games, toys AND more!

❏ **I want 12 HUGE issues of SHONEN JUMP for only $29.95*!**

NAME

ADDRESS

CITY/STATE/ZIP

EMAIL ADDRESS   **DATE OF BIRTH**

❏ YES, send me via email information, advertising, offers, and promotions related to VIZ Media, SHONEN JUMP, and/or their business partners.

❏ **CHECK ENCLOSED** (payable to SHONEN JUMP)   ❏ **BILL ME LATER**

CREDIT CARD: ❏ **Visa**   ❏ **Mastercard**

ACCOUNT NUMBER   **EXP. DATE**

SIGNATURE

CLIP&MAIL TO:
SHONEN JUMP Subscriptions Service Dept.
P.O. Box 515
Mount Morris, IL 61054-0515

P9GNC1

* Canada price: $41.95 USD, including GST, HST, and QST. US/CAN orders only. Allow 6-8 weeks for delivery.
ONE PIECE © 1997 by Eiichiro Oda/SHUEISHA Inc. BLEACH © 2001 by Tite Kubo/SHUEISHA Inc.
NARUTO © 1999 by Masashi Kishimoto/SHUEISHA Inc.

RATED **T** TEEN
ratings.viz.com

VIZ media
www.viz.com

ONE PIECE

Story and Art by Eiichiro Oda

Want even MORE?

Visit **onepiece.viz.com/wanted**
and enter the name of the character featured on this
sticker for a *One Piece* speed-up bonus!

And DON'T
FORGET to
check out these
other GREAT
TITLES from
SHONEN JUMP
THE WORLD'S MOST POPULAR MANGA

Find more at shonenjump.viz.com